PERESTROIKA AND INTERNATIONAL LAW

PERESTROIKA
AND
INTERNATIONAL LAW

edited by

W. E. BUTLER

MARTINUS NIJHOFF PUBLISHERS

DORDRECHT / BOSTON / LONDON

Library of Congress Cataloging in Publication Data

```
Perestroika and international law / edited by W.E. Butler.
      p.   cm.
   Includes bibliographical references.
   ISBN 0-7923-0483-7
   1. Soviet Union--Foreign relations--1985---Congresses.
 2. International law--Soviet Union--Congresses.  3. Perestroika-
 -Congresses.   I. Butler, William Elliott, 1939-
 JX1555.P47   1990
 341'.04'0947--dc20                                    89-36001
```

Published by Martinus Nijhoff Publishers.
P.O. Box 163, 3300 AA Dordrecht, The Netherlands.

Sold and distributed in the U.S.A. and Canada
by Kluwer Academic Publishers,
101 Philip Drive, Norwell, MA 02061, U.S.A.

In all other countries, sold and distributed
by Kluwer Academic Publishers Group,
P.O. Box 322, 3300 AH Dordrecht, The Netherlands.

Printed on acid-free paper

Printed in the Netherlands

TABLE OF CONTENTS

PERESTROIKA AND INTERNATIONAL LAW

W. E. BUTLER

Unlike no other dimension of Soviet domestic or foreign policy in the twentieth century, perestroika and glasnost, in capturing the imagination of the West, have begun to affect the international legal process and perhaps the substance of international law itself. Indeed the terms have been officially acknowledged to be part of the English tongue.

The initial ingredient from the Soviet Union was "new thinking," combined almost immediately with foreign policy decisions that are contributing to a de facto restructuring of the post-1945 international order. The precise sequence will remain for the diplomatic historians to reconstruct, but strong candidates, from the short-range perspective, of major readjustments must include: the decision to disengage in Afghanistan, the repayment of arrears to the United Nations and a host of proposals to enhance the role of international institutions, active interest in seeking association with or membership in international economic and monetary institutions or communities, the conclusion of bilateral arms control agreements coupled with an active acceptance of intrusive monitoring and control machinery, the establishment of direct links with States or entities such as South Korea, Israel, Taiwan, and Saudi Arabia, acceptance of the compulsory jurisdiction of the ICJ under certain human rights conventions, and a reassessment of the rule-of-law within the USSR, which has considerable implications for the Soviet perception of international law as well.

New thinking is likewise leading to a restructuring of the past.[1] The so-called "Brezhnev Doctrine," set out in doctrinal documents and writings from September 1968, is being criticised in the same media as a "deformation" of socialism "inconceivable" under modern conditions. Criticism of earlier Soviet diplomacy proceeds explicitly and implicitly in various guises. A special Commission has been appointed to look into the Soviet-German agreements concerning the Baltic States and another to assess the evidence surrounding the Katyn massacre. Soviet diplomats and international lawyers who were victimised or executed in the Stalin era are being rehabilitated or, where this already had been done, restored to public visibility. Amongst them are individuals associated with the improvement of relations with the non-socialist world: G. V. Chicherin, M. M. Litvinov, S. B. Krylov, V. E. Grabar, A. V. Sabanin, V. Potemkin, S. A. Lozovskii, and N. N. Krestinskii.

The USSR Ministry of Foreign Affairs has been internally reorganised to make foreign policy formulation more open within the Ministry. Certain ambassadorships have been filled by competitive application rather than selection from above. Some

W. E. Butler, Perestroika and International Law, 1–4.

foreign policy decisions have been placed under parliamantary control, including the use of military force beyond Soviet frontiers and the defence budget.

Are these changes purely cosmetic, or are other reconceptualisations in process that reinforce perceptions of a fundamental reassessment of the Soviet role in the international system? Soviet concepts of and approaches to international law are useful points of reference. Whereas the foreign policies of States may change from one day to another, the rules of law accepted as such by States in their international relations necessarily change at a slower pace. In the case of socialist States international law has posed a conundrum for Marxist-Leninist legal theory ever since the Soviet Government came to power in October 1917. Given the Marxian view that State and Law are elements of social superstructure determined by the economic relations and activities of the ruling classes of a particular society, how could a new socialist State be the subject of the pre-existing international legal order created entirely by bourgeois States? And since the differences among imperialist and socialist States were *a priori* deemed to be irreconcilable, with Revolution imminently inevitable in capitalist countries, what possibility existed for the creation of rules common to both social systems?

The tension between ideological presumption and diplomatic requirements was considerable. The Soviet Union stood alone in the international community for several years, eventually joined by the Mongolian People's Republic in 1921-24 after revolutions in Hungary, the Baltic republics, and Germany proved to be short-lived. Peace treaties needed to be negotiated, trade and consular relations re-established, diplomatic recognition achieved, frontiers demarcated. International law, whether bourgeois or otherwise, served simultaneously as an instrument of protection, of opportunity, of creativity, as well as a potential constraint upon the impact and influence of the Revolution.

Broadly speaking, there emerged two strains of "theory" in Soviet international legal doctrine. The first – sweeping, dismissive, combative – originated in the writings of chiefly academic scholars involved in practical international legal matters on a part-time basis. The principal figures were E. A. Korovin, E. B. Pashukanis, A. Ia. Vyshinskii, and G. I. Tunkin. The second strain – tentative, realistic, conciliatory – emerged in the articles and utterances of international legal advisers who engaged in part-time teaching and research. Among the major figures were: V. E. Grabar, A. V. Sabanin, V. L. Lakhtin, S. B. Krylov, V. N. Dur-denevskii, and again G. I. Tunkin, who in a sense bridged both approaches.

By 1952 there were indications that Soviet theory would move in the direction of accepting that a single superstructure of international legal rules exists, constituted by agreement between States of opposed social systems.[2] The principal architect of this postulate was G. I. Tunkin, whose subsequent writings, one building upon the other, have dominated Soviet international legal theory since 1956.[3] His notion of "agreement" became a cornerstone of the doctrine of peaceful coexistence, for agreement implied participation, involvement, and consensus vis-a-vis the international legal process. By the 1960s Soviet international legal doctrine accepted the existence of a "new international law," by which they meant an entire system of rules in whose formation the Soviet Union has been involved and to which it has assented.

In the course of time and events Soviet doctrine has declared that new States would have to accept the international system as they entered it (thereby dispensing with the right of new States to pick and choose the rules of international law by which they are bound). Methods of rule-formation other than the international treaty are deemed to be acceptable (customary international law) or helpful (certain documents of international institutions). Constructive as these notions have been in East-West relations, however, perestroika has occasioned a considered appraisal of their shortcomings as well as their virtues, for it is evident that the doctrines of the past are not wholly suitable to the modern day.

The implications of "new thinking" for Soviet approaches to international law were first explored extensively by Vereshchetin and Müllerson. A cardinal tenet is the establishment of the primacy of international law over State policy. This will require, they suggest, "a number of rather material changes in international law itself and a rethinking of certain of our traditional notions about international law."[4] Among the material changes is a reformulation of the doctrine of peaceful coexistence to become not, as previously, a form of class struggle in the international arena but rather a principle of general international law universal in application and binding in the relations of States. Further they propose to alter the traditional accent on "peaceful coexistence as the struggle and cooperation of States." Cooperation, they suggest, ought to be placed first in the equation as the most important element and "struggle" replaced by the expression "peaceful competition."

The papers in the present volume develop the approach of Müllerson and Vereshchetin in two senses. First, Soviet international lawyers have been invited to expound upon the "new thinking" and international law by addressing the principal branches of the discipline systematically and suggesting new lines of enquiry. Appropriately, Professor Tunkin inaugurates the investigation by addressing the primacy of international law in politics. An example of the new thinking in a tangible sense is the syllabus on human rights law translated at the end of the volume. Second, and uncharacteristically, English international lawyers have been asked to be "future-minded" with a view to identifying areas for or approaches to restructuring international law, extending a domestic Soviet preoccupation quite legitimately to the international plane.

The "new thinking" which emerges is not merely novel and original. Often it involves a reassertion of what might be called traditional or "middle-ground" positions in the interests of consensus. In the case of international institutions, it is remarkable how relevant the dreams cherished by their early architects seem so pertinent again. Underpinning these reformulations is the conviction that mankind shares a common fate and confronts common threats; that the hostilities of old, the risks of nuclear accident, the certainties of irreparable environmental harm, the horrors of war, whether local or otherwise, bear too high a price for the former patterns of inter-State relations to continue.

The papers published herein originated in the III Anglo-Soviet Symposium on Public International Law[5] held at University College London on 20-22 March 1989 under the auspices of the Centre for the Study of Socialist Legal Systems, University College London, and the Soviet Association of International Law. For material assistance in arranging the Symposium, we are especially grateful to the Foreign and Commonwealth Office for grant support administered by The British Academy. All Soviet contributions except that by Danilenko have been translated from the Russian language by the Editor.

Notes

1. See, for example, R. Müllerson, "The History of the Soviet Science of International Law," *Yearbook on Socialist Legal Systems 1988*, III (1989).
2. See W. E. Butler, "International Law, Foreign Policy, and the Gorbachev Style," *Columbia Journal of International Affairs*, XXII (1989), 363–375.
3. See G. I. Tunkin, *Osnovy sovremennogo mezhdunarodnogo prava* (1956); *id, Voprosy teorii mezhdunarodnogo prava* (1962); *id, Ideologicheskaia bor'ba i mezhdunarodnoe pravo* (1976); *id, Teoriia mezhdunarodnogo prava* (1970), revised in W. E. Butler (transl.), *Theory of International Law* (1974); *id, Pravo i sila v mezhdunarodnoi sisteme* (1983).
4. V.S. Vereshchetin and R. A. Müllerson, "Novoe myshlenie i mezhdunarodnoe pravo," *Sovetskoe gosudarstvo i pravo*, no. 3 (1988), p. 4.
5. The papers of the first symposium appear in W. E. Butler (ed.), *International Law and the International System* (Dordrecht, Nijhoff, 1987), and of the second symposium in Butler (ed.), *The Non-Use of Force in International Law* (Dordrecht, Nijhoff, 1989).

ON THE PRIMACY OF INTERNATIONAL LAW IN POLITICS

G. I. TUNKIN

The primacy of international law in politics or, to put it another way, the supremacy of international law in inter-State relations, is not a new issue. What is new is the situation in which the Soviet Union has raised this virtually forgotten question. "The world in which we live today," said M. S. Gorbachev in his address to the United Nations, "is fundamentally different from that at the beginning and even the middle of this century. And it continues to change in all its basic aspects."[1]

The world of today is a world of scientific-technical revolutions following one after another. The sphere of influence of various human problems is changing decisively. Many of those which were previously resolved at national levels have been transformed into global problems whose resolution requires the cooperation of not many, but all States.

But it not only a matter of this. The fate of human civilization has come to depend on the resolution of these global problems. The problem of survival has for the first time confronted mankind. Now mankind is bound together not merely by a joint existence on the planet Earth, but by a common fate. Together we survive, or together we perish is now the issue.

In order to survive mankind must ensure the normal functioning of an inter-State system which would preclude not only the possibility of nuclear war but likewise the possiblity of any large-scale armed conflicts and would create the essential prerequisites for resolving global problems. The most important condition for the normal functioning of the inter-State system is the primacy of international law in politics. It is from this that the question is posed anew.

International politics and international law

International politics is the process of the interaction of the foreign policies of various States. How does this interaction influence the creation of norms of international law and their functioning? According to the concept which is predominant in world international legal doctrine, norms of international law are created in relations between States and are not introduced from without. It follows that international politics influences the creation thereof.

The creation of norms of international law is the process of bringing the wills of States into concordance. The content of the will of a State is its international legal position, which constitutes part of the foreign policy position of a State. In the

W. E. Butler, Perestroika and International Law, 5–12.
© 1990 *Kluwer Academic Publishers. Printed in the Netherlands.*

6

course of forming new norms of international law there occurs the bringing into concordance of the international legal positions of States, bringing their wills into concordance relative to the content of rules of behaviour and recognising them to be legally binding. This process takes place within the framework of the inter-State system. An international legal norm is formed when the bringing of the wills of States into concordance is completed. One may thus believe that politics has primacy when norms of international law are created. The former Chief Legal Adviser of the French Ministry of Foreign Affairs, and later member of the International Court of Justice, Guy de Lacharriere, wrote: "Nothing prevents us from regarding international law as that which politics desired, at least the politics of the dominant States."[2]

Although born in the sphere of international politics, norms of international law are distinct from the phenomenon of politics. The fact that norms of international law are formed in the sphere of international politics objectively has facilitated the emergence of the concept of international law being mixed with politics. The notion most prevalent at present is the "policy-oriented international law" of Myres McDougal, in the creation of which the sociologist Harold Lasswell had an important part. McDougal formulates the essence of this notion as follows:

international law is most realistically regarded, after the model of the American Legal Realists with respect to the law of any community, as that comprehensive process of authoritative decision by which the members of the larger community of humankind seek to clarify and secure their common interests in the shaping and sharing of all values. The inherited body of rules, described as international law in the positivist frame, with its abundant complementarities, ambiguities and incompletions, has meaning only insofar as it refers to past decision or to the guidance, not command, of future decision.[3]

Thus is international law dissolved into politics, since "the process of authoritative decision" is politics. As Stanley Hoffmann writes: "international law is one of the aspects of international politics."[4]

However, life persuasively bears witness that international law exists as an independent social phenomenon. References to international law embellish international documents: diplomatic correspondence, resolutions of international organisations, declarations of social organisations, and so forth. There are various views on the role of international law, but even those who believe that this role is insignificant acknowledge the existence of international law as a phenomenon distinct from politics.

Norms of international law are the scale for the behaviour of States and other subjects of international law and are legally binding upon them. They establish the legal parametres for politics. The legally binding nature of norms of international law distinguish them from other social norms which function in the inter-State system (norms of recommendatory resolutions of international organisations, political norms, norms of international morality, and others). This specific feature is analogous in general to the specific features of norms of municipal law. It consists of the fact that norms of law make provision for the possibility of applying State coercion to secure compliance with those norms.

Since norms of international law are created in the sphere of politics, this means that politics determines the framework within which it may juridically operate. It is appropriate in this connection to dwell on a delusion of diplomacy: that it is essential to endeavour to resolve international problems by political means. This is quite correct if one has in mind that international problems must not be resolved with the aid of force. But it is only partially true. Political means alone can never secure the normal functioning of the inter-State system. Together with politics it is essential to have a system of legal norms which establish the parametres of politics, that is, an order, a legal order, which is obligatory for States.

Norms of international law seemingly program the behaviour of States, being to a certain extent not merely a means of regulating, but also of planning those relations. They comprise a normative system making it possible to foresee the reaction of other actors in the inter-State system to particular actions of a State. Other social norms which function in the international system also play a certain, albeit subordinate, role with respect to international law.

Therefore their negotiations on important international issues States endeavour wherever possible to complete with the conclusion of international treaties, and not merely agreements about intentions. International treaties create legally binding norms, that is, norms of international law. Experience shows that to achieve positive results in negotiations on international matters both the art of politics and the art of law are needed. Only in that event can one achieve a "balance of interests" as the basis for the effectiveness of norms of international law and the legal perfection thereof, which is another important condition for the effectiveness of those norms.

Thus, international politics and international law are in constant interaction. Norms of international law are created in relations between States, that is, in the sphere of international politics. Having emerged as a special social phenomenon, they exert influence on international politics. This interaction is clearly manifest in the stabilising and creative role of international law. International law legally consolidates relations between States created by politics, and simultaneously is the legal basis for the creation of new relations between them, which again are created by politics.

This can be demonstrated, for example, in the United Nations. At the outset politics were directed toward the creation of a universal international organisation for the maintenance of international peace and security. As a result of those politics, international legal norms were worked out: the United Nations Charter. On the basis of the Charter; the United Nations was created by political means. As a result of the further interaction between politics and law, it grew into an enormous international machinery.

Concept of the primacy of international law in politics

The task of ensuring the primacy of international law in international politics comes down to ensuring that the norms of international law created by States through agreement encompass all spheres of vitally important relations between States and that these norms are complied with by States. The problem is a multi-faceted one, connected in one way or another with all aspects of social life. On the political-legal level, the following above all are required to ensure the primacy of international law in politics:

[1]. The rejection of an obsolete and dangerous anachronism of a conceptual model of an inter-State system according to which the relations between sovereign States, above which there is no supreme authority, are built or may be built on force, above all armed force. The acceptance of a new conceptual model of an inter-State system, according to which in order to save human civilisation from perishing it is essential that relations between States be based not on force, but on equal negotiations and agreements, that is, on international law.

This model includes cessation of the arms race and a reduction of arms to the level of reasonable sufficiency, and the elimination of nuclear weapons and other means of mass destruction, the very existence of which is a danger to mankind.

This model means a humanisation and democratisation of inter-State relations, since all States irrespective of their might will act as truly equal subjects of international law.

[2]. Acknowledgement of the priority of general humanitarian values. The growth of the significance of general humanitarian values is the result of the growing interconnections and unity of the fate of all people on earth. The priority of general humanitarian values over national and class values is not a pious wish but an imperative requirement of the modern age. It is reflected above all in the fact that the quantity of global problems on whose resolution the very existence of human civilisation depends is growing. This is not merely the threat of nuclear self-destruction, but the ecological threat, the threat of underdevelopment, the threat of despoiling natural resources, and others.

Every State is a component of the system of global problems and since the well-being and even the existence of individual States depends on the resolution of these problems, as does that of mankind as a whole, the global problems objectively take priority over national problems.

[3]. The inter-State system and the municipal system interact, and States are the principal components of the inter-State system, of the politics on which its functioning depends. The peculiarities of this system and its functioning exert a

great influence on the foreign policy of a State. Beyond doubt a State in which democracy and legality predominate and respect for human rights is ensured can be expected to respect international law in the international arena more than a State in which arbitrariness predominates. Therefore, the existence of the greatest possible number of rule-of-law States which can set the tone of international life is an important prerequisite for the primacy of international law in politics. As M. S. Gorbachev said in his address at the United Nations on 7 December 1988: "Our ideal is a world community of rule-of-law States which are subordinate to law also in their foreign policy activity."[5]

[4]. The further development of international law. Even before the emergence of nuclear weapons international law had taken a gigantic step forward on the path of a non-coercive world. The 1928 Pact of Paris prohibited recourse to war, and the United Nations Charter went further, prohibiting the use or threat of force in relations between States. The emergence in international law of such important new principles as the principles of peaceful coexistence, equality, and self-determination of peoples had great importance, as did the further development of the old democratic principles of international law. Considerable success was achieved in the progressive development of international law after the creation of the United Nations. Contemporary international law is an extensive system of norms which can be called the legal minimum for peaceful coexistence and the normal functioning of the inter-State system.

At the same time, contemporary international law does not contain a sufficient number of norms on such vitally important global problems as disarmament, the protection and rational use of the environment, ensuring the accelerated development of economically backward countries, and the like. The further rapid development of international law is especially essential in the most important and dangerous areas of inter-State relations.

[5]. The creation of effective international machinery for the functioning of international law and enhancing its effectiveness. Such machinery is essential both to make international law effective and to enforce it with respect to States which violate international law. There is such machinery at present, but it is insufficiently effective, especially as regards enforcement.

The possibility of using State coercion to secure compliance with norms of law is a specific feature of both municipal and international law. Appropriate agencies exist in a State to ensure compliance with norms of law; they may in the instances established by law use coercion with respect to a subject of law irrespective of its consent.

In the inter-State system the principal actors and potential violators of international law are States, above whom there is no supreme authority. Therefore, the possiblity of creating norms of international law making provision for the use of coercion with respect to States depends upon agreement between States. At the moment those possiblities are rather limited in international law.

10

At present according to international law individual States may apply a rather broad group of enforcement measures to violator-States. Such measures may include diplomatic representations and protests, various forms of economic and other restrictions, the rupture of diplomatic relations, and other actions with the exception of the use of armed force.

Together with these, States are to a greater degree endowing international organisations with the right to take enforcement measures against States which violate international law on the basis of the agreement of all. The United Nations has especially extensive powers with respect to taking enforcement measures. The list of enforcement measures which may be applied by the United Nations goes beyond measures which States may use. Whereas States may use armed force against other States only in the event of an armed attack (Article 51, United Nations Charter), the United Nations may use armed force not merely in the event of an armed attack against a State (Article 42, United Nations Charter). In so doing, decisions to use enforcement measures are taken by the Security Council, that is, by an organ with a limited membership. This is already an element of supranationality.

The inter-State system needs a strengthening of normative regulation, the principal means of which are international law and international organisations, further possess possibilities for such strengthening.

The way forward

The question arises of how far in this direction may we go in the foreseeable future.

There exist two types of laws of societal development which have direct application to this matter. First, there is the process of the growing interconnections and interdependence of States and the emergence of global problems on whose resolution depends the fate of civilisation and which can be resolved only through the collective efforts of States. This law is manifest, in particular, in the rapid development of international law and international organisations and the enhancement of their role in society. If we proceed only from this law of societal development, the road is open for the creation of a world government.

However, there are other laws of societal development which operate in another direction. These are above all and principally the existence of sovereign States and two socio-economic systems.

Of course, State sovereignty is not absolute and does not mean complete freedom of action. States may, while preserving the attributes of sovereignty, by means of agreements concluded on the basis of equality and voluntariness, limit their freedom of action. It is on this path that the development of international law has proceeded. For example, in the nineteenth century international law recognised the "right of a State to go to war," which was regarded as a major attribute of State sovereignty. On the basis of agreement, States have renounced this right, and a major principle of contemporary international law is the principle of the non-use of force, which includes first and foremost a prohibition to resort to war. State sovereignty is exercised within the framework of international law, whose norms are created by means of agreement between States.

The matter is similar with respect to international organisations. While remaining sovereign, States in creating international organisations by means of concluding treaties endow them with specific powers. These may be supranational powers, the essence of which in accepting resolutions of international organisations as binding upon their members. However, such an international organisation with specific supranational powers is an inter-State organisation, and not a world government.

Thus, the existence of sovereign States does not preclude the creation of an effective international organisation possessing supranational powers and functions in specific questions.

As regards differences of socio-economic systems, this fact undoubtedly is an insuperable obstacle to the creation of a world government and a world State. It also is an obstacle to the creation of an effective international organisation, but that obstacle can be overcome. States, having transferred part of their prerogatives to an international organisation, continue to remain sovereign, and the questions of socio-economic system as before are relegated to the exclusive domestic jurisdiction of States, and the international organisation may not interfere in those.

Consequently, insuperable obstacles on the path of enhancing the effectiveness of international organisations, above all of the United Nations, do not exist, and the need to save human civilisation will be an important stimulus for overcoming those difficulties in the way.

In order to move forward on the path toward the primacy of international law in politics, the full use of other machinery for the functioning of international law presently existing has enormous significance: direct negotiations, mediation, conciliation procedures, international arbitration, and courts. Of course, the International Court of Justice has special significance in this respect, the acceptance of the compulsory jurisdiction of which by all States on the largest possible number of questions would be a significant step forward.

In order to preserve the civilisation created in the course of thousands of years and even its own life, mankind must make the greatest effort in history to replace the law of force with the force of law. This requires a cardinal restructuring of thinking. But there is no other way.

Notes

1. *Pravda*, 8 December 1988.
2. G. de Lacharrière, *La politique juridique extérieure* (1983), p. 199.
3. M. McDougal, "The Dorsey Comment: A Modest Retrogression," *American Journal of*

12

International Law, LXXXII (1988), 53–54.
4. S. Hoffmann, "International System and International Law," in K. Knorr and S. Verba (eds.), *The International System: Theoretical Essays* (1967), p. 205.
5. See note 1 above.

CHANGING MODELS OF THE INTERNATIONAL SYSTEM

J. A. CARTY

If international law is supposed to rest upon the practice of States then it is surely not out of place to give serious consideration to the thoughts of the chairman of one of the two superpowers on the nature of the international system. The reflections of international lawyers on that system are in fact what lawyers call international law. The system itself is created and maintained by statesmen such as M. S.Gorbachev. Therefore his writings have a quality which is much more primary than, for instance, the reflections of international lawyers in an institution such as the ICJ.

The memoirs and speeches of a prominent politician that do not relate to specific disputes which engage his State may easily be passed over by a profession so deeply averse to theory as is that of international law. After all, this person is not a prominent legal publicist. His opinions are perhaps influential, but even if this be the case, one should look to where these opinions find expression in State acts. However it is a movement such as perestroika which underlies attempts, coming primarily from the Socialist bloc, and the Soviet Union itself, to reshape the entire international system. Perestroika underlies the new Soviet policy which leads Gorbachev's proposal to strengthen the ICJ. The interest of perestroika lies at the deeper level of the assumptions it makes about how, and how far, the international system can be changed.

Perestroika, from the book of the same name and subtitled in its English edition "New Thinking for our Country and the World" is a definite reaffirmation of the values of liberalism, thought to be Western, but in fact here demonstrated to be part of, at the very least, wider European tradition. In a word, it supposes, as an ideal to be vigorously implemented, that the shaping of national and international society, is to be achieved through the most widespread critical debate possible. This debate has to be seen as an unstoppable process, the impact of which is as dynamic as the uncertainties which no one would deny underlie the whole of international relations. For instance, a treaty on any matter which affects the serious political interests of States, for example, that concerning intermediate nuclear weapons) cannot be taken to freeze in legal terms the military relations of States. The compromise which it represents will soon be destabilised if States do not work to complete it in other areas and refrain from upsetting the balance of military forces underlying the conclusion of the treaty. So there has to be sustained an overall dynamic of critical debate which engages the forces that impede progress.

How does this concern international lawyers, always so reluctant to engage in political controversy? At one level Gorbachev's work is yet another call to respect the basic liberal principles of international law, above all, equality and non-

W. E. Butler, Perestroika and International Law, 13–30.

intervention. Lawyers might then be taken as charged with interpreting how these principles are applied in the practice of States. The vigorous debate among American international lawyers at the time of the Vietnam War about the legality of the American involvement must surely represent a remarkable example of a critical and independent reflection of an international legal profession on its country's conduct.[1] Such a debate may be unusual among international lawyers from other Western countries who do not often find themselves at the centre of dialogue about the vital foreign policy interests of their States. However, it has not been argued that such debate is beyond the scope of the profession.

Yet such an interpretation of the Vietnam debate does not go to the heart of the perestroika enterprise. It leaves unanswered such queries as: what is the significance of the interpretations given by those who call themselves international lawyers and the principles which they are defending (usually in a contradictory manner, and at cross-purposes; for instance it would be difficult to say that a common view emerged out of the legal debate on the Vietnam War). By "significance" is meant not merely on what authority do these people hold forth on the public scene and what impact do they expect to have? Even such questions are rarely asked, and were they there would be general agreement that a reference to Article 38(1)(c) of the Statute of the ICJ would be regarded as arcane (primarily because of the type of audience the lawyers would have been trying to reach and influence, i.e. the politicised American general public, rather than the international judiciary).

Can it be said that such persons constitute an independent and critical intelligentsia engaged in a debate for the heart of the "res publica." In this view their contribution to public life would be decisive. The vague and contradictory nature of the basic liberal principles of international society – again equality, non-intervention, respect for the autonomy of national communities, absence of hegemonial and imperialist ambitions (short terms for the denial of liberalism stated in a positive form) – is then resolved through informed public dialogue which must have some break-off point, but which, by its very nature, does not have to be given a systematic, logically consistent, and definitive form. The desire for such debate and, above all, the belief that it can and should be significant, is the very essence of perestroika; it promises a remarkable rejuvenation for the profession of international law precisely as a liberal profession. The question, of course, remains whether perestroika is still possible.

What follows intends to explain how perestroika is a development of a liberal democratic concept of international society which, at least at the level of doctrine, has been a consistent feature of some Soviet international legal theory since before Gorbachev. How closely this resembles classical liberal theory as to the nature and function of public debate will be shown, concluding with a presentation of how the "high liberal" concept of the international law profession in the 1870s corresponds closely to the same model. There will follow an introduction to the recent debate within social and literary theory – particularly in West Germany and the Soviet Union – about the continued possibility of such debate in late twentieth century "Euro-American" societies. The concluding part will offer modest notes about how at the micro-level of detailed legal argument a liberal approach could and should permeate the profession of international law in terms of a critical hermeneutic.

Perestroika and democratic international law

Gorbachev stresses a substantive rather than a formal concept of democracy. Restructuring is to come from the triumph of reason and conscience over passivity and indifference. The mass media are to provide the forum for every citizen to voice his opinion confidently, thereby guaranteeing the correctness of decisions and their conformity with the interests of the masses. The key to this revitalization is that the press should prefer dialogue to monologue (pp. 76–77). Criticism is not only self-expression, a fulfilment of personal interets and ambitions, but a matter of public importance, a dialogue of those who criticize and those who are criticized (p.78). An intelligentsia even of individuals who consider themselves to be their own foremost authorities is preferable to an antagonistic class struggle. It is a quest to include every honestly held perspective, which is bound to reflect some real aspects of life. In this the intelligentsia exercises a civic responsibility (p. 82).

This notion of democratic debate is linked directly to economic democracy. Resourceful quality performance must come from real social demands, with the growth of direct ties between the manufacturers and consumers, with the employee's income depending upon the fulfilment of contract commitments. Gorbachev calls this a socialist market (pp. 83–92). This is not an equalizing doctrine. It is a matter of each according to his work (pp. 100–101), and the direct link with political democracy is that the work-place itself, where a great part of modern existence is spent, must be democratized. That is, the internal structures of social groups must permit full debate (p. 104). The removal of the command economy system of management is necessary if the people are to exercise their constitutional right to have direct involvement in the affairs of the State (p. 111).

It is with this substantive notion of critical democrary that Gorbachev passes from national to international affairs. The principle of critical dialogue is rooted in the basis liberal postulates of liberty and equality, the foundations of humanism at all levels of human society:

> I for one am sick of the attempts by some politicians to teach others how to live and what policies to conduct. They proceed from the arrogant assumption that the life and policy of their own country is an example and model of freedom, democracy, economic activity and social standard. I think it would be far more democratic to assume that other nations can disagree with this point of view. In

our own complicated and troubled world it is impossible to measure everything by one's own yardstick. Attempts at military diktat as well as at moral, political and economic pressure, are out of fashion today (p. 132).

Gorbachev does not stop with equality in the form of peaceful coexistence. He considers that the impossibility of war means that international politics have to be based on ethical and moral norms that are common to all mankind. Mutually advantageous agreements have to be based upon supreme common interest (pp. 140–143). This is not to ignore the importance of class conflict, nor the presence of interest groups such as the military-industrial complex in the United States (pp. 148–149). Yet the principle of self-determination of peoples is seen by Gorbachev primarily as a principle of critical reason. It means that the complexities of the modern world are such that dialogue has to be undertaken with people from different philosophical and political systems. Gorbachev takes a subtle step forward to the humanist position that it is a matter of interpenetration of different world views, coming from scientists, writers, and cultural personalities. It is a matter of listening to the concerns of an international intellectual elite when it expresses views for a common humanity (pp. 152–153). Even the opinion of one man matters where it reflects the thoughts and concerns of millions (p. 155).

For such an approach to international politics there must be first-hand information about the intentions of statesmen (p. 156). We must return to the original meaning of the words we use in international contacts. The avoidance of double-faced policies is essential for stability. This implies a new style extending beyond the traditional diplomatic process. Once again it is not merely a matter of governments and even Parliaments. One must recognize the invasion of this domain by public opinion. People's diplomacy, a way of addressing the peoples directly, is becoming a standard means of inter-State contact.

There is no doubt that, in theoretical terms, Gorbachev has changed the parameters of the previous Soviet doctrine of peaceful coexistence. He does not envisage a static model of self-restraining yet still mutually opposed ideological systems. Instead he speaks of foreign policy not being made subject to ideological differences. A responsible attitude to policy requires scientific substantiation. With the threat of nuclear annihilation, there is need for humanity to develop the priority of human values so as to bring States of different social systems to cooperate with one another (pp. 143–147).

This differs from the notion of the democratic model of the global system which G. I. Tunkin has expounded in *Law and Force in the International System*, published in Russian (1983). However, Tunkin does insist that while socialist and bourgeois democracy are radically different types of democracy, both are nonetheless democratic, and so it is possible for the general international system to reflect that reality in our consciousness (pp. 239–240). Tunkin accepts that there are other progressive forces besides socialism shaping the democratic character of international law, so that for the first time it can reflect the interests of the entire human race and not merely those of a narrower ruling class (p. 241). As Tunkin envisages the democratic character of peace, it is not limited to refraining from the use of force. It is necessary to undertake positive actions to avoid violations of the peace (p. 245). He stresses that there is an ideological aspect of the socialist concept of peaceful coexistence which Western States cannot be expected to share. Therefore, it is also necessary to stress the general-democratic character of peaceful coexistence which the West can share. This requires not merely tolerance, but living together on the basis of principles of good neighbourliness. There has to be active cooperation to resolve international problems.

Nonetheless, it is clear that Tunkin has in mind primarily questions of security and that he believes it neither desirable nor possible to harmonize ideologies (pp. 247–249). The most that can be required is that the law prohibiting propaganda of a warlike character against an opposing ideological system (p. 249). The notion of democracy itself is limited to State structures. Relations among sovereign States can and must be based on negotiations which lead to binding agreements resting upon respect for the equality of the parties (pp. 226–228). While Gorbachev could be expected to endorse this perspective in strictly legal terms, he does elaborate upon a more diffuse and substantive rather than formal notion of democracy in international relations.

If a Western international lawyer reacts sceptically to what might appear fine distinctions about the democratic character of international law and relations, it should be worth noting that Tunkin makes forceful remarks about Western and in particular American perspectives on the nature and scope of international law. When one considers this aspect of his study alongside Gorbachev's own work, there is a clear continuity of thought. This is explicable in terms of the elementary fact that the West and in particular the United States are not considered to have susbstantially modified their hostility to and distrust of socialist States. The problem still remains, as Gorbachev puts it, that universal security "rests on the recognition of the right of every nation to choose its own path of social development ... on respect for others in combination with an objective self-critical view of one's own society" (p. 143).

So a large part of Tunkin's work objects to the manner in which many Western international lawyers treat their discipline primarily in the area of technical, everyday matters, leaving aside as beyond feasible legal regulation, matters of substantial political importance. These will be, in the final analysis, decided by States in the light of their vital interests (esp. pp. 176–178, but generally, pp. 171–190; also p. 289). In other words, the argument can be stated by default, that there is not a serious academic literature in the West which attempts to grapple with the issues, however apparently scholastic, that Tunkin is handling. It may come as a surprise to Western international lawyers that the most prominent Soviet international lawyer considers that their academic view of their subject is not significantly distinguishable from the extreme Hegelianism current in Germany in the late nineteenth century (esp. pp. 170–172).

The second major theme of Tunkin's analysis concerns what he takes to be the imperialist character of United States foreign policy. The stress placed on the litany of United States "misdemeanours" may be a matter of judgment or taste, but there is a definite continuity to the present when Tunkin quotes at length the comments of George Kennan on Reagan's foreign policy in 1982. In particular he concludes by noting how Kennan accuses the Reagan administration's failure "to recognise the commonality of many of their problems and ours as we move inexorably into the modern technological age; and this corresponding tendency to view all aspects of the relationship in terms of a supposed total and irreconcilable conflict of concerns ..." (p. 283).

The common ground between these two perspectives is that the most vital part of international law is its democratic character, and that the essence of that part is an ethical component of liberal values of respect for the autonomy of the "other," whether an individual and his human rights, or a community and its right of independence. These are, as Tunkin pointed out, also Western values. Bourgeois democracy is definitely not fascist (p. 239). The question is how these ethical matters might be a central professional concern of Western international lawyers.

The classical role of liberal opinion and the most "highly qualified" international publicists

An exhaustive account of the development of the liberal notion of intellectual political life in the nineteenth century and of the place of international scholarship within it is not possible here. The more modest ambitions here entertained are to understand how such a life was thought to be possible; what could be achieved and why; and finally, the continuing relevance of this experience. Our subject remains the possibility of effective public debate, a form of substantive democracy. Essentially the concern resembles that of Habermas: how there can be unconstrained public debate in advanced industrial societies dominated by powerful economic, social, and bureaucratic interest groups. In fact Habermas' question – how such debate is to be rediscovered – is the same as the anxiety as to whether perestroika is possible. So it seems that a suitable historical framework in which to examine the question is afforded by his "Changing Structures of the Public Space" and the context which it helps us to set as regards the founding of the Institute of International Law in 1873.

The classical liberal public space was not the sole prerogative of State power, but belonged as well to civil society, which saw the public interest as an "affair" to which it might contribute with a public use of its reasoning powers (Habermas, pp. 34, 38). This capacity for reasoned public debate was seen as rooted in the untrammelled subjectivity of the individual, protected by his economic independence and by the (perhaps) emotional privacy guaranteed by the family (p. 39). For this notion of debate each participant is taken as a simple person without hierarchy or status, equality is assumed, and the laws of the market are suspended, to achieve a detachment beyond mere competitiveness (p. 47). Ideas of public reasoning were intimately related to the notion of conversation and dialogue. The independence of the individual conscience was decisive (p. 53). The very idea of "humanity" in this liberal sense rested on free will, the intimacy of the family (i.e., free of compelling social constraints) and an independent intellectual culture (pp. 56–57). This internalised sentiment of independence provided the foundation for a critical approach to all established social constraints, hence the connection between Enlightenment and emancipation (p. 58).

Such a notion of liberal political rationality is tied to a substantive and therefore elusive view of constitutional legality. The constitutional State has to guarantee the connection between law and public opinion. The reign of law signifies the representation of the people. However, law is not simply an expression of the will of a particular group of people, but also a guarantee of a "ratio" which puts aside a dimension of domination, precisely because it is the outcome of a continuing spirit of public debate. In so far as law is an expression of agreement based upon rational public discussion, the inevitable arbitrariness of actual laws has to be submitted to the constant pressure of public debate, so that a positive legal order cannot be seen as a static phenomenon. There must be a constant pressure to turn "voluntas" into "ratio" (pp. 91–93). Clearly there is presupposed the possibility that each person can attain the independence of property and culture which will permit a detached concern for the general public welfare, the res publica, a dream which harks back to the classical Greek polity, still very much an ideal for Habermas. Once this public transforms itself into a dominant class, reason will become dogma and opinion will become command. Nevertheless, the bourgeois idea of legality remains that truth, not authority, makes law and that liberal political rationality is able to untie the dominant force of group interest (pp. 96–98). Clearly Habermas does not attempt to argue that the entire Western political tradition fits into such a mould. It is Kant, rather than Rousseau or Hobbes, who is his mentor. Nor is it every educated lay person who lifts his pen. The spirit of the Enlightenment does depend, above all, upon an intellectual class. They must be independent vis-a-vis the State and elaborate critical principles for their own sake. In his view it is to philosophy that one must look and not to law, theology, and medicine, all of which rest upon authority, erudition, and a certain supervision by the State (pp. 114–115). However, there is no hierarchy of rational authority. That is a contradiction in terms. Nor are professional demarcations clear. The general principles of bourgeois legality in question have to serve to remove or at least assuage the element of command and domination in public life. This means a conflation of law and morality (p. 118). The task of public instruction then falls to what Kant calls, in his Critique of the

Faculties, "professeurs de Droit libres," which really presupposes an underlying pre-statist natural law (pp. 125–126).

In 1873 the founders of the Institute of International Law stated[2] that recent events in Europe and America had given rise to a general awareness of the imperfections of international law. Although there was a huge proliferation of international legislation, it was confined to administrative and technical fields.[3] It might be wondered how international lawyers thought they could hope to direct or regulate the activities of powerful, centralised States. Even in the most democratic of States the foreign offices and diplomatic services continued to be staffed from a minute section of society. Parliament and public opinion were not important, although they exercised influence at certain intervals. Foreign affairs were still the prerogative of a largely pre-bourgeois aristocratic class, who nonetheless were mostly honourable men. They really experienced a conflict of loyalties between the defence of their country and the claims of a common heritage and unity in the civilisation of Europe.[4] What is incongruous about the growth of a bourgeois perspective on international law at this time is that the most distinctive feature of a continuing "ancien regime" was the secrecy with which its affairs were conducted.[5]

Nonetheless, the Institute was set up by academic lawyers "to serve as an organ for the legal opinion of the civilised world on the subject of international law."[6] These men were attracted by the establishment of associations in other disciplines, such as history and medicine. They wished to set up an institution which could, without the bias of belonging to one nationality, give "… au sentiment élevé du droit et à la conscience du genre humain son expression la plus haute et la plus pure." While it is difficult to assess the exact nature of this sentiment, it is not to be found simply in the practice of States, for they were careful to distinguish the role of the jurist from that of the diplomat in these terms:

> D'une part les dipomates, quelle que soient leurs lumières et leurs expérience, n'arrivent pas facilement à discerner et à formuler les règles absolues de droit, parcequ'ils ne peuvent oublier ni les instructions des souverains qu'ils représentent, ni l'intérêt particulier des nations qu'ils ont mission de défendre."[7]

The nature of the preferred international system is profoundly liberal. International law would be negated by a world federation. Individual nationalities must be preserved, but must submit to the laws of justice. These lawyers rely upon an ethical sense of mankind, for they see their task in the following terms.

> de découvrir et de préciser les règles de justice, de morale et de fraternité, qu'il reconnaissent comme devant être la base des relations des peuples entre eux, voilà, nous a-t-il semblé, le moyen de faire contribuer au science collective."[8]

The law which had to be acceptable to States was one whose guiding principles were: "Verité et Justice à tous, Independence de tous les peuples, et surtout Guarantie des faibles contre les abus de la force.[9] Jurists have to state the juridical opinion of the civilised world as clearly as possible, so that it can be accepted by States as regulating their relations.[10]

The founders of the Institute said that without the support of public opinion even the unanimity of men of science would be of no effect. This is not to say that they relied upon public opinion alone. There was a law of progress and there were the imperfections of human nature.[11] In spite of the vicissitudes of politics, the society of fact existing between nations is becoming a society of law, because it is difficult for an individual or a State to confine its activities to its own territory. In these circumstances rules of law are not merely a moral and scientific necessity, but also a political necessity of the first order.[12]

Perhaps a representative and more detailed exposition of the assumptions underlying this theory of law might be gleaned from the writings of Alfonse Rivier, who succeeded Rolin-Jaequemyns as the second secretary-general of the Institute. His "Principles du Droit des Gens" was not, in his view, a digest of material but a guide to politicians and diplomats which aimed to draw out from the multiplicity of facts certain general and dependable principles and rules of law universally and habitually respected "de façon à faire ressortir ce qu'il appelle "la conscience juridique des nations".[13] In the preface to the Serbian edition of his work, Rivier, a Swiss national, said that he thought the task of the jurists was:

> de contrôler les actes des politiques et de les juger, non d'après un code arbitraire, mais du point de vue le plus élevé du juste et de l'injuste; il proclame que c'est abaisser le droit des gens envisagé comme science que de lui assigner le rôle presque passif d'un simple enrégistreur et classification des faits internationaux; il affirme qu'il doit constamment s'inspirer des principes supérieurs de la morale, de la justice et de la fraternité.[14]

So for Rivier the notion of general customary law itself had to be understood in the context of a wider concept of liberal legality which it was the function of jurists to uphold by their power of legal reasoning in public debate. Rivier says that States are independent, but that, in their autonomy, they adopt certain rules and submit to certain principles, whose necessity they recognise, this voluntary consent expressing itself in custom and treaties.[15] However voluntary it may be, the positive law is not merely changeable and relative. It is not arbitrary: "Ses principes decoulent des relations effectives des peuples, de l'ordre universal, tel que Dieu l'a crée et continue à le créer."[16] He says the definition of the law of nations supposes a plurality of States which submit their relations to common juridical principles:

> Ils montrent ainsi qu'ils possédent une conscience juridique commune, laquelle

se modifie et se perfectionne à mesure qu'eux-mêmes progressent et que leurs relations mutuelles se développent et se multiplient.[17]

The twilight of liberalism and the risks of perestroika

It is a commonplace of recent debate that perestroika risks floundering on the immobile power of vested interests, that the military, industrial, and bureaucratic structures do not allow for the reasoned debate about the public interest which may have been possible to a limited extent in the rarified governing circles of mid-nineteenth century Europe. It is equally a commonplace of classical Marxist theory that such debate can be no more than the reflection of economic interest groups impelled forward in terms of their own internal dynamics. Habermas is perfectly aware of this last objection and takes it as his point of departure for the preparation of a solution, to which we shall return later (Habermas, pp. 131–138).

A study on problems of theory in international law suggests a series of obstacles to a continued role for international lawyers as the Institute originally envisaged. Basically the State appears as an instrumental superstructure providing a framework for the modern industrial State within such a context, the role of law is purely technical and the lawyer furnishes, at most, a legal information service.[18] One has only to state the problem in these terms to see how ambitious is the idea of perestroika. That is to say, even if the profession of international law is persuaded to resume the type of debate once thought to be possible, it must be obvious to Marxists above all that its "real" impact will be negligible. The work of restructuring international law could only be an immense task.

The terms of the problem were set quite brilliantly by a rather unusual Englishman, Thomas Baty, in two works, *The Canons of International Law* (1930) and *International Law in Twilight* (1954). He undertook a panoramic, although thoroughly destructive, survey of the remnants of classical liberal international law theory. He retains a liberal model of the role of law. He does not accept the view that law consists merely of regulations issuing from a definite authority, because any law must have a foundation in the conscience of the general public (Twilight, p. 10). This signifies that a connected tissue of rules is felt by the generality of people to exercise a binding force of stringency.

To be sure, his view of the public is elitist in the traditional sense. So the Law of Nations operates upon the minds of statesmen and publicists who have a direct share in controlling the affairs of nations. It follows that it does not bind the mass of private individuals who hardly know of its existence (Twilight, pp. 1–2). The character of the law should ideally reflect this fact. It may be supported by physical force but it cannot originate in it, as that would involve a degraded consciousness of a simple necessity (Canons, p. 24). In his view:

Resting on the deep consciousness of unrelated and uncommunicative individuals, differing from each other literally, as East from West, unable to agreee on simple refinements, and still less to articulate their agreement or difference, the Law of Nations must be simple … Deriving its force from the common belief of a multitude of heterogeneous elements, the Law of Nations contains an element of weakness, due to the fact that common belief is extremely difficult to prove … (Canons, p. 27).

The question must arise whether law understood in this sense continues to exist. Baty thinks that a crucial obstacle has been, since the First World War, the ideological constitution of States which reduce everything to their own absolutes. Marxism and fascism are obvious targets, but Baty outlines another category: Anglo-American democracy which is "bureaucracy designed as freedom: the rule of party politicians and the party machine" (Twilight, p. 10). It is the way lawyers consider the personality of the State which makes the whole subject of international law sterile. States appear to be regarded as indestructible entities (Twilight, p. 45). After the eclipse of the human sovereign, whether monarch or oligarchy, a number of factors contributed to the view that not only the form of a government but even the fact of it was non-essential to the continued existence of the State (Twilight, p. 30). These factors included the Hegelian philosophy of the State, the Anglo-American theory of the joint-stock company, State socialism and, once again Anglo-American, plutocratic bureaucracy. He said that the joint-stock company in particular:

familiarized the minds of practical people with the conception of an artificial person, not as a thing of poetry and fancy, but as a practical business proposition, with definite effects in the field of human action.

He added that such a theory suits a bureaucratic view of the State: under which the activities and interests of the ordinary individual are subordinated to an inelastic system administered for the furtherance of an abstract national objective (Twilight, pp. 42–44).

The symbiotic relationship of the "State" lawyer to inter-State law is well summed up by Habermas in his assertion that the loss of independence of the intellectual is rooted both in the loss of a private, interior life and in the exclusion from active, in the sense of spontaneous, participation in public life (Habermas, p. 165). A process of "disinteriorisation" is the converse of the social absorption by an all-embracing State regulatory apparatus (p. 167). An independent critical standard becomes inconceivable as a matter of the sociology of knowledge. On a matter of apparent detail, which has nonetheless enormous significance for perestroika, Habermas draws a sharp contrast between the private culture of the traditional bourgeois, who engages in independent investigation and integration of material, and the "ready-made" debate furnished by the mass media, in which the vast majority can participate only at a voyeuristic level that cannot possibly unpack the rigid social structures of modern society. Such public debate becomes one more form of production and consumption which will inevitably obey its own laws of the social market, without necessarily having any impact on the rest of the system (pp. 170–172). Public discussion takes the form of fabricating an acclamatory consensus as a passive social response and is a far cry from the Enlightenment ideal of civil society as the foundation for independently directed criticism of public power. Such a picture cannot survive the totally integrative function of the production-consumption cycle of the social market (p. 203).

As Baty himself had indicated, power is now transferred to groupings, whether public or private, whose interests are reflected in attitudes, and which use publicity, the mediation of pre-digested views, as part of a bargaining process, where "consensus" reflects what a traditional liberal rationalist would regard as a stalemate or a stand-off. If there is "real" debate, it is secretive and takes place within these groupings (p. 208). The public sphere is refeudalised by formalistic acts of self-representation by these groups, struggling for the prestige and reputation (p. 209).

Other things being equal, a project such as Gorbachev's perestroika appears bound to fail. There is as much chance of free public debate unpacking the power of interest groups as there is of an independent association of international lawyers, such as the International Law Association, having a critical impact on the conduct of States. Unless some new dimension can be added, the New Thinking is unlikely to lead to a modification of the present influence of international law reasoning on international society. A way out which Habermas considers is to create further institutions which might undertake the task of publicising and popularising the opinions of an elite qualified by a special level of intelligence and information. This is openly to sacrifice universality in order to retain rationality (p. 248), a form of government by expert opinion or "doctrine." Such institutions could embrace governmental commissions, the secretariats of trade unions, the "quality" press, and the like. The difficulty is that they do not amount to public debate in the classical liberal sense because there is no relationship of reciprocity between them and the general, unorganised mass of the population. They owe their profile to a prior conferring of privilege by institutions (p. 257). The only fragmentary public debate which is still possible is between persons who are "private" intellectuals in the classical liberal sense and the members of those social groups or institutions which are willing to permit their internal structures to function on a basis of democratic discussion (pp. 259–260).

The first conclusion for an international lawyer who has the confidence, impertinence, or conceit to consider himself a private person in this classical liberal sense is to be aware that he will have to confront and attempt to enter into dialogue with a variety, probably an infinite plurality, of quasi-official discourses, rather than imagine that there is a single "State" discourse which is for him authoritative and which he can either influence directly or simply absorb and reproduce. These rather simple propositions have utterly radical implications for the work of international lawyers, if one supposes that the so-called orthodox criteria for the identification of law – above all general custom and treaty practice – cannot yield any evidence of the *opinio juris* of States which could serve the noble purposes set by the Institutes of International Law at its foundation, but subsequently lost for the reasons so passionately explained by Baty. There is no single authoritative monologue to which we have simply to listen, any more than there is a possibility of universalised rational public discourse, in the sense understood by the classical liberal political tradition. Instead we all, and the international lawyer is here included, face a cacaphony of discordant monologue and a bewildering plurality of more or less imperfect dialogue.

It is here that perestroika can find support from outstanding developments in Soviet literary theory favouring a dialogic and horizontal rather than monologic and vertical approach to legal phenomena and legal normativity. In *The Dialogic Imagination*, and in particular in the essay "Discourse in the Novel," M. M. Bakhtin writes that there has always been an assumption behind the philosophy of language, linguistics, and stylistics, that one should postulate a simple and un-mediated relation of speaker to his unitary and singular "own" language, at the same time as supposing a simple realisation of this language in the monologic utterance of the individual. So there are only two poles: the system of the unitary language and the individual speaking in this language (Bakhtin, p. 269). In fact language, "directed towards its object, enters a dialogically agitated and tension-filled environment of alien words, value judgments and accents ... " (p. 276). For Bakhtin the novel is the prose form most resembling the actual shape of social discourse. It entails a deliberate intensification of differences in representation, opposing them in unresolvable dialogues (p. 291); as one point of view, accent and evaluation is opposed to another; the author may use one language, then another to avoid giving himself up to either and to remain a neutral third party (p. 314). It is this deliberate reconstruction which enables the author to give a heightened sense of his own social vision.

The literary form is potentially more realistic than the social reporting form because, far from submitting to a supposedly singular, sacrosanct unconditional language, it recognises how far oppositions between individuals are merely surface upheavals of those elements which play on such individual oppositions. Manifest dialogue and mere conversation are always stratified in unconscious structures (pp. 324–326). In order to be understood they call for creative reconstruction (perestroika). The literary form of reconstruction recognises rather than denies the acute difficulty, if not impossibility, of achieving dialogue. The dialogic imagination means, for Bakhtin, the task of coordinating and exposing languages to one another. The legal doctrinal reconstruction of differing statist discourses could also organise the exposure of social languages and ideologies to one another. "What is realised in the novel is the process of coming to know one's own language as it is perceived in someone else's, coming to know one's own belief system in someone else's. There takes place within the novel an ideological translation of another's language, and an overcoming of its otherness" (p. 365). For this reason the novelist, and also the legal theoretician, will make no effort to achieve a linguistically exact reproduction of the empirical data of alien languages: "He attempts merely to achieve an artistic consistency among the images of these languages" (p. 366).

The role of dialogic imagination is vital because there is no denying, at least according to Bakhtin, that the specific nature of discourse as a topic of speech, one that requires the transmission and reprocessing of another's word, has not been understood (p. 355). The most that can be undertaken readily is to identify where wounds will open up. Bakhtin draws a distinction between what purports to be authoritative discourse and internally persuasive discourse. The authoritative model bears an obvious resemblance to the pretensions of the juridical. It demands that we acknowledge it; it binds us without any power to persuade us internally: "Its authority was already acknowledged in the past. It is a prior discourse" (p. 342).

International lawyers devote virtually all of their time to "proving" that their opponents have tied themselves up in such authoritative knots. In the absence of a definitive, centralised authority, it appears obvious that this exercise is tendentious and sterile, however much arcane references may be made to the supposed practice of States under the rubric of general customary law. As Bakhtin put it so beautifully, the conclusions of such "scientific research" will "enter our verbal consciousness as a compact and indivisible mass" (p. 343). Where another's ideological discourse is acknowledged as internally persuasive, thought has begun to work in an independent, experimental and discriminating way. This comes precisely at the point where the individual subject separates authoritative and internally persuasive discourse. This liberating experience wakens new words, organises masses of words from within, and transforms their isolated and static condition (p. 345). That it involves intense interaction and struggle is obvious (p. 346). How, it will occur remains a mystery; hence the hopes placed in the dialogic imagination.

It might be too ambitious to proceed to exercises in dialogic legal imagination while the major part of the profession adheres to what Bakhtin calls an authoritarian discourse. It might first be necessary to persist in efforts to deconstruct and decenter this discourse. Baty gives a vivid description of the twilight of any model of international law based on the assumption that nation-States come together to form an international community united by a common moral-legal consciousness to be found in their virtually uniform State practice. General international law as usually conceived is in my view a conceptual system which is in a state of advanced decay. It is not simply that it is rightly ignored by other disciplines, but it does not cohere internally. Baty has not provoked much interest. Bakhtin warns of what it means to speak of the decay of a language:

A sealed-off interest group, caste or class, existing within an internally unitary and unchanging core of its own, cannot serve as socially productive soil for the development of the novel unless it becomes riddled with decay or shifted from its state of internal balance and self-sufficiency. This is the case because a literary and language consciousness operating from the heights of its own uncontestably authoritative unitary language fails to take into account the fact of heteroglossia and multi languagedness ... This verbal-ideological decentering will occur only when a national culture loses its sealed-off and self-sufficient character ...

There will arise an acute feeling for language boundaries and only then will language reveal its essentially human character; from behind its words, forms etc ... begin to emerge the images of speaking human beings (pp. 368, 370).

Perestroika restructuring and a critical approach to international law

To summarize the argument, there is a definite place for the classical liberal style of reasoning and debate within the framework of international legal structures. These structures continue to profess a commitment to classical liberal values of freedom and equality. Autonomy, the ability to determine the course of one's own destiny, is regarded as the primary value. Equality is above all a logical consequence of the acceptance of autonomy. Democracy might be described as a "process" value. It stresses how the other values are to be given effect, i.e. above all through free discussion and uncoerced cooperation.

This humanist paradigm is not peculiar to international society. It comes from the very idea of human relationship. From a recognition of this fact flows most intellectual work of a critical approach to international law. That is to say, the paradigm does not fit comfortably into existing international structures. Perestroika may be interpreted as a determination to pursue the liberal paradigm as far as possible, using the humble and fragile tool of free discussion and debate to identify obstacles which stand in the way of an opening up and humanising of international society. The extensive historical criticism herein of the actual functioning of the classical liberal paradigm as applied to the methodology of international law is intended to demonstrate that legal orthodoxy continues to assume a central feature of the classical liberal paradigm, that there is a single, global, thinking public, with a conscience to which appeal can be made in the form of rational debate and in the form of a scientific distilling of the essentials of that debate. Hence this methodology still retains globalist pretensions; it assumes that there are single, authoritative legal answers still somehow addressed by everyone to everyone, and which retain sufficient essential humanist values to make the enterprise worth continuing. In general terms such orthodoxy is obviously unsound. However, the great value of perestroika is an invitation to reexamine the possibility of the revitalisation of the liberal paradigm at the micro-level.

Here the work of Habermas has been invoiced to enable us to identify realistically how much might be possible in the way of "the new thinking." This is a retreat from the global ambitions of classical liberalism. It entails a pluralism of discourse which may well not be, and most probably is not, sufficient to hold the entire system together. Yet there is nothing else for the critical individual international lawyer to do but engage in open debate those aspects of the structures of international sociedty which are sufficiently open to engage in such debate.

Clearly this is a matter of looking where one can, and there is no sense in assuming that such structures are confined to States and that the latter are equally open to be engaged in debate. As Habermas puts it, that is entirely a matter of how they are internally constituted. The subject of one's enterprise is and remains international society.

Bakhtin has been looked to for a method to engage in this debate. He defines in a vivid manner the distinctions between monologue and dialogue, between authoritarian and internally persuasive discourse, and between expansive and decaying language structures.

By way of concluding we shall examine how one might progress concretely with a critical method in international law by drawing on developments in hermaneutic approaches to the study of international relations.

The critical approach is not quite the dialogic imagination. Taken on its own it supposes a monopoly of virtue on the side of the critic. This may be tactically realistic where the initiative for the review of an institution's conduct, e.g. the legal department of a foreign ministry, is itself relatively closed and uninterested in a critical review of its conduct. In other words, it is more practical than the dialogic imagination. The latter confines itself to a reflective and essentially solitary exercise of colliding, conflating, and otherwise reconstructing discourses. It is the work of the international legal novelist. The critic is the dramatist who is out to engage and provoke directly, to make himself part of a series of colliding monologues, perhaps in the hope that the mysterious transformation, to which Bakhtin alludes, may occur. Should the "engaged" institution deign to respond to its critic it may well, in turn, employ the same method. Indeed, it will be more inclined to do so should it wish to engage another structure which impinges upon it, e.g. a department of an international institution which has the power to affect the country of that same foreign ministry.

In his *Towards a Normative Theory of International Relations*, Mervyn Frost draws a clear distinction between a hermaneutic which simply accepts a subject's self-understanding and one which goes beyond that person's initial self-understanding, to point out deep-seated internal contradictions, and thereby show the way to changing the practice expressed by this understanding (Frost, pp. 27–28). Frost points out that the democratic dimension of the exercise is that the investigator is required to actively participate with the investigatees in a discussion about the proper reasons for their actions. Because this will frequently involve argument about fundamental values, the investigator cannot focus simply on the unreflective or immediate reaction of the subject, but will have to examine the subject's considered response to a critical dialogue which he investigator himself undertakes in good faith (p. 35). It is the insistence upon this sense of the democratic element in critical dialogue which allows Frost to oppose his method to that of the "scientific" positivist. The latter believes that in analysing interventions, actions in defence of the national interest, etc. it is enough somehow to describe what are supposed to be actions, although they are in fact barely observable as events. Such an approach will not draw out the substantive moral theory underlying the events (p. 36).

Frost's confidence is misplaced that the whole international system can be seen as an interacting network of State-based norms, even if much of the rhetoric employed does refer repeatedly to concepts of modernisation, increased autonomy, democratisation, and the like, which existing State apparatuses are supposed to serve (pp. 121–128). This is to take the legal rhetoric of modern international relations at its face value. It contradicts the assumption behind the method which Frost would employ, that State conduct is riddled with internal contradictions and that these are not normally subjected to effective criticism. This is the point made by Baty several generations ago and amounts merely to a restatement of the problem, i.e. simply whether the opaque structures of international society are in fact amenable to public debate and critique. However, this is not to reject the addition which Frost makes to new ways of thinking about international relations. Thinking about a matter does not mean that one believes it can be effectively thought through. It simply means that one can "think" of nothing better to do.

Nonetheless, the conceptual framework devised by Frost to draw together the notions of commitment (conviction, or if one wishes, *opinio juris*), identity (the issue of recognigtion of subjecthood), and normative standards is useful. He says that it is not possible to conceive of a State independently of it making and recognising claims based on some code of right conduct: "Recognizing such rules and being recognized in terms of them is what is involved in being a State" (p. 49). His choice of a State as the subject of inquiry, however, is too large for his "critical investigator" to engage. The latter has to be able to find a social structure (institution) whose internal constitution is sufficiently democratic to allow debate with the "private" intellectual without that structure. Here Habermas's thesis is to be preferred. Nonetheless, Frost's starting point is a basic humanist analogy applied to States. He insists that what is involved in being a person or in being a State cannot be explicated without some reference to a common commitment (p. 51). Perhaps it is clearer what Frost means by a State when he speaks of the normative assumptions which underlie and therefore limit the exercise of power by persons such as Reagan or the Ayatollah Khomeini. They are tied up with aspects of the self-understanding of American and Iranian societies (pp. 66–69). These are quite

30

clearly not statist phenomena. But the conceptual triangle proposed by Frost is a starting point for a critical hermaneutic, and eventually, a vivid flow of dialogic imagination.

Notes

The text discusses a number of writers at length, in particular Gorbachev, Tunkin, Habermas, Baty, Bakhtin and Frost. These are cited in the text, with a full reference in the bibliography after the enumerated notes.

1. See, above all, R. Falk (ed.), *The Vietnam War and International Law* (1968–1976). 4 vols.
2. G. Rolin-Jaequemyns, "De la Necessité d'Organiser une Institution Scientifique Permanente Pour Favoriser l'Etude et les Progres du Droit International," *Revue de droit international*, V (1873), 463, 703.
3. F. H. Hinsley, *Power and the Pursuit of Peace* (1967), pp. 261–262.
4. R. Albrecht-Carrie, *A Diplomatic History of Europe* (1967), pp. 152–153.
5. See generally A. J. Mayer, *The Persistence of the Old Regime* (1981), esp. pp. 79–127.
6. R. P. Dhokalia, *The Codifiction of International Law* (1970).
7. Note 5 above, p. 704.
8. *Ibid.*
9. Speech of M. Mancini at the Foundation of the Institute. *Ibid.*, p. 675.
10. *Ibid.*, p. 705.
11. *Ibid.*, p. 706.
12. *Ibid.*, p. 463.
13. Obituary of A. Rivier by M. E. Lehr, *Annuaire de l'Institut de Droit International*, XVII (1898), 342, 344.
14. E. Nys, "Alphonse Rivier, Sa Vie et Ses Oeuvres," *Revue de droit international*, XXXI (1899), 415, 429.
15. A. Rivier, *Principes du droit des gens*, I, p. 27.
16. *Ibid.*, p. 29.
17. *Ibid.*, pp. 7–8.
18. A. Carty, *The Decay of International Law?* (1986), esp. pp. 108–115.

Bibliography

Bakhtin, M. M., *The Dialogic Imagination*, ed. M. Holquist (1981).
Baty, T., *The Canons of International Law* (1930).
Frost, M., *Towards a Normative Theory of International Relations* (1986).
Gorbachev, M. S. *Perestroika* (1987).
Habermas, J., *L'Espace Public* (1986).
Tunkin, G. I. *Law and Force in the International System* (1985).

NEW TRENDS IN THE THEORY AND METHODOLOGY OF INTERNATIONAL LAW

D. I. FELDMAN

Theory and methodology are the two summits in any science, including the science of international law. But the relationship between them is not always specially examined in works on the theory of international law or in studies of the problems of methodology. For example, in the book on the methodology of international law by M. Boss of the University of Utrecht it is difficult to discern the line between the theory and the methodology of international law. The author stresses (despite the fact that the book is entitled "A Methodology of International Law") that the work illuminates issues of the binding force of international law and that the application of the last is of an obligatory character "independent from the will of States."[1]

Theory in the broad sense is understood usually to mean a complex of views, notions, ideas directed toward the interpretation and explanation of phenomena; in its narrower and specialised meaning theory is regarded as the highest and most developed form of organising scientific knowledge which gives a thorough picture of the natural developmental laws and material links in a specific domain of reality: the object of the particular theory.[2]

As regards methodology, it is understood to be the system of principles and ways of organising and structuring theoretical and practical activities, as well as the doctrine concerning this system. Methodology accents the methods, the ways of achieving true and practical knowledge.[3] To be sure, methods are different in various sciences and very particular in some, and in others have a very specific content. The essence of each is that the philosophical prerequisites of humanitarian cognition and its peculiarities in specific sciences, including the science of international law, has characteristic features. It it these which are directly addressed in studies on problems of methodology and are presumed but not specially emphasised in works on the theory of a particular science.[4]

Significance of methodology

The importance of new philosophical approaches, and consequently of the methodological aspects in each humanitarian science, especially in the theory of international law, is of special significance under modern conditions since "a change in philosophical approaches and in political relations is a serious prerequisite for giving a powerful impulse to efforts directed toward the establishment of new relations between States while relying on objective processes of a world scale."[5]

W. E. Butler, *Perestroika and International Law*, 31–40.
© 1990 *Kluwer Academic Publishers. Printed in the Netherlands.*

It is now wholly evident that the problem of survival, of the self-preservation of mankind, is of great magnitude. The very idea of democratising the entire world order has been transformed into a powerful socio-political force. A number of global problems have emerged whose resolution is impossible without international political and legal regulation. A resolute review of views on "the entire sum of the problems of international cooperation as the major element of universal security" is required inexorably. The new realities are changing the entire world situation. And insofar as we are in an age when the basis of progress is the general humanitarian interest, this inevitably requires that world politics and international law be determined by the priority of general humanitarian values. And, of course, under these conditions "the world community must learn how to form and direct processes so as to preserve civilisation and make it safe for all and appropriate for normal life."[6]

Under conditions of a scientific-technical revolution general humanitarian values must be placed at the forefront. It is obvious that any new large step along the path of progress will be linked by thousands of threads with an entire system of externally remote phenomena and events, and that the very definition of general humanitarian values requires new scientific elaboration. Not by accident did the USSR Minister of Foreign Affairs E. A. Shevardnadze note that "thorough work on a modern treatment of such comparatively new concepts as 'general humanitarian interest' and 'general humanitarian values'" is essential. Our possibilities for completing the task are insufficient. "It will require cooperation also with the forces of big science, of all the social sciences."[7]

For the last a considerable if not the leading role in resolving the task is undoubtedly allocated to the science of international law. And at once the question is inevitably raised of how appropriate the old methods are for resolving new tasks? Is a fundamental renewal required of the methodological arsenal or may traditional methods be combined with the new methodology?

When we speak of the latter, we have in view above all the possibility or even the necessity of using mathematical modelling in the science of international law, of which Academician A. A. Samarskii spoke in such detail and so interestingly in his article on the "Inevitability of a New Methodology." The article convincingly showed the role of mathematics in the methodological renewal of science and drew the conclusion that "on the basis of a new methodology ponderable results are now being obtained not only in the technical sciences, but also in the socio-economic and political domains. Moreover, they go beyond to those frontiers where with its assistance it is possible if not to 'compute' the future, at least to play with various scenarios of regional and global development."[8] Consequently, in the science of international law too when its theoretical problems of highest priority are considered, the new methodology is called upon to play a leading role, especially if one takes into account that there is a significant potential in contemporary international law which, regrettably, is not fully imbued into international practice. In this connection it is wholly just to say that "legal science, while engaging in studies of the basic principles and norms of international law, clearly has devoted inadequate attention to investigating the gap between the requirements and principles and the international realities and the working out of scientifically well-founded proposals to overcome that gap."[9] And of course Vereshchetin and Müllerson are right to stress that it is these issues which must become the priority questions for the science of international law.

Implications for Soviet theory

The Soviet theory of international law must develop further the theory of the very essence of forming norms of contemporary international law, the author of which is Professor G. I. Tunkin. This concept in recent decades has been recognised not only in the socialist doctrine of international law, but likewise in a number of works by Western international lawyers.

We speak here of the theory of the concordance of wills, according to which in an international system consisting principally of sovereign and equal States there is no other means of forming legal norms binding upon those States except by bringing the wills of States into concordance. In Tunkin's view the wills of States which are either identical or different in their class nature clash in the process of creating norms of contemporary international law. It is sufficient that they come into concordance as regards the content of a rule of behaviour and recognise it as legally binding.[10]

To be sure, this theory has stood the test of time. However, in modern conditions of new political thinking, having regard to the fact that an organic link exists between world politics and international law and that general humanitarian values have top priority, the theory of the concordance of wills must take into account this new element. Since world progress is possible only through seeking a general humanitarian consensus in moving towards a new world order, any agreement relative to rules of behaviour and recognising them as legally binding must conform to the priority of general humanitarian values. The classification of the latter, as noted above, requires comprehensive studies. The Soviet doctrine of international law confronts the priority task of determining the socialist component of general humanitarian values. As yet there is no concise and exhaustive answer to this important question.

Both here and in resolving other urgent theoretical problems of the science of international law the optimal methodological instrumentation is essential. The task of forming a *philosophy of international law* is exceptionally urgent. This is an unconditional demand of the age, of new thinking, and an urgent task of the methodological renewal of the science of international law. The very system of methods previously postulated in the Soviet science of international law required renewal.[11] Whereas in our 1971 study modelling was regarded merely as one of the general-scientific and special methods of research, now mathematical modelling is characterised as "a universal methodology, the principal method of mathematising scientific-technical progress" (A. Samarskii). The 1971 study devoted to methodological aspects of international law spoke of the applicability of mathematical methods in the domain of international legal realities. However, it cautioned against excessive optimism in this realm and emphasised the need to refrain from overestimating these methods both in the domain of research on international relations and international law.[12] Now the position should be reconsidered. Although there are no fundamental works in the science of international law in which a triad has been created (model-algorithm-programme) which would show the applicability of mathematical modelling when resolving multifaceted aspects of the theory and practice of international law, it may be supposed that this universal methodology has prospects and serious studies will commence in the near future in this sphere, especially as regards such urgent problems as the interaction between municipal and international law.

Whereas the Hegelian philosophy of law had as its core the doctrine of external State law which, despite being contradictory, "was inclined to the conservative side" and attached priority to municipal law, the world has changed so much in the past nearly two centuries that one speaks rather of the need to create a system of universal world order ensuring the primacy of international law in politics. The creation of the triad (model-algorithm, programme) in the sphere of the interaction of international and municipal law has, apart from its theoretical significance, incalculable practical importance in the cause of bringing municipal legislation into full conformity with those international treaties to which they are parties.

The role of mathematics

It is difficult to overestimate the role of mathematical modelling when studying international legal aspects of global problems of the modern day and, in particular, the significance of international law as a regulator of inter-State relations with regard to the environment. This is determined by the rapid development of international nature-protection cooperation characteristic of recent decades, the avalanche of rules of international law in this domain, and the need to create international legal machinery for averting harm to the environment. Be it a special Declaration of the United Nations General Assembly on the principles of international environmental law, or be those principles formed as an international agreement, or be the institute of responsibility applied in the sphere of international environmental protection including well-developed machinery for responsibility in connection with the basic types of activities causing ecological damage,[13] thought-provoking results undoubtedly can be obtained by means of the magic lantern of mathematics and mathematical modelling.

Under these conditions it is very important that international lawyers be so trained that the general theoretical level of future specialists would include in addition to the fundamental knowledge of the science of international law also a sound knowledge of mathematical modelling and computer applications.

The last has become especially obvious in compiling the bibliographies of Soviet works on international law and facing the task of creating an international bibliography in the process of developing information systems in the near future on the basis of automatic data processing of international legal information with the aid of computers with a gradual transition in the direction of creating a world scientific information centre on international law.[14] And, of course, in the realm of the theory of international law in general the need has grown for a thorough examination of the problem of the system of international law. And it is no accident that two recently published monographs on the theory of international law gave considerable space to this issue in the Soviet Union.[15] A number of books which touch upon the system of international law also have been published in the West. Suffice it to mention monographs by W. E. Butler, F. Malekian, S. Rosenne, I. De Lupis, and others.[16]

Systems approaches

Without dwelling on the complexities of building a system of international law and allotting its principal branches and institutes, one may note that the science of international law confronts the important theoretical and practical task of creating a generally-recognised system of international law, which would have great significance with respect to the codification and progressive development of international law, eliminating gaps, and generally in the process of realising all the multifaceted aspects of the application of the principles and norms of contemporary international law.

A systems approach may play a major role in resolving this problem, having regard to system of norms comprising international law, that is, "the question of international law as a special-purpose complex of interconnected interrelations of elements that are legal norms and subordinate to certain rules."[17] In the view of E. T. Usenko, the entire problem of the system of international law requires, together with other factors, the use of the "achievements of the systems approach."[18] He distinguishes the so-called variable and nonvariable parts of the system and asserts that thanks to the nonvariable (constant) basis, international law "has continued at all stages of its development to remain and now remains law."[19] And this brings Usenko to conclude that the stability of the constant part of the system is relative, whereas the nonvariable part of the system performs the role of guarantor for the development of the entire system as a whole in accordance with the essence thereof.[20] V. A. Vasilenko, who has used the systems approach, shares this view and distinguishes four subsystems in the system of international law:

(1) the unified normative complex of norms and principles which determine the basis of the fundamentals of inter-State interaction;
(2) the institutes and branches whose norms determine the status of subjects of international law and establish the procedure, forms, and means of their interaction;
(3) the institutes and branches whose norms determine the procedure of inter-State interaction in special spheres;
(4) individual complexes of norms which have limited spheres of effect and do not possess the qualities of institutes and branches.[21]

In his view the notion based on such an approach

precludes the arbitrary grouping of complexes of norms, institutes, and branches, enables the place and role of each to be determined in accordance with the notion created with the aid of the systems approach; international law represents a system incorporating above all the principles of the United Nations Charter and other basic and generally-recognised principles of general international law, next the law of international legal personality, the law of foreign relations, the law of international treaties, the law of international responsibility, the law of procedure, and finally, international humanitarian law, international economic law, international environmental law, international law of the sea, international air law, international space law, and others.[22]

Without dwelling on the merits and shortcomings of this system, we note only Vasilenko's conclusion is correct that "a certain order of systemic links exists"[23] between the groups of legal communities and within their framework and that the complexes of norms are mobile and under the influence of changes in the external environment "individual institutes and branches may lose their significance, disappear, or develop rapidly."[24]

Finally, in recalling the fact that in the Soviet doctrine of international law the view is widely held that a branch has been formed such as the law of international security, which Vasilenko does not mention in his system, but nonetheless writes that in light of the idea of the concept of creating a universal system of international law and security, "it is possible to presuppose that in the system of international law of the future there will be formed not a separate branch of the international law of security, but rather material changes will occur which transform it into a law of peace, peaceful coexistence, and universal and all-encompassing security."[25] Without disputing the very prospects for the transformation of international law thus, we note that from the standpoint of the systems approach the author should in general introduce such criteria as the role of international law in resolving global problems of the modern day, and in this event the place of all those branches in the system which directly lead into global problems of the day should be precisely determined.

It is likewise clear that some international lawyers such as, for example, the Frenchman Combacau do not have recourse to systems analysis when considering the problem of the system of international law and generally express doubt as to whether international law is a system or "bric-a-brac."[26] Although ultimately he is forced to state that the aggregate of elements in international law is not accidental, that it forms an "order" in that they are linked with one another and from the aggregate of those links, which can be seen as isolated from such elements only through false analysis.[27] However, without giving the details of the entire problem of the system of international law, we note merely that in and of itself the use of systems words and concepts does not produce systems studies, that the matter is not one of the semantic likeness of the terms "system" and "systems approach," and of course not that the systems approach is fashionable in the Soviet Union and the West, but that the systems movement is one of the concrete manifestations of the "dialectical trend in modern cognition."[28]

Reflections

New trends in modern international life, in international relations and their regulation by international law, require the rethinking of certain of our traditional notions about international law.[29] Under these circumstances the possibilities of the systems approach, which might be used extensively when considering such important legal problems as the delimitation of world order, international order as a whole, and the international legal order, retain significance so as to give a new appreciation of the world order which emerged during the past forty years and single out the most progressive trends of its development.[30]

To be sure, the list of issues which require rethinking in the theory of international law in connection with the New Thinking and the new methodology may be materially enlarged and here again may play both a role both through traditional methods of research and the new methodological approach.

In speaking of the methods of research in international law, it is difficult to accept the view that they do not differ from those which are used when investigating problems of municipal law, especially given the basic differences between the two systems of law. Thus, S. Rosenne asserts that the "methods and methodology of research in international law do not differ fundamentally from the respective methods and methodologies usually applied in municipal legal systems."[31] However, Rosenne himself stresses this material distinction, noting that international law is a coordinating law, which cannot be said of municipal law, since it is created and applied by the subjects themselves, above all by independent States (directly or indirectly), that this law has no "higher sovereign power," nor properly adopted legislation, nor a precise demarcation between executive, legislative, and judicial authorities, nor ordinary hierarchical judicial system, nor suitable machinery for the "rectification" of possible undesirable consequences of legal decisions, nor a clear system of "precedents" or demarcation between political and judicial precedents, and no centralisation – "in fact not a single trait or element characteristic of 'law' within the State." He stresses finally that international law is the result of the coordinated wills of its subjects and calls it the "rules of the game."[32]

Although Rosenne finds certain similarities with individual branches of municipal law (State, labour, and so forth), there is no doubt of the material differences existing between the two systems of law. Various methods of research are understandable in this connection, so it is difficult to accept that these methods coincide.

Regrettably, neither Rosenne nor a number of other writers distinguish sharply between methodology in the application of international law, methodology in the study of international law, and methods applicable in various branches of the very science of international law. As a result, a certain mixing of concepts occurs which complicates the consideration of many aspects of methodology.

The core question of methodology is the methodological instrumentation in the science of international law. And, to be sure, it materially differs in comparison with the research methods in the science of municipal law, although no mediaeval wall exists between them.

The use of the historical method in the science of international law is particularly specific, for controversy continues on the issues of when international law itself originated, the periodisation of its development, and the establishment of the body of norms which has passed into contemporary international law and function at present. This is especially complex when investigating the history of the origin, renewal, and establishment of the category of sources of international law relegated to custom.[33]

Interesting results have been achieved, as the works of Professor W. E. Butler and many other international lawyers who use comparison in the science of international law, by applying the comparative method in international law, which in its numerous facets differs significantly from the analogous method in the general theory of law.[34]

Strictly speaking, a certain difference exists also when investigating the institutes and norms of international law in its various branches. Some are extensively used in the law of the sea, others in air law, and yet others in space law, and there are many peculiarities in the research methodology of the international protection of human rights. A consideration of such specific features is one of the most important tasks of the methodology of international law.

Finally, there are still no works specially devoted to delimiting the methodologies of international law and the science of international law, on one hand, and the methodology of teaching, as well as the methods of teaching, international law on the other. This is especially important in modern conditions when the study of international law in schools and non-law faculties of universities and other institutes is acquiring such significance in principle. It is difficult to overestimate the introduction of knowledge about the fundamental principles of international law to the entire rising generation. Today, as never before, active efforts in forming the international legal consciousness are vital. It is not merely that international law is an integral part of world culture, a major general humanitarian value. It is also the fact that the resolution of global problems of the modern day, as noted above, presupposes the broadest application of the principles, institutes, and norms of contemporary international as the greatest legacy of mankind.

Under these conditions the problem of methodology in international law bears not only a general theoretical, but also an exceptionally important political and even moral significance.

A cohesive methodology also is invaluable in a forecasting role, which makes the urgency of the problem herein investigated the more acute.

Notes

1. M. Boss, *A Methodology of International Law* (1984), p. 357.
2. V. I. Lenin, "Filosofskie tetradi," *Polnoe sobranie sochinenii*, XXIX; V. S. Shvyrev, *Teoreticheskoe i empiricheskoe v nauchnom poznanii* (1978); I. D. Andreev, *Teoriia kak forma organizatsii nauchnogo znaniia* (1979).
3. E. G. Iudin, *Sistemnyi podkhod i printsip deiatel'nosti. Metodologicheskie problemy sovremennoi nauki* (1978).
4. See, for example, *Problemy gumanitarnogo poznaniia* (1986), pp. 33–54, and others.
5. M. S. Gorbachev, *Vystuplenie v Organizatsii Obedinennykh Natsii 7 dekabria 1986 g.* (1988), p. 12.
6. *Ibid.*, p. 8.
7. "Chto zabstit sovetskikh diplomativ? Realizuia idei i initsiativy, vydvinutye Mikhailom Gorbachevym v OON. Interv'iu s chlenom Politbiuro TsK KPSS, ministrom inostrannykh del SSSR E. A. Shevardnadze," *Moskovskie novosti*, no. 52 (25 December 1988), p. 8.
8. A. Samarskii, "Neizbezhnost' novoi metodologii," *Kommunist*, no. 1 (1989), p. 92.
9. See V. S. Vereshchetin and R. A. Müllerson, "Novoe myshlenie i mezhdunarodnoe pravo," *Sovetskoe gosudarstvo i pravo*, no. 3 (1988), p. 6.
10. See G. I. Tunkin, *Teoriia mezhdunarodnogo prava* (1970), pp.236–243; *id*, et al. (eds.), *Mezhdunarodnoe pravo* (1982), pp. 45–48.
11. See Iu. Ia. Baskin and D. I. Feldman, *Mezhdunarodnoe pravo: problemy metodologii. Ocherki metodov issledovaniia* (1971), pp. 76–90.
12. *Ibid.*, p. 103.
13. For details see A. S. Timoshenko, *Formirovanie i razvitie mezhdunarodnogo prava*

okruzhaiushchei sredy (1986).
14. See D. I. Feldman (ed.), *Mezhdunarodnoe pravo. Bibliografiia, 1917–1972* (1976), p. 15; *id, Mezhdunarodnoe pravo. Bibliografiia, 1973 1985 gg.* (1987), p. 4.
15. See N. A. Ushakov, *Problemy teorii mezhdunarodnogo prava* (1988), pp. 35–81; V. A. Vasilenko, *Osnovy teorii mezhdunarodnogo prava* (1988), pp. 204–264; also see E. T. Usenko, "O sisteme mezhdunarodnogo prava," *Sovetskoe gosudarstvo i pravo*, no. 4 (1988), pp. 117–127.
16. W. E. Butler (ed.), *International Law and the International System* (1987); F. Malekian, *The System of International Law* (1987); S. Rosenne, *Practice and Methods of International Law* (1984); I. Detter de Lupis, *The Concept of International Law* (1987).
17. N. A. Ushakov, *Problemy teorii mezhdunarodnogo prava* (1988), p. 35.
18. Usenko, note 15 above, p. 118.
19. *Ibid.*, p. 118.
20. *Ibid*, p. 118.
21. V. A. Vasilenko, *Osnovy teorii mezhdunarodnogo prava* (1988), p. 223.
22. *Ibid*, p. 226.
23. *Ibid*, p. 224.
24. *Ibid.*, p. 227.
25. *Ibid.*, p. 228.
26. J. Combacau, "Le droit international: bric-a-brac ou systeme?," *Archives de philosophie du droit*, XXXI (1986), 85–105.
27. *Ibid.*, p. 85.
28. See I. V. Blauberg and E. G. Iudin, *Stanovlenie i sushchnost' sistemnogo podkhoda* (1976), p. 85; V. G. Afanas'ev, *Sistemnost' i obshchestvo* (1980), p. 9. See Chapter I, "The Role of Systems Approach in the Study of the System of International Law," in Feldman, *Sistema mezhdunarodnogo prava* (1983), pp. 6–14.
29. Note 9 above, p. 4.
30. See N. E. Tiurina, *Sovremennyi mezhdunarodnyi pravoporiadok i amerikanskie proekty ego preobrazqvaniia* (1988) (kand. diss.)
31. Rosenne, note 16 above, p. 1.
32. *Ibid.*, p. 2.
33. See G. M. Danilenko, *Obychai v sovremennom mezhdunarodnom prave* (1988), p. 5.
34. W. E. Butler, "International Law and the Comparative Method," in *id* (ed.), *International Law in Comparative Perspective* (1980), pp. 25–27.

THE THEORY OF INTERNATIONAL LAW: IS THERE AN ENGLISH CONTRIBUTION?

C. J. WARBRICK

The answer to this question is "no" or "not much", at least on the surface. The predominant attitude among English international lawyers is to remainder or denigrate theory.[1] The case should not be overstated. Not all English international lawyers, all of the time, are dismissive of the claims of theory. Furthermore, we seek here a distinctively English approach. This excludes the Scots, but it also excludes those who have received "foreign" influences in their susceptible periods: the interest in theory at all and particular theories in particular of, say, Hersch Lauterpacht and Rosalyn Higgins may be traced to the fact that they were exposed to educational experiences outside English law schools. Of course, all international lawyers are to some degree influenced by forces outside their own jurisdictions and we should not expect to find a "pure" English school of international law; what we do find is a general approach to the subject largely shared by English international lawyers, whether professional or academic or, as is often the case, both. This last observation is important because generally the division between the practising and academic sectors in domestic English law is marked and will be commented on below.

The uses of theory

First, some remarks about the uses of theory with respect to international law. These are not epistemological remarks about what is really meant by theory but descriptions of the way "theory" is used in connection with international law. It may be possible to identify others; it may be possible to break down the categories below even further; the categories may not be self-contained: but they are sufficient for the discussion to follow. What it means, of course, is that no theory is offered, only description. Accordingly, the following notions of "theory" are identified:

(1) *"Grand"* theory, which asks the question what part, if any, international law plays in the actual conduct of international relations. In the English tradition this has largely been left to experts in international relations.[2]
(2) *"Nature"* theory, which asks what international law is like, what it consists of. There is a tendency in English writing to leave this to the jurisprudes,[3] who have considered the matter, if they have considered it at all, as an afterthought to their speculations about domestic law.

W. E. Butler, *Perestroika and International Law*, 41–59.
© 1990 *Kluwer Academic Publishers. Printed in the Netherlands.*

(3) *"Sources"* theory, which asks about the basis of obligation in international law and, particularly, how we identify the sources of the obligations of international law. Here, we are in a field where English international lawyers have had their say, though whether we should always regard their contributions as "theoretical" is not so obvious.[4]

(4) *"Technical"* theory, which asks questions about the various legal concepts and rules within the international legal system, for example about international personality or the concept of jurisdiction. This is the very stuff of international law.[5] Not all work done by international lawyers on these questions is theoretical but there is some general sympathy for the view that their work is done best if it is informed by an understanding of the theoretical structure and relationship of the bits and pieces of the international legal system.

(5) *"Justice"* theory, which asks questions about what international law is *for*, what ends should it pursue, what values should it embrace.[6] Using the conditional gives the game away somewhat because those writers who address such questions would usually put them in terms of what ends *does* international law pursue, what values *does* it embrace. These questions, it appears, are hardly the concern of contemporary English international lawyers and, if this has not always been the case, it reflects a realism about the role of international law among its propounders which contrasts with earlier ambitions for international law as the foundation for international peace. If international lawyers in England do not address themselves directly to the "Grand" theory questions of category (1), it is perhaps because they have been chastened by the over-optimistic claims made in the past for the decisive impact of international law over the less salubrious but enduring influences of self-interest and accommodation. Modern ambitions are more mundane: to oil the wheels, not to build the engine.

Professional and academic international lawyers

Before turning to the ways in which English international lawyers use theory (when they do), it is necessary to return to the earlier observation about the blurring of the line between professional and academic international lawyers. That this is not the case in English domestic law has been remarked upon by Patrick Atiyah in his Hamlyn Lectures, where he bemoaned the estrangement of the practitioners in the courts and the writers in the schools in England.[7] He began his addresses with the following:

I shall start with the fairly uncontroversial suggestion that English lawyers are not only more inclined to the pragmatic and somewhat hostile to the theoretical approach, but positively glory in this preference.[8]

Professor Atiyah was writing about merely a small part of the whole edifice of the "law": when he spoke of "English law", he referred almost exclusively to the decisions of the appellate courts and of such legislation as had been brought to their attention.

If consideration of international law were to be similarly restricted, it would be a small and distorted picture. International law is not exactly like municipal law (still less like English law) and we should not necessarily expect that the deprecation of theory so characteristic of practising lawyers would be shared by international lawyers. If Atiyah was concerned about the disadvantages to the professional world because of its ostracism of the academic, perhaps academic international lawyers should be more concerned that the universities will lose the energies of their leading lights to the demands of practice: perhaps there is no English theory of international law because the professors are in the Temple rather than the schools. These days there is scarcely a case before the International Court of Justice which does not feature one or other and sometimes both of the senior professors of international law in this country.[9] Half a dozen academic lawyers have been engaged in the *International Tin Council* litigation.[10] There is a long tradition of British judges on the International Court being academics.[11] A recent President of the European Commission of Human Rights,[12] the present member of the United Nations Human Rights Committee,[13] and an Advocate-General of the Court of Justice of the European Communities were or are academics.[14] Some members of the Foreign and Commonwealth Legal Adviser's staff have been academics and some academics were once Legal Advisers. Legal writing by the Legal Advisers is frequent and impressive.

The question is whether this intense cross-fertilisation has led to the infection of academic law by predominantly practical considerations or whether the law school practitioners have carried with them theoretical virtue into the court rooms and chancellories. In general, as intimated already, the answer is an easy one: pragmatism has supplanted theory. The explanations for this are not restricted to a priority for briefs over books. When English jurists have turned their attentions to international law, which has not been often, they have not treated it very kindly. While it is to Bentham that we owe the name "international law,"[15] he did not concern himself much with its substance. His successor, John Austin, began the whole sterile debate about whether international law is "really" law. He regarded international law as an example of what he called "positive morality,"[16] a conclusion not surprising when it is realised that he consigned customary law in general to the same category.[17] Austin's criticisms were later dismissed by Sir Henry Maine as "very interesting and quite innocuous,"[18] but Maine, who was after all giving the Whewell lectures, instead rather damned international law by faint praise. He was willing to concede that there were points of connection between positive law (in Austin's sense) and international law and he made the important observation that the founders of international law, though they did not create a sanction, created a law-abiding sentiment.[19]

Nonetheless, he saw real defects in international law compared with positive law, particularly the absence of law-developing and law-enforcing mechanisms.[20] Austin had spotted these same gaps and pronounced the system not law. Later, T. E. Holland, who was both an international lawyer and a jurisprudent, held, only marginally more favourably, that international law was the "vanishing point" of jurisprudence.[21]

More disappointingly, H. L. A. Hart, who has exerted more influence on English lawyers of this generation than any other legal theorist, concludes that international law merits only the third-class status of a "primitive legal system."[22] The regret at this conclusion, to which we shall return, is more pronounced because Hart has dealt convincingly with those who would seek to deny altogether the title of law to the international legal system. Hart does this, in keeping with his general method, by insisting that the questions must be answered by examining "the actual practice of States,"[23] a reference which does find a favourable echo from English international lawyers: for if theory is eschewed or avoided, what is left? What is left is practice and, in this context, practice is what States do.

The emphasis on practice of states

Here we are on familiar ground. Holland on another occasion said that, whatever international law was about, it was generally agreed that it had something to do with States.[24] Today, most of us might be inclined to say that it has something to do with State practice. English international lawyers have had less trouble with Kelsen's *grundnorm* – "that international custom is a law-creating fact"[25] – or the inverted language of Article 38(1)(b) of the Statute of the Court – "international custom as evidence of a general practice accepted as law" – than have theoreticians. It is true, though perhaps not surprising, that the accounts of custom are not very elaborate. A notable exception is Michael Akehurst's article,[26] which is more inquiring than usual and comes to a conclusion which goes beyond the orthodoxy of English international law in ascribing a significance to the words of States equal to their practice.[27] The theoretical objections to the ordinary understanding are well enough known: that the basis of the obligation is obscure and that the psychological requirement of the *opinio iuris* means it cannot account for change in existing rules or for the emergence of new ones. What matters to English international lawyers is that the process does work. Custom can change, e.g. the breadth of the territorial sea;[28] new custom can emerge, e.g. the continental shelf;[29] and in each case it does so by the practice of States.

This emphasis on State practice has two consequences: first, the practitioners of international law exert a great deal of influence on what counts as international law in Britain. Disputes of the kind which arise in the United States between the Department of State lawyers and the academic community are rare in England: what the Legal Adviser said is (international) law! What the Legal Advisers think, say, and do about international law is, then, of great importance to English international lawyers. Finding out what they think, say, and do is not always easy. As in so many areas of English public life, the canon of secrecy overrides the interests of the concerned or the curious about how the government is taking its decisions. In recent years, more information has become available, although it tends to be the outputs of the decision-making process, what Ministers have done, rather than what the legal advisers have told them.[30] However, there are indications that Ministers have sought advice,even on politically sensitive matters, and we take comfort from Sir Gerald Fitzmaurice's view (though here he was talking about the Law Officers" Opinions) that "whether the advice was good or bad, governments tended to *act* upon it – at least as regards the United Kingdm."[31] Furthermore, the Legal Advisers, or some of them, have written quite extensively about international law or the legal adviser's role, of whom Fitzmaurice is the most important example.

The other consequence which follows from ascribing priority to State practice is that it *all* counts. Clive Parry used to say, or pinched from somebody else, that international law had no history, it *was* its history.[32] What this meant was that for custom, for title to territory, for treaty obligations, everything counted, old age was no exclusion. It was an approach which reached its height in the *Minquiers case*,[33] where both Britain and France thought that it was worth putting to the International Court evidence from Norman times, evidence of events before the start of the modern international legal system, no matter how early a date is fixed for that. Accordingly, Parry set out to make available the evidence of British State practice. He followed the example of Lord McNair, of whom Fitzmaurice wrote, "this was essentially a practical rather than a theoretical approach to law ... In this, he was typical of much of Anglo-Saxon mentality."[34] McNair published his three volumes of law officers' opinions and the Law of Treaties.[35] Parry collected all the law officers' opinions in many volumes[36] and all the treaties ever entered into.[37] He began to collect and publish British State practice in the *British Digest of International Law*. The few volumes of the first series covered the period 1860 to 1914, the cut-off date taking into account the then existing "50 year rule" before official papers could be published.[38] There was, however, no concession that this old practice was not relevant to the doing of international law, no acceptance of the claim that practice from before the Russian Revolution, before the United Nations Charter, before the process of decolonisation, was not part of international law after all, that it was of merely antiquarian interest. The premature termination of Parry's mammoth undertaking almost before it had started suggests that there is a history of international law, that materials of a certain age are of limited significance for modern conditions.[39]

However, to some international lawyers, Parry's approach to the subject remains sound. If there be any genuine theoretician of international law writing in England at present whose approach is not identifiably influenced by foreign ideas, it is Philip Allott, who writes,

> The relevance of the past is that it provides evidence of countless test-tube experiments of conflict resolution. It is not the *theory* of what would be reasonable and what this or that State might seek or achieve or how it would react. It is the *story* of how the continuing problems have been presented and resolved or circumvented over a long period of time.[40]

This approach is a rejection of explicit theory and the substitution of a hidden theory in the guise of the study of practice, a practice, which Allott argues, provides the "best" rules as a result of experience and the amelioration of conflicting interests.

Allott's analysis and explanation gives pragmatism a value beyond its supposed objectivity – practice is what works; what works does so because it is useful; what is useful is valuable. Rules are not good because they are old, but old because they are good.

For English international lawyers it seems to be enough that they observe that States *do* international law (without needing to ask *why* they do it). States refer to international law, they (largely) comply with it, they employ international lawyers, who argue in legal terms, they go to courts (sometimes), they distinguish between their legal and their political obligations. International law simply "*is.*"[41] As for the identification of international law, given the historic approach, much weight is ascribed to custom. The United Nations Charter notwithstanding, Parry has remarked:

> It ... remains essentially true that one can have a fair idea of international law without having read a single treaty; and that one cannot gain any very coherent idea of the essence of international law by reading alone.[42]

This is a claim which these days can only be sustained if one accepts the finding of the International Court of Justice in the *Nicaragua case* that the principal substantive provisions of the Charter are also part of customary international law.[43]

Treaties and custom

The Charter presents the biggest objection to a view widely held among English international lawyers that treaties should not be considered as a source of law but as sources of obligation for the parties which had taken advantage of the customary rule of *pacta sunt servanda*.[44] Sir Ian Sinclair presents the generally received English view of the relationship between multilateral treaties and customary international law when he embraces the rather strict requirements set out by the Court in the *North Sea Continental Shelf Case*.[45] In view of the traditional reluctance to find obligations for non-parties in or deriving from treaties, it is an interesting development to see that the Anglo-French Declaration issued in conjunction with the Channel Boundary Agreement[46] is couched in the language of the 1982 United Nations Convention on the Law of the Sea.[47]

Generally, though, there is little evidence of the United Kingdom accepting the "law-making" or "institution-creating" effects of treaties for non-parties. This formality is reinforced by the reluctance to concede legal consequences to resolutions of the General Assembly, even for members of the United Nations.[48] There is a measure of difference between the attitudes of English academics on this matter, although, in bald terms at least, the government's attitude has been consistent, i.e. that General Assembly resolutions do not create binding obligations for States. It is something which will bear re-examination in the light of the *Nicaragua case*.[49] A strong example of the line taken by the British government is its explanation of its position about South Africa's rights with respect to South West Africa. While agreeing with the International Court that South Africa had lost its legal claim to occupy the territory of South West Africa, the British government would not endorse the Court's explanation that this was because the General Assembly had terminated the Mandate. Instead, in the British view, South Africa was in fundamental breach of its obligations under the Mandate agreement, which had resulted in its termination.[50] Likewise the government has not be willing to recognise or accept the United Nations Council on Namibia as having any authority, especially authority to promulgate laws binding on third States.[51]

This is not the place to resolve the correctness of the government's understanding of the legal position. On the other hand, it is worth noting the relationship between theory and practice in making such an assessment. Plainly the Charter itself provides no basis for the binding effect of General Assembly resolutions. Equally plainly, all General Assembly resolutions could not create legal obligations: they are sometimes hortatory or prospective or specifically recommendatory. So if *any* General Assembly resolutions are legally significant, we need some way of ascertaining which. It is not enough that States actually do comply with their terms because that ignores the possibility, in the words of J. E. S. Fawcett, that States intend to comply with resolutions but do not intend to be bound by them.[52] What is needed is some demonstration that States intend to be bound by the content of a particular resolution. Practically, we are thrown back on custom and treaty, not merely as the explanations but as the identifiers of which resolutions generate legal obligations: custom, because practice has fallen in line with the terms of the resolution, treaty because the Resolution can be said to be an explication of existing Charter obligations. If we are to take Hart's approach, the process of which we determine whether there is a new source of law does not seem substantially different from determining whether there is an existing customary rule. If we proceed with Kelsen, we would have to accept this precisely, unless we wish to demonstrate that there is a new addition to the international grundnorm. With the possible exception that the *Nicaragua case* may have shifted the burden of proof for establishing the binding effect of any particular resolution, it does not seem that English practice or English international legal writing in general (though there are obvious exceptions) would concede the latter. The system is essentially the same historic legal system throughout the whole of international law, which often goes by the name of the Westphalian System.

"Technical" theory

At this point the English approach to international law seems, in general, to be one of "modern positivism," that is to say, it sees law as a set or system of rules emanating from a narrow variety of accepted sources, but recognises that the rules themselves require identification (or proof), interpretation, and application, processes which leave scope for the legal imagination but which are, nonetheless, sufficiently confined to leave the international legal process distinct from politics or morality. There may, it is true, be a question as to whether some of the alleged rules of the system are sufficiently concrete to merit the term "law" or whether the discretions that they allow in their application are so wide as to allow ad hoc, virtual legislative authority to the person charged with applying them.[53]

Our attention should turn naturally to questions of "technical" theory. There are two broad categories here. The first is questions about the rules themselves, which are common to all legal systems: are they accessible? are they consistent?, are they general or particular? do they impose duties or confer discretions?

While these are not unimportant, they are not the main concern: certain aspects of those rules which form the foundations of the international legal system. The rules about sources are, on one view, part of this group (though they may find their origins outside the legal system). The topics in mind, and this is only a selection, are the matters of personality – who are the actors in the legal system? – the relationship of the international legal order with other, domestic systems, and the regime of responsibility. It is remarkable how little impact theory makes on the way English international lawyers deal with these issues. Personality is bound to be a problem for any legal system which concedes that primary law-making is in some way the role of actors within the legal system. How were the rules which gave these persons that capacity arrived at? Most English international lawyers would accept James Crawford's view that there are rules of international law which tell us what things are States: entitles satisfying those criteria are, as a matter of law, States; those which don't, are not.[54] The application of the rules to controversial cases can be difficult. The question of statehood will seldom be a matter for third-party determination.[55] Accordingly, attention focuses on the role of recognition in establishing statehood. It is an area of law which has almost drowned in theory.[56] Despite Lauterpacht's influential work on recognition,[57] which did exert an influence on Briish practice,[58] most academic writing has been doubtful about the value of either the declaratory or the constitutive theories of recognition.[59]

If Lauterpacht exercised some influence on the practice of the British government on recognition, he was less persuasive about the status of individuals. He argued strongly that individuals did enjoy rights in international law,[60] but the government's reaction to this proposition has been extremely cautious. Even though it was prepared to ratify the European Convention on Human Rights in 1953, the United Kingdom did not accept the right of individual petition until 1966[61] and it continues to emphasise the international nature of the Conventions system,[62] despite the substantial changes in the procedure of the system to the benefit of individual applicants.[63] Although she starts from a different point, Rosalyn Higgins's claims for the recognition of the international status of individuals have similarly had little influence on British practice.[64] The prevailing view is that international law concerns practically entirely relations between States and that the basis for even obligations owed under human rights agreements is the treaties themselves, that is, inter-State agreements.[65] Theory has played practically no part in widening the official position on this question.

The narrow view is reflected also in the relations between international law and English law. While it is the case that in recent years the British courts have become more receptive to arguments based on international law, the relationship is largely formal. If the *Trendtex* case[66] has established finally that customary international law is part of English law, it is important to understand that that statement is to be understood literally: customary international law confers none or only the rarest of rights on individuals; accordingly, individuals will seldom, if ever, be in a position to rely on customary law in an English court.[67] For treaties, the general rule is that implementing legislation is required, so that an English court will invariably be faced with a question of statutory interpretation where a treaty matter arises before them. There has been an encouraging practice in recent years for the domestic courts to approach treaty interpretation, even when mediated through a domestic statute, in the way an international tribunal would do so.[68] Sometimes the courts have been willing to take notice of "unimplemented" treaties, an example being the European Convention on Human Rights.[69] For custom, the inability of the leading text books even to agree on the term to describe the relationship between international and domestic law is an indication of the lack of influence of theory.[70] For treaties, equally, the need to account for the courts' occasional reliance on unimplemented treaties has meant that a single theoretical perspective is inadequate. The theoretical approaches through monism and dualism are almost universally derided. Even Sir Gerald Fitzmaurice's attempt to dissolve away the problem by the rigid separation of the international and domestic legal spheres is inadequate.[71] Ultimately, the best account is D. P. O'Connell's explanation of the phenomenon as one of the "harmonisation" of legal obligations.[72] It would be too much to confer the title "theory" on his account. Rather it is a description of the practice of the courts and for that reason, doubtless, commends itself to English international lawyers and to domestic judges.[73]

There have been some recent exceptions[74] but, on the whole, there has not been a great deal of interest among English international lawyers in the work of the International Law Commission on State responsibility. Although the rapporteurs have collected a vast quantity of practice, the theme of their reports has been theoretical.[75] It has demonstrated how central the understanding of the law of State responsibility is to the nature of the international legal system.[76] The English approach remains wedded to a bilateral, delictual and reparative view of the nature of State responsibility. It is an understanding founded in and reinforced by its own practice.[77] To take one example, at least as far as its public pronouncements indicate, the government has couched representations made to other States about human rights matters, including the treatment of their own nationals, in terms which obscure the basis of them. The government has relied on instruments of uncertain legal stature, like the Helsinki Final Act or the Universal Declaration.[78] It is often far from clear whether the representations are a legal protest or a political complaint. These ambiguities are particularly likely when the issue concerns a specific individual. In another direction, criticising the ILC proposal for State criminal responsibility, Ian Brownlie draws attention to the practical objections to its introduction.[79] These matters, sometimes on the margin between *lex lata* and *lex ferenda*, seem invariably to be determined in a way which excludes any development in the international legal system of the equivalent to domestic public law.[80]

On recognition and on the relationship between domestic and international law, the English experience is hostile to any of the theoretical accounts which have commended themselves to other jurisdictions. This may not be merely a chauvanistic rejection of things foreign. In any system, a general level of abstraction to which theory aspires will fail to explain *some* deviant examples. Given the small size of the international system, deviant examples soon cease to be anomalous but become significant. The matter is exacerbated because the requirements of international law are seldom peremptory and so States can recognise, acquiesce in, or make reservations to condone situations which are out of line with the general rule.[81]

States can, of course, make specific exceptions to general customary law by treaty. The debate about compensation for nationalised or expropriated property is an example of the uncertainties that can arise. If (and it is a big if) the general rule requires prompt, adequate, and effective compensation, what is the impact of settlements between States which embrace a lesser standard? Richard Lillich and

Burns Weston (Americans, admittedly!) have argued that from the various claims treaties can be derived evidence for a new and different customary rule.[82] F. A. Mann has strenuously contested this proposition.[83] It is not clear how it is to be resolved. Similarly, it is not always easy to distinguish practice which violates an existing customary rule and that which is establishing a new rule. As Hart has said, sometimes we just have to wait and see.[84] Judge Jennings instanced the operation of the principle of self-determination on the rules relating to title of the territory as one where the outcome of conflict may depend, not upon the assertion of a sure legal rule, but upon the reaction of other States, acting in a kind of legislative role if they were to accept the new situation in preference to the old.[85] Against a system which permits so many deviations and where the deviations may be of significant dimensions compared with the number of standard cases, it is hardly surprising that even technical theory sometimes fails to enlighten.[86]

However good technical theory is, there is always the problem of the open-textured rule: what is meant by "domestic jurisdiction" in Article 2(7) of the United Nations Charter? When is a State exercising its high seas rights with "reasonable regard" to the interests of other States? What is a "civil right or obligation" in Article 6(1) of the European Convention on Human Rights? Modern jurisprudence generally teaches us that there are no right answers to these questions. Ronald Dworkin has sought to explain how this kind of dilemma should be resolved in a municipal legal system[87] but the difficulty for the international legal system is identifying Dworkin's "principles" and "policies."[88] There have been English international lawyers who have regarded international law as an exercise with substantive purpose, but some of them recanted in the light of a fuller consideration of State practice.[89] Brierly was one of them, acknowledging that the previous emphasis he had put on the need to assure peaceful change was misplaced.[90] The predominant objective was a system of collective security with an informal non-coercive process for the adjustment of disputes: international law would be the product of this process, in the form of agreements or accommodations, not its generator.[91] Others have been more consistent, none more so than Lauterpacht. His insistence that the "legal rights and duties of States are essentially the legal rights and duties of individuals who act on their behalf"[92] led him to the conclusion that the depersonification of the State would reduce the tendency to operate two moral systems, one for States and one for individuals and that,

> the individual human being is the ultimate unit and end of all law, national and international, and that the effective recognition and protection of the dignity and worth of the human person and the development of the human personality is the final object of all law.[93]

This humane evangelism led to Lauterpacht's inspiring work, *International Law and Human Rights*.[94] That book may have helped inspire the developments in positive international law which have moved the system in the direction that Lauterpacht would have wished, but they are sentiments which have not been widely echoed in British practice and writing.

In contrast, one may refer to Fitzmaurice's remarks when he said:

> Law aimed at ultimate justice, but achieved it indirectly, by methods the immediate object of which was not so much justice as such, but order, stability, certainty, and the elimination of that subjective element that cannot fail to enter into any attempt to apply justice directly, and which often vitiates it.[95]

There may not be many who are prepared to accept Fitzmaurice's "neutral principles" account of law as realistic, but the other values to which he refers can and do inform the interpretation and application of international law.

The result is, as Brierly noted, that law is a conservative force, a force favouring the *status quo*,[96] an outcome of particular weight given the cumbersome mechanism for change in the international legal system. Much of the argument about the basis of obligation in international law and the sources of international law has been directed at this perceived weakness. Law-making by consensus in all its guises – weakening the generality for custom, undermining the position of the objector, decision-making at codification conferences, reliance on General Assembly resolutions – the introduction of something like majority decision-making – has generally been resisted in English writing and English practice.[97] The indications are that the process is of limited effectiveness. The failure of the United Kingdom to ratify the 1982 U. N. Convention on the Law of the Sea and the Protocols to the Geneva conventions are part of a pattern of resistance to accepting as binding the products of a consensual process.

Latent theory

We return to Atiyah and what he calls the "Theory Beneath the Surface." The constant disavowals of theory by English legal professionals, he says, reveals

> [a] very elitist theory in which those who wield power do not want to justify or explain too carefully what they are doing or why they are doing it.[98]

and, he goes on,

> The pure pragmatist who professes to scorn all theory is himself usually proceeding on the basis of some theory, seeking (albeit perhaps unconsciously) some rational objective; and his pragmatism may simply amount to an unwillingness to discuss his objectives, to examine his premises, to open himself to accountability.[99]

This must strike a chord in any English international lawyer, at least as concerns one aspect of matters: that is the claim of the government and the acquiescence of the domestic courts in the claim that "foreign affairs are different," in particular, they are non-justiciable, even, or, perhaps, especially, where the claim is to review the conduct of the British government against the standards of international law. Indeed, it appears that the government itself might be prepared to concede more by way of accountability than the courts will demand of them.[100]

If we take Atiyah's observations outside the domestic arena to international law, what hidden theory or values might we find being covertly pursued under the "It's what States do" approach. First, we should recognise that there is little interest among contemporary English international lawyers in "Grand" theory. Disillusionment with the inflated claims of international law as the guarantor of international peace and justice accounts for this. The disappointment of the utopian aspirations of the early part of this century has been repeated in lesser measure with respect to the United Nations. It is accepted that the individual State is the predominant repository of power and authority. Lawyers have lowered their sights – but not too far. They need no convincing of the need for international law to be effective. The importance of technical theory is not just a matter of professional pride but increases the practical influence by showing its consistency, its predictability, in short, its *usefulness* to political decision-makers.[101] It is for the lawyer to show them how to do it. Reliance on practice, on custom and treaty, apparently allows the lawyer to maintain his independence of political values. This reliance on practice, combined with a strict approach to the sources of law – very general practice for custom, only participation for treaties – reinforces the natural conservatism of the law with special barriers against change. The English approach to international law provides a protection against unwelcome obligations (and explains why there is so little divergence between its legal advice and what the government actually does).[102] Its weakness is at times of change: the post-Charter regime, the expansion of the number of States, concern for human rights, economic development. In a recent book on collective human rights Brownlie was dismissive of those who sought new rules or new concepts to protect the rights of peoples. He wrote, exhorting the professional vocation, that lawyers should look harder to find protection in the existing regime.[103] His antagonists argued that the present rules were demonstrably inadequate: a "legislative" initiative was needed in which Western States were singularly unwilling to participate.[104]

Conclusion

The values of the hidden theory are preserving the maximum freedom to act commensurate with the minimum obligations necessary to allow useful independence and practical security. Beyond this bare minimum, the source of obligation is

54

precise consent. The values of the international system are largely formal rather than substantive because, in a society of States with greatly different values, that is the most that can be sought. To go further risks repeating the over-reaching of an earlier generation of international lawyers. History not only gives us our law, it teaches us what we can (and cannot) do with it. Only if we can be persuaded that the international system has or will undergo substantial structural changes, which will allow, *inter alia*, the identification of the values and rules of international law independently of the practice of the States directly involved, will there be any scope for change.

Notes

1. For instance: "There is no doubt room for a whole treatise on the harm caused to the business of legal investigation by theory," I. Brownlie "Recognition in Theory and Practice," in R. St. J. Macdonald and D. M. Johnston (eds), *The Structure and Process of International Law* (1983), p. 627.
2. See H. Bull, *The Anarchical Society: A Study of Order in World Politics* (1977). For a notable exception of an international lawyer being concerned with these matters, see G. Schwarzenberger, *Power Politics: A Study of World Society* (3d ed., 1964). It is hardly surprising that an expert in international relations, Hedley Bull, contributed the chapter on international law to a recent English jurisprudential study of Kelsen. See R. Tur and W. Twining (eds.), *Essays on Kelsen* (1988).
3. I. Brownlie, *Principles of Public International Law* (1966), pp.v-vi: "No chapter appears on the basis of obligation in international law because it is thought that, as part of the problem of defining law, the topic belongs to books on legal theory;" I. Sinclair, *The Vienna Convention on the Law of Treaties* (2d ed., 1984), pp. 2–3; "It is easy enough to posit the rule that every treaty in force is binding upon the parties to it; but the source of that rule rests ... on considerations relating to the binding force of international law in general, which of necessity leads us into somewhat metaphysical regions."
4. C. Parry, *The Sources and Evidences of International Law* (1965); G. G. Fitzmaurice, "Some Problems Regarding the Formal Sources of International Law," in *Symbolae Verzijl* (1956), pp. 153–176.
5. Brownlie's textbook, *Principles of Public International Law* (3d ed., 1979) has no real rival, despite the profusion of textbooks published in recent years in England. Note also the various English contributions to the General Course on Public International Law at the Hague Academy; G. Schwarzenberger, "The Fundamental Principles of International Law," *Recueil des cours*, LXXXVII (1955) 191; G. G. Fitzmaurice, "The General Principles of International Law considered from the standpoint of the rule of law," *Recueil des cours*, XCII (1957), 1; R. Y. Jennings, "General Course on Principles of Public International Law," *Recueil des cours*, CXXI (1967), 1; J. E. S. Fawcett, "General Course on Public International Law," *Recueil des cours*, CXXVII (1969), 363.
6. H. Lauterpacht, for a very short encapsulation of his view which was pervasive through his writing, see *id*, *International Law, being the Collected Papers of Hersch Lauterpacht*, ed. E. Lauterpacht (1970), I, pp. 33–36, 51–56; R. Higgins, "Policy

Considerations and the International Judicial Process," *International and Comparative Law Quarterly*, XVII (1968), 58; C. W. Jenks, *The Common Law of Mankind* (1958).

7. P. Atiyah, *Pragmatism and Theory in English Law* (1987).
8. *Ibid.*, p. 3,
9. For example, *Libya* v *Malta (Continental Shelf)*, ICJ Rep. (1985) 13.
10. *Maclaine Watson & Co. Ltd.* v *Department of Trade and Industry etc.* [1988] 3 All E. R. 257.
11. Of the postwar judges, McNair, Lauterpacht, Waldock, and Jennings were academics; only Fitzmaurice had not been.
12. J. E. S. Fawcett.
13. R. Higgins.
14. Francis Jacobs.
15. J. Bentham, *An Introduction to the Principles of Morals and Legislation*, eds. J. Burns and H. L. A. Hart (1970), p. 296.
16. J. Austin, *Lectures on Jurisprudence or the Philosophy of Positive Law*, ed. R. Campbell (5th ed., 1911), I, pp. 225–226.
17. *Ibid.*, II, pp. 536–537. See N. MacCormick, *H. L. A. Hart* (1981), p. 114.
18. H. S. Maine, *International Law* (2d ed., 1894), p. 49.
19. *Ibid.*, p. 51.
20. *Ibid.*, pp. 52–53.
21. T. E. Holland, *The Elements of Jurisprudence* (13th ed., 1924), p. 391.
22. H. L. A. Hart, *The Concept of Law* (1961), Chapters X and V.
23. *Ibid.*, pp. 210–220. Hart has not accomplished this to the satisfaction of all international lawyers, see Brownlie, note 41 above, pp. 6–8.
24. I cannot now relocate the source of this remark but would be glad to be reminded of it by anyone who knows it!
25. H. Kelsen, *Principles of International Law*, ed. R. W. Tucker (2d ed., 1966), p. 446.
26. M. Akehurst, "Custom as a Source of International Law," *British Yearbook of International Law*, XLVII (1974–75), 1.
27. Akehurst, "Nicaragua v United States," *Indian Journal of International Law*, XXVII (1982), 357, 357–364.
28. Territorial Sea Act 1987, extending UK territorial waters to 12 miles; see "Current Legal Developments," *International and Comparative Law Quarterly*, XXXVII (1987), 412–415 (R. R, Churchill).
29. *North Sea Continental Shelf cases*, ICJ Rep.(1969), pp. 3, 23. For anticipation of change in customary law, see "Current Legal Developments," *International and Comparative Law Quarterly*, XXXVII (1988), 415–418 (R. R. Churchill), on the decommissioning of off-shore installations.
30. G. Marston, "United Kingdom Materials on International Law," in the *British Yearbook of International Law* since 1978; E. Lauterpacht, British Practice in International Law, 1963–1967. A. V. Lowe and C. Warbrick, "Current Legal Developments" in the *International and Comparative Law Quarterly* since 1986. English academic international lawyers have reason to be grateful to the cooperation of recent FCO Legal Advisers and their staff.
31. G. G. Fitzmaurice, "Lord McNair," *British Yearbook of International Law*, XLVIII (1974–75), xi, xvi.
32. Like many of his remarks, it was not entirely serious; see C. Parry, "The Function of Law in the International Community," in M. Sorensen (ed.), *Manual of Public International Law* (1968), pp. 8–26.
33. *France* v *United Kingdom (Minquiers and Ecrehos case)* ICJ Rep. (1953), p. 47.

34. Note 31 above, p. xiv.
35. A. D. McNair, *International Law Opinions* (1956); *id.*, *The Law of Treaties* (1961).
36. C. Parry (ed.), *Law Officers' Opinions to the Foreign Office, 1793–1860* (1975).
37. C. Parry (ed.), *The Consolidated Treaty Series* (1969-).
38. C. Parry (ed.), *British Digest of International Law* (1965).
39. Though, certainly, all practice before 1917 or 1945 cannot be rejected as having no contemporary importance; for example, *The Caroline Case*, *British and Foreign State Papers*, XXIX, 1137; XXX, 195; *Alabama Claims Arbitration*, J. B. Moore, *International Arbitrations*, I, p. 495; *Island of Palmas case*, *United Nations Reports of International Arbitral Awards*, I, p. 829.
40. P. Allott, "Language, Method and the Nature of International Law," *British Yearbook of International Law*, XLV (1970), 79, 131.
41. G. G. Fitzmaurice, "The Foundations of the Authority of International Law and the Problem of Enforcement," *Modern Law Review*, XIX (1956), 1, 9: ... "international lawyers, who must take things as they find them." For a particularly strong defence of this position, see Brownlie, "The Reality and Efficacy of International Law," *British Yearbook of International Law*, LIII (1982), 1.
42. Note 4 above, pp. 34–35.
43. *Nicaragua* v *United States*, ICJ Rep. (1986), pp. 14, 97–111.
44. G. G. Fitzmaurice, note 4 above. Mr Allott makes a more subtle point, arguing that this significance of treaties should not be overrated because they are the product of temporary balances of power and not to be compared to the enduring weight of custom. Note 40 above, p. 133.
45. Note 3 above, pp. 22–24.
46. See "Current Developments," *International and Comparative Law Quarterly*, XXXVIII (1989), 000 (R. R. Churchill).
47. Text in *ILM*, XXIX (1982), 1245. Article 38.
48. Academic opinion is not uniform; see I. MacGibbon, "Means for the Identification of International Law," and R. Higgins, "The Identity of International Law," in B. Cheng (ed.), *International Law: Teaching and Practice* (1982), pp. 10–26, 27–44.
49. Note 43 above.
50. H. C. Hansard, MCCCLXXXII, cols. 1564–66, 4 December 1974.
51. H. L. Hansard, CCCCVIII, col. 758.
52. *International Law and the Uses of Outer Space* (1968), p. 9.
53. An example is the rule (or rules) for dividing shared areas of coastal jurisdiction. For a recent account concluding that the flexibility of the rule (or rules) is a virtue, see M. Evans, *Relevant Circumstances and Maritime Delimitation* (1987), p. 241.
54. J. Crawford, *The Creation of States in International Law* (1979), p. 32.
55. That is to say, in general. Within certain specific contexts in international organisations, questions of statehood may be for collective determination.
56. See Brownlie, note 1 above, theory as "theological," (p. 634); "unhelpful and uninspiring," (p. 639).
57. H. Lauterpacht, *Recognition in International Law* (1950).
58. H. C. Hansard, CCCCLXXXV, cols. 2410–2411, 21 March 1951.
59. It is important to remember that, unless Lauterpacht, note 57 above, were right, recognition is a matter of conditional discretion and not of duty. Certainly, pragmatic considerations rather than considerations of theory persuaded the British government to change its policy on the recognition of governments. H. L. Hansard, CCCCVIII, cols. 1121–1122, 28 April 1980. See C. Warbrick, "The New British Policy on the Recognition of Governments," *International and Comparative Law Quarterly*, XXX

(1981), 568.
60. H. Lauterpacht, "The Subject of the Law of Nations," *Law Quarterly Review*, LXIII (1947), 438; LXIV (1948), 97.
61. For an explanation of the United Kingdom position, see A. Lester, "Fundamental Rights: The United Kingdom Isolated?" *Public Law* (1984), pp. 46, 49–55, 58–61.
62. See the remarks of Paul Fifoot, an FCO Legal Adviser at the Neuchatel Seminar on the Merger of the European Commission and European Court of Human Rights, *Human Rights Law Journal*, VIII (1987), 107–108.
63. See P. Mahoney, "Developments in the Procedure of the European Court of Human Rights: the Revised Rules of the Court," *Yearbook of European Law*, III (1983), 127.
64. R. Higgins, "The Individual in International Law," BIISI (1978), 1. There have from time to time been claims by individuals to have some status with respect to international law, a recent example being Greenpeace's claim to be enforcing the international obligations of parties to the Antarctic Treaty. For some of the complications which can arise in this context, see G. Plant, "Civilian Protest Vessels and the Law of the Sea," *Netherlands Yearbook of International Law*, XIV (1987), 133.
65. The most conspicuous demonstration of this was the approach taken to the interpretation of the European Convention on Human Rights by Judge Fitzmaurice; see J. Merrills, "Sir Gerald Fitzmaurice's Contribution to the Jurisprudence of the European Court of Human Rights," *British Yearbook of International Law*, LIII (1982), 115; and see, for example, *ibid.*, LVII (1986), 546–547.
66. *Trendtex Trading Corporation* v *Central Bank of Nigeria* [1987] 1 Q. B. 529.
67. One such example, the right of a refugee, has probably been transformed into domestic law; see *Bugdaycay* v *Secretary of State for the Home Department* [1987] 1 All E. R. 940.
68. See F. A. Mann, *Foreign Affairs in English Courts* (1986), pp. 84–114 and R. Higgins, "United Kingdom," in F. Jacobs and S. Roberts (eds.), *The Effect of Treaties in Domestic Law* (1987), pp. 123–140.
69. But they have been showing an increasing unwillingness to do so; see *R* v *Immigration Appeal Tribunal ex parte Chundawara* (1987) Imkm. A. R. 227.
70. Brownlie, note 5 above, uses "incorporation" and "transformation;" (pp. 445, 447); D. Greig, *International Law* (2d ed.) uses "adoption" and "incorporation;" (p. 57); D. P. O'Connell, *International Law* (2d ed., 1970), uses "adoption" and "transformation."
71. Fitzmaurice, note 5 above, pp. 70–80. The *International Tin cases*, note 10 above; relatively rare cases like *R* v *Secretary of State for Transport ex parte Iberia Lineas Aereas de España* (unreported, 1985) see "Current Legal Developments," *International and Comparative Law Quarterly*, XXXV (1986), 425 (C. Warbrick) and human rights cases show the limits of this explanation.
72. O'Connell, note 70 above, I, pp. 50–54.
73. See Lord Templeman (in an extra-judicial capacity): "In English Law, the power of the Crown to enter into treaties and the supremacy of Parliament over the law are harmonised in a typical compromise way." Note 65 above (1986), p. 495.
74. Brownlie, *System of the Law of Nations: State Responsibility (Part I)* (1988); C. Gray, *Judicial Remedies in International Law* (1987); O. Elagab, *The Legality of Non-Forcible Counter-Measures in International Law* (1988).
75. For example, M. Spinedi and B. Simmie (eds.), *United Nations Codification of State Responsibility* (1987); E. Zoller, *Peacetime Unilateral Remedies* (1984).
76. See W. Riphagen, "State Responsibility: New Theories of Obligation in Inter-State Relations," in Macdonald and Johnston, note 1 above, pp. 555–580.
77. See Allott, "State Responsibility and the Unmaking of International Law," *Harvard*

International Law Journal, XXIX (1988), 1.

78. For example, FCO Press Release, 6 August 1987 (Soviet Emigration).
79. Note 74 above, pp. 32–33.
80. The extreme caution with which the British government has approached the notion of obligations erga omnes and the content of *ius cogens* are the manifestations of this.
81. See, for example, Brownlie, note 70 above, p. 75; not all the conditions for Statehood are peremptory; D. Bowett, "Estoppel Before International Tribunals," *British Yearbook of International Law,* XXXIII (1957), 197; MacGibbon, "Some Observations On the Part of Protest in International Law," *ibid.,* XXX (1953), 293; Sinclair, note 3 above, Chapter III; Parry, note 4 above, p. 59: "In a community containing as few members as the international community, the difference between introducing a change into the law which is of universal application and merely asserting and establishing for oneself a claim to the benefit of an exception to the existing law, which nevertheless remains unchanged, is not enormous."
82. R. B. Lillich and B. H. Weston, "Lump-Sum Agreements: Their Continuing Contribution to the Law of International Claims," *American Journal of International Law,* LXXXII (1988), 69.
83. F. A. Mann, "Correspondence," *ibid.,* LXXXII (1988), 801. On United Kingdom practice, see E. Denza and S. Brookes, "Investment Protection Treaties; United Kingdom Experience," *International and Comparative Law Quarterly,* XXXVI (1987), 908; "Current Legal Developments, *ibid.,* p. 929 (I. Cheyne).
84. Note 22 above, p. 229.
85. R. Y. Jennings, *Title to Territory in International Law* (1963), pp. 78–87, while denying that there was a legislative process for deciding territorial questions in international law, does seem to leave open the possibility of the validation of dubious situations.
86. See A. V. Lowe, "Do General Rules of International Law Exist?" *Review of International Studies,* IX (1983), 207–213.
87. R. Dworkin, *Taking Rights Seriously* (1977).
88. For a brief attempt to enlist Dworkin's methodology in the service of International Law, see Macdonald, "The Role of the Legal Adviser of Ministries of Foreign Affairs," *Recueil des cours,* CLVI (1977), 377, 398–404.
89. See Higgins, *International Law and the Reasonable Need of Governments to Govern* (1983), inaugural lecture, London School of Economics and Political Science, p. 16, noting that reasonable expectations of subjecting government conduct to scrutiny against international legal standards in domestic courts are thwarted by "the practical realities."
90. J. L. Brierly, *The Outlook for International Law* (1944), pp. 125–131.
91. It is important to distinguish between law as a product of a process and law as the process itself; compare M. McDougal and associates, *Studies in World Public Order* (1960).
92. Note 6 above, p. 34.
93. *Ibid.,* pp. 148–149.
94. H. Lauterpacht, *International Law and Human Rights* (1950). Compare the criticism of Schwarzenberger, "The Misery and the Grandeur of International Law," *Current Legal Problems,* XVII (1964), 184, 204.
95. Note 41 above, p. 12.
96. Brierly, note 90 above, p. 125.
97. Sinclair, "The Impact of the Unratified Codification Conventions," in A. Bos and H. Siblesz (eds.), *Realism in International Law-Making: Essays on International Law in*

Honour of Willem Riphagen (1986), p. 211.

98. Note 7 above.
99. *Ibid.*
100. See the argument of the Attorney-General in *Westinghouse* v *Rio Tinto Zinc* [1978] A. C. 547, 593–4. For the orthodox view, see Mann, note 68 above, p. 1.
101. Brownlie, note 41 above, p. 8.
102. Macdonald, note 88 above, points out that the role of the legal adviser will depend, *inter alia*, on the overall view of his State of its international interests.
103. In Crawford (ed), *The Right of Peoples* (1988), Chapter 1.
104. *Ibid.*, R. Rich, Chapter 3; G. Triggs, Chapter 9.

SOURCES OF INTERNATIONAL LAW IN A CHANGING INTERNATIONAL COMMUNITY: THEORY AND PRACTICE

G. M. DANILENKO

In any legal system a set of rules determining the procedures by which rules of law can be created, altered, or terminated is part of a body of fundamental provisions functioning as constitutional principles. By defining the tests of validity, these principles provide for certainty and stability in the creation and identification of law. International law, like other systems of law, also contains a number of rules defining the means of making and changing substantive legal prescriptions. As a result, the law-making activities of the members of the international community take place within the framework of specified procedures traditionally called sources of law.

The international community of States is passing through a period of profound change. The emergence of a large group of independent States promoting new ideas of international justice revolutionary technological transformations, and the growing number of global problems require the rapid generation of new international legal norms. The need of the more interdependent international community to create new rules, accompanied by the development of international organisations providing universal forums for the exchange of views among all States, creates strong pressure to modify the traditional law-making techniques. The reassessment of the existing sources of international law gives evidence of different approaches. The radical approach is reflected in claims that wholly new sources of international law corresponding to structural changes in international relations have come into being. A more moderate view tends to deny that the changes in the international community have resulted in the emergence of completely new sources. However, the contention is often made that those changes have contributed to transforming the traditional sources into essentially new modes of law-making.

This article assesses to what extent the transformations in the social and legal infrastructures of the international community have affected the traditional rules determining how international law is to be made or changed. It clarifies the content and significance of the present consensus concerning sources of international law and then discusses the possibilities of change in those sources. Some recent claims regarding the emergence of new sources of international law or relating to the changing nature of the existing sources are examined. Finally, some conclusions concerning the current state of the law governing the sources of international law are drawn.

W. E. Butler, Perestroika and International Law, 61–79.
© 1990 Kluwer Academic Publishers. Printed in the Netherlands.

The existing consensus

Consensus on the sources of law is an indispensable prerequisite for the smooth operation of any system of law as an institutional entity. Law in general and international law in particular cannot exist as a specific normative phenomenon without a certain set of rules defining the criteria of the validity of rules belonging to a particular system of law. From this perspective, it is often contended that only a concept of law based on the doctrine of sources could help to draw a distinction between law and other kinds of rules, particularly moral and political norms.[1]

In international law, as in any other legal system, law-creation can take place only within the framework of specified legal procedures serving as generally recognised modes of manifesting agreement of its subjects with a view to establishing legally binding rules of conduct. These procedures provide criteria which allow subjects of law to determine what observable or proclaimed rules of conduct have to be considered as law and therefore complied with in international relations.

The existing consensus on the criteria of validity is reflected in Article 38 of the Statute of the International Court of Justice (ICJ). According to Article 38(1), the Court, "whose function is to decide in accordance with international law such disputes as are submitted to it," is to apply: "a. international conventions, whether general or particular, establishing rules expressly recognised by the contesting states; b. international custom, as evidence of a general practice accepted as law; c. the general principles of law recognised by civilised nations."

Article 38(1) of the Statute of the ICJ is of major significance in at least two respects. First, it reflects the consensus of the members of the international community that all rules of international law are created by the consent of States. Second, it provides an authoritative statement of the legitimate sources of international law.

(1) The role of consent

Article 38(1) of the Statute of the ICJ reflects the basic principle that rules of international law are created only by the consent of States. In the case of conventions, Article 38(1) determines that customary general practice should be "accepted as law." Finally, "the general principles of law" should also be "recognised" by civilised nations. This essentially consensualist view of international law is confirmed and developed by abundant international practice and case law.

In the case of treaties, the 1969 Vienna Convention on the Law of Treaties[2] stressed the importance of consent in the process of treaty-making in its preamble. The same idea lies behind many of its specific provisions, including those relating to the effect of treaties on third States.[3] The 1986 Vienna Convention on the Law of Treaties[4] also stresses "the consensual nature of treaties in its preamble and text."

With respect to customary international law, there are various theories rejecting its consensual character. Many international lawyers are inclined to deny that customary law-making is based on the consent of States. In particular, it is often contended that custom requires only general acceptance. The recognition of emerging customary rules on the part of States that are considered to be bound by them is said to be not necessary. In discussing the practice of the ICJ, many authorities claim that the Court does not enquire into the question of whether the contesting parties have consented to the applicable customary rule.[5]

An analysis of the practice of the World Court indicates, however, that it shares the view that the contesting States must have consented to the rule in question in order to be bound by it. The basic approach of the World Court to international law-making was expressed in the famous *dicta* of the Permanent Court of International Justice in the *Lotus* case. The Court stated: "International law governs relations between independent states. The rules of law binding upon states therefore emanate from their own free will as expressed in conventions or by usages generally accepted as expressing principles of law."[6] The ICJ has expressed essentially the same attitude in the *Case Concerning Military and Paramilitary Activities In and Against Nicaragua*: "In international law there are no rules, other than such rules as may be accepted by the states concerned."[7]

In dealing with customary law, the ICJ has had many occasions to elaborate this basic approach in specific situations. In its judgment in the *Fisheries Case* the ICJ expressed a fundamental principle of customary law-making, according to which States that have persistently objected to the practice of other States are not bound by the relevant customary rule.[8] In a number of cases the ICJ did take account of the attitude of the contesting parties to applicable custom. Thus, in its judgment in the *Case Concerning Delimitation of the Maritime Boundary in the Gulf of Maine* the ICJ has taken into account the attitude towards applicable customary law not only of "all states," but also of "the parties to the present dispute."[9] In the *Nicaragua Case* the Court noted the "shared view of the parties as to the content of what they regard as the rule."[10] In considering the applicability of a number of customary rules, the ICJ pointed out that the parties to the dispute had expressed "recognition of the validity thereof as customary international law."[11] The ICJ examined, among other things, "the attitude of the parties" towards certain United Nations General Assembly resolutions in order to determine whether the effect of consent to the text of such resolutions "may be understood as an acceptance of the validity of the rule or set of rules declared by the resolution."[12] In particular, the ICJ carefully evaluated the available evidence which testified to "the existence, and the acceptance by the United States, of a customary principle which has universal application."[13]

The actual practice of States from different parts of the world is based on the essentially consensualist approach to international law-making. The traditional position of the Soviet Union, that it cannot be considered bound by a rule of international law without its consent,[14] remains unchanged. The international legal policy of other States is likewise based on the assumption that, as the representative of Belgium at the Third United Nations Conference on the Law of the Sea (UNCLOS) put it, "no state could be bound by international law without its consent."[15] Because in the final analysis the methods of international law-making are determined by the basic features of the international community, one can hardly expect a different approach. So long as the international community remains a society of sovereign and independent States, international law-making will necessarily be based on their consent, expressed in one form or another.

(2) Article 38(1) of the statute of the ICJ as a statement of sources

When Article 38(1) was included in the Statute of the Permanent Court of International Justice, it was not intended to be an enumeration of sources of international law. Technically, Article 38(1) did not refer to sources of international law as such; it merely contained a direction to the Court to apply different categories of rules in resolving disputes submitted to it. At the San Francisco Conference, the original text of Article 38 of the Statute of the Permanent Court of International Justice was amended through the insertion of the words "in accordance with international law" into the opening phrase. This amendment clarified that the enumerated categories of rules constitute applicable international law. However, technically speaking, the situation remained the same: Article 38 remained a direction to the Court to apply rules listed in Paragraph 1. Indeed, it could not be otherwise: the Court cannot apply sources of law or procedures of law-making as such. It can only apply the normative results of such procedures: established rules of law.

While this restrictive view of Article 38(1) *per se* is technically correct, the subsequent practice of States and of the ICJ has created political legal grounds for a broader interpretation of its significance and effect. It was beyond dispute that each listed category of rules was the result of the operation of a particular source. Therefore, a tendency has emerged to regard Article 38(1) as the definition of the sources of international law and, moreover, as "the codification of this aspect of international law."[16] Thus, during a debate which touched upon the role of the U. N. General Assembly resolutions in the decisions of the ICJ, the majority of States participating in the discussion expressed the opinion that Article 38(1) enumerates the sources of international law.[17] The same approach has been endorsed by the ICJ. In the *Nicaragua case* the Court held that Article 38 of the Statute requires the Court to apply "the sources of international law."[18] In the same judgment the Court maintained that Article 38 "enumerated" sources of law.[19]

A system of sources can ensure certainty and stability in the functioning of international law only if it contains an exhaustive list of procedures by which law can be made or changed at a given moment. International practice indicates that there is a strong tendency to regard Article 38(1) as an exhaustive enumeration of sources of international law. This view of sources has been expressly supported by a number of States.[20] This approach is strengthened by the tendency to regard Article 38(1) as the only authoritative guide to the content of modern international law. There are important instances of State practice where States defined international law exclusively through reference to Article 38. Thus, Articles 74 and 83 of the 1982 U. N. Convention on the Law of the Sea[21] require that the delimitation of maritime boundaries should be effected by agreement on the basis of international law "as referred to in Article 38 of the Statute of the International Court of Justice."[22]

It is important to note that the tendency to define international law exclusively in terms of Article 38 of the Statute of the ICJ amounts to a rejection of the view that the sources of international law could be different in the judicial and extrajudicial contexts.[23] States support the unity of international law, which has the same sources in different operational contexts.

(3) The possibility of change in the existing sources

The fact that Article 38(1) is regarded as an exhaustive enumeration of procedures by which international law can be made does not mean that it precludes the possibility of change in the sources of law. As a treaty provision relating to the functions of the ICJ, it acquired constitutional significance as a result of the development of the subsequent practice of States. It is beyond dispute that as law-givers in the international society States can reach a new agreement modifying or amending the existing constitutional principles reflected in the provisions of Article 38(1).

This does not mean, however, that States are completely free to adopt wholly new procedures for making or changing the law. The first important limitation follows from the fact that constitutional provisions supported by the consensus of the international community can be changed only by provisions having similar broad community support. Until a new community consensus on procedures for law-making is established, individual States seeking new general international law cannot disregard the procedures for law-making prescribed by the existing law. Otherwise, their alleged law-making activities would not be recognised as such by other members of the international community.

Second, because the matter under discussion is already regulated by rules of international law, consensus-legitimating new sources must necessarily partake of the nature of a legal rule. It is obvious that in practice States can provide the new constitutional rule with adequate legal form only within a the framework of an already recognised source. This would mean that the establishment of a new source requires the adoption by all or almost all States of a new treaty provision to this effect or the acceptance of a new general practice, legitimating a new source, as law.

Experience indicates that in a number of instances States were able to reach an agreement legitimating new autonomous procedures of rule-making in specific treaty regimes. Thus, members of the United Nations have recognised certain resolutions of the U. N. General Assembly on internal organisational matters as having binding effect. States have also recognised the legally binding character of some enactments of international organisations in specified technical fields of international co-operation.[24]

While these exceptional arrangements, expressly provided for in international treaties, are beyond dispute, the alleged appearance of wholly new sources on the level of general international law remains controversial. The most frequest examples cited in this connection are the United Nations General Assembly resolutions and community consensus. These alleged new sources will be briefly examined here.

The alleged new sources

(1) United Nations General Assembly resolutions

In view of the relatively slow pace of treaty and customary law-making the proponents of a radical reform of international law have focused their attention on United Nations General Assembly resolutions as a most promising candidate for a new source of law. Political realities in the General Assembly, where the developing countries have a stable majority, tend to generate pressure to endow the General Assembly with quasi-legislative authority.

In a number of situations the developing countries maintain that a General Assembly resolution addressing issues of international law can of itself create legal obligations for States who joined a consensus supporting it. An illustration of this trend may provide the argumentation of the developing countries on the legal consequences of the 1970 Declaration of Principles Governing the Sea-Bed and the Ocean Floor, and the Subsoil thereof, Beyond the Limits of National Jurisdiction.[25] The Declaration proclaimed the seabed and its resources to be the common heritage of mankind. During a debate on the Declaration at the Third UNCLOS the Chairman of the Group of 77 stated that as "a solemn pronouncement by the most representative organ of the international community" the Declaration "established a principle of law precisely in the meaning of Article 38 of the Statute of the International Court of Justice."[26] The Declaration was claimed to be "the embodiment of current international law with regard to the regime of the seabeds."[27] As a result, the developing States maintained that the Declaration had led to abrogation of the previously existing international law governing the seabed.[28]

On the theoretical level, arguments supporting the law-making authority of the General Assembly tend to question the very basis of obligation in international law. It is contended that the General Assembly produces legally binding norms because many rules proclaimed in resolutions operate as effective standards influencing the actual behaviour of States. The actual effectiveness of the proclaimed rules transforms the General Assembly into a quasi-legislative body.[29] From a broader perspective, it is asserted that the traditional concept and the sources of international law are too restrictive and obsolete. Many authorities claim that in the international normative system there is no clear line separating legally binding rules from non-binding norms governing international behaviour. It is contended that, from a law-making perspective, there is also no definite threshhold between pre-law and law. Within the framework of this trend of thought the General Assembly resolutions are often regarded as a source of "soft law."[30]

Whatever the theoretical merit of these arguments, they cannot alter the basic fact that the United Nations Charter accords the General Assembly no authority to enact, alter, or repeal rules of international law. According to the United Nations Charter the General Assembly can only make recommendations. True, some rules proclaimed by the General Assembly have been effective in influencing the actual conduct of States. However, effectiveness is not the only characteristic of law. There are various kinds of rules, for example, moral and political norms, which may be effective in the international system. But this fact alone does not automatically transform them into legal rules. To acquire legal quality, such rules have to be recognised as law within a specified law-making procedure. It is clear, for instance, that as a matter of law the ICJ could "take account of moral principles only in so far as these are given a sufficient expression in legal form."[31]

It is also important to emphasise that as a normative system international law continues to operate on the assumption that there exists a threshhold of validity separating rules still in the process of formation from the established legal norms. While the distinction between *lex ferenda* and *lex lata* may be difficult to apply in specific situations, the recognition of such a distinction is crucial for the concept of law. In the *Fisheries Jurisdiction case* the ICJ has clearly endorsed such an approach. The Court held that "the Court as a court of law, cannot render judgment *sub specia legis ferendae*, or anticipate the law before the legislator has laid it down."[32]

These trends provide sufficient evidence for rejecting the assertion that we are witnessing a complete blurring of the distinction between legal and non-legal rules, between law and pre-law. From this perspective, it is clear that the so-called "soft law" rules allegedly produced by the General Assembly resolutions remain below the established threshhold of validity. In other words, they remain outside the law proper.

This line of argument is strengthened by the fact that generally States do not support the view of U. N. General Assembly resolutions in themselves generating legal rules. There is only a broad consensus, as expressed in the U. N. General Assembly resolution 3232(XXIX), that "the development of international law may be reflected, *inter alia*, by declarations and resolutions of the General Assembly which may to that extent be taken into consideration by the International Court of Justice."[33]

An analysis of statements by States during a debate concerning the General Assembly resolution 3232(XXIX) just cited indicates that it was not intended to modify Article 38(1) of the Statute of the ICJ.[34] During the debate several States stressed that they did not consider General Assembly resolutions to be a source of international law. Thus, the representative of the Soviet Union stated: "In accordance with the U. N. Charter and the Statute of the International Court of Justice, in particular Article 38, resolutions and declarations of the General Assembly do not constitute a source of international law."[35] Similarly, the representative of Venezuela stated: "We cannot consider that the resolutions of the General Assembly constitute sources of international law within the meaning of Article 38 of the Statute of the Court."[36] Many States stressed that General Assembly resolutions could not of themselves develop international law because they are not legally binding.[37]

It is important to note that States continue to maintain the same approach with regard to specific General Assembly resolutions. Thus, during the adoption of the Declaration on the seabed[38] the representative of the Soviet Union has stated that the Declaration could not give rise to legal consequences for States in view of the well-known fact that the decisions of the General Assembly were merely recommendations.[39] During a debate on the legal consequences of this Declaration within the framework of the Third UNCLOS, the representative of the United States also stated that "United Nations General Assembly resolutions, irrespective of the majorities by which they were adopted, were not legally binding on any State."[40]

In view of this clear record, any contention that the U. N. General Assembly resolutions have emerged as an autonomous source of international law remains groundless. United Nations General Assembly resolutions *per se* cannot create international legal obligations; nor can they of themselves lead to abrogation of an existing rule of treaty or customary law. Such an abrogation would require the creation of a new legal rule. Because the requirements for modification or abrogation of an existing legal rule are generally the same as for the creation of a new legal rule, simple recommendations cannot change the existing legal situation.

(2) Community consensus

A number of commentators maintain that States continue to use not only the formalised law-making procedures enumerated in Article 38(1) of the Statute of the ICJ, but also the formless methods of law-creation. The argument is that "formless" inter-State consensus remains the primary source of international law which operates irrespective of Article 38(1).[41] It is asserted, in particular, that if all States meeting at a conference or at the United Nations General Assembly reach a consensus to be bound by a particular rule, this would suffice to establish the legally binding quality of the rule in question.[42]

As indicated earlier, in their capacity of law-givers in the international system States can in principle legitimate any method of law-making, including the proposed formless consensus. There are, however, a number of arguments which undermine the possibility of using "formless" consensus as a direct source of international law. It should be borne in mind that the recognition by States of the formalised methods of law-making creates at least a strong presumption, if not a legal requirement, that their law-making activities would follow the prescribed procedures. From this perspective, any claim as to the emergence of a direct law-making consensus should be backed by sufficient evidence that States have indeed expressed a clear intention to create legal obligations outside the existing sources. This would mean that community consensus on substantive issues should be accompanied by a consensus that the relevant rules automatically become binding as law in the absence of any treaty or custom which would normally give them legal effect.

It is submitted that while in the modern international community there are instances of consensus on substantive issues, there is no consensus on the constitutional requirement transforming it into a direct source of law. On the contrary, States participating in international law-making conferences or in the United Nations General Assembly proceed from the assumption that consensus on substantive issues can become law only if confirmed through the treaty or customary process.

It is submitted, furthermore, that the emergence of consensus on the constitutional requirement is highly unlikely becuse the proposed "formless" consensus would lack recognisable forms of manifestation. States rely on the established sources because they provide specific criteria which may be used in the search for consensus on substantive issues. In the absence of these criteria, determining the existence of consensus would be practically impossible.

The alleged modifications of the traditional sources

Where the radical proposals aimed at restructuring the existing system of sources are not accepted, the proponents of reforming international law-making seek to achieve similar results by promoting far-reaching changes within the traditional sources. The proposed changes relate not only to the technical issues of law-making. Some touch upon the very basis of obligation in international law.

(1) Conventions

The growing number of global problems calling for global solutions has increased the need for normative instruments of a universally binding character. New political and legal concepts, such as the common heritage of mankind, by their very nature require universal application. Therefore, the search has intensified for a means to ensure that States which are not parties to conventions on issues of vital importance to the international community as a whole would comply with legal requirements imposed by such conventions.

The trend in this direction became particularly evident with the adoption of the 1982 Convention on the Law of the Sea.[43] During the debate on the Convention, some States have expressed the view that the Convention created the only valid law for ocean space binding on all States irrespective of their participation. Many developing States claimed, in particular, that the Convention "would be law for all States – even those that are outside its framework."[44]

It is clear that the present international law relating to law-making cannot support such far-reaching legislative claims. There is no evidence that the international community is ready to adopt legislative techniques based on majority law-making. On the contrary, States participating in the Third UNCLOS proceeded on the assumption that "the conference was not a parliament, and a majority vote would not result in legislation."[45]

There is also no evidence that the principles of the law of treaties, including those relating to the effect of treaties on third States, codified by the Vienna Convention on the Law of Treaties[46] are not applicable to the 1982 Law of the Sea Convention. Therefore, as a matter of law the conventional regime cannot be imposed on third States. The 1982 Law of the Sea Convention, like any other international treaty, may have the desired legal effects only between States which have expressed their consent to be bound by it.

It is generally recognised that more subtle means to ensure the universal applicability of treaties are provided by the treaty-custom relationship. Provisions of a treaty may become binding on all States via international customary law. The basic requirement in this connection is established by the 1969 Vienna Convention on the Law of Treaties. According to the Convention, a rule set forth in a treaty may become "binding upon a third State as a customary rule of international law, recognised as such."[47]

In recent years some commentators have advanced the theory that a multilateral convention can itself produce general customary law. It is contended that the international community "has accepted a constitutive rule to the effect that generalisable norms in treaties generate equivalent norms of customary law."[48] This would mean that treaties (especially multilateral treaties) constitute or generate customary rules of law *ipso facto*, that is directly and without the need for subsequent practice.[49]

Proponents of the concept according to which customary law can be generated through the adoption of a multilateral convention often support their theoretical constructions with references to an unhappily formulated passage in the judgment in the *North Sea Continental Shelf case*. In this judgment the ICJ stated that "with respect to the other elements usually regarded as necessary before a conventional rule can be considered to have become a general rule of international law, it might be that ... a very widespread and representative participation in the convention might suffice of itself, provided it included that of states whose interests were specially affected."[50] A number of authors[51] interpret this provision out of the context of the Court's subsequent argumentation. This leads them to conclude that in the view of the Court a widespread participation in a convention "of itself" creates customary law. In reality, however, when describing the transformation process of a treaty rule into a rule of general customary international law the Court required the existence of the uniformity of subsequent practice, the passage of a certain period of time, and, what is most important, the acceptance of a treaty norm by the *opinio juris* of States.[52]

The same approach is required by the 1969 Vienna Convention on the Law of Treaties, which stipulates that a rule set forth in a treaty should be "recognised" as a customary rule of international law.[53]

It is submitted that generally such recognition can not be established in the framework of the treaty process itself. More particularly, contrary to the recent pronouncement of the ICJ in the *Nicaragua case*,[54] the "weight of an expression of *opinio juris*" cannot be attached to the ratification of a convention. This follows from the fact that treaty and customary law-creating procedures are being conducted within different sets of rules. According to the 1969 Vienna Convention on the Law of Treaties, signature and ratification should be considered only as "a means of expressing consent to be bound by a treaty."[55] By signing and then ratifying a treaty, States assume treaty obligations and not wider customary law commitments. These acts cannot express the *opinio juris* of States because *opinio juris* implies not just recognition of a norm's legally binding character, but recognition of such a norm as a rule of international customary law operating irrespective of the treaty. The ICJ has stated that "where two states agree to incorporate a particular rule in a treaty, their agreement suffices to make that rule a legal one, binding upon them; but in the field of customary international law, the shared view of the parties as to the content of what they regard as the rule is not enough."[56] The Court then stressed the need for *opinio juris* which should be "confirmed by practice."[57] Such *opinio juris* would enable States, apart from the treaty commitments binding them to the rule in question, to express "recognition of the validity thereof as customary international law."[58]

It follows from the preceding observations that the adoption of a treaty in itself is not sufficient for the emergence of customary legal obligations. Other forms of practice outside the treaty context are necessary to serve as evidence of the recognition by the relevant States of the customary nature of rules contained in a treaty. In other words, conventions *per se* cannot generate general international law either directly or via custom.

(2) Custom

The customary law-making process has undergone profound changes under the impact of structural changes in international relations. Major innovations were brought by new forms of State practice in the framework of international conferences and international organisations. In particular, methods of "parliamentary diplomacy" have substantially accelerated the pace of customary law formation.[59]

The emergence of new verbal forms of State practice in the framework of international organisations and international conferences has led to the theory that customary law-making had radically changed its traditional characteristics. Custom is no longer considered to be a source of law essentially based on the actual practice of States. The contention is made that official pronouncements in international organisations or similar forums are sufficient for the creation of customary law.[60] Some authorities claim that a mere repetition of principles in subsequent United Nations Assembly resolutions,[61] or the accumulation of resolutions on the same matters in the same, or diverse international organisations,[62] establishes a sufficient international practice leading to customary rules. The most radical claim is that a single U. N. General Assembly resolution can create "instant" customary law.[63]

A survey of recent legal argumentation of governments reveals that this approach is supported on the official level. Thus, the developing States have based their claims as to the existence of a customary rule proclaiming the seabed to be the common heritage of mankind exclusively on "examination of the attitude of states in different international fora."[64] More particularly, they claimed that "a customary rule may be crystallised through the intermediary of a declaration of the United Nations."[65]

However, there are grounds to believe that recent innovations in customary law-making have not altered the basic characteristics of international custom. Actual State practice continues to be a decisive factor in custom-formation. As the ICJ has pointed out, it is "the actual practice of States which is expressive, or creative, of customary rules."[66] In other words, as a source of law, custom continues to be based on real and concrete legal relationships. Experience indicates that the convergence of the positions of States on the verbal level does not necessarily mean that the proclaimed rules will be applied in actual practice. For this reason, the official pronouncements in themselves cannot lead to the creation of customary rules. As the ICJ has emphasised, "the shared view of the parties as to the content of what they regard as the rule" should be "confirmed by practice."[67]

It is clear that recent claims to the effect that U. N. General Assembly resolutions in themselves can create customary law are largely caused by the blurring of the distinction between the verbal and actual State practice. Another factor contributing to the emergence of such claims is the tendency to regard General Assembly resolutions as adequate vehicles for expressing both State practice and *opinio juris*.

Indeed, the unqualified equating of resolutions with State practice leading to the formation of custom coupled with the contention that such resolutions may express *opinio juris* inevitably leads to the assumption that a single resolution or at least a number of resolutions are sufficient to create customary law. It appears that in dealing with the impact of General Assembly resolutions in the *Nicaragua case*, the ICJ has come dangerously close to such an equating. The Court regarded the voting for resolutions not only as a form of State practice but also as evidence of *opinio juris*.

The ICJ held, specifically, that *opinio juris* may be deduced from the attitude of States towards certain General Assembly resolutions.[68] The Court, in particular, stated that the acceptance by States of the text of Resolution 2625(XXV) containing the Declaration of Principles of International Law Concerning Friendly Relations and Cooperation Among States in Accordance with the Charter of the United Nations amounted to "an *opinio juris*" respecting rules or set of rules declared by the resolution.[69] The major argument used by the Court in this connection was that the consent to the text of such resolutions may be understood as "an acceptance of the validity of the rule or set of rules declared by the resolution."[70] The Court also drew attention to the fact that Resolution 2625(XXV) set out principles which the General Assembly declared to be "basic principles" of international law.[71]

It is submitted that the concept according to which U. N. General Assembly resolutions can of themselves express *opinio juris* of States disregards the indisputable fact that under the United Nations Charter (Articles 10, 11) the General Assembly may only adopt recommendations. Correspondingly, the voting for the relevant resolutions cannot be regarded as an expression of the will of States towards recognition of the legal validity of the norms contained in resolutions. The provision of the Charter on the recommendatory nature of General Assembly resolutions sets a clear-cut threshhold for law-formation that cannot be overridden by resolutions. Obviously, in this case the formation of customary rules requires other forms of State practice that can express *opinio juris*.

In its assessment of the role of Resolution 2625(XXV) the ICJ attached special significance to the fact that the Declaration of Principles of International Law contained a provision proclaiming the principles therein as "principles of international law." The weakness of this argument is clear in light of the fact that under the United Nations Charter all resolutions, including resolutions of this type, are recommendations. Therefore, the cited provision of the Declaration is merely a recommendation to States to regard the proclaimed principles as rules of international law. Although on the politico-legal plane the international legal character of the proclaimed principles gives this Declaration a special significance, from a strictly legal point of view it cannot change the recommendatory nature of the whole resolution and bind the States that have voted for it.

It would follow from these observations that the voting for an instrument which is not binding cannot amount to acceptance of the relevant rules as law. Even if resolutions would be regarded as sufficient for the establishment of the necessary general practice, they cannot meet the requirement of the acceptance as law laid down by Article 38(1)(b) of the Statute of the ICJ for customary law-making.

This conclusion is supported by broader considerations. The theory that General Assembly resolutions can of themselves generate customary international law is a disguised form of the contention that resolutions constitute an autonomous source of international law. To that extent this theory is subject to all objections developed earlier. The international community has not granted the General Assembly express or implied legislative powers, nor is the community ready to allow the General Assembly to exercise such powers in a disguised form via alleged customary law-making through its own resolutions.

(3) "The general principles of law"

For a long time the nature and even the role of "the general principles of law" as an autonomous source of international law has been controversial.[72] The continued uncertainty over the nature of "the general principles' is a major factor explaining why they have not played a major role in the development of modern international law. There are recent attempts to revive this source by suggesting that General Assembly resolutions can express the required "recognition" of "the general principles of law" by "civilised nations."[73] It appears that this approach is supported by some States.[74]

While theoretical backgrounds for such an approach may be different, it seems clear that its political and legal background is largely provided by the desire to avoid the specific requirements of law-creation recognised by the other two principal sources. In assessing these recent claims, it should be borne in mind that as a source of law "the general principles of law" are traditionally regarded as a vehicle for transposing into the international legal order some very general notions recognised in domestic legal systems. It is doubtful that States are prepared to radically change this traditional nature of the third source by accepting the idea of a direct recognition of new rules through an international instrument of a recommendatory nature. One may even assume that such a development is highly unlikely in view of the fact that it would accord the U. N. General Assembly *de facto* legislative powers under the guise of an established source of international law.

(4) The impact of the jus cogens concept

The *jus cogens* concept is often regarded as a radical departure from the consensual nature of international law. By referring to Article 53 of the 1969 Vienna Convention on the Law of Treaties,[75] some commentators claim that the creation of peremptory norms does not require the consent of individual States. They believe that because Article 53 requires the acceptance of norms under discussion not by individual States but by "the international community of States as a whole" we are witnessing a trend towards majority rule in international law-making. An examination of the legal argumentation of governments indicates that some States also tend to use the notion of *jus cogens* in order to impose specific normative solutions on dissenters.[76]

In reality, however, Article 53 of the Vienna Convention does not abolish the requirement of consent. Following the requirements established by Article 38(1) of the Statute of the ICJ, it calls for "acceptance" and "recognition" of emerging peremptory norms by States constituting the international community. It also requires that the relevant norm first become a norm of "general" international law. International law does not have a specific source designed to generate rules of "general" international law which are going to be accepted as norms *jus cogens*. Therefore, such rules have to be created within the framework of the established sources. This would require the application of the traditional criteria of validity for establishing a rule of general international law.

As the ICJ has indicated in the *Nicaragua case*, the evidence supporting the peremptory character of a rule may have relevance in the process of ascertaining the required generality.[77] However, this does not mean that the requirement of generality as such can be relaxed. In particular, general recognition of a rule cannot be reduced to recognition by only "the essential components of the international community,"[78] a requirement that is generally considered as sufficient for the establishment of the peremptory character of an existing general rule.

It would follow from these observations that although the concept of *jus cogens* may represent a major breakthrough in the development of the international legal order, it cannot be considered as indicating a trend towards law-making based on majority rule. The rules of *jus cogens* are and will continue to be created in the framework of the existing sources which remain essentially consensual in their nature.

Conclusion

The preceding analysis indicates that changes in the international community have not resulted in a reform of constitutional principles governing law-making. While structural changes in international relations have a major impact on law-making within the framework of the traditional sources, it appears that in the modern international community there is no consensus legitimating wholly new procedures of law-creation. From a theoretical perspective, it appears that such fundamental constitutional reforms are unlikely so long as the international community based on the coexistence and cooperation of sovereign States retains its present basic features. In view of the growing number of global problems calling for global normative responses, the international community may be in need of international quasi-legislative techniques. The elaboration of such techniques remains, however, a major challenge for future generations which hopefully will live in a more homogeneous and closely-knit World Community.

Notes

1. See H. Kelsen, *Allgemeine Theorie der Normen* (1979), p. 94.
2. *UNTS*, DCLV, 331.
3. *Ibid.*, Articles 34–38.
4. 1986 Vienna Convention on the Law of Treaties Between States and International Organisations or Between International Organisations, U. N. Doc. A/Conf. 129/15 (1986).
5. See A. Verdross and B. Simma, *Universelles Volkerrecht. Theorie und Praxis* (1984), p. 349; A. D'Amato, *The Concept of Custom in International Law* (1971), p. 190; P. Haggenmacher, "La doctrine des deux elements du droit coutumier dans la pratique de la Cour internationale," *Revue générale de droit international public*, XC (1986), 26–30.
6. PCIJ, Ser. A, No. 10, p. 19 (1927).
7. ICJ Reports (1986), p. 135 [hereinafter cited as *Nicaragua case*].
8. See ICJ Reports (1951), p. 131.
9. ICJ Reports 1984), p. 299.
10. Note 7 above, p. 98.
11. *Ibid.*
12. *Ibid.*, p. 100.
13. *Ibid.*, p. 107.
14. For details see G. I. Tunkin, "Soviet Theory of Sources of International Law," P. Fischer et al (eds.), *Völkerrecht und Rechtsphilosophie.* (1980) pp. 67–77.
15. Third UNCLOS. Official Records, IX, p. 107. In the course of the debate on the legal status of the seabed the United States stated their position on the general issue of law-making in the following manner: "The United States could not accept the suggestion that, without its consent, other states would be able, by resolutions or statements, to deny or alter its rights under international law." *Ibid.*, p. 104.
16. This was suggested already in "The Survey of International Law, in Relation to the Work of Codification, submitted by the U. N. Secretary General to the International Law Commission," U. N. Doc. A/CN. 4/1/Rev. 1, p. 22 (1949).
17. See, for example, the statements of the representative of Mexico (U. N. Doc. A/C. 6/29/SR 1486, para. 9 (1974)), Brazil (U. N. Doc. A/C. 6/29/SR 1486, para. 3 (1974)), Israel (*Ibid.*, para. 8) and Japan (*Ibid.*, para. 32).
18. Note 7 above, p. 38.
19. *Ibid.*, p. 92.
20. See the statements of the representatives of Brazil (U. N. Doc. A/C. A/29/SR 1492, para. 3 (1974) and Japan (para. 32).
21. U. N. Doc. A/Conf. 62/122 (1982).
22. It is interesting to note that during a debate on Articles 74 and 83 at the Third UN-CLOS, various States maintained that Article 38 of the Statute of the ICJ defined "sources of international law." See the statements of the representative of the GDR

(Third UNCLOS. Official Records, XV, p. 41) and Venezuela *Ibid.*, XVI, p. 15).

23. Cf. M. Sörensen, "Theory and Reality in International Law," Proceedings of the American Society of International Law, (1981), p. 148.

24. Standards relating to air navigation over the high seas established by the ICAO in accordance with Article 12 of the Chicago Convention on International Civil Aviation of 1944 (UNTS, XV, p. 295) may be an example in this connection.

25. G. A. Res. 1749(XXV) (1970.

26. Third UNCLOS. Official Records, IX, p. 103.

27. *Ibid.*

28. See U. N. Doc. A/.Conf. 62/77 (1979) – Third UNCLOS. Official Records, XI, p. 82 (Letter from the Chairman of the Group of 77 to the President of the Third UNCLOS).

29. See, for example, R. A. Falk, "On the Quasi-Legislative Competence of the General Assembly," *American Journal of International Law*, LX (1966), V. 60, pp. 782. A similar line of argument is developed by the proponents of the policy-oriented approach to international law. See generally M. S. McDougal and W. M. Reisman, "The Prescribing Function in World Constitutive Process: How International Law is Made," *Yale Studies in World Public Order*, V1 (I1980), 249.

30. See, for example R.-J. Dupuy, *La Communité international entre le mythe et l'histoire* (1986), pp. 135ff.

31. ICJ Reports (1966), p. 34.

32. ICJ Reports (1974) pp. 23–24.

33. Review of the Role of the International Court of Justice. G. A. Res. 3232 (XXIX) (1974).

34. See the statements of the representatives of Mexico (U. N. Doc. A/C. 6/29/SR 1486, para. 5 (1974)), Brazil (U. N. Doc. A/C. 6/29/SR 1492, para. 5 (1974)), Israel (para. 8), Turkey (para. 23), Ukrainian SSR (para. 25) and Ireland (U. N. Doc. A/29/PV 2280, para. 77 (1974).

35. U. N. Doc. A/C. 6/29/SR 1492, para. 12 (1974) (Translation from the Russian record by the author).

36. U. N. Doc. A/29/PV 2280, para. 84 (1974). See also the statements of the representatives of Turkey (U. N. Doc. A/C. 6/29/SR 1492, para. 23 (1974)), Japan (para. 32), Byelorussian SSR (para. 39), GDR (para. 48) and Mongolia (U. N. Doc. A/29/PV 2280, para. 79 (1974)).

37. See, for example, the statements of the United Kingdom representatives (U. N. Doc. A/C. 6/29/SR 1492, para. 16 (1974)), Japan (para. 32) and Mongolia (U. N. Doc. A/29/PV 2280, para. 79 (1974)).

38. See note 25 above.

39. U. N. Doc. A/C. 1/25/SR 1798, para. 65 (1970).

40. Third UNCLOS. Official Records, XII, p. 14.

41. See note 5 above, pp. 324–327.

42. See L. B. Sohn, "'Generally Accepted' International Rules," *Washington Law Review*, LXI (1986) 1079–1080.

43. See note 21 above.

44. The statement of the representative of Trinidad and Tobago. Third UNCLOS. Official Records, XVII, p. 23. See also the statements of the representatives of Cameroon (p. 16), Peru (speaking on behalf of the Group of 77) (p. 22), Kenya (p. 47) and Chile (p. 67).

45. The statement of the representative of Bahamas. Third UNCLOS. Official Records, I, p. 138. See also the statement of the United States delegation: "Neither the Conference nor the States indicating an intention to become parties to the convention have bveen

78

granted global legislative powers." Third UNCLOS. Official Records, XVII, p. 243.

46. See notes 2 and 3 above, and accompanying text.
47. Note 2 above, Article 38.
48. A. D'Amato, "An Alternative to the Law of the Sea Convention," *American Journal of International Law*, LXXVII (1983), 281–282.
49. See A. D'Amato, *International Law: Process and Prospect* (1987), pp. 129, 145.
50. See ICJ Reports (1969), p. 42.
51. See H. W. A. Thirlway, *International Customary Law and Codification* (1972), pp. 86–89; Haggenmacher, note 5 above, pp. 94–96.
52. See Note 50 above, pp. 41–44.
53. See Note 47 above and accompanying text.
54. See Note 7 above p. 100.
55. Note 2 above Article 11.
56. Note 7 above p. 98.
57. *Ibid.*
58. *Ibid.*
59. For details see G. M. Danilenko, "The Theory of International Customary Law," *German Yearbook of International Law*, XXXI, (1988).
60. See B. Cheng, "Custom: The Future of General State Practice in a Divided World," in R. St. J. Macdonald and D. M. Johnston (eds.), *The Structure and Process of International Law: Essays in Legal Philosophy, Doctrine and Theory* (1983), p. 531. Also see A. Bleckmann, "Die Praxis des Völkergewohnheits rechts als konsekutive Rechtssetzungf" in R. Bernhard et al. (eds.), *Völkerrecht als Rechtsordnung. Internationale Gerichtsbarkeit. Menschenrechte.* (1983), pp. 91–92.
61. See E. Suy, "Innovations in International Law-Making Processes," in Macdonald et al. (eds.), *The International Law and Policy of Human Welfare* (1978), p. 190.
62. See the dissenting opinion of Judge Kotaro Tanaka in ICJ Reports (1966), pp. 291–292.
63. See Cheng, "United Nations Resolutions on Outer Space: "Instant" International Customary Law?," *Indian Journal of International Law*, V (1965), 23.
64. U. N. Doc. A/Conf. 62/106 (1980) – Third UNCLOS. Official Records, XIV, p. 112 (Letter from the Chairman of the Group of 77 to the President of the Third UNCLOS).
65. *Ibid.*
66. I. C. J. Reports (1982), p. 46.
67. Note 7 above, p. 98.
68. Note 7 above, pp. 99–100.
69. *Ibid.*, p. 101.
70. *Ibid.*, p. 100.
71. *Ibid.*, p. 107.
72. For details see G. I. Tunkin, "'General Principles of Law' in International Law," in R. Marcic et al. (eds.), *Internationale Festschrift für Alfred Verdross* (1971), pp. 523–532; id., "International Law in the International System," *Recueil des cours*, CFXLVII (1975) 98.
73. See A. Verdross, "Les principes généraux de droit dans le système des sources du droit international public," in *Recueil d'études de droit international en hommage à Paul Guggenheim* (1968), p. 525; E. Hambro, "Some Notes on the Development of the Sources of International Law," *Scandinavian Studies in Law*, XVII (1973), 90, 92.
74. See the statement of the representative of Mexico,. U. N. Doc. A/C. 6/29/SR 1486, para. 13 (1974). See also the argumentation of the Group of 77 regarding legal consequences of the U. N. General Assembly resolution on the seabed, note 26 above and accompanying text.

75. See note 2 above. Article 53 of the Convention, which is considered to be a generally accepted definition of *jus cogens* norms, reads: "For the purposes of the present Convention, a peremptory norm of general international law is a norm accepted and recognised by the international community of states as a whole as a norm from which no derogation is permitted and which can be modified only by a subsequent norm of general international law having the same character." See also the definition of a peremptory norm in Article 53 of the 1986 Vienna Convention on the Law of Treaties note 4 above.

76. One illustration is the references to the *jus cogens* character of the common heritage of mankind principle in the law of the sea. See U. N. Doc. A/Conf. 62/106 (1980), note 64 above.

77. The Court has expressed this approach in the following manner: "A further confirmation of the validity as customary international law of the principle of the prohibition of the use of force expressed in Article 2, Paragraph 4, of the Charter of the United Nations may be found in the fact that it is frequently referred to in statements by state representatives as being not only a principle of customary international law but also a fundamental or cardinal principle of such law." The Court referred then to the opinion of the International Law Commission, which regarded the principle under discussion as having "the character of *jus cogens*. Note 7 above, p. 100.

78. See R. Ago, "Droit des traites à la lumière de la Convention de Vienne," *Recueil des courfs*, CXXXIV (1971) 32 3. The expression "the essential components of the international community" was used by the International Law Commission in its commentary to Article 19 of the Draft Articles on State responsibility. Article 19 deals with international obligations which "are essential for the protection of fundamental interests of the international community." See *Yearbook of the International Law Commission*, II(2) (1976), pp. 95ff.

ARE TREATIES MERELY A SOURCE OF OBLIGATION?

M. H. MENDELSON

In an article written in 1958,[1] the late Sir Gerald Fitzmaurice argued that treaties are not a formal source of law, but merely a source of obligation:[2]

> It is often said, and sometimes simply assumed that in the international field *treaties*, and international agreements generally, are the equivalent of the domestic law statute, or at least a substitute for it, and serve a substantially similar purpose. But this is certainly an overstatement, if it is accurate at all, and it has had particularly unfortunate consequences in promoting a readiness to view treaties as a source of law of basically the same kind as statutes. Actually, if treaties (so constantly coupled with custom as one of the two main *formal* sources of international law) are a source of law at all (which is not strictly the case), this is never in the same sense as a statute. Treaties are, if anything, a *material* rather than a formal source of law. Even so called 'law making' treaties do not really create law in the proper sense of the term [i.e. as meaning rules of general validity for and application to the subjects of the legal system, not arising from particular obligations or undertakings on their part], though they may lead to its emergence if their provisions are eventually caught up, so to speak, into the general body of customary international law, so as to bind even non-parties; or they may reflect it, where these provisions are simply declaratory or codificatory of existing general rules of law. They are then evidences of law, and of course a given treaty may (and many treaties do) have a double aspect, both declaring existing law and creating (not new law but) new conventional obligations that may lead to or become law.
>
> Considered in themselves, and particularly in their inception, treaties are formally a source of obligation rather than a source of law. In their contractual aspect, they are no more a source of law than an ordinary private law contract, which simply creates rights and obligations. Such instruments (as also, on the international plane, a commercial treaty, for example) create obligations and rights, not law. In this connexion, the attempts which have been made to ascribe a law-making character to *all* treaties irrespective of the character of their content or the number of the parties to them, by postulating that some treaties create 'particular' international law and others 'general', is of extremely dubious validity. There is really no such thing as 'particular' international treaty law, though there are particular international treaty rights and obligations. The only 'law' that enters into these is derived, not from the treaty creating them – or

W. E. Butler, *Perestroika and International Law*, 81–88.
© 1990 *Kluwer Academic Publishers. Printed in the Netherlands.*

from any treaty – but from the principle *pacta sunt servanda* – an antecedent general principle of law (pp. 157–158).

This view has had a certain influence, being espoused by such authorities as Brownlie,[3] Jennings,[4] O'Connell,[5] and Parry.[6] Insofar as it emphasizes that treaties do not, in general, create obligations for States not party to them, it is incontestable and, indeed, trite law.[7] But it is submitted that, in his comparison with bilateral contracts in municipal law, Fitzmaurice drew an inappropriate analogy which can lead the unwary to underestimate the place of treaties in the international legal process.

The roles of contract and legislation in municipal law

In the first place, the model of contract as a unique bargain between two parties distorts the reality even of municipal law. Many agreements do follow this model, but others do not. Consider the so-called "adhesion contracts." These are agreements, in standard form, which consumers enter into with, for instance, public utility companies supplying electricity, gas, rail transport, and so on. The member of the public is theoretically free to propose variations in the contractual terms to the supplier; but in practice he will meet with a polite refusal, if not incredulity and ridicule. He is not compelled to avail himself of the service if he is not content with the terms offered. But in modern society it is usually regarded as a sign of major eccentricity, if not worse, for a person voluntarily to forego the supply of power, water, public transport, and so on; and few would consider life without these amenities agreeable. In short, there is no genuine choice as to whether or not to accept the proffered terms.

It may also be asked, parenthetically, whether it is not true of legislation, also, that one often has a choice as to whether to be subjected to its regime? The motorist who does not wish to be subjected to traffic regulations is free not to drive; and the baker who finds the regulations about the conduct of his trade irksome is equally free, at least in theory, to pursue another calling. Fitzmaurice appreciated this point, at least to some extent, when he said:[8]

A genuine law may of course be applicable only to certain particular subjects of the legal system, but if so it is usually as members of a class, not as individuals. For instance, a law relating to married women obviously applies only to women who are married. But it applies automatically and *ipso facto* to *all* such women, not merely to those individual women who have set their hands to some particular instrument.

This may be so, but it is as a result of having voluntarily entered into the marriage contract that women find themselves subject to this statute, somewhat in the same way as consumers find themselves subject to a code (this time arising directly *ex contractu*) when they sign an agreement for the supply of electricity.

For the normal consumer, then, the adhesion contract performs something akin to a legislative role: the standard terms set out the conditions under which the facility is supplied, with no practical possibility of variation. These conditions represent a *code*. In whole areas of activity standard contracts play a central part. In Great Britain, for instance, a book on the law pertaining to architects which did not consider in detail the standard conditions of contract of the Royal Institute of British Architects, or on the international carriage of goods by air which did not explore in depth the International Air Transport Association standard conditions of carriage, would be a slender volume indeed. In a real sense, these contractual terms are "the law" on most aspects of these activities.

It can, moreover, be a matter of chance whether the rules concerned are contained in a contract or in legislation. At about the time that Fitzmaurice wrote his article, if he had taken an underground train to Euston Station in London, he would have been governed by London Transport's bye-laws – a legislative code made by the local transport authority under the authority of Parliament. If he had then taken a steam train from Euston main line station, however, his journey would have been governed by the standard (contractual) conditions of carriage of British Railways.[9] Even Sir Gerald would have called London Transport's bye-laws legislation; but their terms were in substance virtually identical to the contractual conditions of British Railways. In functional terms, both codes performed a legislative role to the same extent.

Nor is it the case that legislation is necessarily more extensive in scope than contracts. *Ratione materiae*, this can be seen from the railways example just given; and there are many pieces of legislation, particularly subordinate legislation, very narrow in scope. *Ratione personae*, there are pieces of legislation which apply, and are capable of applying, only to small numbers of people. It is even possible for statutes to be *in personam*, such as the statute dissolving the marriage of King Henry VIII,[10] or the various acts of attainder etc.[11] passed during his reign.[12]

It would be mistaken to think that, even in municipal law, contracts can produce legal consequences only bilaterally, *in personam*. For example, in England, certain contracts to dispose of interests in land have effect also as a *conveyance*; that is to say, as a transfer of ownership. To the extent that property is transferred, the legal consequences are valid *erga omnes*; or, as Wesley Newcomb Hohfeld put it, the rights created are multital, not merely paucital.[13]

To summarize, it is submitted that, when Fitzmaurice compared treaties to legislation and contracts, his account of the role of the latter was too simplistic, even as a matter of municipal law. Let us now consider how far it was in any case appropriate to draw an analogy between domestic law and international law in considering whether treaties are a source of law, or merely of obligation.

84

Comparison between municipal and international law

In *municipal* law it is *arguable* that the role of contract is interstitial, in the sense that a great deal of law is made – or, to use more neutral terminology which Fitzmaurice might have preferred, a great many obligations are created – otherwise than by contract. Every year in the United Kingdom, for instance, Parliament enacts two or three thick volumes of laws. In addition, several volumes of subordinate legislation are enacted (under the ultimate authority of Parliament) by Government ministers, local authorities, and a variety of other bodies. In a precedent-based system such as the common law, moreover, the judges have what might be termed a delegated legislative role; every year there are published several volumes of reports of judicial decisions which not only determine the dispute with which they are concerned, but also lay down rules applicable in other, similar cases. Nor are we governed by a single year's legislation and decisions alone, but also by those of all the previous years.[14] The consequence is that, even if we confine ourselves to the "primary" sources of British law, hundreds of volumes are needed to contain it all. *Mutatis mutandis*, the same is true of Soviet law and any developed legal system.

It is in these circumstances that it is even plausible to argue that the role of the contract is in some sense interstitial, or even subsidiary.[15] But how different is the position in international relations! Apart from treaties – the subject under discussion – the only major source of positive international law is custom.[16] There is no denying that custom plays an important part in the international legal process; for various reasons it even seems to be enjoying a new lease of life. Nevertheless, whatever the merits or demerits of the customary, as opposed to the treaty, mode of rule-creation – a discussion which will have to be left to another occasion – it can hardly be disputed that the amount of new international law which custom contributes each year is limited, and that treaties are, quantitatively and qualitatively, an important source of rules for the subjects of the international legal system.

This point can be put in another way. Fitzmaurice was quite right in saying that treaties are not legislation. For one thing, they do not bind those who do not agree to be bound by them. Second, reservations to legislation are not permitted. Furthermore, whereas members of a national legislature would, one hopes, feel ashamed to admit that their decision whether to vote for or against a certain measure was motivated by purely selfish reasons – voting, for example, against increasing taxes on the ground that the member of parliament would himself have to pay higher taxes – States feel no embarrassment about opposing some proposed law-reforming treaty on the ground that it is against their national interest. But it is precisely because there is no such thing as international legislation proper that treaties perform such an important function as a source of rules for States. Nor is it satisfactory to say that custom performs the role of legislation: the ability of States to prevent new rules of customary law from coming into being, or at any rate to exempt themselves from their scope, by means of persistent dissent, makes custom rather similar to treaty in this regard. So there is a legislative void which so-called "law-making" treaties do much to fill.[17]

Even treaties which appear similar to commercial contracts are often more than that. As Sir Humphrey Waldock pointed out:[18]

> The parties to treaties – whether States or international organizations – are themselves organs of government and their agreements on the international plane tend inevitably to have in a certain degree a law-making character. ... The great majority even of bilateral treaties are essentially of a law-making character so far as concerns the States parties to them. They establish a legal régime binding upon the two States.

It might be objected that Waldock is here mixing up levels: he seems to be saying that, as governments are national bureaucratic systems, a treaty obligation will often be transmuted into legal or bureaucratic rules on the domestic plane. Strictly speaking, this may tell us nothing about whether the treaty is law-making on the *international* plane. Nevertheless, this quotation does underline some important differences between bilateral contracts and bilateral treaties.

As is well known, moreover, treaties perform many more functions than a simple bilateral contract. They can also serve as a conveyance of territory, the basis of an alliance, the constitution of an international organization, an instrument for the codification and/or reform of the law, and so on. One particular treaty, the Charter of the United Nations, is in fact the nearest thing to the constitution of international society that exists. In short, treaties are, so to speak, the maids-of-all-work of the international system, and their role is far from merely interstitial or subordinate.

Imagine a South Sea island with 165 inhabitants. They have a simple and primitive economy, largely based on fishing. They have no legislature, but a system of customary law, which amongst other things ordains how the catch of fish is to be shared out: five for the chief, four for the priest, and the rest divided amongst the heads of families according to time-honoured rules. Suddenly, whales frequent the waters around the island, and once a month, on average, the islanders catch one. They have a problem as to how to divide them up, which their customary fishing rules cannot resolve; for those rules are designed to deal with the allocation of numerous units, not fractions of a single unit, not all of whose parts are as desirable as the others. These islanders, though primitive, are not stupid; they hold a meeting and discuss what to do. A wise man amongst them proposes a code of how to divide up whales, to be embodied in an agreement. 155 of the inhabitants accept this proposal and sign the agreement; 10 refuse to do so. Now, if an anthropologist were describing the laws of this South Sea island, he could accurately use the term "law" to describe the rules regarding the apportionment of catches of *fish* – and this notwithstanding that there might be persistent dissenters not bound by those rules. It is submitted that, for such a society, it would not be a misuse of language to describe the rules for the division of whales as the "law" relating to these mammals, notwithstanding its contractual origin and notwithstanding that the scrupulous commentator, in giving an account of this law, may wish to add that, here too, the rules do not bind non-signatories *inter se*, or in their relations to those who have signed.

So far, we have been considering the role of treaties only insofar as they *directly* create rights for the parties. And it has been seen that the importance of this obligation-generating process in the international system is such that it is not inappropriate to speak of it as a source of law. But in fact treaties can have a wider role, both as evidence of the law and as material sources of the law.

In the first place, it is well known that treaties – particularly multilateral treaties – can codify existing customary international law. For instance, the preamble to the 1958 Geneva Convention on the High Seas states that its provisions are "generally declaratory of established principles of international law;" and at any rate certain provisions of the 1969 Vienna Convention on the Law of Treaties have been held by the highest international and national tribunals to represent customary law – *and this even before the entry into force of the Convention*. Here, the treaty is, strictly, *evidence* of the law, not a *source* of it. But plainly, if there is some doubt whether a rule is or is not a rule of customary law, the assertion that it is, or its reiteration, in a treaty may have a decisive effect, either tilting the evidential scales or as adding to the *quantum* of State practice.[19]

Add to this the fact that in the international community multilateral treaties can sometimes have a "gravitational pull:" non-parties (and parties in relation to non-parties) may come to adopt practices similar to those required by the treaty, so that a rule of customary law of like content comes into being.[20] Well known examples are the abolition of privateering by the 1856 Declaration of Paris and the provisions of the United Nations Charter prohibiting the use or threat of force. It is not suggested that such treaties are a *formal* source of law so far as concerns non-parties; in that respect they are merely a *material* or *historic* source, the formal source being the custom which replicates the treaty rule. But it does mean that, in this way too, treaties are an important source of legal rules and obligations.

It is not suggested that treaties, even multilateral treaties sponsored by the United Nations, *necessarily* evidence existing customary rules or give rise to new ones. The *North Sea Continental Shelf cases*[21] are a sufficient corrective to any such facile assumption. But equally, there are many instances of such phenomena; and the recent decision of the International Court of Justice in the case of *Nicaragua v. United States*[22] seems to indicate a greater readiness of that tribunal, rightly or wrongly,[23] to draw inferences of this kind.

In short, as well as having great importance – in the absence of an international legislature – as a source of obligations for the parties to them, treaties, and particularly multilateral ones, have an important part to play in the formation, determination, and acceptance of customary norms.

Concluding remarks

It might be argued that, even if the points above are well taken, all that the objection to Fitzmaurice boils down to is a terminological quibble. In a sense this is true, though the fact that it was Fitzmaurice who first raised the quibble suggests that it is not inappropriate to try to meet him on his own ground. But in any case it is submitted that, behind this merely semantic problem, there lies an issue of substance. The inference can easily be drawn from Fitzmaurice's argument that, if treaties are merely (not his word) sources of obligation, they are of a lower rank than custom, which is a source of *law*. Such an inference would not only give an erroneous impression of hierarchical relations between treaties and custom – since the former in fact normally prevail over the latter; it could also lead to an underestimation of the great importance and value of the treaty in the international legal process. Even if one would not necessarily wish to go so far as G.I. Tunkin in his vigorous championing of the cause of the treaty as the dominant source of international law,[24] certainly they do and should play an important role in the structuring and restructuring of international law which it would be a grave error to underestimate.

It is for this reason that issue has been taken here with Fitzmaurice' description.

Notes

1. G. Fitzmaurice "Some Problems Regarding the Formal Sources of International Law," *Symbolae Verzijl* (1958), p. 153.
2. Fitzmaurice drew a distinction between "sources of law" and "evidences of the law," and also between "formal" and "material" sources of the law. "Evidences" included, for example, the documents recording State practice, such as diplomatic correspondence. So far as concerns the difference between "formal" and "material" sources, he said that the latter

   > represent, so to speak, the stuff out of which the law is made. It is they which go to form the *content* of the law. ... The formal ... sources consist of the acts or facts whereby this content, whatever it may be and from whatever material source it may be drawn, is clothed with legal validity and obligatory force. The essence of the distinction therefore is between the thing which inspires the content of the law, and the thing which gives that content its obligatory character as law.

   Ibid., pp. 153–154. For these distinctions, see *International Law Association, Warsaw Conference (1988)*, 1st Interim Report of the International Committee on the Formation of Rules of Customary (General) International Law, Appendix to 2nd Report of the Rapporteur (Mendelson).
3. I. Brownlie, *Principles of Public International Law* (3d ed., 1979) p. 2.
4. R.Y. Jennings, "General Course on Principles of International Law," *Recueil des cours*, cxxi (1967), p. 331.

88

5. D. P. O'Connell, *International Law* (2d ed., 1970), I, p. 21.
6. C. Parry, *The Sources & Evidences of International Law* (1965), p. 53.
7. See e.g. *Status of Eastern Carelia* (1923), PCIJ Ser. B/5, p. 27; *German Interests in Polish Upper Silesia* (1926), *ibid.*, Ser. A/7, pp. 28–29; *International Commission of the River Oder* (1929), *ibid.*, Ser. A/23, pp. 18–22; *Aerial Incident of July 27, 1955*, ICJ Rep. 1959, p. 127, 136–38; Articles 34–38, 1969 Vienna Convention on the Law of Treaties.
8. Note 1 above, p. 158.
9. See O. Kahn-Freund, *The Law of Carriage by Inland Transport* (4th ed., 1965).
10. 32 Hen. VIII, c. 25.
11. E.g. 26 Hen. VIII, Private Acts, c. 3 & 4.
12. 22 Hen. VIII c. 8, although laying down certain general rules regarding the crime of poisoning, also had as one of its main provisions the direction that Richard Roose, who had poisoned various people whilst the Bishop of Rochester's cook, be boiled to death. This penalty was, of course *in personam* rather than related to the office of cook to the Bishop; otherwise, it is hard to believe that His Grace would have had many applicants for the replacement appointment.
13. W. N. Hohfeld, "Some Fundamental Legal Conceptions as Applied in Judicial Reasoning, II," *Yale Law Journal*, XXVI (1917), 710; reprinted in Hohfeld, *Fundamental Legal Conceptions*, ed. Cook (1919), Chap. 2.
14. Unless they have been repealed or overturned.
15. This may be to underestimate the importance of the contract in daily life; in many countries most people would be unable to obtain even the bare necessities of life if they could not buy or lease them. But it has nevertheless to be conceded that many legal obligations arise by other, more legislative, means.
16. Whilst some (including Fitzmaurice, p. 161ff.) would suggest that natural law or some analogue thereof is a major source of international law, many others would deny it, and in any case an extra-legal reason why certain processes are regarded as sources of law does not make that reason itself a source, or at any rate not in the same sense. Other "sources" may also exist, such as "general principles of law recognized by civilized nations," judicial and arbitral decisions, and the "teachings of the most highly qualified publicists of the various nations;" but they perform a very subordinate role and/or are merely evidentiary.
17. This is not the place to go into alleged distinction between "law-making" and "contractual" treaties. For a valuable discussion, see G.I. Tunkin, *Theory of International Law*, transl. W.E. Butler (1974), pp. 93–97.
18. C. H. M. Waldock, "General Course on Public International Law," *Recueil des cours*, CVI (1962), 76.
19. There is some doubt how far it is legitimate to count treaty practice as a form of State practice for the purposes of ascertaining the existence of rules of customary law; but, whether legitimate or not, there is no doubt that it *is* sometimes counted.
20. See M. H. Mendelson, Panel Discussion on "Disentangling Treaty and Custom," *1987 Proceedings of the American Society of International Law* (in press).
21. *ICJ Rep.* (1969), p. 3.
22. *ICJ Rep.* (1969), p. 14.
23. See M. H. Mendelson, "The *Nicaragua Case* and Customary International Law," *Coexistence*, XXVI,(1989), 85.
24. Note 17 above, pp. 133–38.

PEOPLE'S DIPLOMACY AND INTERNATIONAL LAWYERS

I. I. LUKASHUK

International law is becoming an ever more important general humanitarian value. Its role is growing in the protection of vitally important social interests. As a result its social foundation is expanding and its links with the social milieu on a global scale. It is in these links that the principle source for the effective functioning of international law are concealed. Regrettably, neither jurists nor governments devote adequate attention to this source. We propose to discuss one of the new aspects of this problem, namely the link between international law and the broad popular masses, with public opinion.

The growth in the role of international relations in the life of human society is a general law of historical development. The principal social problems have today taken on a global character. Saving of man from nuclear and ecological catastrophe is possible only on a world scale. Social progress occurs on the same scale. Contemporary international law protects the interests of man not only as a part of a nation and the State, but also as an individual. A vivid expression of this phenomenon is to be found in the institute of the protection of human rights, which as influenced the legal status of man in capitalist, socialist, and developing countries alike.

An understanding of all this is penetrating the consciousness of broad strata of the populace, giving rise to an aspiration not only to grasp the course of world events but also to influence it. The character, size, and complexity of the historical task of ensuring peace and international cooperation requires the conscious activities of the broadest masses throughout the world to resolve it. The growth in the role of international law in ensuring the normal functioning of the international system and in resolving global problems is attracting the attention of the broadest strata of the populace, which leads to strengthening their influence on the functioning of international law. We note that the Soviet science of international law has devoted considerable attention to this problem.[1] True, in recent years the interest in this matter has unjustifiably declined.

The rise of people's diplomacy

It is under these conditions that the new phenomenon has arisen: people's, or citizen, diplomacy. The concept has two aspects: (a) the "diplomacy of peoples or citizen diplomacy" means the activities of nongovernmental social organisations and movements, as well as of individuals who pursue the purpose of influencing

W. E. Butler, Perestroika and International Law, 89–107.
© 1990 Kluwer Academic Publishers. Printed in the Netherlands.

foreign policy, international relations, and law; (b) "people's diplomacy" is the foreign policy activity of States addressed to peoples, to public opinion. Both forms of activity are closely intertwined. The principal orientation of the diplomacy of peoples consists of influencing the diplomacy of States and inter-State relations, which have the central position in the international system. This orientation is of special significance for international law, which is created by States.

The diplomacy of peoples has its own specific forms of activity, its own paths for influencing the functioning of international law. Among them are bilateral and multilateral meetings and conferences, the activities of private individuals and nongovernmental organisations on the national and international scale.[2] The very fact of the creation of numerous and diverse international nongovernmental organisations testifies to the increased attention of broad strata of the populace to international life and their desire to influence it.[3] Of special significance is the fact that these organisations are devoting increasing attention to international norms in their activities.

The forms of international activities of the public have their advantages. The principal one is that, being free from diplomatic conventions, these forms enable complex and controversial problems to be raised and discussed more freely and extensively.[4]

The new political thinking gives people's diplomacy a rather important place in the functioning of the inter-State system. M. S. Gorbachev writes: "Citizen, people's, diplomacy is an appeal directly to the people – is becoming a normal means of inter-State communion."[5] The significance of people's diplomacy for the functioning of international law is emphasised in Soviet doctrine.[6]

The increased significance of public opinion for the implementation of foreign policy has given birth to a special function of diplomacy – the link with the public. Without this diplomacy could not function. It informs the populace about its activities and endeavours to secure its support or weaken its resistance.[7] This fact has more than once been stated by international lawyers.[8] However, its significance for international law has not received enough attention. The greater the scale of foreign policy measures, the more active should be the influence of public opinion. The growth of the influence of foreign policy on the life of each country, on the interests of every person, determines the development of the functions here considered, which occupy an increasingly important place in diplomatic activity. These also appertain to international law. The greater the effort which a particular international legal act requires from a country, the more well-founded must be the preparation of public opinion to conclude and implement it.

The scientific-revolution in the domain of information has raised the level of knowledge of the populace about international events. At the same time, the monopolisation of these means has opened the possibility of controlling the awareness and, consequently, the will of the popular masses, of spiritually colonising them. They could not avoid taking advantage of this for their own purposes. A special form of political activity emerged – the manipulation of public opinion.[9] It is engaged in by both the State apparatus and private organisations. Having analysed the activities of State institutions in this sphere, researchers have come to rather critical conclusions.[10]

The character of information depends upon in whose hands the respective means for disseminating it are located.[11] Lloyd George wrote in his day that "Northcliffe took advantage of his great influence as owner of the most widely read daily newspaper and most influential journal in the United Kingdom and was not unwilling to display and demonstrate his power. When he behaved in that way, the majority of political figures bowed to him. Often he acted dishonestly and gave false information on the true state of affairs."[12]

Lloyd George's statement can be illustrated by the following facts. The *Times* on 25 May 1935 wrote that the Secretary for Foreign Affairs would act correctly if he persuaded the French Government that nine-tenths of the English people loathed the Franco-Soviet pact and wished that it be dissolved. Two months later the results of the so-called "peace plebiscite" were published, which showed that the respective policy of the English cabinet was not approved by the overwhelming majority of the people. And a Gallup poll in 1939 established that 92% of English people questioned favored an alliance with the USSR.[13]

There exist a number of extremely critical evaluations of the influence of the mass media on public awareness. W. Lederer came to the conclusion that the stupefication of ordinary Americans with the aid of radio, the press, and television had transformed them into a "nation of sheep."[14] This created a growing distrust of the mass media. A Harris poll on the origins of the "cold war" showed that only one American in four trusted the news about international events.[15]

The control of public opinion by the mass media is greatly developed in the United States, as many writers have stated for a long time.[16] However, this phenomenon also is characteristic in some measure of other countries. It cannot be said that the monopolisation of the mass media by the State produces good results. The experience of socialist and other countries bears witness to this.[17] Therefore perestroika in the USSR in the realm of the mass media is raising significant hopes.

Both private and State monopolisation of the mass media lead to their being transformed into an instrument of a specific policy which does not always coincide with public opinion. Therefore, it would be advisable to form an association of subscribers who through elected representatives would direct the activities of a respective newspaper, journal, and the like. Having regard to the enormous power which the mass media have in society, it must be placed under social control. It is essential to create instruments which would prevent the dissemination of disinformation.[18]

The harm caused to international relations and international law through the "psychological warfare" of the mass media is well known. This is an intolerable position. One means of normalising information activity could be the conclusion of

92

a convention on the mass media which would make provision for the creation of appropriate control machinery. An important role could be played by an international information agency attached to UNESCO. This would have special significance for disseminating reliable international legal information, on which to a significant degree the effective functioning of international law is dependent.

Thus, the mass media have an important place in the socio-political machinery for the functioning of international law. Without the aid of the media, the last cannot function normally. Using their influence on the broad strata of the populace and on political and public figures, the mass media are capable of appreciably influencing the creation of particular international legal acts and their implementation after they enter into force. The greater the efforts and resources which an international legal act requires and the more directly it affects the interests of the populace, the greater support is required from the mass media.

This is merely some evidence of those significant transformations which have occurred in the socio-political machinery for the functioning of international law. As its significance grows, international law is enlarging the ambit of socio-political phenomena with which it is connected. As a result the functioning of the socio-political machinery is more complex. Without studying the machinery, especially its new elements and the nature of the links between them, it is doubtful whether the effectiveness of contemporary international law can be ensured. Herein is one of the principal tasks of the science of international law.

The enhanced role of public opinion

We already have spoken about the significance of people's diplomacy both for politics and for international law. The functioning of international law is part of the general political process. We turn to certain basic moments affecting only international law. Above all, we state a general proposition: the influence of public opinion on the formation and effectuation of international law, which increasingly reflects the interests of the people's masses, is growing. Jurists in the first decade after the war said a great deal about this.[19]

The proposition also was noted in subsequent years. The United Nations document on the "Final Stage of Work on the Codification of International Law" is illustrative, where is said that the active support of public opinion "being so valuable at any stage of the process of codifying international law, can be decisive at the concluding stage on the State level. The mobilisation of forces may influence administrative, governmental, and parliamentary organs and persuade them to take the necessary measures, which is a task that the United Nations could with benefit begin."[20]

We note that the literature, with very rare exceptions, adheres to the position that norms of international law are created directly by States, and the popular masses influence this process through governments. The practice of States firmly also adheres to this position. In this unity is the guarantee of success. Therein is the essence of people's diplomacy. Therefore, the formula of the preamble of the Charter of UNESCO is not a happy one, for it may be interpreted as contraposing in some way the treaties of governments with the peoples.[21]

Science attaches material significance to the influence of peoples on the process of effectuating norms of international law.[22] And, as already noted, an increasing number of international treaties require in the course of their implementation the support of the general public of the parties. State practice has long since observed that treaties in and of themselves can not lead to fundamental changes in the relations of the parties without the support of the peoples.[23]

This view is taken into account by diplomacy, which is devoting greater attention to persuading peoples that the treaties concluded are consistent with their interests and wishes. However, if such consistency is truly lacking, diplomatic propaganda does not provide a stable result.[24]

One of the tasks of science is to seek ways for further strengthening the influence of the populace on the process of effectuating norms of international law. Obviously new organisational forms can be suggested too. The draft convention on the reduction of armaments submitted by the USSR to the preparatory commission of the 1928 conference on disarmament is to be recalled in this connection. The draft provided for the founding of a permanent international control commission which should consist of the representatives of legislative bodies and professional or other organisations of workers. Subsequently it was suggested that representatives of international social organisations be included.[25]

The task of science also consists in studying ways of enabling the resolutions of international organisations, especially of the United Nations General Assembly, to influence the consciousness and will of the broad strata of the populace in the interests of ensuring respect for international law. This type of resolution is capable of exerting a substantial influence on public opinion and mobilising its support for particular norms. Moreover, such resolutions are capable of being an important means for forming an internationalist public awareness and affirming the general humanitarian values therein, which is of the utmost importance for the functioning of international law. Regretfully it must be noted that the mass media do not devote sufficient attention to these important acts. As a result the contents thereof are not brought to public notice, which materially depreciates the activities of organisations such as the United Nations. This makes it easier for governments not to respect the resolutions adopted, or the norms of international law. Doctrine stresses the significance of resolutions as a means of condemning violations of law, as a means of "mobilising shame."[26]

This all once again testifies to the fact that international organisations are becoming a more important sphere for people's diplomacy and are capable of playing a serious role in it.

People's diplomacy also has been reflected in the provisions of international legal acts making provision for promoting the development of direct links between the publics of participating countries. The significance of these links has for many years been emphasised in State practice.[27] In the majority of instances the respective provisions are incorporated in an agreement on cultural cooperation.[28] We note that significant attention is devoted in this type of agreement to the development of links between scholars and their organisations.

Other examples might be cited as to how international legal acts reflect the growing role of international links of the general public. However, as a whole international law inadequately reflects the role of people's diplomacy. At the same time, greater attention is being devoted to such issues in non-legal international acts. The Concluding Document of the Vienna Meeting of Representatives of the Participating States of the Conference on Security and Co-operation in Europe contains an entire body of rules affecting the basic aspects of people's diplomacy. The parties are obliged to promote cooperation beween their peoples. Contacts between people are regulated in detail, as are the activities of the mass media and cooperation and exchanges in the realm of culture and education. Note the obligation of the parties relating to the fact that the Document must be "published in each participating State, which will disseminate it and make it known as widely as possible." Even more material is the provision that the parties "will encourage their relevant governmental agencies or educational institutions to include, as appropriate, the Final Act as a whole in the curricula of schools and universities."[29] It is to be hoped that this is a first step towards including a course on the "Fundamental Principles of International Law" in the curricula of schools and universities.

In general there is a trend towards regulating links between people and nations primarily with the aid of international political rather than legal acts. This will create yet another channel for strengthening the influence of political normative acts on the functioning of international law. This phenomenon merits the attention of doctrine.

People's diplomacy and the science of international law

It is evident from the foregoing that people's diplomacy sets before the science of international law many complex problems of material importance for the functioning of that law. From the outset must be noted the general trend towards an ever deeper penetration of science into politics. Today politics cannot do without science. The price to be paid for political errors is too dear. And, as experience shows, quite a few mistakes have been made.[30] Under conditions of a scientific and technological revolution, it is essential that the "reins of government should not slip out of people's hands."[31]

Science is penetrating politics to a significant degree through the apparatus of executive power. The leaders of States create whole complexes of scholarly advisers and experts and resort to scholarly organisations for assistance. They are provided with information obtained by the State apparatus. A distinctive political and academic complex is created.[32] One result of this phenomenon is the strengthening of the executive, frequently at the expense of parliament. Sometimes public opinion also promotes this. The leaders of the State work out a policy jointly with their advisers. Then, using the mass media, they appeal to public opinion for support. Having obtained it, they implement the political decisions. These tactics are most frequently to be seen in the popular press.[33] Adherence to such tactics also is reflected in the speeches of public figures.[34]

The new political thinking adheres to the concept of directly incorporating science into world politics. It proceeds from the Leninist thesis about the need to "aspire to a scientific study of the facts underlying our policy."[35] Commenting on this issue, M. S. Gorbachev notes that we "conduct affairs on the basis of a scientific analysis and well-tested internal and foreign policy conception."[36]

The role of science in politics determines the high responsibility of scholars to ensure that their achievements serve the purposes of peace and international cooperation. In the domain of ensuring the normal functioning of the international system the responsibility of legal scholars is especially great. It has two aspects, positive and negative. The first is the responsibility for resolving legal problems relative to the maintenance of peace and the development of cooperation. The significance of this responsibility has been repeatedly noted by public figures. N. I. Ryzhkov stated that the "world community has the right to expect from jurists a growing contribution to working out the legal aspects of a universal system of international peace and security, ensuring the natural right of each person and all peoples to life and free development."[37]

The negative responsibility of jurists consists in ensuring that science is not used to the detriment of the interests of peace and the international legal order. Stressing this, E. A. Shevardnadze at the same time pointed to a number of facts when "with truly mediaeval chicanery attempts are made to rehash agreements and remove restrictions on the arms race, to adapt jurisprudence so as to justify an armed encroachment on peaceful outer space belonging to all mankind, and to subordinate science to these dangerous aims."[38]

The responsibility of jurists has been noted by the governments of many countries.[39] Legal scholars have themselves begun to write about it.[40] But little has been done in a practical way to give effect to this responsibility. Frequently the responsibility for this situation is placed by Western authors on the science of "communist States," accusing it of lacking objectivity and being of an "official" character. But even those authors conclude that the situation "is not hopeless."[41] As regards those Western scholars who know the science of international law in socialist countries well (and regrettably there are very few), they too in the past came out against the tendency to "exaggerate the monolithic nature and 'official' character of [Soviet] legal scholarship," pointing to the community of principle in Western and Soviet approaches to many specific issues, for example, the law of the sea.[42] Now the opportunities for cooperation between Soviet and Western scholars in working out problems of international law are significantly broader.

Important steps have been taken in the USSR in the direction of strengthening the links between foreign policy and science. The USSR Ministry of Foreign Affairs is regularly holding scientific-practical conferences with the participation of a large group of scholars at which issues of international law have an important place. The report of E. A. Shevardnadze to the first such conference devoted a special section to the link between science and the public. The significance of that link was stressed, and a number of organisational measures were announced with the object of developing them. In particular, a Scientific Coordinating Council has been created within the USSR Ministry of Foreign Affairs and is called upon to ensure the maintenance of permanent links with science and with scholarly centres in the country and abroad.[43]

The USSR also is proposing new forms of international cooperation in the cause of scientific support for politics. During his meeting with the President of the United States in Washington D. C., M. S. Gorbachev proposed the creation of a Soviet-American Commission of Scholars which might offer advice and recommendations both to the American administration and to the leadership of the Soviet Union.[44] In international practice the role of scholars who represent the most competent part of world public opinion is being stressed.[45]

All this beyond doubt testifies to the growing role of scholars in politics. Yet all the same the growth lags behind the requirements of politics, which needs to resolve more important and complex problems. We are still far away from overcoming the gap so typical of the history of mankind between the intellect, knowledge, and political leadership. The importance of intellect and knowledge in politics has been remarked on by thinkers since ancient times. The legendary Hindu philosopher Kautilya asserted that "a wise king will outwit a courageous ruler as a hunter outwits an elephant."[46] And nonetheless the intellectual level of world politics has continued to lag behind. Oxienstern, a wise Swedish chancellor during the Thirty Years War, supposedly said: "You cannot imagine, dear boy, how miserable is the mind which rules the world." L. von Bertalanfi remarked on this: "The reading of modern newspapers and listening to the radio shows that this is more true of the twentieth and of the seventeenth century."[47]

Numerous facts could be cited and utterances quoted which affirm this notion, demonstrating that decisions taken are often of an anecdotal nature.[48] This all confirms Lenin's statement that "politics is a science and an art that does not fall from the heavens or come as a gift."[49]

It is especially important for us to note the fact that the leaders not only of States, but also of departments of foreign affairs often do not possess the requisite knowledge of international law. No one is allowed to sit at the wheel of an automobile without knowing the rules of the road. Why are individuals at the helm of a State not obliged to have a knowledge of the rules for inter-State communion? This cannot but have a negative effect on the functioning of international law. A cursory familiarity with the major foreign policy addresses of State leaders is enough to persuade that they give little room to international law. In light of this, the significance of the new political thinking concerning the supremacy of law in politics is especially important.

The attitude towards international law goes far beyond the limits of jurisprudence. This law is one of the highest general humanitarian values called upon to establish the humanitarian values of civilised relations between peoples. A knowledge of international law is an element of general humanitarian culture. International law is the result of the development over many centuries of an internationalist communion, a concentrated expression of historical experience in a most complex social sphere. The supremacy of law is an integral indicia of civilised international relations. To ensure such supremacy without the respective international legal knowledge on the part of the leaders and broad strata of the populace is impossible. All this is reason to suppose that today a resolution of the problem of the effective functioning of international law should be sought above all in the intra-State sphere. In our view, there are two basic orientations of activity: the development of the international legal consciousness of the masses, and the formation of a rule-of-law State.

The facts show that today the effective functioning of international law, especially in the crucial areas of the maintenance of peace and security, is inconceivable without the support of the broad strata of the populace. In stressing the significance of this factor, we are far from idealising mass consciousness. A truly revolutionary transformation of this consciousness is required. In significant measure a national consciousness needs to be transformed into an internationalist consciousness. Jurists have constantly pointed to nationalism as the principal danger to international law.[50] Sir Gerald Fitzmaurice noted: "This is the supreme paradox – that a world of separate nation-States cannot do without international law, and yet that nationalism they engender is the worst enemy of progress in the international law ..." By nationalism is meant "the policy of asserting the interests of one's own nation, viewed as separate from the interests of other nations or the common interests of other nations or the common interests of all nations."[51] The significance of these propositions is also reflected in multilateral inter-State acts emphasising the role of an internationalist approach to counterbalance the unilateral activities of States.[52]

It should be borne in mind that strengthening international security and affirming the supremacy of law in and of itself will not bring nationalism to an end. Moreover, there is reason to suppose that as internationalist interests are secured, individual States, especially small ones, and social groups will struggle actively to achieve their specific interests. Therefore in the future attention will need to be devoted to the dangers of nationalism. Yet all this reinforces the significance of the primacy of general humanitarian interests over national, class, and group interests which are contrary to them, propositions underlying the new political thinking. The internationalisation of social consciousness, affirmation of the notions of human community therein – these are essential conditions for the normal functioning of the international system and international law.

Legal consciousness and international law

International legality can be reliably ensured only in relations of rule-of-law States. Domestic and international legality are closely interconnected. Just as a rule-of-law State can not function without an adequately high level of legal consciousness and legal culture, so too does international law require an appropriate international legal consciousness and culture from leaders and the populace.[53] Both types of legal consciousness are connected, as leaders in foreign policy have noted. E. A. Shevardnadze has commented: "A legal consciousness which ignores the fact that international law operates in inter-State relations, that only on the base thereof can affairs be conducted between sovereign entities, is harmful."[54] General legal consciousness is the basis of international legal consciousness, and the development of the last is a more complex process.

The problem of knowledge of the law is an important and complex one of jurisprudence as a whole. It has long attracted the attention of jurists since without such knowledge law cannot function properly. In studying the problem, scholars have come to conclude that the legal knowledge of individuals is acquired mostly in daily life.[55] The most vital information is obtained "mouth to mouth." The role of the mass media is significantly lower.[56] In the acquisition of international legal knowledge both sources play a much smaller role. The opportunities for the majority of the populace to acquire personal experience are minimal. A few may pass information "mouth to mouth." Therefore, the principal channel for obtaining international legal knowledge must be the mass media, as well as the practice of States and international organisations. National legislation is able to play an important role. As an example, there is the principle of conscientious fulfillment of international legal obligations as a principle of Soviet foreign policy consolidated in the USSR Constitution. Of great significance are international acts of States and international organisations, the addresses of public figures, and acts of national and international social organisations.

Regrettably, those documents do not have regard to the task of developing international legal consciousness. For example, when enumerating the principles underlying the mutual relations of States, official acts do not mention the principle of conscientiously fulfilling international legal obligations.[57] Popular literature on international law or on international problems can have serious significance. However, both journalists and many specialists in the realm of international relations have vague ideas about international law. This leads to either international law being ignored in their works or misinterpreted. And jurists writing about the crisis of international law render a disservice to the development of the international legal consciousness.[58]

A practical problem is the extent of requisite international legal knowledge. International law has reached a stage of development when even specialists cannot know all of its norms. The amount of international legal information is virtually boundless, and the channels of information are overloaded.[59] There is no need for public figures and the populace to know all of international law. They should have a command of the basic general notions of international law and especially the basic principles which in concentrated form express the principle content of that law.

For all of its significance, international legal knowledge in and of itself will not ensure the effective functioning of international law. The knowledge must be accompanied by the conviction that international law requires respect. This conviction is the most important indicator of the level of international legal consciousness and culture.

It is from this vantage point that we must resolve the issue of the international legal consciousness of foreign policy leaders. Historical experience offers many examples of jurists who headed departments of foreign affairs causing material harm to international legality. There are many instances when the leaders were knowledgable but did little to solidify relations of politics with science. On the other hand, there are examples when leaders who were not jurists by education did much to strengthen the international legal basis of the foreign policy of the State. Foreign policy leaders need, in addition to basic notions about international law, the conviction of possibly finding alternative solutions and means of satisfying the needs of the State without going outside the framework of international law.

Legal scholars, pooling their efforts, have been called upon to play an exceptional role in the development of the international legal consciousness. The requisite conditions exist for this. Numerous reproaches have been made in Western literature with respect to Soviet international legal doctrine. It has been said that it "remains in large measure a fighting international law rather than a thinking international law."[60] They write that Soviet internatinal lawyers do not influence policy and cannot objectively comment on it.[61] They assert that an official monolithic unity dominates with respect to basic issues.[62] In recent years it has been recognised that Soviet doctrine plays a certain role in politics.[63]

On their part, Soviet jurists have not been found wanting and have devoted much attention to sharp and not always well-founded criticism of works by Western scholars. And much that is just has been expressed on both sides. Notwithstanding all this, working independently and cooperating within international agencies and organisations, including social organisations, the scholars of East and West have done a great deal to develop the science of international law and to prepare universal international legal acts. One may point to the productive work of the International Law Commission, which consists primarily of scholars. The delegations of States to diplomatic conferences engaged in the codification of international law include a significant number of scholars.

To be sure, we cannot discount the heavy legacy of the "psychological warfare" rooted in the consciousness of broad strata of the populace. This is stressed both by public figures and many authors.[64] Public opinion polls testify to the same. However, tangible shifts are occurring in the mass consciousness.[65]

All this could not but affect the science of international law. But if States are making a transition from confrontation to more active cooperation in the interests of ensuring a peaceful world order, the more timely for scholars to do so. Only through joint efforts can they make a proper contribution to strengthening the position of international law, on whose effective functioning depends in no small way the fate of mankind.

Scholars have great opportunities for moulding the international legal consciousness of the masses. But they cannot close their eyes to the difficulties in resolving this grandiose task. The underdeveloped state of international legal consciousness is constantly noted by jurists. Okeke writes: "The general attitude of both students of international law and laymen towards international law is usually the same. It is often a reaction of scepticism. When first a mention of international law is made, a feeling of doubt as to its usefulness arises in the minds of many people. Then comes the question whether it is really law or just should be classified in the realm of ethics rather than law."[66]

Nonetheless, broad strata of the populace are on the whole positive towards international law and international organisations. This fact also is reflected in belles lettres. One of the heroines of Erve Basin was Mariette, a common woman engaged exclusively with family concerns who, in the words of her husband, was in favour of the United Nations which seemed to her more akin to a society for the protection of animals, but only for people.[67]

This once again confirms that the populace evaluate the behaviour of States chiefly on the basis of moral, and not legal consciousness.[68] Moral consciousness dominates, which is only natural. At the same time, it opens opportunities for abuse of moral consciousness to the prejudice of the interests of international legality. The manipulation of moral consciousness with significant elements of nationalism enables it to be juxtaposed to international law and facilitates the commission of violations of law. The moral legitimation of violations of international law is extensive in State practice. This phenomenon also occurred in the past. Appealing to national morality, the mobilisation of popular support occurred with special significance when waging war. As the significance of the popular masses grew in the implementation of foreign policy, this method was developed further. Illustrative on this plane is the practice of the United States, which violates international law under the pretext of protecting its citizens, fighting terrorism, and the like.

A way out of this situation is seen in the affirmation of general humanitarian morality as a counterweight to a nationalistic morality. The requirements of morality frequently go farther than the requirements of law and thereby promote the realisation of legal norms. On the other hand, international law and legal consciousness contribute to the affirmation of general humanitarian morality. Therefore, the development of international legal consciousness is essential also in the interests of strengthening general humanitarian morality in international relations.

A considerable share of the responsibility for the inadequate development of international legal consciousness lies on international lawyers. They have done little to popularise a knowledge of international law. They are inadequately organised on both the national and international scales. Their participation in people's diplomacy is not consistent with the role of international law in the modern world. World associations of the struggle for peace of doctors and natural scientists have been created. But there is no such association of international lawyers, who should be pioneers in the struggle for a peaceful world order. The existing organisations of international lawyers, the "World Peace Through Law" centre, the International Law Association, and the Institute of International Law, have concentrated their attention chiefly on specific issues. No one would deny the importance of their activities for the development of the theory of international law and politics. Yet it is difficult to understand the inadequate attention of those organisations to the fundamental problems of securing international legal order, to the dissemination of a knowledge of international law, and to the formation of an international legal consciousness.[69]

It is essential to regularly ascertain and publicly express the opinion of jurists on fundamental problems of international law. To this end, for example, it would be desirable under the aegis of UNESCO to publish a journal or a yearbook of international law. On the national level jurists must combine their efforts in the interest of promoting a rule-of-law foreign policy by their State.

International organisations, especially the United Nations and UNESCO, are called upon to play an important role in the development of an international legal consciousness, which undoubtedly strengthens their own positions and facilitates their activities. Some steps are being taken in this direction. Deserving of special mention is the 1978 Declaration on Educating Societies in the Spirit of Peace, adopted by the United Nations General Assembly at the initiative of Poland. The obligations of educating societies in the spirit of peace, respect for international law, and human rights also have been established by international political acts, for example, the 1975 Final Act of the Conference on Security and Co-operation in Europe and the 1989 Concluding Document of the Vienna Meeting of Representatives of the Participating States of the Conference on Security and Cooperation in Europe.

Education in a spirit of peace fosters an internationalist consciousness which is of primary importance for the functioning of international law. Referring to this, Symonides wrote: "A result of the realisation of the idea of education in the spirit of peace is the formation of a committed public opinion and thereby the operation of a special social sanction as a reaction of world public opinion against a violation of the principles of peaceful coexistence and cooperation ..."[70]

The United Nations General Assembly adopted a special resolution on the broader dissemination of a knowledge of international law. However, the steps taken have shortcomings. The Declaration on Educating Societies in the Spirit of Peace does not contain a section on education in a spirit of respect for international law. Yet this is an integral element of education in the spirit of peace. The United Nations programme for a broader dissemination of a knowledge of international law still has not produced tangible results. It must be invigorated. It would be advisable to suggest that the General Assembly adopt a resolution recommending to States that all law schools introduce into their curricula compulsory courses on international law of sufficient scope. In secondary schools and universities a course on the "Principles of Relations between Peoples" should be studied. Man must imbibe with his mother's milk the idea of internationalist friendship, general humanitarian values, principles of international communion, and human rights. This is essential for the normal functioning of the international system and international law

Conclusion

Perhaps the author is to be reproached for overestimating the potential of the science of international law. Therefore in conclusion it is appropriate to recall that historical experience shows how many ideas advanced by thinkers of the parts and declared to be idealistic have subsequently become part of international life. The very idea of international law was put forward by thinkers of the sixteenth and seventeenth centuries and sceptically greeted by public figures of the day. Perez de Cuellar has said: "At one stage of history the ideas in the United Nations Charter seemed fantastic and even strange. Those ideas were born in the minds not of statesmen, but of thinkers such as Hugo Grotius in the course of his activities as a trail-blazer in working out the norms of war and peace, and of Immanuel Kant in his essay on perpetual peace. Ruling circles have hardly given attention to them ..."[71] These days scholars have incomparably more opportunities for influencing the policies of States and public opinion and the functioning and development of international law.

Notes

1. See I. I. Lukashuk, "Znachenie Oktiabr'skoi revoliutsii i deiatel'nosti Sovetskogo gosudarstva dlia bor'by narodov za demokratizm mezhdunarodnykh dogovorov," *Sbornik nauchnykh rabot Saratovskogo iuridicheskogo instituta* (1958); V. S. Semenov, "Mirovaia demokraticheskaia obshchestvennost' i mezhdunarodnoe pravo," *Sovetskii ezhegodnik mezhdunarodnogo prava 1965* (1965); M. I. Lazarev, "Mezhdunarodno-pravovye voprosy dvizheniia narodov za mir," *ibid.*; V. V. Kravchenko, *Sovetskie obshchestvennye organizatsii v mezhdunarodnykh otnosheniiakh* (1976); A. A. Berkov and A. I. Poltorak, "Mirovaia obshchestvennost' i mezhdunarodnoe pravo," in *Obshchestvennost' i problemy voiny i mira* (1976).
2. See *Unofficial Diplomats* (1977).
3. See G. I. Morozov, *Mezhdunarodnye organizatsii* (1974), p. 288.
4. The importance of these occasions also is noted by the participants in social movements themselves. See, for example, "Torzhestvennaia Deklaratsiia Assamblei obshchestven-nykh sil za bezopasnost' i sotrudnichestvo v Evrope," *Pravda*, 7 June 1972.
5. M. S. Gorbachev, *Perestroika i novoe myshlenie dlia nashei strany i dlia vsego mira* (1987), p.164.
6. See V. S. Vereshchetin, "Sovetskie mirnye initsiativy i razvitie mezhdunarodnogo prava," *Sovetskii ezhegodnik mezhdunarodnogo prava 1987* (1988), pp.13–14.
7. See J. Rosenau, *The Scientific Study of Foreign Policy* (1976), p.433.
8. G. Schwarzenberger wrote: "Corresponding to the increasing importance of public opinion in present-day mass society, States have found it necessary to seek closer contact with this elusive phenomenon. Thus, propaganda has become a junior branch of the foreign service." G. Schwarzenberger, *The Frontiers of International Law* (1962), p. 23.
9. Senator Fulbright wrote that "so-called public opinion manipulators represent not only domestic clients of every description, but foreign governments as well. The total of efforts and investment devoted to opinion-manipulating, or molding, in this country now represents one of the major undertakings." See J. W. Fulbright, *A Legislator's Thoughts on World Issues* (1963).
10. The American publicist Wise wrote that "through official secrecy, we now have a system of institutional lying. The resulting erosion of confidence between the people and their Government is perhaps the single most important political development in the United States in the past decade." D. Wise, "The Institution of Lying," *New York Times*, 18 November 1971.
11. See K. Deutsch, *The Analysis of International Relations* (1968), pp. 54–55.
12. D. Lloyd George, *The Truth About the Peace Treaties* (1938), II, pp. 232–233.
13. See J. Wheeler-Bennett, *Munich – Prologue to Tragedy* (1948), p. 394.
14. W. Lederer, *A Nation of Sheep* (1961), p. 8.
15. *Pravda*, 15 September 1969.
16. See B. Cohen, *The Press and Foreign Policy* (1963); J. Reston, *The Artillery of the Press: Its Influence on American Foreign Policy* (1967); J. Robinson, *Public Information About World Affairs* (1967); T. Sorenson, *The World War: The Story of American Propaganda* (1968).
17. See A. Pankin, "Glasnost' vo vneshnei politike: konechnaia tsel' i promezhutochnye etapy," *Mezhdunarodnaia zhizn'*, no. 2 (1989).
18. See Iu. M. Kolosov, *Massovaia informatsiia i mezhdunarodnoe pravo* (1974); Iu. M. Kolosov and B. A. Tsepov, *Novyi mezhdunarodnyi informatsionnyi poriadok i problema podderzhaniia mira* (1983).

19. Manfred Lachs wrote: "Since international law is one of the factors of history, such an essential historical factor as the will of peoples can not but influence its development and effect." M. Lachs, "Sistema kollektivnoi bezopasnosti i voprosy obespecheniia bezopasnosti," *Problema kollektivnoi bezopasnosti v Evrope* (1955), p. 53. D. B. Levin went even farther, believing that "the major peaceful and democratic principles of international relations are formed under the influence of the popular masses." D. B. Levin, *Osnovnye problemy sovremennogo mezhdunarodnogo prava* (1958), p. 23.

20. U.N. Doc. A/CN.4/205/Rev. 1, 29 July 1968, p. 24.

21. The following provision is what is in view: "Peace based only on the economic and political agreements of governments can not ensure the unanimous, stable, and sincere support of peoples, and consequently peace must be created on the basis of the intellectual and moral solidarity of mankind." *IUNESKO i sovremennost'* (1968), p. 223.

22. D. B. Levin wrote that the movement of the popular masses for peace "is acquiring a certain significance as one of the means of ensuring the true force of norms of international law." Levin, note 19 above, p. 110. Also see B. I. Melekhin, "Vozdeistvie mirovogo obshchestvennogo mneniia na mezhdunarodnoe pravo," *Sovetskoe gosudarstvo i pravo*, no. 2 (1964), p. 83.

23. J. Tito stated: "One cannot achieve with the aid of various military pacts that to which some States or leaders aspire, that is, the devotion and sympathy of a particular country or people. It leads to the opposite results." *Pravda*, 14 January 1956.

24. The fate of the Baghdad Pact is illustrative. They attempted to persuade the populace of the participating countries that it was based on the wishes of the peoples of the region. See, for example, the Communique of the session of the Council of the Baghdad Pact, 30 January 1958. *Department of State Bulletin*, no. 973 (1958), p. 255. But the true position was otherwise. The Egyptian President, Nasser, stated that "The Baghdad Pact aroused the opposition of the Arab peoples and ended with the alliance becoming static and lifeless." *Al-Ahram*, 9 September 1958. The subsequent development of events confirmed the well-foundedness of this statement.

25. See *Dokumenty vneshnei politiki SSSR*, XI, p. 228; also see pp. 47 and 105.

26. See "The Mobilization of Shame," in *The Effectiveness of International Decisions* (1971), pp. 447–455.

27. Thus in a Soviet-Yugoslav Statement, the governments expressed the "firm conviction that one of the essential conditions for improving the international situation is ... the greater involvement of the people's masses in international cooperation." *Pravda*, 21 June 1956; also see "Sovmestnoe sovetsko-zambiiskoi kommiunike," *Pravda*, 28 November 1974.

28. Article XI of the Anglo-Soviet Agreement on Links in Science, Education, and Culture for 1985–87 provided that the parties "will encourage links between nongovernmental organisations," in particular on topics which "further the development of cultural ties and friendly relations between the public and peoples of both countries." *SDD*, XLI, p. 359; also see Article 11 of the 1978 Agreement between the governments of Czechoslovakia and the German Democratic Republic on cultural cooperation. *Rude pravo*, 12 dubna 1978.

29. *Izvestiia*, 26 January 1989; *International Legal Materials*, XXVIII (1989), 547.

30. Robert McNamara, who took part directly in a significant number of foreign policy and strategy decisions of the American administration, declares that some were erroneous. At the time they seemed "rational and unavoidable." In fact, the most important decisions were taken on the spur of the moment, on the basis of "incomplete and frequently contradictory and constantly changing information." In particular, he

acknowledges that "we had a wrong idea of the Soviets' intentions." R. McNamara, *Blundering into Disaster* (1986), pp.53–54.

31. M. S. Gorbachev, "K luchshemu miru. Slovo k amerikanskomu chitateliu," *Kommunist*, no. 7 (1987), p. 7.
32. See V. F. Petrovskii, *Amerikanskaia vneshne-politicheskaia mysl'* (1976), chapter 1.
33. Professor R. Shiratory wrote that the Prime Minister of Japan, Mr. Nakasone, "first of all receives private advisory reports from councils or private advisory bodies. Next, he seeks the support of the Japanese people through the mass media. He then puts his policy into practice." R. Shiratory, "Wind of Change in Policy Making," *Manichi Daily News*, 7 July 1987.
34. See the remarks by Prime Minister Nakasone, *Manichi Daily News*, 2 February 1987.
35. V. I. Lenin, *Polnoe sobranie sochinenii*, XXXIV, p. 109.
36. *Izvestiia*, 17 July 1987.
37. "Poslanie predsedatelia Soveta Ministrov SSSR N. I. Ryzhkova uchastnika Mezhdunarodnoi Konferentsii iuristov v g. Deli," *Pravda*, 13 February 1988.
38. E. A. Shevardnadze, "Vystuplenie na vstreche s ministrom inostrannykh del Italii Dzh. Andreotti," *Pravda*, 28 February 1987.
39. See B. Brittin and C. Watson, *International Law for Seagoing Officers* (1972), p.15.
40. See K. Wolfke, *Rozwoj i kodyfikacja prawa miedzynarodowego* (1972), Section VII; G. I. Tunkin, "The Nuclear Age and a Jurist in an Ivory Tower," in *International Law at the Time of its Codification* (1987).
41. See K. Hailbronner, "Die Autoritat der Volkerrechtsordnung," in *Die Autoritat des Rechts* (1985), p. 37.
42. See W. E. Butler, *The Soviet Union and the Law of the Sea* (1971), p. 3.
43. *Mezhdunarodnaia zhizn'*, no. 9 (1988), pp. 26–27.
44. Gorbachev, "Vystuplenie na press-konferentsii v Vashingtone," *Izvestiia*, 12 December 1987.
45. During M. S. Gorbachev's meeting with Perez de Cuellar, the last agreed that science is now entering politics "also through the public thought of concerned scholars. This has great potential for peace, the most competent part of world public opinion. It is at the disposal of mankind, and this means the United Nations too." *Izvestiia*, 30 June 1987.
46. Kautilya, *Arthasastra* (1967), p. 346.
47. L. von Bertalanfi, "Obshchaia teoriia sistem – kriticheskii obzor," *Issledovaniia po obshchei teorii sistem* (1969), p. 74.
48. H. Kissinger says: "Since many of our policy-makers first address themselves to an issue when it emerges as their area of responsibility, their approach to it is often highly anecdotal." H. Kissinger, "Domestic Structure and Foreign Policy," in *International Politics and Foreign Policy* (1969), p. 269. In his view, "in almost every democratic country so much energy is absorbed in getting into office that leaders are not always as well prepared as they could be and have to learn their job by doing it. All of this has created a crisis of leadership in many democratic countries." *id.*, interview in *Time*, 27 October 1975. He suggests that the situation is even worse in communist countries.
49. Lenin, *Polnoe sobranie sochinenii*, XLI, p. 65.
50. See B.Cheng, "Aviation, Criminal Jurisdiction and Terrorism," in *Contemporary Problems of International Law* (1988), p. 31.
51. G. Fitzmaurice, "The Future of Public International Law and the International Legal System in the Circumstances of Today," in Institut de droit international, *Livre du Centenaire 1873–1973* (1973), p. 317.
52. See the Declaration on a World Order, adopted at a Meeting of the Heads of Government of the Commonwealth in 1985, in *Report of the Commonwealth Secretary-*

106

General 1987 (1987), p. vii.
53. See M. Sh. Patsatsiia, "Sovremennoe sostoianie problemy mezhdunarodno-pravovogo soznaniia," *Metodologiia issledovaniia teoreticheskikh problem mezhdunarodnogo prava* (1986).
54. Shevardnadze, "Doklad na konferentsii konsul'skikh rabotnikov MID SSSR," *Mezhdunarodnaia zhizn'*, no. 2 (1989), p. 12.
55. See V. P. Kazimirchuk and S. V. Bobotov, "Znanie prava: iuridiko-sotsiologicheskie aspekty printsipa 'neznanie zakona ne est' opravdanie'," in *SSSR-Frantsiia: sotsiologicheskii i mezhdunarodno-pravovoi aspekty sravnitel'nogo pravovedeniia* (1987), p. 12.
56. See J. Carbonier, "Printsip 'nekto ne vprave ssylat'sia na neznanie zakona' vo frantsuzskom prave," *ibid.*, p. 15.
57. See the "Kommiunike zasedaniia Komiteta ministrov inostrannykh del gosudarstv-uchastnikov Varshavskogo Dogovora," *Pravda*, 27 March 1987.
58. See J. Frowein, "Die Verpflichtungen erga omnes im Volkerrecht und ihre Durchsetzung," *Volkerrecht als Rechtsordnung* (1983), p. 242; A. Carty, *The Decay of International Law?* (1986).
59. See I. I. Lukashuk, "Teoriia informatsii i mezhdunarodno-pravovoe regulirovanie," *Vestnik Kievskogo universiteta*, no. 7 (1978).
60. L. Lipson, "Peaceful Coexistence," in H. W. Baade (ed.), *The Soviet Impact on International Law* (1965), p. 27.
61. R. A. Falk, *The Status of Law in International Society* (1970), p. 451.
62. See *Osterreichisches handbuch des Volkerrechts* (1983), I, p. 28.
63. H. Uibopuu, "International and Municipal Law in Soviet Doctrine and Practice," *Jus Humanitatis* (1980), p.670.
64. Shevardnadze said: "We have all passed through the decades of "cold war" and "iron curtain," through the division of the world into blocs and alliances, and survived the periods of sharp confrontation. All of this did little to contribute to the spiritual unity of the world. Moreover, we must acknowledge that the past – both distant and recent – has profoundly deformed the spiritual life of mankind, leaving a heavy legacy for us." Shevardnadze, "Vystuplenie v shtab-kvartire IUNESKO," *Pravda*, 13 October 1988. W. Hyland wrote that after many years of anti-communism, troubles, and crises in the relations of the United States with the Soviet Union and China, any restructuring of those relations could not find a rapid response in public consciousness; it requires a shattering of intellectual standards." W. Hyland, *Mortal Rivals. Superpower Relations from Nixon to Reagan* (1987), p. 197.
65. 68% of Americans polled agreed that "Soviet leaders cannot be trusted so that reactions to Soviet initiatives must be slow and cautious." Simultaneously, 67% believe that in the next ten years both countries would act jointly in the United Nations, and 41% admit that they could even become military allies. *Pravda*, 12 May 1988.
66. Ch. Okeke, *The Theory and Practice of International Law in Nigeria* (1986), p.1. W. Coplin said: "The general publics in most Western states are apathetic towards international law although they have definite ideas about international politics." W. Coplin, *The Functions of International Law* (1966), p. 182. Also see Ch. de Visscher, *Theory and Reality in Public International Law* (1957), pp. 139–240.
67. E. Basin, *Supruzheskaia zhizn'* (1972), p.328.
68. See G. K. Dmitrieva, "Printsip spravedlivosti v mezhdunarodnom prave," *Sovetskii ezhegodnik mezhdunarodnogo prava 1983* (1984), p. 69.
69. The Centre for "World Peace Through Law" gives some attention to these matters. However, its activities are confined to general appeals to comply with international law.

Its resolutions affect the development of legal education in general, and not education in the realm of international law. See *Resolutions Adopted by the Cairo Conference on the Law of the World* (1983), pp. 20–27; *The Berlin Declaration and Resolutions Adopted by the Twelfth Conference on the Law of the World* (1985), p. 12.

70. J. Symonides, *Wychowanie dla pokoju* (1980), p. 11.
71. J. Perez de Cuellar, *Poslaniia i zaivleniia, posviashchennye Mezhdunarodnomu godu mira – 1986* (1987), p. 33.

FOREIGN RELATIONS LAW AS STATE PRACTICE

W. E. BUTLER

"Foreign relations law" enjoys an ambivalent status in international law, comparative law, and municipal legislation. International lawyers have daily recourse to the legislation of States governing diplomatic and consular affairs, the conclusion and ratification of international treaties, territory, nationality, foreign trade, the legal status of aliens, piracy, terrorism, and other areas where there is a direct legal interface between a municipal legal system and the international legal system. In their eyes such legislation represents the implementation of obligations assumed under customary international law or international treaties or the assertion of a claim on behalf or against the incipient formation of a rule of international law. It may be one form or expression of the "practice of States" engaged in by reason of *opinio juris*.

These are not necessarily wholly compatible roles for foreign relations law. Assertions of a claim on behalf or against the incipient formation of a rule of international law may constitute a violation of the existing rule of international law and occasion protests from other States. More commonly, foreign relations legislation restates, adopts, elaborates, or clarifies rules of international law within a domestic law context, and in doing so may contribute creatively to the development of international law.

Viewed through a comparative municipal law prism, foreign relations law is comprised of both law and "non-law:" it is law to the extent that legislation is utilised as the means for articulating rules of normative behaviour but "non-law" when a means not recognised as "law-creative" for a municipal legal system is used on the international plane and is deemed by international law to be a source or subsidiary source of international law. Most, if not all, municipal legal systems have avoided addressing the "non-law" dimension of domestic foreign relations law, as has the world of comparative law.

There are nonetheless tentative moves in the direction of defining the contours of foreign affairs legislation. Official systematic collections of legislation in several major powers contain sections on the subject. The Digest of Laws of the Union of Soviet Socialist Republics devotes Section V to "Legislation on International Relations," which consists of two parts: so-called "general questions," encompassing enactments treating war crimes, the procedure for the conclusion, execution, and denunciation of international treaties, and diplomatic and consular legislation.[1] The second part contains Soviet legislation on foreign trade and on economic scientific-technical, and cultural co-operation with foreign countries, by which is meant enactments authorising foreign economic activities within the USSR, the

W. E. Butler, *Perestroika and International Law*, 109–119.
© 1990 *Kluwer Academic Publishers. Printed in the Netherlands.*

statutes of Soviet agencies involved in foreign economic relations, and customs and shipping regulations. Legislation on other matters of direct "foreign relations" concern, including territorial boundaries and innocent passage, is dispersed amongst other sections of the Digest.

The official revised edition of the United Kingdom *Statutes in Force* employs an analogous category,[2] denominated "International Relations," divided into two parts: (1) Privileges and Immunities; and (2) International Agreements. Grouped under Part One are the German Conventions Act 1935, the International Headquarters and Defence Organisations Act 1964, the Diplomatic Privileges Act 1964, the Consular Relations Act 1968, the International Organisations Act 1968 and 1981, the State Immunity Act 1978, the Diplomatic and Consular Premises Act 1987, the Arms Control and Disarmament (Privileges and Immunities) Act 1988, among others. Part Two contains acts appertaining to individual treaties. Cross references are given to 23 other relevant subject classifications within the looseleaf edition.

Halsbury's Statutes of England and Wales (4th ed.) contains no separate subject heading for foreign or international relations, distributing the materials amongst a myriad of other classifications, most of which have no obvious immediate relevance to international law.[3] Happily Lord Hailsham took a different view in *Halsbury's Laws of England* where there is a thorough chapter entitled "Foreign Relations Law."[4] Even so the editors have selected individual topics for separate treatment – Fisheries, Extradition and Fugitive Offenders – which seem to fall squarely within the definition of foreign relations law.

Not surprisingly in the jurisdiction where a Restatement of Foreign Relations Law has been compiled, the United States Code devotes Title 22 to "Foreign Relations and Intercourse" consisting of fifty-three subdivisions. Nevertheless, vast areas of foreign relations matters are relegated to other Titles: aliens and nationality, arbitration, certain aspects of commerce and trade, conservation, customs duties, navigation, shipping, territories and insular possessions, and war and national defense, among others. And the fifty-three headings are themselves a ragbag choice giving no evidence of a rational, cohesive approach to legislation on the subject.[5] The unofficial annotated versions of Federal legislation are superior in this regard, but they too show little evidence of thorough systematisation of the subject.

A thorough survey of all official, quasi-official, and unofficial systematic collections of municipal legislation is beyond the scope of this article, but perhaps the selection of three major influential jurisdictions is sufficient to suggest that in some measure at least official recognition has been accorded to foreign relations legislation in one form or another as a branch of legislation. And in this limited sense foreign relations law is *law*.

Whether foreign relations law can be said to constitute a distinct branch of law or legal science is rather more difficult. The most ambitious attempt by far to reduce foreign relations law to a unified exposition of principles and rules has occurred in a jurisdiction least disposed to acknowledge law as a branch of science or learning, i.e., the United States. Those legal systems most preoccupied with the structure and substance of legal science have done the least with respect to foreign relations law. Nevertheless, there are signs of progress. The number of monographs on international law which rest primarily or exclusively on foreign affairs legislation continue to multiply.[6] Studies of individual national legal systems are beginning to devote attention to foreign relations law,[7] but monographs by international lawyers on the subject are narrowly conceived and often confined merely to diplomatic and consular law.[8]

In law schools, courses are beginning to be introduced on foreign affairs law; the first in the United Kingdom offered at University College London as part of the postgraduate LL.M. degree by Richard Gardiner. Its concern is the relationship between public international law and national systems of law examined through the "mechanisms" by which international law has "effect on and in municipal law." Beginning with the doctrines of monism and dualism, the course examines the constitutional dimension of foreign relations, the respective roles of international and municipal law in defining persons "who may act on, or be affected by, law" made on the international plane. Consideration is given to international law as a formal source of municipal legal rules and to municipal law as a source of international law. Special attention is given to treaties, dispute settlement, and other areas of interaction between international and municipal law.[9] Within the admittedly loose categorisation of subjects in the University of London LL.M. degree, it is viewed as an international rather than comparative law subject.

Definitions of foreign relations law

Foreign relations law viewed from a municipal law perspective is normally perceived as having two principal components by those who have undertaken a formal definition: (1) international law as it applies to the municipal legal system concerned; and (2) municipal law concerned with foreign relations matters. The *Restatement* defines foreign relations law as consisting of:[10]

(a) international law as it applies to the United States; and
(b) domestic law that has substantial significance for the foreign relations of the United States or has other substantial international consequences.

English definitions differ slightly. Parry and Collier wrote that

Foreign Relations Law consists of rules of public international law which are binding upon the United Kingdom, and such parts of English law as are concerned with the means by which effect is given to the rules of public international law or which involve matters of concern to the United Kingdom in the conduct of its relations with foreign States and governments or their nationals.[11]

There are intriguing nuances in the two definitions which may or may not masque differences. The American definition, for example, seems broader in its reference to international law as it *applies to* the United States vis-à-vis the English formulation of rules *binding upon* the United Kingdom. The second portion of the definition is rather sweeping in both cases. English doctrine speaks of "matters of concern" to the conduct of relations with "foreign States and governments or the nationals," omitting any reference to international institutions. On this point the official systematic collection of United Kingdom legislation would appear to go further, for it clearly encompasses international organisations under this rubric.

The *Restatement* definition is reminiscent to European ears of American "long-arm" legislation: "substantial significance" or "other substantial international consequences," although no mention is made of nationals.

In both instances, however, it should be observed that the definitions speak of domestic *law* and not other forms[12] of State practice which may have standing as a source of law under international law. Moreover, the definitions are based essentially upon the subject matter or consequences of the legislation, that is, they classify the legislation and do not in any way attempt to evaluate the quality of its contribution to international law.

The practice of states: international law

The practice of States as a source of international law is a concept of *international law* and not municipal law. Wheresoever municipal organs may invoke State practice, it is believed that they do so pursuant to international law and not as a source of domestic law, although they may act under domestic laws which require them to apply the law of nations.

Article 38 of the Statute of the International Court of Justice is perhaps the principal authority for regarding State practice as an important element contributing to the formation of rules of international law. Commonly the reference is to Article 38(1)(b), where the ICJ is instructed to apply international custom, "as evidence of a general practice accepted as law." Equally pertinent, at least from a comparative law perspective, as State practice must be the "general principles of law" recognised by civilised nations, assuming of course that the Statute has reference to general principles of *municipal* law. Some would argue that Article 38(1)(a) is apt on the premise that international conventions, whether general or particular, are a form of State practice.

Doctrinal writings to be sure show some ambivalence with regard to the role of

State practice. Positivism is perhaps responsible for raising the behaviour of subjects of international law to the elevated stature it enjoys. Theories of international law which visualise the international system on the basis of other values or dynamics are disposed axiomatically to accord less weight to the conduct of States. On the other hand, some writers look upon all State conduct as constitutive of international law through the policy processes of claim and counterclaim.

Deliberations on the subject of State practice in 1983 led the architects of the discussion to define it as a legal practice (la pratique du droit), which excluded doctrine and the practice of "individuals" as they are not subjects of international law. The general reporter formulated his definition as follows: "in international law practice is the conduct in international relations of organs of subjects of international law which is imputable to those subjects."[13] Leaving aside international organisations and other entities enjoying qualified legal personality under international law, State practice emanates most often from government bodies, including parliamentary and judicial organs, and conceivably even from quasi-public bodies whose behaviour is equated to that of State organs.

The quality of the practice of States as evidence of a rule of international law, it is widely acknowledged, may vary from one situation to another. It may be material, for example, as to whether the practice of States appertains to an area where there is no rule of international law, or whether it reinforces a developing rule, or whether it clarifies or elaborates an existing rule, or whether – as noted above – it is contrary to the existing rule and is asserted with a view to modifying or abolishing the rule.[14] Opinio juris would would appear to be essential in every instance.

No a priori distinction is drawn in international law amongst the types or forms of the practice of States. Legislation would seem to carry the same weight in principle as a national court judgment or a diplomatic note, although doubtless in the event of conflict an international tribunal might ask how the municipal jurisdiction itself equated these forms of practice. Neither does international law impose a priori standards, procedural or substantive, upon the quality of the evidence of State practice. There seems to be an assumption that the expression of State will is sufficient irrespective of whether municipal or conceivably even international standards are satisfied with respect to the disclosure or publication of that will.

Foreign relations law under this approach is but one form of the practice of States which enjoys no predetermined stature vis-a-vis other forms of State practice either by the same State or other subjects of international law. Whether foreign relations law acts in a procedural capacity to incorporate[15] rules of international law into municipal law or in a rule-creative or rule-enforcement capacity with regard to the substance of international law is a matter for determination in each individual instance, apparently ad hoc unless the learning and lore of comparative law – as this article will argue – can be of assistance.

The practice of states: comparative law

If the traditional objects of comparative legal studies are national legal systems, it follows that Article 38(1)(c) affords the principal access for the ICJ to municipal law as a source of international law: "general principles of law" recognised by civilised nations. Accepting that "general principles of law" here refer to principles of municipal law, there seems to be an unspoken assumption that principles of domestic law wholly unrelated to international law are contemplated.

From the comparative lawyer's point of view, the municipal law of a State is a legal unity subject to comparison with the law of other States. Whether the rules or practices concern matters of tort, contract, estoppel, unjust enrichment, social security, property, or foreign relations is immaterial. What matters is the quality of comparison and generalisation. That foreign relations law has until recently been outside the purview of traditional comparative legal studies is a comment on the myopia of comparatists and not on the relevance of comparative law to foreign relations law. Accordingly, from the comparatist's standpoint, there is no reason why foreign relations law should not be the object of scrutiny for general principles of law which constitute evidence of a rule of international law.

On this reasoning, to the comparatist there is a certain redundancy in using the practice of States in the form of foreign relations law as evidence of an international custom when the same result might be obtained through foreign relations law as the repository of general principles of law. Yet invariably foreign relations law as comparative law data is analysed discretely together with other evidence of State practice on the international rather than the comparative plane.

Should "general principles of law" in Article 38(1)(c) of the Statute of the ICJ be understood to mean not merely principles of domestic law, but also principles of domestic law with no foreign relations dimension whatever? International judicial and arbitral practice tends to sustain such a distinction. However, under the approach taken in the *Restatement*, it might well be argued that any domestic law which constitutes a general principle of law recognised by civilised nations *ipso facto* has "substantial significance" for the foreign relations of a country or "other substantial international consequences" because it is, or is capable of, being drawn upon as evidence of a rule of international law.

While the comparatist may be sceptical about the division between foreign relations law and other types of domestic law, he is likely to see complexities in identifying general principles of law recognised by civilised nations for reasons that inhere in comparative legal studies and are not obvious to the international lawyer. "Civilised nation" is now an archaic expression; nonetheless, it does contain a sense of limitation. Must an international tribunal seek a general principle of law in *all* legal systems of the world? Does the absence of the general principle in certain legal systems defeat the quest of the tribunal on the principle of universality, or is it sufficient to locate the principle in the major or principal legal systems of the world? If the last, what are the criteria for "major" or "principal"? Should one, for example, treat the five members of the United Nations Security Council as "major" for these purposes (which would exclude Islamic, Scandinavian, Hindu, Japanese, and other significant legal traditions)? Perhaps classifications widely employed in comparative legal studies should be invoked; for example, the notion of families of legal systems.

Further, is it imperative that a general principle in a municipal legal system have been identified or articulated within the system itself, whether by legislation, customary law, judicial decision, or doctrinal gloss, or is the international tribunal at liberty to employ its own methods of search and identification? This leads to an important and virtually unexplored dimension of general principles of law as a source of international law. In its capacity as municipal legislation, foreign relations law is a form of the practice of States which, if general, consistent, and followed from a sense of legal obligation – to use the words of the *Restatement* – may result in the creation of customary international law. Equally, as suggested above, foreign relations law might contain a general principle of law common to the principal legal systems of the world – to paraphrase the *Restatement* again – from which a rule of international law may be derived.

From the comparative lawyer's perspective it is of no consequence whether domestic law, be it foreign relations law or other law, is used in one way or the other. To the international lawyer, however, the distinction may be vital, for foreign relations law as evidence of customary international law is presumed to be consciously enacted by States against the fabric of the international legal system; it is unlikely that a State could persuasively argue that it was unaware of the impact its foreign affairs legislation would have upon the formation or shaping of a rule of international law. And for this reason foreign affairs law as the practice of States may be construed as consent to the formation or existence of a customary rule of international law.

The same does not necessarily follow from other general principles of municipal law. Their concurrent existence in the principal legal systems of the world may transpire for reasons that differ from one legal culture to another, and the reasons may affect the configuration or application or the rule. The coincidental existence of a rule, conceivably the universal existence of a general principle of law, is not evidence that the States concerned had consented to be governed by the rule as a rule of international law. When we address the issue of the application of the law of nations in a municipal legal system, we speak of a process of assimilation – adoption, incorporation, transformation – all based on a consensual act of the municipal State at some point in its history. General principles of law is a reverse process without, however, the element of consent by the municipal legal system to the rule in its capacity as a rule of international law. "Derivation" of the rule is to occur without an element of State will being present, i.e., that the rule was also intended to be binding on the international plane.

Foreign relations law: quality of the evidence

In a world in which general humanitarian and democratic values are to help forge an international law appropriate to the circumstances, it is relevant to ask what might be done to "democratise" the international legal process and the general public's awareness of and involvement in it. The creation of an international minimum standard for the publication and dissemination of the practice of States taking the form of foreign relations law is one step in this direction.

International law contains no rule regarding the forms of State practice, and in fact a vast array of forms and devices are employed to express the will of States: treaties, protocols, notes, statements, declarations, resolutions, legislation, tacit acquiescence are but a few examples. Disputes submitted for judicial or arbitral settlement are likely to confront those resolving the disagreement with a considerable variety of examples of State practice, each to be weighed and evaluated without any formal priority of place attached to each. The First World War provoked a strong reaction against secret treaties and agreements, leading in due course to arrangements within the League of Nations and the United Nations for the registration, translation, and publication of treaties. Although the service has been extensively utilised, far from all treaties are registered and, as a rule, no legal consequences flow from the failure to register.

The evaluation and generalisation of the practice of States is a principal responsibility of doctrinal writings. International lawyers find themselves deluged, on one hand, by a flood of texts, enactments, documents, resolutions, and the like difficult to cope with and are deprived of access, on the other hand, to vital areas of State practice because of security classification or simple lack of publication. How to weigh the respective merits of this morass of material is increasingly perplexing.

One means of reducing the scope of the dilemma would be to introduce and operate a presumption based on a practice found in some municipal legal systems with respect to the validity of legislation: to be valid and enforceable, legislation must be published for general information in a readily accessible and inexpensive official gazette. This is a requirement that in late-twentieth century democratic societies is being imposed upon so-called "subordinate" or "delegated" legislation.[16] Translated to international law, the presumption might be formulated at various threshholds, as follows:

1. unpublished forms of State practice create no obligations under international law and have no evidentiary or other value as regards the formation or existence of a rule of international law; or
2. unpublished forms of State practice may create obligations between parties, but these are unenforceable under international law and have no evidentiary or other value as regards the formation of existence of a rule of international law; or

3. unpublished forms of State practice create enforceable obligations between the parties, if consistent with international law, but have no evidentiary or other value as regards the existence of a rule of international law.

Formulation (3) is perhaps the most flexible from the standpoint of States. They retain maximum flexibility to develop State practice in accordance with international law but are presumed to refrain from utilising that practice to create or reinforce a rule of international law unless the practice is suitably published. Publication itself becomes a constituent element of *opinio juris*. Presumably international law would have no objection if municipal legal systems introduced a higher standard for publication than the international standard.

"Publication" as contemplated in this proposal means a full and official text and not merely disclosure of the existence of a respective document. The latter practice is widely used, sometimes even with foreign affairs legislation, and can lead to serious distortions or omissions in State practice. It does little good to produce the full and official text at dispute stage when availability at issuance or promulgation stage may have averted the dispute.

Consider, for example, the case of Peter the Great Bay, which on 4 July 1957 was declared to be an historic bay.[17] The existence of the decree adopted by the USSR Council of Ministers was disclosed in a communique published in *Izvestiia* on 21 July of the same year,[18] and as the official gazette of the USSR Council of Ministers in 1957 was just resuming publication and not subject to export, Western writings on the subject assumed that the date of enactment was the date of notification in the press.[19] Moreover, the press announcement made reference to foreign vessels and aircraft being excluded from Peter the Great Bay unless competent authorities issued an appropriate authorisation;[20] while this was a logical conclusion to draw from the enactment of the legislation, the Decree itself did not so stipulate. Several diplomatic protests were lodged by foreign governments, but none of those published suggests that the protesting governments had actually seen the Decree,[21] which provided as follows:

"ON THE ESTABLISHMENT OF THE BOUNDARIES OF INTERNAL WATERS OF THE SOVIET UNION IN PETER THE GREAT BAY
[Decree of the USSR Council of Ministers, 4 July 1957, No. 867]

The USSR Council of Ministers decrees:

1. To establish, having regard to the geographic conditions of Peter the Great Bay and its special economic and defence significance, and to the fact that the waters of this Bay historically are waters of the Soviet Union, that the line connecting the mouth of the Tiumen-Ula River with Cape Povorotnyi shall be

the boundary of internal waters of the Soviet Union in this area and the baseline for calculating seaward the breadth of Soviet territorial waters.

2. To oblige the USSR Ministry of Defence to notify in *Izveshcheniia moreplavateliam* that the waters of Peter the Great Bay delimited landward by the line connecting the mouth of the Tiumen-Ula River with Cape Povorotnyi are internal waters of the Soviet Union as they are waters of an historic bay.

The navigation of foreign vessels to the open port of Nakhodka shall be authorised along a channel established by the USSR Ministry of Defence, which also shall be proclaimed in *Izveshcheniia moreplavateliam*."

Examples of similar disclosure practices could be compounded manyfold with respect to dozens of governments. Foreign affairs legislation of this nature is normative in character, affects boundaries and therefore foreign citizens as well as the issuing State's own nationals, and as the assertion of a claim to territory is involved, inevitably the legislation becomes the object of doctrinal gloss and reaction from other governments. Knowledge of the law simply cannot be served or presumed in the absence of *glasnost'* in regard to State practice.

Conclusion

Manley O. Hudson was amongst those of the interwar generation of international lawyers who popularised the expression "international legislation" with reference to multilateral conventions. Perhaps the moment is opportune on another plane to introduce municipal standards for the publication of legislation into the international arena with the appropriate evidentiary consequences. *Glasnost'* needs to be brought to the practice of States in the form of foreign relations law. To be construed as norm-reinforcing or norm-creative, foreign relations law should be required to satisfy minimum standards of procedure and form: full official text in an inexpensive and readily accessible public gazette. Insofar as international law is concerned, the failure to meet the standards would mean that a State would be deprived of the right to invoke this form of State practice as evidence of a rule of international law, *opinio juris*, or a general principle of law recognised by the major legal systems of the world.

Notes

1. *Svod zakonov SSSR*, IX.
2. *Statutes in Force*, Section 68
3. *Halsbury's Statutes of England and Wales* (4th ed., 1977).

4. Lord Hailsham, *Halsbury's Laws of England* (4th ed.), XVIII, 713–994. The Chapter was written by the late Professor Clive Parry and J. G. Collier.
5. *United States Code (1982 ed.)* (1983), IX, Title 22. See esp. p. xix.
6. Many works on national approaches to the law of the sea are of this nature, to mention one example among many,
7. See for example, W. E. Butler, *Soviet Law* (2d ed., 1988), pp. 366–402; G. L. Certoma, *The Italian Legal System* (1985), pp. 103–137; H. Oda, *Modern Japanese Law* (1990)
8. See among others K. K. Sandrovskii, *Pravo vneshnikh snoshenii* (1986).
9. See University of London, *Syllabuses for the LL.M. Degree for Internal Students 1988–9* ([1988]), pp. 84–85.
10. The American Law Institute, *Restatement of the Law: The Foreign Relations Law of the United States* (1987), p. 7.
11. Note 4 above, p. 717, para. 1401.
12. Compare the definition of foreign relations law with the range of materials extracted as evidence of State practice in the Digests of international law compiled by J. B. Moore, G. H. Hackworth, M. Whiteman, C. Parry, A. C. Kiss, J. Charpentier, P. Guggenheim, C. Rousseau, and others.
13. W. Goralczyk, "Rapport Général," in *Travaux de l'Association Henri Capitant: le role de la pratique dans la formation du droit*, XXXIV (1983), 539.
14. See *ibid.*, pp 540–541, where Professor Goralczyk offers examples of each situation.
15. On the variant forms of international law becoming part of English law, see W. E. Butler, "International and Municipal Law: Some Reflections on British Practice," *Coexistence*, XXIV (1987), 67–76.
16. For an influential article that contributed to publication of the Code of Federal Regulations, see E. N. Griswold, "Government in Ignorance of the Law – A Plea for Better Publication of Executive Legislation," *Harvard Law Review*, XLVIII (1934), 198–215.
17. *Sobranie deistvuiushchego zakonodatel'stva SSSR*, I (1973), 40–41. Curiously, the *Svod zakonov SSSR* does not contain this Decree, nor that of 1926 regarding land territories in the Soviet Arctic. Given the official stature of the latter publication, it may create the impression that both acts have lost force, although neither has done so in fact.
18. *Izvestiia*, 21 July 1957, p. 1.
19. See W. E. Butler, *The Soviet Union and the Law of the Sea* (1971), p. 108. The official gazette of the USSR Council of Ministers became available abroad from 1972.
20. See the text translated in Butler, *The Law of Soviet Territorial Waters* (1967), pp. 108–109.
21. The Japanese note appears in the *Japanese Annual of International Law*, II (1958), 215.

THE LAW OF THE SEA IN LIGHT OF THE
NEW POLITICAL THINKING

A. P. MOVCHAN

According to the new political thinking, there is proceeding at the moment, gathering momentum, an objective process: "the process of the formation of an interconnected and integral world."[1] The basis of progress in this world is the general humanitarian interest and, consequently, world politics will be determined by the priority of general humaniarian values. One of those values is general international law, an integral part of which is the law of the sea.

The concept of universal security being advanced by the new political thinking "is based on the principles of the United Nations Charter and proceeds from the binding nature of *international law* for all States."[2] It is advisable to stress too that among the guarantees of military-political, economic, and humanitarian universal security, the *new thinking elevates legal guarantees* to the top place.[3] All this testifies to the fact that the new thinking devoted significant attention to international law and allocates to it an important role in future world progress.

According to the new political thinking, the progress of mankind towards a new world order means the creation of a system of universal legal order under which the primacy of international law in politics will be secured.

World order on the World Ocean is an integral component of the contemporary world legal order. Therefore, all generally recognised principles and norms of international relations constitute the foundation stone of the entire legal regulation of relations and activities of States regarding the research, use, and exploitation of the expanses and resources of the World Ocean and its subsoil.

The modern law of the sea

The law of the sea is a branch of contemporary international law and a system of norms which defines the legal status and regime of marine expanses and resources and regulates relations between States in the process of their activities on the World Ocean so that they are effected exclusively for peaceful purposes. These days the law of the sea has acquired extremely important socio-economic and political-legal significance. This is first and foremost because the World Ocean plays an enormous role in creating the requisite conditions for life on earth. All of mankind is a concern that the World Ocean and its economic potential be rationally and effectively used for peaceful purposes and the benefit of peoples of our planet.

The objective necessity for universal, comprehensive, and all-round exploitation

W. E. Butler, *Perestroika and International Law,* 121–132.
© 1990 *Kluwer Academic Publishers. Printed in the Netherlands.*

of the expanses and natural resources of the World Ocean and its subsoil are being realised under specific historical conditions of the existence of very different States. The differences in social system, levels of economic development, and geographic location (coastal, strait, archipelagic, landlocked, etc.) of modern States is overcoming significant differences in the degree of maritime productive forces and scientific-technical potential of those countries, and consequently, in their approach to the ways and means of resolving the global problem of exploiting the World Ocean.

Under these conditions the world need for establishing and confirming unified rules for any State activities on the seas and oceans has increased, as too for the creation and application to the behaviour of all State parties of relations in the exploitation of the World Ocean of a single standard for evaluating what is admissible or inadmissible as lawful or unlawful activities by States and governments. The aggregate of all these rules comprise the content and object of the law of the sea as a uniform regulator of the relations of all States in the process of their activities in all expanses of the World Ocean.

The principles and norms of the law of the sea were created in the course of centuries of State practice under the influence of socio-political and economic factors of social development, as well as the level of scientific-technical achievements and opportunities for exploiting the economic potential of the sea expanses, especially their biological and mineral resources. In the past the oceans and seas had importance for the development of world economic exchange primarily in the realm of transport, as "the common spacious road of all nations" (K. Marx). As regards the potential of marine resources, until the middle of this century it was used in part, primarily in the form of fishing.

The principal radical changes in exploitation of the World Ocean, especially of its natural resources, occurred in the period of scientific-technical revolution which began in the mid-1940s. The unprecedented growth in the development of productive forces and remarkable expansion of scientific-technical possibilities and means for conducting marine scientific research, and the emergence of a wholly new marine technology created real conditions for a transition to a multi-faceted, highly effective, and comprehensive exploitation of marine resources and expanses.

All this has told on the development of the law of the sea. Whereas initially it arose and developed as customary law which basically concentrated on defining the legal status of sea expanses and the regulation of navigation and fishing, by the mid-20th century the law of the sea, reflecting the dynamic requirements of contemporary international relations and scientific-technical progress, began to develop as conventional law and to extend the sphere of its effect, encompassing ever newer and intensively expanding types of State activities in the domain of the comprehensive research and use of sea expanses and their biological and mineral resources (commercial, trade, naval, and others; survey and operational drilling for oil and gas; scientific-research vessels and installations; exploration and exploitation of minerals, both coastal and in the deep seabed, and the like).

Codification of the law of the sea

Commencing the process of the codification and progressive development of the modern law of the sea was in essence vested in the United Nations. In 1948 the work programme of the International Law Commission emphasised that "codification in the broad sense of the word of all the branches of the law of the sea into a unified and agreed 'code of rules' or analogous more authoritative document will significantly enhance the value of both work on codification and of international law as a whole."[4] The 1982 Convention on the Law of the Sea is the most recent such document.

The new thinking and its active proponents see the validity of international law above all in the fact that it rests on *norms reflecting the balance of interests of States*. Universally recognised norms of international law undoubtedly reflect and symbolise the optimal balance of interests of West and East, of North and South. The working out of such norms requires a joint search for generally-acceptable decisions, mutual concessions and compromises, reasonable and just satisfaction of the real interests of different States or groups of States. In essence one is speaking of a form of cooperation which M. S. Gorbachev in his address to the United Nations called "co-creativity" or "co-development." It is extremely essential to enhance the effectiveness of international law, to resolve other urgent problems, and, of course, to resolve global problems positively.

The world community already has some experience of such an approach to resolving, for example, the global problem of ensuring that the modern practice of exploiting the expanses and resources of the World Ocean rationally serves the interests of all mankind. This experience was manifested in the works and concluding documents of the III United Nations Conference on the Law of the Sea (1973–82) [UNCLOS]. The social value of this experience is various, for it can be used also in resolving other urgent problems of international life.

It should be emphasised above all that the UNCLOS achieved a mutually acceptable and agreed politico-legal decision of one of the modern global problems. The new thinking has appealed for this more than once. M. S. Gorbachev in his address to the United Nations indicated that "in urging the demilitarisation of international relations, we want to see politico-legal methods predominate when resolving problems that arise."

The UNCLOS was genuinely universal; virtually all the States known to the modern political map of the world took part in it. The existence of sovereign States is an objective reality of our age. Under these conditions the joint resolution by mankind of global problems is possible only through the combined and agreed activities of all modern States. To be sure, a study of the character and nature of global problems and searches for scientifically well-founded methods for resolving them is possible also on the non-interState level. National scientific studies and drafts, meetings and conferences of scholars and socio-political leaders of various countries and of various types, and the activities of nongovernmental national and international organisations have important significance for promoting the positive settlement of particular problems confronting mankind. However, the resolution of those problems and the implementation of those decisions is impossible without the direct participation of States and governments in this process. Such is the socio-political reality of the modern age.

With a view to achieving not merely a universal legal order but one generally-acceptable to all States on the World Ocean, special political-legal methods of drafting and adopting decisions of conferences have been used; for example, the "consensus" method and the rules of approving agreed decisions in "a single package." Here we speak of a real consensus, which is created by a constructive and business-like atmosphere of "co-creativity" in international forums. The essence of the "package" approach was that all the principal problems of exploiting the World Ocean (legal status and regime of sea expanses and international straits, exploration and exploitation of natural marine resources, protecting the marine environment against pollution, conducting marine scientific research, and others) must be regarded and resolved as closely interconnected. This method directly served the task of achieving a "balance of interests" of very different States – coastal, polar, and landlocked; those possessing developed marine technology as well as those just embarking on the exploitation of marine natural wealth, and the like.

Ultimately the UNCLOS drafted a new code of the law of the sea which combines both the "traditional" and completely new norms of international law. They all are de facto observed in practice by the international community of States. The exception may to some extent be only the section of the "code" relating to deep-water resources of the seabed and its subsoil. And this is to be explained chiefly by the fact that here there was not achieved the optimal balance of interests of all States, nor was there either a creative or official consensus process when ultimately adopting the decisions relative to the legal fate of the seabed. But this exception once again confirms the vital importance of the proposition that the effectiveness of international legal decisions and of international law as a whole depends of to what extent they reflect the balance of interests of modern States, both large and small.

Finally, one must note a characteristic feature of the UNCLOS, that all of its ideas and decisions were directed toward truly ensuring the use of the expanses and resources of the World Ocean *exclusively for peaceful purposes*, as was officially proclaimed and consolidated in the 1982 Convention on the Law of the Sea. The general humanitarian value of this experience and the bases of the legal order on the World Ocean is beyond doubt. He serves as a real confirmation of the thesis of the new political thinking that "forces have formed in the world which in one way or another are impelling us to enter a period of peace" (M. S. Gorbachev).

A characteristic peculiarity of the 1982 Convention is that it determines the legal procedure for exploiting the World Ocean as a whole. It establishes the legal status of all sea expaneses, as well as the living and mineral resources of the World Ocean and its seabed. Having regard to the achievements of scientific-technical progress, the convention regulates all the principal types and spheres of State activities regarding the research, use, and exploitation of sea expanses and their resources. Therefore, it is fully possible to say that the new convention is of an all-embracing character. The international community has no other single international legal act which encompasses such an extensive ambit of questions.

The consolidation in a single convention, constituting a "balanced package of compromise arrangements," of all the basic principles and norms of the contemporary legal regime of the World Ocean is undoubtedly facilitated by the fact that the Convention provisions are inter-connected, inter-conditional, and mutually agreed. These characteristic peculiarities of the convention could not but further the unity of the international legal order on the seas and oceans and its acceptability to all countries and peoples and, consequently, the effectiveness of this legal order.

The nature of the 1982 Convention

The political-legal resolution of the global problem of exploiting the ocean, reflected in the 1982 Convention, enables certain conclusions to be drawn which are of a certain significance also for various studies of the present and rising world order. First, it is a universal politico-legal document (just as the method for preparing it) which undoubtedly can serve as a model for the real restructuring of international relations in many other areas of contemporary international life.

The extensive revolutionary and democratic transformations in many countries, assistance to the struggle of States in strengthening universal peace, as well as the dynamics of international life and the achievements of scientific-technical progress urgently require that the international legal resolution of urgent problems of international relations be rapidly and adequately reflected in the changes taking place in the world, in the mutual relations of countries and peoples, and in the various activities of States in sundry spheres of their cooperation. Only in this event man the development of international law be progressive, and its conformity to the principles and norms of the social laws of development of our age be a guarantee that it will effectively serve the aims of developing peaceloving and friendly ties and cooperation between peoples. The 1982 Convention was drafted by maximally taking into account under modern conditions the requirements of social development.

The entire previous positive experience of mankind in the domain of the politico-legal resolution of questions of exploiting the World Ocean, in particular of certain provisions of the 1958 Geneva Conventions and many other multilateral maritime agreements, were reflected in it, as were recent changes in the exploitation of the World Ocean dictated by the newest changes in socio-economic development and the requirements of the scientific-technical revolution.

A dialectical combination of international and national interests also is characteristic of the Convention; it is based to the maximal extent on two major trends of contemporary international relations: the constantly growing development of world links and various extensive cooperation of States, on one hand, and the trend towards the further strengthening of and respect for the sovereign rights and national jurisdiction of various States. Many contradictory national interests and requirements, sometimes rather extremist, were reduced to a mutually acceptable, albeit compromise, single denominator.

The achievement of such a unified approach by all members of the modern international community was possible only as a result of the shared purpose in creating a single universal international document through mutually-agreed arrangements on the basis of consensus and in a single "package." It was confirmed with persuasive clarity that the politico-legal resolution of the global problem of exploiting the World Ocean must in our era occur on a multilateral and universal basis, and not with the aid of a multiplicity of bilateral transactions, treaties, and regional agreements of individual States or groups of States.

It is appropriate to note in this connection that insufficient attention is still devoted in the theory of international law to social purposes when establishing a legal order on an international scale. The studies available basically concentrate on the correlation of the concepts of "legal order" and "legality," or enumerate the basic international legal acts and foreign policy initiatives relating to the achievement of a particular order in international relations. But, as is justly noted in recent studies on legal theory, the principal theoretical burden which the abstraction of "legal order" bears is that "it reflects both the social purposes and the objective result of legal regulation." The "bringing of social relations into a state of regularity and order with the aid of all legal means of forming social relations" serves, in this instance, as the result.[5]

Since in each specific historical era the international legal order is formed on the basis of those socio-political aims and purposes which States pursue and strengthen as specific legal requirements in the principles and norms of international law, then these two inter-connected elements – the socio-political and the legal – also inhere in the concept of "international legal order."

In this rather complex age in which there are States with very diverse socio-political systems, it can and must be said that the contemporary international legal order is an order (or system) of international relations responsive to the interests of the entire international community as a whole; those relations arise and are effectuated on the basis of and in accordance with the requirements of prevailing general (for all members of the community) international law.

For the creation and existence of such a legal order it is essential that the underlying principles and norms of international law are responsive in their socio-political content to the interests of the entire world community and in their legal character are legally binding upon all participants of contemporary international relations without exception.

Securing an identical socio-political approach for all the very different States with respect to the rational exploitation of the economic, including resource, potential of the World Ocean and its seabed can be effected in the modern age only through the creation of a single legal regime for the use of the spaces and resources of all the seas and oceans, inexorably obligatory for all members of the world community. The extremely urgent role and important significance of general international law in resolving the global problems of humanity and other essential requirements of international relations and world is conditioned by this above all. This regretfully is still insufficiently appreciated by some politologists.

The 1982 Convention contains comprehensive provisions relative to the fate of the expanses and natural resources of the World Ocean. And this is a significant achievement of the entire international community. Characteristic of our period are the social laws of the development of mankind, as well as the basic leading trends in international relations, including the intensive growth and deepening of international links, the undoubted strengthening of interdependence of various actions of States, especially on issues of war and peace, that is, the so-called indivisibility of the world in our age, which in significant measure has promoted the higher level of the general understanding of the unalterable fact that the limits of free discretion of all States must be strictly outlined and brought within a legal framework, a withdrawal from which would be considered to be illegal, unlawful, and even criminal. Otherwise, not merely the interests and rights of other States may be harmed, but also the interests of the international community as a whole.

The results of UNCLOS also are a very persuasive manifestation of the objective necessity for the existence, progressive development, and further strengthening of international legal frameworks, rules, and norms binding upon all members of the international community with respect to their behaviour and mutual relations. The general acceptability of these results, that is, of the new legal order on the World Ocean, for the entire international community is attested to by their having been approved by virtually all existing States. The fact that even though the Convention has not yet entered into force (according to the procedure provided therein), it already has acquired extensive politico-legal recognition as an important international document of the modern period whose provisions and requirements are being absorbed and complied with in practice by virtually all States also is testimony to this.

The very dynamic process of the codification and progressive development of the principles and norms of the law of the sea has led to material qualitative and quantitative changes. By its legal nature the law of the sea has become conventional law. In essence all the principal customary-law principles and norms have been subjected to codification and consolidated in written international instruments – conventions, agreements, treaties, United Nations declarations, and the like. This has brought clarity and precision to the prevailing rules of the international community on the seas and oceans, facilitated their exact exposition, comprehension, and interpretation by various participants in this community, and, consequently, a more consistent practical implementation of all those rules.

This has been facilitated also by changes in the social nature of the law of the sea. All its principles and norms have become general-democratic in nature since they are the result of the joint law-creation of socialist, capitalist, and developing States. A similar transformation in the social essence of the modern law of the sea undoubtedly is an important contribution to the strengthening of international legal order on the seas and oceans.

Finally, striking changes have occurred in the socio-legal content and role of the modern law of the sea. One can even speak of a certain acceleration in the development of its normative content since in a very brief period of time the law of the sea has come to encompass in substance all types of State activities with regard to research and exploitation of the expanses and resources of the World Ocean which are known and accessible to the modern practice of international relations. Thus, together with the traditional types of use of sea expanses, new relations of States have become the subject of international legal regulation, brought to life by the socio-economic and scientific-technical progress in the realm of exploiting sea expanses and resources. Completely new legal concepts and categories in the law of the sea have emerged and been confirmed – the economic zone, waters of archipelagic States, the international area of the seabed, and others. New institutes of the law of the sea have arisen and the content of previously existing one has been much enriched. Now one can say without exaggeration that in the number of institutes and specific norms the law of the sea significantly determines the development of all other branches of general international law.

The modern law of the sea can be characterised as a whole as a very developed harmonious system of interconnected and mutually agreed principles and norms which are responsive to the urgent requirements of international relations with regard to exploitation of the World Ocean and to the tasks and interests of strengthening the legal order on the seas and oceans. All this has led to the fact that in our era the social value of the law of the sea has significantly grown.

The legal structure of the entire system of principles and norms of the existing law of the sea is not complex. The centre (the active centre of the entire system) is the basic principles of the law of the sea. Their requirements permeate the entire system of the law of the sea and therefore should be constantly taken into account when studying, interpreting, or applying in practice any individual rules or provisions of the law of the sea.

All the basic principles of the law of the sea are among the generally-accepted norms of international relations, which are closely and dialectically linked with other generally-recognised principles of international law and have an important place in ensuring the modern international legal order as a whole. Thus, for example, the principle of freedom of the high seas is not only a cornerstone and fundamental principle of the law of the sea, but is one of the most important principles of general international law. In characterising its significance, and also when classifying the generally-accepted principles of international relations, the principle of freedom of the high seas must be placed on the same level as such principles of international cooperation as the principles of respect for State sovereignty, territorial integrity, inviolability of frontiers, equality, and others, and not be relegated to the sphere of the law of the sea only. This conclusion is confirmed both by the history of the origin and subsequent progressive development of the principle of the freedom of the high seas and by the extremely urgent politico-legal significance it has for international cooperation today in resolving one of the global problems of mankind – exploitation of the World Ocean.

New principles of the law of the sea

The urgent requirement of international cooperation on the seas and oceans also is giving rise to other new principles of the law of the sea. Thus, in the process of formation, in particular, are the principles of the rational use and preservation of living marine resources, the principle of the freedom of marine scientific research, the principle of protection of the marine environment, and the principle of use of the World Ocean for peaceful purposes.

The essence and central arrangement or basic and principal legal requirement of the principle of the use of the World Ocean for peaceful purposes is to exclude the use or threat of force in the maritime activities of States and, consequently, to ultimately prohibit military activities of States on the seas and oceans and ensure in fact that they are used only for peaceful purposes. However, the practical realisation of this main requirement is possible only through specific prohibitions of military activities in certain specific expanses of the World Ocean or specific types of such activities. The 1982 Convention was drafted with this in view with regard to the principle of using the seas for peaceful purposes.

The purpose of the legal order on the World Ocean established by the Convention is to ensure the peaceful national economic exploitation of the seas and their natural resources. The entire content and all the principles and norms of the law of the sea consolidated in the Convention are directed towards this. The spirit and letter of the Convention come down to the fact that only "peaceful activities" are the "normal activity" of States on the World Ocean. But in so doing the Convention is obliged to take into account that "military activity" exists all the same and therefore specific limits and frameworks for such activities are provided in the Convention with a view to ultimately being prohibited and terminated on the World Ocean.

Soviet studies justly indicate in this connection that "States who participated in drafting the unified Convention at UNCLOS had the task of working out a regime for using the World Ocean for peaceful purposes."[6] Therefore the principle of the use of the World Ocean "reflects the aspiration of the majority of States that the seas and oceans always be an arena of peace, cooperation, and development of mutually advantageous relations between countries."[7] The contents of this principle, in particular, the "content of the formulation 'use for peaceful purposes' in the Convention may be correctly understood if it is linked not only with the United Nations Charter but also with the text of the entire Convention."[8]

The entire text of the Convention attests that only the peaceful exploitation and use of the expanses and resources of the World Ocean are lawful. On this basis all the provisions of the Convention relative to the legal status and legal regime of specific expanses of the World Ocean (territorial sea, exclusive economic zone, waters of international straits and archipelagic States, high seas), as well as the natural resources (economic zones, continental shelf, and international area of the seabed). This also appertains to the legal regulation of various types of functional activities of States, for example, the regulation of marine scientific research.

Priority is accorded to peaceful, economic, and scientific activities of States on the World Ocean, including the peaceful use by all countries of the sea lanes ordinarily used for international navigation, irrespective of whether such routes lie in the high seas or territorial seas, or in straits or archipelagic waters.

Therein lies the principal element of the normative content of the principle of the use of the World Ocean for peaceful purposes as the basic principle of the modern law of the sea.

Since the existing general international law does not yet prohibit "military activities" or a "military presence" on the World Ocean, but constantly and gradually augments the specific prohibitions relative to the types, individual acts, and spatial sea areas for such activities, the 1982 Convention takes this trend into account and the modern state of international legal regulation of armaments and military activities of States on the seas and oceans.

Therefore, a dialectical combination of the ultimate purpose of not permitting military activities on the World Ocean together with specific prohibitions of certain types or manifestations of such activity that have become truly attainable and agreed in a legal manner within the international community at the present stage of its historical development are characteristic of the normative content of the principle of the use of the World Ocean for peaceful purposes. An example of such a specific prohibition is the 1971 Treaty on the Prohibition of the Emplacement of Nuclear Weapons and Other Weapons of Mass Destruction on the Sea-Bed and Ocean Floor and in the Subsoil Thereof, as well as the 1985 South Pacific Nuclear

Free Zone Treaty. And these trends toward ensuring the peaceful use of the World Ocean are continuing and constantly being strengthened each day. Therefore, the Convention justly proceeds from the fact that similar specific prohibitions will grow and expand, enhancing thereby the progressively developing specific normative content of the principle of peaceful use of the seas and oceans.

The special position of the principle of using the World Ocean for peaceful purposes is sharply manifested in such central provisions of the 1982 Convention as those which speak of the high seas being *"reserved* for peaceful purposes," and the international seabed area being *"open* to use exclusively for peaceful purposes" (Articles 88 and 141; emphasis added).

As regards the prohibited types and and manifestations of military activities on the World Ocean, the provision that any military activity contrary to the United Nations Charter and other generally-recognised norms of international law is inadmissible and unlawful permeates many specific Convention provisions relating to legal order on the World Ocean. Illustrative in this respect, for example, are the Convention provisions ensuring the safety and peaceful character of international navigation, historically the major type of use of the World Ocean.

In recent years the USSR and other socialist countries favour considering the issue of limiting and reducing the level of military presence and military activity in appropriate regions of the World Ocean: the Atlantic, Pacific, and Indian oceans, and the Mediterranean Sea. A specific programme for a global resolution of naval problems and applicable to specific waters was set out in addresses by M. S. Gorbachev in Vladivostok (1986), with respect to the Asian Pacific Region; in Delhi (1986), with respect to the Indian Ocean; in Murmansk (1987), with respect to the North of Europe; and in Belgrade (1988), with respect to the Mediterranean Sea. It also was proposed to convoke a special conference to discuss questions of limiting the activities of naval forces and of reducing them.

This programme, in particular, makes provision for the prohibition of naval activities in agreed zones of international straits and areas of intensive international navigation and fishing; limiting the number of large-scale naval exercises in each ocean and sea theatre of military operations; and limiting the navigation of warships carrying nuclear weapons.

As a whole, the Soviet initiatives are persuasive evidence of the adherence of the new thinking to strengthening the principle of use of the World Ocean for peaceful purposes; their practical realisation undoubtedly will serve the future enrichment of the normative content of this important principle of the modern law of the sea.

Notes

1. M. S. Gorbachev, "Vystuplenie v Organizatsii Obedinennykh Natsii," *Pravda*, 8 December 1988.

132

2. *Ibid.* (emphasis added).
3. E. A. Shevardnadze, "Vystuplenie na 43-i sessii General'noi Assamblei OON," *Pravda*, 28 September 1988.
4. Quoted from A. P. Movchan, *Kodifikatsiia i progressivnoe razvitie mezhdunarodnogo prava* (1972).
5. A. M. Vasil'ev, *Pravovye kategorii* (1976), p. 181.
6. *Mirovoi okean: ekonomika i politika* (1986), p.515.
7. *Mirovoi okean i mezhdunarodnoe pravo: osnovy sovremennogo pravoporiadka v Mirovom okeane* (1986), p. 240.
8. S. V. Molodtsov, *Mezhdunarodnoe morskoe pravo* (1987), pp. 183–184.

DEEP SEABED MINING: THE PROTECTION OF PIONEER INVESTMENT UNDER THE UNITED NATIONS PREPARATORY COMMISSION

KENNETH R. SIMMONDS

There has been no more sustained, more complex, or more ambitious attempt the evolution of the law of the sea. During the last weeks of the Third United Nations Conference on the Law of the Sea (UNCLOS III), strenuous efforts were made on many sides to induce the group of industrialised States, led by the United States, to reconsider their objections to the deep seabed mining provisions in Part XI of what was then the Draft Convention on the Law of the Sea.[1] Of the various concessions offered, most important was the scheme for preparatory investment protection, or PIP, which was, on the final day of the Conference, incorporated as Resolution II annexed to the Final Act of the Conference.[2] The principal progenitor of the PIP scheme was Leigh S. Ratiner, then deputy chairman of the United States delegation to UNCLOS III. He has described his objective as to "... negotiate a grandfather clause, a mini-treaty within the Convention."[3] The "grandfather rights" would accrue to those consortia and State enterprises that had been engaged in preliminary exploration at certain deep seabed sites before the Convention was opened for signature. The consortia and State enterprises would be enabled to seek licences from the Preparatory Commission for the exploration of defined seabed mine sites; after the Convention came into force, they would have priority in the issuing of production authorisations, and their plans of work for the exploitation of seabed mineral resources would secure automatic approval by the future International Seabed Authority (ISBA).[4]

It was an imaginative scheme, and, after intensive negotiations in March and April 1982, appeared to have emerged as a viable compromise between the interests of the developing countries and of the mining industry elements in the industrialised countries for the interim period before ratification of the Convention. Yet the olive branch was not grasped by those to whom it was offered, and, since 1983, the protection of pioneer investors has been proceeded with in the Preparatory Commission in parallel with, and quite separately from, what has become known as the "reciprocating States' regime," which was established by the signature, on 2 September 1982, of a multilateral Agreement concerning Interim Arrangements relating to Polymetallic Nodules of the Deep Sea-Bed.[5] This Agreement, to which the original signatories were the United States, the United Kingdom, France, and the Federal Republic of Germany, was widened in 1984 to include also as signatories Belgium, Italy, Japan, and The Netherlands.[6] It thus

W. E. Butler, *Perestroika and International Law*, 133–146.
© 1990 *Kluwer Academic Publishers. Printed in the Netherlands.*

came to comprehend, within two years of the opening for signature of the 1982 United Nations Convention on the Law of the Sea on 10 December 1982, eight States with advanced ocean mining technology who were linked together in a regime entirely contrary to the PIP scheme and one that has been widely perceived as supplanting for all practical purposes the Part XI provisions of the 1982 Convention.[7]

It is the purpose of this article to review briefly the operation of the PIP scheme within the Preparatory Commission between 1983 and 1988 and to examine the registration of the first four applications received for the protection of pioneer investors. Such a review must, of course, take into account the parallel progress of the "reciprocating States' regime" and also seek to identify the principal elements in the continuing confrontation over the meaning and application of the concept of "the common heritage of mankind" in its application to the resources of the deep seabed.[8]

The PIP scheme

The Preparatory Commission, established under Resolution I annexed to the Final Act of the Conference, was given special responsibility for the establishment of the International Sea-Bed Authority (ISBA) and the International Tribunal for the Law of the Sea.[9] Membership of that Commission is open to States and other entities which have signed the Convention whilst observer status at its meetings is open to States and other entities which have signed the Final Act of the Conference.[10] Of the major potential ocean mining States which have been referred to, all, except for the Federal Republic of Germany, the United Kingdom, and the United States, have signed the Convention.[11] Although it was expected initially that there would be considerable pressure upon States to sign the Convention in order to secure full membership of the Preparatory Commission, so far the Commission has, like the Conference itself, proceeded by consensus rather than by vote for most items on its agenda.[12]

Resolution II had itself identified as potential pioneer investors a group of four States with State-owned or controlled enterprises (France, Japan, India, and the USSR)[13] and also a second group of four consortia, whose component corporations or enterprises came from one or more of eight States (Belgium, Canada, the Federal Republic of Germany, Italy, Japan, The Netherlands, the United Kingdom, and the United States).[14] It also allowed developing States to qualify for pioneer investor protection.[15] To be registered as a "pioneer investor" an enterprise, corporation, or consortium must have "a certifying State" which has signed the Convention.[16] The pioneer investor applicant is required to propose a seabed area large enough for two commercial mining operations but not larger than 150,000 square kilometres.[17] The application undergoes an examination process through committees appointed by the

Preparatory Commission, and, if approved, leads to the allocation of one portion of the site area to the pioneer investor and to the reservation of the other, commercially equivalent, portion for development by the Enterprise (established under the Convention as a separate legal entity to carry out mining activities on behalf of the ISBA either directly or through joint ventures with national or private entities).[18] The Enterprise is authorised to exploit its "reserved" site either alone, in joint ventures, or in collaboration with developing States; it may, alternatively, relinquish its "reserved" site for the benefit of developing States.[19] Essentially, therefore, the PIP scheme was designed not only to attract established consortia within the industrialised States, but also to underpin and to service the parallel system of mining promoted by the Part XI provisions of the Convention.[20]

The registration of pioneer investors by the Preparatory Commission

The Preparatory Commission held its first (two-stage) session at Kingston, Jamaica, from 15 March to 8 April and from 15 August to 9 September 1983.[21] During its first session, it established four Special Commissions of equal status with the Plenary.[22] These are (i) Special Commission 1 on the problems that could be encountered by developing land-based producer States likely to be most seriously affected by the production of minerals derived from the International Sea-Bed Area, (ii) Special Commission 2, for the adoption of measures necessary for the entry into effective operation of the Enterprise, (iii) Special Commission 3, for the preparation of rules, regulations, and procedures for the exploration and exploitation of the ISBA – the sea-bed mining code, and (iv) Special Commission 4, to prepare recommendations regarding practical arrangements for the establishment of the International Tribunal for the Law of the Sea. The Preparatory Commission also established a General Committee consisting of the Chairman and other officers of the Preparatory Commission and of the Special Commissions.[23] The General Committee acts on behalf of the Preparatory Commission as the executive organ for the administration of Resolution II on preparatory investment in pioneer activities relating to polymetallic nodules. The Preparatory Commission also agreed to take decisions by consensus on rules and procedures for the implementation of Resolution II.[24]

Meanwhile, in July 1983 the USSR became the first country to submit an application for the registration of a pioneer investor.[25] This move was followed by an application from India in January 1984.[26] France and Japan followed this lead and submitted applications for registration in August 1984.[27]

During its second session in 1984, the Preparatory Commission adopted a number of the draft rules on registration which had been prepared for it by the Law of the Sea Secretariat.[28] It also began discussion on issues such as the confidentiality of information supplied by pioneer investors and the composition and functions of the group of technical experts who were to study applications for registration.[29] It was not, however, able to take action on the applications already received from the USSR and from India because of a failure to reach agreement as to whether or not the applicants had satisfied the requirement that overlapping claims had been satisfactorily resolved between all prospective claimants to the prospective USSR and Indian mine sites.[30] Since the last date for the signature of the Convention had been set at 9 December 1984,[31] it was strenuously argued by a group of industrialized States that no potential claimant should be excluded at this stage and that the Commission was not yet ready to receive applications in conformity with Resolution II.[32]

These objections were eventually overruled but only after some acrimony. Multilateral consultations, initiated by Canada, had begun in July 1982 on arrangements for the exchange of claims coordinates and on procedures for the resolution of conflicts over boundaries.[33] The USSR took part initially in these consultations but later withdrew when Western countries insisted that even States which had not signed the Convention should be allowed to participate in resolving conflicts over boundaries. This demand, in the view of the USSR, was an attempt to circumvent the requirements of Resolution II. During the debates the Indian delegation claimed that India had offered to exchange coordinates with other potential pioneer investors and had in fact done so with the USSR.[34]

The agenda item on the adoption of regulations for the registration of pioneer investors and the consideration of the initial applications was not dealt with in the formal meetings of the Preparatory Commission in 1985 but consultations were undertaken informally by the Chairman with a view to resolving overlapping claims. Overlap problems existed between the proposed minesite areas of Japan and the USSR, and between those of France and the USSR, which were situated on the seabed between the Clarion and Clipperton fracture zones of the North East Pacific.[35] These east-west fracture zones are narrow bands of high fault scarps and volcanic ridges that are the inactive scars of transform faulting at the East Pacific Rise. No overlap problems were faced in respect of the Indian application, which concerned a seabed area in the Central Indian Basin of the Indian Ocean.

At the Geneva meeting of the Preparatory Commission in 1985 the Chairman was able to report that there had been a provisional resolution of the conflict between the overlapping claims of Japan and the USSR, but that the problems between France and the USSR had not yet been resolved.[36] At the same meeting the Commission adopted, on 30 August, 1985, a Declaration asserting that claims incompatible with the Convention regime for deep seabed mining "... shall not be recognized ..." and "... were illegal ..."[37] This followed a complaint submitted by the USSR following the receipt by the Soviet enterprise Iuzhmorgeologiia of a letter from the US-based Ocean Mining Associates (OMA) consortium stating that it had been issued, on 29 August 1984, with a licence from the United States National Oceanic and Atmospheric Administration (NOAA) for exploration in part of the International Sea-Bed Area of the Pacific Ocean.[38] This licence purported to grant to OMA exclusive rights to manganese nodules in the area identified and priority in respect of other seabed resources. At the adoption of the Declaration, the Chairman of the Commission said that it was his understanding that the Declaration commanded "... a large majority in the Preparatory Commission ..." but that a number of delegations present could not support it because of their concerns over some aspects of its substance and effects.

The NOAA in fact issued licences to four of the major United States-based consortia in 1984 and 1985; licences for seabed exploration were granted to the Kennecott Consortium, Ocean Management Inc. (OMI), and to Ocean Minerals Company (OMCO), as well as to OMA.[39] The coordinates of those licence areas lie between 14° and 11° N latitude, and 138° and 122° W longitude. The OMA affair appears to have spurred on the Preparatory Commission to a resolution of the original difficulties over the registration of pioneer investors, for, at the end of its fourth session, on 5 September 1986, it arrived finally at a comprehensive understanding on the procedures and a formula for the registration of the claims submitted by the USSR, Japan, France, and India.[40] This agreement on the implementation of Resolution II was probably the most significant development since the adoption of the Convention in 1982. It gave the four applicant States until 25 March 1987, to submit revised applications for registration. The applicants agreed that, upon the satisfactory completion of registration, they would relinquish parts of their application areas which might overlap with other potential applications by four consortia whose component elements were legally based within Belgium, Canada, the Federal Republic of Germany, Italy, Japan, The Netherlands, the United Kingdom, and the United States.[41] The understanding further gave any developing country the right to apply for registration as a pioneer investor provided that it had signed the Convention and satisfied the registration requirements.[42] It also gave to a group of all or several socialist states of Eastern Europe the right to apply for one pioneer minesite area before the Convention enters into force.[43]

This understanding was designed not only to speed up the initial registration procedures, but also, as was the negotiation of Resolution II itself in 1982, to convince potential pioneer investors at large that the Preparatory Commission was prepared and able to act equitably in the interests of all groups of States (including those so far outside the Convention) as well as those of the Enterprise. Once again, an olive branch was offered – but it was accompanied by a warning. Earlier in the year, on 11 April 1986, the Preparatory Commission had adopted a further Declaration, this time by vote, which reaffirmed its earlier Declaration of 30 August 1985 and rejected any claim, agreement, or action that was incompatible with the Convention and its related Resolutions as wholly illegal and devoid of a basis for the creation of legal rights.[44] It took this action in response to the issuance of licences for the exploration of parts of the International Sea-Bed Area by the United Kingdom, the United States, and the Federal Republic of Germany under parallel national legislation within the "reciprocating States' regime."[45]

The two meetings of the fifth regular session of the Preparatory Commission which were held in 1987 saw the culmination of almost five years of intensive negotiation. It had been expected that, following the understanding of the previous year, the revised applications of the USSR, Japan, France, and India would have been proceeded with immediately. Instead the applicant States requested, and were granted, a further extension of time until one week before the commencement of the second (summer) meeting of the Commission. The Group of Technical Experts, established in accordance with the terms of the understanding of 5 September 1986, was then convened in order to examine the applications and to report on them to the General Committee.[46] It was agreed that the application from India, on which there were no overlap problems, could be registered separately and individually. The applications from the USSR, Japan, and France were to be considered and registered simultaneously. The consideration of the revised application of India was concluded and the Preparatory Commission decided to register India as the first pioneer investor in the International Sea-Bed Area on the basis of the report it received from the Group of Technical Experts.[47]

The Indian application concerned an area of 150,000 square kilometres on the floor of the southern portion of the Central Indian Ocean basin. The Commission reserved from the Indian application an equal areas of equal estimated commercial value to that allocated to India for future development by the International Sea-Bed Authority.[48] The average element concentration of copper and nickel in the polymetallic nodules here is said to compare favourably with that of the nodules within the Clarion/Clipperton fracture zones area. There is, however, a wide variation in the density and population of deposits. India has in recent years predicted a rising demand for nickel, copper, cobalt, and manganese and taken the view that her national interests are well served by the regulatory regime set out in the provisions of Part XI of the Convention.[49] Whether she will be willing over a number of years to meet the costs of establishing her capability to prospect must, however, remain in doubt.

The registration of the Indian application for pioneer investor protection undoubtedly marked a significant step forward for the work of the Preparatory Commission. The Group of Technical Experts met again between 23 November and 5 December 1987 to examine the other three applications. The Group reported favourably[50] on each of the three applications, and on 17 December 1987 the General Committee formally adopted a decision to register the three applicants as pioneer investors under Resolution II.[51] The first round of registration was completed and the Preparatory Commission was thus enabled, at its most recent sixth regular session meetings, held between 14 March and 8 April and between 15 August and 2 September 1988, to turn its attention to the obligations, flowing from registration, of the pioneer investors and their certifying states.[52]

The pioneer investors

The Indian application for registration was submitted on behalf of the Department of Ocean Development of the Government of India.[53] The USSR application was made on behalf of the Soviet State enterprise Iuzhmorgeologiia.[54] The Japanese application was made on behalf of the Japanese enterprise Deep Ocean Resources Development Co. Ltd. (DORD);[55] this is a joint government-private industry enterprise which is the successor to the former Deep Ocean Minerals Association (DOMA). The French application was made on behalf of the Institut français de recherche pour l'exploitation de la mer (IFREMER), acting on behalf of the Association française d'études et de recherche des nodules (AFERNOD).[56] The various registration documents contain schedules of the co-ordinates of the areas allocated to the applicants and of those reserved for the use of the Authority. The diagram shows the disposition of the allocated and reserved areas in the Clarion/Clipperton fracture zone region in the Northeast Pacific Ocean following upon the decision of the General Committee of the Preparatory Commission to register the pioneer investor applications of the USSR, Japan and France on 17 December 1987.

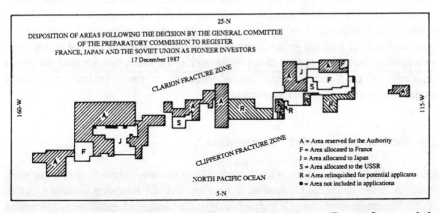

Areas in the Pacific allocated by the Preparatory Commission to France, Japan and the Societ Union as pioneer investors for manganese nodule exploitation, and areas reserved for the International Seabed Authority.

In the same region, as indicated above, but before the completion of the first round of pioneer investor application registrations within the Preparatory Commission, eight mining licences were granted to four licensees within the umbrella of the "reciprocating States' regime" outside the 1982 Convention.[57] Five of these licences were granted by the NOAA, which is an agency of the United States Department of Commerce, under the terms of the Deep Seabed Hard Mineral Resources Act of 1980.[58] Two were granted by the Federal Republic of Germany and one by the United Kingdom under national legislation.[59] The four licensees were the Kennecott Consortium,[60] Ocean Management Inc. (OMI),[61] Ocean Minerals Company (OMCO),[62] and Ocean Mining Associates (OMA).[63] These exploration licences fall clearly within the International Seabed Area as defined in Part XI of the Convention.[64] The performance requirements under these licences include ten-year exploration periods with obligations to conduct operations diligently and to submit annual reports and detailed, regularly amended, exploration plans to the licensor. There have been indications that OMCO may intend to file a commercial recovery permit with the NOAA by 1994.

There is a substantial current debate within the United States as to the degree to which the United States Government, as a resource owner and manager, should be involved in encouraging the pace of exploitation. There is more interest, however, at the present time in that country – and elsewhere – in hard minerals with development potential that occur within territorial seas or exclusive economic zones. Nevertheless, the NOAA has the authority to issue deep seabed exploration licences and commercial recovery permits for the area beyond the boundaries of national jurisdiction. This, under Articles 1 and 76 of the 1982 Convention,[65] is beyond the outermost edge of the continental margins as defined in the Convention. Licences give an authorisation of business activity to corporations which are subject to the jurisdiction of the licensing body and which are applicable outside the boundaries of national jurisdiction. It is precisely in the assertion of jurisdiction by a national licensing agency to activities within the ISBA that we find the prime challenge of the "reciprocating States' regime" to the regulatory machinery established in Part XI of the Convention.

The confrontation and the Convention

The principal new factors which have fundamentally altered the underlying premises upon which the confrontation between the UN licensing scheme and that of the "reciprocating states' regime" originally depended have been discussed elsewhere.[66] Market prices for the principal deep seabed products, nickel and cobalt, have become, and have remained, too low for short or medium-term operations to be regarded as economically viable. Many States have begun to look to meet their strategic needs for these resources in other ways. The discovery of polymetallic sulfides, phosphate nodules, and manganese crusts, some of which are found *within* areas of national jurisdiction, has transformed, from the point of view of the ocean mining industry, the context of the debate over the international regulation of deep seabed mining.[67] The considerable progress made in sonar technology has to some extent been offset by a lag in the development of efficient sampling tools because the market has not been large enough to encourage manufacturers to make the necessary investment of capital.[68] Above all, the almost exponential increase in the area of seabed *within* national jurisdiction over the past twenty-five years, added to an increasing uncertainty over the status of mining rights both inside and outside the Convention, has tended to divert attention from what was the prime concern of the UNCLOS III negotiations – the mining of polymetallic nodules within the ISBA.[69]

The confrontation and the polarisation of attitudes remains essentially based upon an ideologically-oriented division of objectives. The dangers inherent in such a confrontation were succinctly predicted by the late Deputy Secretary-General of the United Nations, Bernardo Zuleta, in a speech in Canberra in May 1983:

> The Law of the Sea Convention proved, if anything, that global accommodation is still possible. The Convention has now been signed by countries that represent 75% of the world population, 76% of the land portion of the earth and 80% of the total coastlines of the globe, and this includes all the political systems, all the regions of the world, highly industrialized countries and small island states, coastal states as well as landlocked countries. It is true that some countries have yet to realize that there is no viable alternative to global co-operation...[70]

Although the Convention is still inchoate,[71] it is increasingly influential. We must redirect our attention to Zuleta's words "... no viable alternative ..." The 1982 Convention has many grave flaws, not only in the Part XI provisions, and has in many respects failed to permit a secure, flexible and equitable accommodation of exclusive and inclusive interests in, and uses of, the marine environment. Yet, as Arvid Pardo, the progenitor of UNCLOS III, wrote recently,

> ... The conference ... is not the end, but rather the beginning of a long process which eventually must lead to a more cooperative and equitable world order if mankind is to survive.[72]

An historic step in that "long process" has been taken by the Preparatory Commission in its registration of the first four pioneer investors. Yet the registration itself will inevitably underscore the nature and the depth of the confrontation. As the Preparatory Commission continues, after its sixth regular session in 1988, to examine the obligations flowing from registration of the pioneer investors and their certifying States,[73] it will certainly watch with even greater attention than in the past the progress and attitudes of the "reciprocating States' regime." Even though the World Bank's recent projection that the growth in demand for the key deep seabed minerals during the 1990s will be lower than that experienced in the 1970s and 1980s[74] has deepened pessimism over the possible time scale for ocean

142

mining,[75] it has not dampened the enthusiasm of the majority of United Nations members for the regulatory system embodied in the provisions of Part XI of the Convention.

The World Commission on Environment and Development was established by the General Assembly of the United Nations in 1983 to formulate a "global agenda for change." Its report, published in 1987 under the title *Our Common Future*,[76] stresses throughout ecological and economic interdependence. The deep ocean floor, one of the so-called three "global commons" of our planet, represents both a resource and a responsibility. That is clearly recognised in the Convention[77] and in the interrelated series of compromises between interests that are reflected in its provisions. Just as that recognition underpins the Convention so it has led the vast majority of States in the world community to believe, or to profess to believe, that the management and disposal of ocean floor resources must rest upon common consent.[78] The UNCLOS III negotiations produced a Convention which demonstrates that the oceans, in part the responsibility of coastal States and in part the heritage of mankind, must be the subject of a global management system. The Convention embraces a socio-economic philosophy, derived from certain of the principles underlying the movement for a new international economic order, and a political philosophy concerned with the redistribution of wealth between nations, both of which proved unacceptable, when translated into the provisions of Part XI, to a small but powerful group of industrialised States. Yet we cannot judge the success or failure of the Convention as a whole by an analysis of the political, legal, and economic implications of the Part XI provisions.

The balance eventually to be achieved has been called "… the interplay of the equities …"[79] and it concerns the totality of maritime access and user, resources management as well as exploitation, and environmental protection and preservation. The confrontation between proponents of the Convention scheme for deep seabed mining and those of the "reciprocating States' regime" threatens the attainment of that balance and the orderly transformation of international law. The position of France, Japan, and the USSR in the continuing Preparatory Commission negotiations must be followed with great care since the philosophy of the "reciprocating States' regime" depends upon the premise that no credible threat to eventual deep seabed mining operations can be mounted by any State which does not itself have the capacity to mine.[80]

We may expect that, under its new administration, the United States will continue to assert that independent deep ocean floor exploration within the ISBA is not in violation of contemporary customary international law. She will be followed in this by the States associated with her in the "reciprocating States' regime," but none of them will seek an outright confrontation with licences or claims that overlap those protected under the Preparatory Commission's "pioneer investor" scheme. There are other hopeful signs. The USSR, which is not a party to the "reciprocating States' regime," adopted in 1982 an Edict on Provisional Measures to Regulate the Activity of Soviet Enterprises Relating to the Exploration and Exploitation of Mineral Resources of Seabed Areas Beyond the Limits of the Continental Shelf.[81] This was done as an interim measure, pending the coming into effect of the Convention, and claims to the establishment of "...sovereignty, sovereign or exclusive rights, jurisdiction, or the right of ownership ..." to seabed areas or resources were expressly denied.[82] More recently, the USSR has participated in a multilateral Agreement on the Preservation of the Confidentiality of Data Concerning Deep Sea Bed Areas, of 5 December 1986, with a group of States, some of which are within the "reciprocating States' regime."[83] The USSR has also joined with a similar group of States in an Exchange of Notes Concerning Deep Sea Bed Areas, of 14 August 1987,[84] designed to implement the provisions of the Agreement on the Resolution of Practical Problems with respect to Deep Sea Bed Mining Areas which was signed at New York on the same date. This last was intended to remove impediments, caused by overlapping or potentially overlapping claims, to the registration of pioneer investor applications with the Preparatory Commission. So the confrontation, although profound, has not prevented sensible, if limited, cooperation during the period of the "ideological stand-off." That cooperation, between all States with potential deep ocean mining capabilities, must be strengthened and widened in the search for a new basis of common interest and common consent.

Notes

1. The 1980 Draft Convention on the Law of the Sea is printed in R. Platzöder, *Third United Nations Conference on the Law of the Sea: Documents* (1982), II, pp. 365-538.
2. See K.R. Simmonds (ed.), *New Directions in the Law of the Sea* (1983-), Document U.1, pp. 19-25 [hereinafter Resolution II].
3. See C. Sanger, *Ordering the Oceans: The Making of the Law of the Sea* (1986), p. 187.
4. Established under Articles 156-169, 1982 United Nations Convention on the Law of the Sea [hereinafter 1982 Convention]. For the text, see note two above, Document U.2. Also see Articles 6-10, Resolution II.
5. This Agreement came into force upon signature and is printed in note 2 above, Document W.1.
6. Provisional Understanding Regarding Deep Sea-Bed Mining, done at Geneva 3 August 1984, entered into force 2 September 1984, and printed in note 2 above as Document W.8.
7. See A. Pardo, "The Law of the Sea. Its Past and its Future," *Oregon Law Review*, LXIII (1984), 7-17; D.L. Larson, "Deep Seabed Mining: A Definition of the Problem," *Ocean Development and International Law*, XVII (1986), 271-308.
8. See Simmonds, "The International Regulation of Deep Seabed Mining," *Oil and Gas Law and Taxation Review*, VI, no. 7 (1987-88), 191-198; no. 9 (1987-88), 246-252; no. 11 (1987-88), 306-310; VII, no. 2 (1988-89), 42-48.
9. By Resolution I, annexed to the Final Act of the UNCLOS [hereinafter Resolution I], Articles 1 and 5; see note 2 above, Document U.1, pp. 17-19.

10. Article 2, Resolution I.
11. A progressively updated table of signatures and ratifications of the 1982 Convention, together with a table of signatories of the Final Act, appears in note 2 above, Document U.3.
12. This was agreed to in a Memorandum of Understanding adopted by the Commission during its first session. All procedural decisions are made by simple majority. See notes 23 and 24 below.
13. Article 1(a)(i), Resolution II.
14. Article 1(a)(ii), Resolution II.
15. Article 1(a)(iii), Resolution II.
16. Article 5(a) and (b), Resolution II.
17. Article 3, Resolution II, and generally the 1982 Convention, Annex III (Basic Conditions of Prospecting, Exploration, and Exploitation).
18. Articles 8 and 9, Annex III, 1982 Convention.
19. Articles 144, 153(2), and 170, 1982 Convention.
20. Sanger, note 3 above, pp. 187-189.
21. UNCLOS, Report of the Secretary-General, GAOR (18 November 1983), pp. 4-6; *Law of the Sea Bulletin*, no. 3 (March 1984), pp. 28-34.
22. See the analysis of the first three regular sessions of the Preparatory Commission in Larson, note 7 above, pp. 286-293.
23. Consensus Statement of Understanding, 8 April 1983; U.N. Doc. LOS/PCN/3. The Rules of Procedure of the Preparatory Commission are contained in U.N. Doc. LOS/PCN/28 of 23 November 1983 and reprinted in note 2 above as Document M.1.
24. Consensus Statement, *ibid.* This Statement extended to the Preparatory Commission the list of decisions requiring consensus in the 1982 Convention (for example, Articles 160(2)(e), 161, 162; Annex IV, Article 11(3)(c)) and added other matters which would require consensus.
25. The documentation submitted by the Soviet Union in support of its application for registration is contained in U.N. Doc. LOS/PCN/99, reprinted in note 2 above as Document M.7.
26. The Indian documentation is contained in U.N. Doc. LOS/PCN/94 and Corr. 1, reprinted in note 2 above as Document M.5.
27. The French and Japanese documentation is contained in U.N. Docs. LOS/OCN/97 and 98 respectively, both reprinted in note 2 above as Documents M.4 and M.5 respectively.
28. U.N. Doc. LOS/OCN/WP.16.
29. The eventual agreement reached on the composition and functions of the group of Technical Experts is contained in Preparatory Commission: Statement on the Implementation of Resolution II (5 September 1986), U.N. Doc. LOS/PCN/L.41/Rev. 1, Annex, 11 September 1986, and reprinted in note 2 above as Document M.3.
30. See GAOR, 39th session, Agenda item 34, Law of the Sea: Report of the Secretary-General, 16 November 1984, pp. 22-23.
31. Article 305(2), 1982 Convention.
32. U.N. Doc. LOS/OCN/40 (Letter from the Canadian delegation to the Chairman of the Preparatory Commission).
33. See U.N. Doc. LOS/PCN/36.
34. See U.N. Docs. LOS/PCN/BUR/INF./R.1 and LOS/PCN/BUR/R.1.
35. See note 8 above, no. 7, p. 192.
36. See GAOR, 40th session, Law of the Sea: Report of the Secretary-General, 27 November 1985, pp. 30-31.
37. Declaration adopted by the Preparatory Commission, 30 August 1985; U.N. Doc.

LOS/PCN/72, reprinted in note 2 above as Document M.2.

38. The USSR complaint is contained in U.N. Doc. LOS/PCN/64.

39. See Larson, note 7 above, pp. 281-282. Also see the Note dated 13 January 1986 from the United States Mission to the United Nations addressed to the Secretary-General of the United Nations, to which is attached extracts from the *Federal Register* relating to the first five licenses issued by the NOAA to the four licensees under the terms of the Deep Seabed Hard Minerals Resources Act of 1980; the Note and attachments are repinted in note 2 above as Document W.10.

40. Note 29 above.

41. The consortia referred to in Article 1(a)(ii), Resolution II.

42. Note 29 above, and Article 1(a)(iii), Resolution II. Point 20 of this Statement in fact extends the scope of operation of Article 1(a)(iii), Resolution II.

43. *Ibid.*, point 21 of the Statement. This applies to Bulgaria, the Belorussian SSR, Czechoslovakia, German Democratic Republic, Hungary, Poland, Ukrainian SSR, and the USSR.

44. U.N. Doc. LOS/PCN/78. The declaration was based upon a proposal from the Group of 77. U.N. Doc. LOS/PCN/L.20.

45. See note 8 above, no. 11, pp. 308-309.

46. See note 26 above.

47. GAOR, 42d session, Law of the Sea: Report of the Secretary-General, 5 November 1987, p. 34. The report of the Group of Technical Experts is contained in U.N. Doc. LOS/PCN/BUR/R.1.

48. Note 26 above. The coordinates of the two areas (Area A allocated to the applicant State and Area B reserved for the conduct of activities by the Authority through the enterprise) are scheduled in the annex to this document, pp. 4-6.

49. On the prospects for a first generation minesite in the Central Indian Ocean, see M.R. Shyam, "Deep Seabed Mining: An Indian Perspective," *Ocean Development and International Law*, XVII (1986), 325-349.

50. U.N. Doc. LOS/PCN/L.55.

51. U.N. Doc. LOS/PCN/97-99.

52. See GAOR, 43d session, Law of the Sea: Report of the Secretary-General, 20 October 1988, pp. 40-41.

53. See notes 26 and 48 above.

54. See note 25 above.

55. See note 27 above.

56. *Ibid.*

57. See note 39 above and note 7 above, no. 11, pp. 308-309.

58. Larson, note 7 above, pp. 279-281; see M.R. Molitor, "The US Deep Seabed Mining Regulations: The Legal Basis for an Alternative Regime," *San Diego Law Review*, XIX (1982), 599-612; and W.B. Jones, "Risk Assessment: Corporate Ventures in Deep Seabed Mining Outside the Framework of the UN Convention on the Law of the Sea," *Ocean Development and International Law*, XVI (1986), 341-351.

59. The details of these two licenses are printed as Documents W.13 (United Kingdom, 21 December 1984) and W.14 (Federal Republic of Germany, 30 November 1985) in note 2 above.

60. The principal components of the Kennecott Consortium were: Kennecott Copper Corporation, Noranda Exploration Inc., Consolidated Gold Fields, Rio Tinto Zinc Ltd., British Petroleum, and the Mitsubishi Corporation.

61. The principal components of Ocean Management Inc. were: INCO, SEDCO, the AMR group (including Preussag AG, Metallgeschaft AB, and Salzgitter AG), and the

DOMCO group (led by Sumitomo).

62. The principal components of Ocean Minerals Company were: Lockheed, Standard Oil of Indiana, Royal Dutch Shell, and Royal Bos Kalis Westminster.

63. The principal components of Ocean Mining Associates were: United States Steel, Union Miniere, Sun Oil Company, and SAMIN.

64. Article 114, 1982 Convention.

65. See especially Articles 76(4) and (6), and 117, 1982 Convention.

66. See Simmonds, note 8 above, VII, no. 2 (1988-89), pp. 42-48.

67. *Ibid.*, pp. 44-45.

68. *Ibid.*, p. 44.

69. Pardo, note 7 above, pp. 14-15.

70. Extracted from a speech made to the Australian Mining Industry Council Minerals Outlook Seminar on 12 May 1983, and printed in *Law of the Sea Bulletin*, note 21 above, p. 6.

71. As of May 1989, 35 instruments have been deposited. The 1982 Convention will come into force twelve months after the date of deposit of the sixtieth instrument of ratification or accession. Article 308(1), 1982 Convention.

72. Pardo, note 7 above, p. 17.

73. Articles 7(b) and 12(a)(ii), Resolution II, among others.

74. See note 52 above, p. 43.

75. See C.G. Welling, "Mining of the Deep Seabed in the Year 2010," *Louisiana Law Review*, XLV (1985), 1249-1267.

76. World Commission on Environment and Development, *Our Common Future* (1987); and see E.M. Borgese, *The Future of the Oceans – A Report to the Club of Rome* (1986).

77. Preamble, paras. four and five, 1982 Convention. The other two areas defined as the "global commons" are space and Antarctica.

78. Former Ambassador Elliot Richardson, who led the United States delegation to UNCLOS III from 1977-80, was one of the first to express this view in Richardson, "Power, Mobility and the Law of the Sea," *Foreign Affairs*, VIII (1980), 918-919. See Larson, "The Reagan Administration and the Law of the Sea," *Ocean Development and International Law*, XI (1982), 297-320; *id*, "The Reagan Rejection of the UN Convention," *Ocean Development and International Law*, XIV (1985), 337-361.

79. Note 66 above, pp. 46-47.

80. *Ibid.*, p. 43.

81. The Edict is translated in W.E. Butler (transl. & ed.), *The USSR, Eastern Europe, and the Law of the Sea* (1983-) as Document F.1, and in note 2 above as Document W.3.

82. Article 2, para. one, *ibid.*

83. The Agreement, to which Belgium, Canada, Italy, and The Netherlands were also parties, is printed in note 2 above as Document W.11. It entered into force upon signature (Article 5).

84. The Agreement and the Exchanges of Notes are printed in note 2 above, as Document W.15. Belgium, Italy, Canada, and The Netherlands were parties, with the USSR, to the Agreement which came into force upon signature (Article 7). In the Exchanges of Notes the United Kingdom, on condition of reciprocity, agreed to be bound by the provisions of the Agreement. A similar Exchange of Notes took place at Moscow on 14 August 1987 between the Embassies of the United States, the Federal republic of Germany, and the USSR Ministry of Foreign Affairs.

INTERNATIONAL LEGAL PROBLEMS OF PREVENTING AN ARMS RACE IN OUTER SPACE

E. P. KAMENETSKAIA

On many occasions in the development of human society the question has presented itself: how should scientific discoveries and achievements be used, for what purposes? Often the answer suggested two opposite possibilities: peaceful and military. As a rule, the reality has been not "either/or," but "both." The "principle of dual usage" has operated.

Outer space has not escaped this fate. To be sure, there a balance exists between peaceful and military, and the balance is not so bad. But all the same, "dual usage" operates in this domain too. Exploitation of outer space is a history of the struggle and mutual influence of two trends: the aspiration to transform outer space into a domain of peaceful cooperation, and attempts to use it as an arena of military hostility.

It was evident even before the space era that outer space offered unique opportunities both for socio-economic progress and for new levels in the development of military technology. "The British dominated at sea and ruled the world. We were dominant in the air and were rulers of the free world. Now the situation is one of who will dominate in outer space."[1] "We strive for outer space ... because this is an expanse where it is possible to engage in military operations of a strategic scale with great effectiveness. The nation ... which enjoys the advantages of a new theatre of military operations ..., inevitably becomes the leading nation."[2] This is the philosophy of one of the two trends in exploiting outer space uttered by the first United States Presidents of the space age, John Kennedy and Lyndon Johnson, and by senior military and political figures at the beginning of the 1960s.

What could and may prevent outer space being transformed into an arena of military competition, into an expanse filled with weapons? The answer lies not on the technical, but on the politico-legal plane. It is a matter of political will, of political decisions, of legal obligations. In this connection it should be emphasised that the essential factor in restraining the militarisation of outer space is international law. It has completely prohibited one action of a military nature and considerably limited others, which has led to the partial prohibition of the militarisation of outer space and the complete prohibition of the militarisation of celestial bodies.

At present the norms of limitation and prohibition with respect to the use of outer space for military purposes are contained, first, in universal agreements on outer space (for example, the 1967 Treaty on Principles Governing Activities of States in the Exploration and Use of Outer Space, Including the Moon and Other Celestial Bodies [Outer Space Treaty], and the Agreement on the Activities of States on the

W. E. Butler, *Perestroika and International Law*, 147–164.

Moon and Other Celestial Bodies [Moon Treaty]; second, in certain multilateral agreements which make provision for specific disarmament measures, a number of which also extend to outer space (the 1963 Treaty on the Prohibition of Nuclear Testing in the Atmosphere, Outer Space, and Under Water [1963 Treaty], the 1977 Convention on the Prohibition of Military or Any Other Hostile Use of Environmental Modification Techniques [1977 Convention]); and third, in bilateral Soviet-American agreements on limiting anti-ballistic missile defence systems (the 1972 Treaty on the Limitation of Anti-Ballistic Missile Systems [ABM Treaty] and the 1974 Protocol thereto) and on limiting strategic offensive weapons (1972 Interim Agreement on Certain Measures with Respect to the Limitation of Strategic Offensive Arms and the 1979 Treaty on the Limitation of Strategic Offensive Arms, which although signed, was not ratified by the American side and therefore has not entered into force).

Terminology

First one must dwell briefly on certain terms used in international agreements, scholarly literature, and the press. No one denies the need for a precise definition of legal concepts. However, no less obvious is the difficulty and sometimes the impossibility of developing them. If one speak of such concepts as "militarisation" (or "nonmilitarisation") of outer space, "military activity," "withdrawal of weapons," "peaceful purposes," and many others relating to the present topic, this difficulty will increase manyfold.[3] Many factors are the responsible for this situation, including the lack of a treaty consolidation of concepts, differences of interpretation in scholarly literature, political and military reasons, linguistic differences, competitive considerations, historical changes in concepts about phenomena, the ignoring or inaccuracy in giving certain facts, and many others.

For example, in Soviet literature military use of outer space is frequently understood as only missiles intended for destroying objects of the adversary. All "spy satellites" have been subjected to criticism. For many years it has not been accepted to speak of the use of space technology by the Soviet Union for military purposes. Only in 1985 did the USSR Minister of Defence bring a certain clarity to the issue, declaring that the Soviet Union also does conduct scientific research work on the military plane while exercising its extensive and multi-faceted space activities. However, this work was not directed towards creating a space strike weapon or anti-missile defence of Soviet territory. The object of similar work is the improvement of *auxiliary* means: early warning space systems, intelligence, communications, navigation.[4]

As regards satellites, in the opinion of Academician B. Raushenbakh, space technology, in particular, satellites, called national means for observing compliance with international agreements, make it possible for a State to gather objective information about the activities of the other party and be convinced of its own security. This situation strengthens the possibility of preserving peace and international stability.[5]

Recently both in the Soviet Union and abroad the term "militarisation" has come to be understood as including various types of military activities, including those of an auxiliary nature. Certain efforts to distort the generally accepted meaning of the word "military" (making it synonymous, for example, with "aggressive")[6] are of doubtful legitimacy; and do not help elucidate the truth. As Vereshchetin has justly commented, "semantic methods can not transform military activity into peaceful activity and vice versa; in any language peaceful activity remains peaceful, and military, military."[7]

Military activities may have an aggressive or a nonaggressive character. It cannot be asserted that international space law prohibits any military activity. Such activity is prohibited only on the moon and other celestial bodies. Only certain types of military activities are prohibited in outer space itself.

In defining militarisation in the broad sense, it should be stressed that the problem of weapons in outer space is a constituent part thereof.[8] This is the most dangerous form of militarizing outer space. Under present conditions it is doubtful whether one can really speak about prohibiting militarisation of outer space as the process of military use of space is taking place and it (with certain exceptions) is not expressly prohibited by international law. The use of space as a whole for peaceful purposes is proclaimed in international space law as an aspiration, as an aim, as a task for the future.

At the moment as a matter of priority the introduction, placing, and use of weapons in outer space must be prohibited. The more so since space is free of weapons. Placing them in outer space could materially complicate the task since, as experience shows, eliminating weapons already available is more difficult that not allowing them to be there at all.

Relationship to disarmament

Outer space has from the outset turned out to be organically linked with general problems of disarmament. Depending on the specific historical situation, this link has been treated superficially. It is noted in Soviet doctrine that the efforts to preclude or limit the military use of space have been pursued by the Soviet Union as part of those connected with the liquidation of American military bases near the boundaries of the USSR and other socialist countries; as a component of the programme for general and complete disarmament; within the framework of proposals for nuclear disarmament; within the framework of proposals to prohibit the placing of weapons of any type in outer space or not to allow the use of force in or from outer space; and within the framework of proposals regarding nuclear and space armaments.[9]

As already noted, even before the space era two trends were evident in exploring outer space, one of which we have mentioned. Now we consider several facts which characterise both the link of outer space with general problems of disarmament and the second trend. On 18 March 1957 the USSR submitted a document to the United Nations entitled "Proposal regarding the Reduction of Armaments and Armed Forces and the Prohibition of Atomic and Hydrogen Weapons."[10] Six weeks later a "Memorandum of the Soviet Government on Implementing Partial Measures in the Domain of Disarmament" was sent to the United Nations.[11]

The first Document spoke, in particular, of prohibiting atomic and hydrogen wapons, "... including missiles with atomic and hydrogen warheads," as well as international control over the prohibition of the use of missiles for military purposes so that such missiles would be "... used exclusively for peaceful purposes." The Memorandum raised the question of liquidating nuclear weapons of all types, including missiles of any size with atomic warheads, which would have meant intercontinental ballistic missiles were useless as strategic weapons. The IBMs, whose creation required significant material expenditures, were intended to launch nuclear weapons; in the absence of nuclear or other weapons of mass destruction, the intercontinental systems would be irrational since their use gave no strategic advantages.

The view was expressed in Soviet doctrine that the realisation of Soviet proposals in 1957 might lead to the complete prohibition of the military use of outer space since those proposals made provision for the prohibition of the principal and only means in those days for military use of outer space – the IBM.[12] But having in view what has been said about military use of outer space, it would be more correct to say that the acceptance of those proposals could have obstructed the path to a more dangerous form of military of outer space, which is connected with the penetration of weapons into space. But there remained other possibilities os using outer space for auxiliary military purposes (space surveillance systems, communications, early warning, and the like).

The Soviet proposals of 1957 also made provision for the liquidation of foreign military bases on the territories of other States and a significant reduction of armed forces and conventional armaments. The reasons for linking space and foreign military bases was obvious. The IBM had become an important means for defending the security of the Soviet Union and ensuring strategic stability. The IBM made it possible to reach the American continent in a short period of time. The United States had placed nuclear means in various countries close to Soviet frontiers as forward basing. In this situation a prohibition of only the IBM would clearly place the United States in a better military strategic position.

The Proposal of the Soviet Government on the prohibition of the use of outer space for military purposes, the liquidation of foreign military bases on the territories of others, and on international cooperation in the domain of studying outer space of 15 March 1958, later submitted to the XIII Session of the United Nations General Assembly, was of importance from the standpoint of the political approach to plans for exploiting outer space.[13] This Document was the first official proposal concerning ways of exploiting outer space after the space era had begun. In its Proposal the Soviet Union set out a position of principle with regard to space research, which included a prohibition of the use of space for military purposes; the liquidation of foreign military bases on the territory of other States; the development of extensive international cooperation in the domain of exploiting outer space; consideration of problems of space activities in the United Nations; the creation of a United Nations organ for international cooperation in space exploitation; and the establishment within the framework of the United Nations of international control over the fulfillment of obligations regarding the prohibition of the use of outer space for military purposes and the liquidation of foreign military bases. However, these proposals by the Soviet Union received a negative reaction on the part of the United States and certain other countries.

The next stage of the Soviet Union's efforts to realise the proposals regarding military outer space were connected with the putting forward of a programme for general and complete disarmament. In September 1959 the USSR submitted to the XIV Session of the United Nations General Assembly a Declaration of General and Complete Disarmament.[14] It was proposed to implement the comprehensive programme for destroying all types of weapons and disbanding all types of armed forces in three stages. In the third stage all types of nuclear weapons and missiles were to be destroyed together with other types of armaments. Thus, as the Declaration noted, "military missiles of all sizes will be liquidated and missile technology will remain merely as a means of transport and exploiting outer space to the benefit of all mankind."

In March 1962 the USSR submitted to the Committee of Eighteen on Disarmament a draft Treaty on general and complete disarmament under strict international control. The destruction of nuclear weapons was to begin with the destruction and cessation of production of all delivery systems for nuclear weapons, including missiles of all calibres and sizes. The destruction of combat missiles was to have been accompanied by the liquidation or, wherever possible, the switching over of launching pads or areas to peaceful requirements. Compliance with this provision was to be ensured through the assistance of specially created control groups which would be present during launches and would examine each missile or satellite before it was launched.[15] The position of the United States and certain other countries did not further consideration of the programme of general and complete disarmament.

From the beginning of the 1960s, work began on the creation of international legal norms directed toward the regulation of relations arising in connection with research in and the use of outer space. Questions of military outer space began to be considered in stages. The solution proceeded along the path of a partial prohibition of certain types of activity of a military character and the full prohibition thereof within specified spatial limits.

Activities regarding the working out of universal agreements on outer space were concentrated in the United Nations and, above all, in the Committee for the Use of Outer Space for Peaceful Purposes as well as in the United Nations General Assembly and other U. N. organs.

Important events in the sphere of limiting military activities in outer space occurred in 1963. Most significant was the conclusion of the Treaty on the prohibition of nuclear weapons tests in the atmosphere, outer space, and underwater. This agreement is not a "purely space" agreement since its substance is broader. However, as already noted, it is among those multilateral treaties on disarmament problems whose provisions have direct connection with outer space.

Article 1 of the 1963 Treaty contains the obligation of States-Parties "... to prohibit, to prevent, and not to carry out any nuclear weapon test explosion, or any other nuclear explosion ..." in the atmosphere, outer space, or underwater. Thus, there appeared in international law the first legally binding norm limiting military activities in outer space, namely prohibiting there any nuclear explosion, that is, explosions not merely for military but also for peaceful purposes.

Two United Nations General Assembly resolutions also were adopted in 1963 which, having the force of recommendations, made their own contribution to the formation of norms of international space law in general and to questions of limiting military activities in particular. The first of them, entitled "The Question of General and Complete Disarmament," called upon all States to refrain from introducing into orbit around the Earth any objects with nuclear weapons or other types of weapons of mass destruction. It consolidated the arrangement previously reached between the USSR and the United States on this issue. The second resolution was the Declaration of Legal Principles Governing the Activities of States in the Exploration and Use of Outer Space. It served as a sort of working variant of the 1967 space treaty.

The Treaty on Principles Governing the Activities of States in the Exploration and Use of Outer Space, Including the Moon and Other Celestial Bodies, laid the basis for the legal regulation of space activities. It consolidated, inter alia, also a number of specific principles prohibiting and limiting specified types of military use of outer space. However, before giving an analysis of the principles directly relating to the military use of outer space (Article IV), it is necessary to mention certain other principles regading all activities relating to the exploitation of outer space.

Thus, Article III of the space treaty consolidated the principle in accordance with which activities relating to exploitation of space must be carried on in accordance with international law, including the Charter of the United Nations, in the interest of maintaining international peace and security and promoting cooperation. It follows from this provision that such principles of international law as refraining from the use or threat of force, non-interference, peaceful settlement of disputes, and others also extend to outer space activities.

The space treaty consolidates a different legal regime for outer space itself and celestial bodies from the standpoint of military use – specified activities of a military character have been prohibited in outer space (partial prohibition of the militarisation of outer space); any activities of a military character are excluded on the moon and other celestial bodies (complete prohibition of the militarisation of celestial bodies).[16]

Thus, the moon and other celestial bodies "shall be used ... exclusively for peaceful purposes." The establishment of "military bases, installations, and fortifications, the testing of any types of weapons and the conduct of military maneuvers" is prohibited on celestial bodies (Article IV). Having regard to the advisability of participation in space flights of military specialists, especially pilots, the space treaty specially emphasises that "the use of military personnel for scientific research or for any other peaceful purposes shall not be prohibited. The use of any equipment or facility necessary for peaceful exploration of the moon and other celestial bodies shall also not be prohibited."

The moon agreement went farther in affirming the respective provisions of the space treaty, developing and clarifying them. First, the agreement extended the prohibition of any military activities to orbits around the moon and other flight trajectories toward the moon or around it.[17] Second, the agreement enlarged the exemplary list of prohibited types of activities on the moon. Thus, the document consolidated the duty not to introduce into orbit around the moon or on another flight trajectory toward the moon or around it objects with nuclear weapons or any other types of weapon of mass destruction, nor to establish or use such weapons on the moon surface or its subsoil. Provision also was made for prohibiting the threat or use of force or any other hostile activities or threat of performing hostile activities on the moon or using the moon with respect to the earth through artificial space objects or their personnel.

Although the space agreements directly provide for using the moon "exclusively for peaceful purposes," and also contain an extensive list of prohibited activities, some authors attempt to assert that so-called "non-aggressive" military activities are permissible on celestial bodies since the enumeration of prohibitions is exhaustive and the use of military personnel is allowed under specified conditions.

As already noted, military personnel may be used only for peaceful purposes; consequently, "pursuers" here has nothing in common with military activities. As regards the list, it is not exhaustive in breadth also because it contains a reservation relative to military specialists. Their special inclusion would not have been required if the list were not illustrative. At the same time, one must concur with Vereshchetin that if the space treaty had used with respect to the list of prohibited activities on the moon the words "in particular," as was done in the Treaty on the Antarctic (which contains practically the same list), the present disagreements could have been avoided.[18]

The space treaty prohibits in outer space only certain types of military activities. In accordance with Article IV, the Treaty prohibits placing in orbit around the earth any objects carrying nuclear weapons or any other kinds of weapons of mass destruction or installing such weapons on celestial bodies or stationing them in outer space in any other manner.

Without withdrawing outer space as a whole from the sphere of military activities, the space treaty proceeds along the path of prohibiting the penetration into outer space of the most dangerous weapons – nuclear and other kinds of weapons of mass destruction.

This article of the space treaty, in making clear on one hand the question that not all weapons but merely specified kinds have been prohibited in outer space, leaves certain problems unresolved. Above all, there is the absence of a definition of weapons of mass destruction. This problem goes beyond the space treaty, but is manifest therein. There are no doubts today the nuclear, chemical, and bacteriological weapons are among weapons of mass destruction.This proposition was consolidated in a resolution of the United Nations General Assembly in 1948.

Efforts to define weapons of mass destruction have been undertaken more than once. Although they have not been successful, an analysis of them enables the conclusion to be drawn that a characteristic feature of such weapons are their mass, indiscriminate character. In this connection it is doubtful that the utterances of certain journalists are correct that laser weapons have been prohibited by the space treaty since they are a weapons of mass destruction. The issue of laser weapons remains open.

In connection with Article IV of the space treaty, the issue is actively discussed in the literature as to whether the prohibitions contained therein extend to space objects of the "Shuttle" type and to intercontinental ballistic missiles. Without commenting in detail on this issue, it seems correct to adhere to the view of those specialists who believe that prevailing international space law does not prohibit the suborbital orbit of IBMs with nuclear weapons.[19] As regards the "Shuttle," to be preferred is the position of those authors who, while regarding it as a *space* object, believe that the principles and norms of international space law extend to the "Shuttle" and, in particular, the prohibitions of Article IV of the space treaty. At the same time, one must concur with the view that the emergence of this new type of space technology raises many legal issues which await resolution.[20]

Article IV of the Space Treaty

Quite a few works can be found in the literature on international space law devoted to Article IV of the space treaty. Those works contain various points of view and assessments, some authors clearly exaggerating the significance of Article IV and expanding its content, whereas others underestimate it.

Adherents of the first approach believe that the 1967 Treaty permits space to be used exclusively for peaceful purposes, that is, it prohibits any military use of outer space.[21]

The positions of proponents of the second approach have their nuances. These are the conclusion that it is impossible to use outer space only for peaceful purposes, and the proposal of carrying out "nonaggressive" military activities on the moon, and rejecting the binding force of space agreements concluded within the framework of the United Nations, and many others.[22] An example of this approach to the space treaty is the article by an American, G. Almond.[23] Some authors, for example, Almond, March,[24] and others, draw from such an evaluation of the treaty the conclusion that a cardinal review is essential.

Proposals to augment or review the space treaty also have been advanced on the official level. Thus, an Italian memorandum submitted in 1979 to the Committee on Disarmament attracted some attention; it proclaimed the intention to wholly prohibit military activities in outer space.[25] However, the memorandum did not prohibit IBMs and auxiliary military means. It spoke merely of the prohibition of anti-satellite systems, and not of the complex of measures ensuring complete demilitarisation of outer space. Similar "additions" would "... only undermine the space treaty, which is the fruit of lengthy negotiations and represents the sole balance of interests attainable under those conditions."[26]

As already noted, specified limitations of certain types of military activities in space are contained in a number of multilateral and bilateral agreements regarding various aspects of restraining the arms race. Thus, in 1977 a Convention was concluded on the prohibition of military or any other hostile use of environmental modification techniques which set out a number of prohibitions also with respect to outer space and celestial bodies.[27]

The bilateral Soviet-American agreements concluded in the 1970s contain very important quantitative and qualitative limitations on the military use of outer space. Thus, they limit to a strictly defined number the quantity of armed IBMs in the USSR and the United States, as well as ballistic missiles of submarines. Also established in the Soviet-American agreements are the qualitative limitations with respect to improving and creating specified new types of the said military space means.

These are the principal prevailing legal norms limiting military activities in space. On the basis thereof a substantiated conclusion has been drawn in Soviet legal literature that "the existence in international space law of prohibitions and limitations on the military use of outer space enables one to speak of the *international legal principles gradually being formed of the use of outer space for peaceful purposes*"[28] (emphasis mine – E.K.).

Trends of the 1980s

In the 1980s the issue of whether outer space should be an arena of cooperation or a sphere for an arms race took on special urgency. It became one of the principal issues of modern international relations. And again in this domain two opposite trends were in evidence whose origin dated back to the early years of the space age. What is to prevail: the "strategic defence initiative," presupposing the presence of objects with the newest weapons in outer space "for struggle against the strategic arms of the adversary" (instead of the complete destruction of nuclear weapons) or the idea of prohibiting any weapons in outer space, the prohibition of the use or threat of force in and from outer space?

The course of events at the end of the 1970s and beginning of the 1980s and later showed that the danger of weapons penetrating into outer space was becoming real. The technology for such a turn of events was ready, and the political decisions for such a "turn" had been taken. In this situation the Soviet Union put forward a whole series of large-scale proposals directed toward not permitting weapons in outer space. Here are some of them:

1981. A draft treaty on the prohibition of placing weapons of any type in outer space was submitted for the consideration of the United Nations.[29] The object of the initiative was to cover the gap left by the space treaty and to prohibit access to outer space not only of weapons of mass destruction but also any other weapons. The basis of the Soviet draft was the obligation "not to place in orbit around the earth objects carrying weapons of any type, not to establish such weapons on celestial bodies, and not to station such weapons in outer space in any other manner, including either on piloted spacecraft for multiple voyages of both existing types or other types which might appear in the States Parties in the future" (Article 1). The Soviet draft made provision for the prohibition of stationing in outer space all types of weapons, including those intended for the destruction of space objects, air objects, missiles in flight, as well as earth objects. With a view to ensuring the safety of space objects the draft consolidated the duty of States not to destroy, nor harm, nor interfere with the normal functioning or alter the flight trajectory of space objects of other States if they were placed in orbit in accordance with the purposes of the proposed draft.

The draft initiative received wide support in the United Nations; however, the United States opposed the proposal, endeavouring to reduce the essence of the problem to anti-satellite systems.

At the same time, certain comments were made in the literature with regard to a number of provisions in the draft. Thus it was noted that the draft does not introduce a prohibition against weapons stationed on earth or in the atmosphere and used against objects in outer space. It was stressed that, being directed against weapons in outer space, the draft did not contain a definition of the concept of weapons. Rather, the draft proceeded along the path of prohibiting specified actions with respect to space objects and not of working out a defintion of "weapons." Those actions prohibited by the draft might be effectuated not only with the aid of weapons, but also by means of an unarmed space object (for example, by means of a collision). It also was noted that the draft did not exclude the use or threat of force in outer space.

Finally, the draft made provision for control over the fulfilment of obligations assumed only with the assistance of national means; however, the idea of combining national and international control is preferable for a broad international agreement.[30]

1983. The USSR submitted to the United Nations a draft treaty on the prohibition of the use of force in outer space and from outer space with respect to the earth.[31] Simultaneously, the Soviet leadership declared that the USSR will assume the obligation not to first place in outer space any types of anti-satellite weapons, that is, to introduce unilaterally a moratorium on such launches so long as other States, including the United States, will refrain from placing anti-satellite weapons of any type in outer space.[32]

Above all it should be noted that the draft treaty, which in orientation and scope went beyond the 1981 proposals, developed and clarified the principle of the nonuse of force with respect to activities in outer space. Article I prohibits recourse to the use or threat of force in outer space, atmosphere, or on earth with the use of space objects in outer space or on celestial bodies. Article II contains an extensive list of prohibitions which should ensure the nonuse of force in space or from space and not allow the threat of force. Thus, the draft does not permit the development and testing of any weapons based in outer space for striking objects in space itself, as well as on earth or in the atmosphere.

Article II of the draft excludes the possibility of using not only space-based weapons as a means of striking objects on earth, in the atmosphere, or in outer space, but also any space objects in outer space or on celestial bodies. This provision of the draft took account of critical remarks made with respect to the 1981 proposals since illegal activities might be effectuated not only with the aid of weapons as such, but also through any space object.

The draft prohibits the destruction, damaging, or interference with the normal functioning, or alteration of the flight trajectory of space objects of other States. A prohibition against the testing and use for military purposes of piloted spacecraft is specially provided.

In accordance with the draft, States must eliminate existing anti-satellite systems and also not allow the testing or creation of new systems.

The XXX Session of the United Nations General Assembly approved this Soviet initiative. The results of voting in the Assembly were curious and illustrative. 147 votes were cast with respect to the Resolution. Only the United States voted against.

The Soviet initiatives of 1981 and 1983, just as later proposals regarding the inadmissibility of weapons in outer space, were considered not in the United Nations Committee on Outer Space, but in the Disarmament Conference at Geneva, in particular, at the Committe specially created in 1985 regarding the prevention of an arms race in outer space. By decision of the General Assembly, the problems connected with not allowing weapons in outer space are considered at the Conference in Geneva, and measures directed toward ensuring the study and use of outer space for peaceful purposes, in the United Nations Outer Space Committee and its subcommittees. There is a certain logic in this division if the problem of weapons in space is considered to be part of the global problem of disarmament; however, the artificial and ineffective division of issues of military and peaceful outer space is obvious. In this situation coordination of the activities of the Conference in Geneva and the U. N. Committee on Outer Space is required. However, as practice shows, this coordination is clearly inadequate. At the Conference in addition to problems on the inadmissibility of weapons of outer space, questions are discussed of the legal status of outer space, traffic rules in space, the immunity of space objects, the creation of safety zones in space, that is, issues far outside the problems of preventing an arms race in outer space and within the jurisdiction of the Legal Subcommittee of the U. N. Outer Space Committee.[33]

The situation cannot but arouse concern. It would be advisable to take measures directed toward ensuring greater coordination and a precise demarcation of the activities of the U. N. Outer Space Committee and the Committee for the prevention of an arms race in outer space of the Geneva Conference on Disarmament.

1985–1986. In 1985 the Soviet Union took an initiative to include on the agenda of the XL Session of the United Nations General Assembly the question "On International Cooperation in Peaceful Exploration of Outer Space Under Conditions of the Nonmilitarisation Thereof."[34] Certain provisions of the document submitted in this connection were materially developed and augmented a year later in a Letter of the Chairman of the USSR Council of Ministers to the United Nations Secretary-General.[35]

The proposals of 1985 and 1986 make provision for the development of cooperation in outer space on a qualitatively new level, define the purposes, tasks, and stages thereof, as well as the forms and methods for a cardinal improvement of the machinery for cooperation in using outer space, in particular through the creation of a World Space Organisation.

These proposals were positively received. But at the same time it must be acknowledged that some provisions of the Soviet documents of the mid-1980s aroused far from the same reaction. The reasons were several and require separate analysis and discussion. Here only two are dealt with briefly. They concern the 1985 proposal.

"Nonmilitarisation" of outer space is the term which was used in the Soviet official document. It is that, or more precisely the differences in its use, which as already noted constituted one of the reasons for a failure to understand the document and to a special distortion thereof. The fact is that in the document the term "nonmilitarisation" was used in a narrow sense; it means, as expressly noted in the text of the proposal, "the renunciation by States of the creation (including scientific research work), testing, and development of space strike weapons." In the West militarisation is understood in a broad sense, that is, relating to military activities in space generally, and not only to the stationing of weapons there. This inconsistency also played a negative role. The explanation of the term given in the document was not accepted, they did not see it or did not wish to see it, and they began to criticise the idea of the unlawfulness of any military activities in space.

The second moment was linked with the fact that in the 1985 proposal the development and improvement of cooperation was expressly and strongly linked with the task of ensuring the "nonmilitarisation" of space. The issue became too direct under the principle of "either/or." Such a categorical approach does not correspond to the realities of our life and therefore did not find great support.[36]

In March 1988 the delegation of the USSR submitted to the Conference on Disarmament in Geneva a Memorandum "On the Creation of an International Control System for Not Allowing the Stationing of Weapons of Any Kind in Outer Space."[37] The proposal again returned to the idea "... on the international legal plane of raising the issue of prohibiting weapons in outer space over the heads of peoples of other countries ..."[38] This idea had been set out in the Soviet draft Treaty on prohibiting the stationing in outer space of any kind of weapons. The Memorandum approaches the same purpose from a somewhat different aspect. The document speaks of the impossibility of creating a system of international control over the non-placement of weapons in space until agreement is reached on the prevention of an arms race in outer space. Thus, the control system (and it is unique in form and extent) becomes a means of not allowing the penetration of weapons in space.

An international space inspectorate could occupy a central place in this system, the chief purpose being to effectuate measures of control to see that any objects placed and stationed in space are not a weapon and have not been equipped as some kind of weapon.[39] The most simple and effective means of control might be an inspectorate at the site immediately before the launch of the object into space effectuated with the assistance of inspector groups which are permanently located at all polygons for launches of space objects. States must have transmitted information concerning each forthcoming launch to representatives of the Inspectorate, including the date and time of the launch, types of missile carriers, orbit parameters, and general information about the object being launched.

The aforementioned proposals of the 1980s concerning the nonadmissiblity of weapons in outer space contraposed the "strategic defence initiative" (SDI) put forward in 1983 by former President Reagan of the United States.

Strategic Defence Initiative

Soviet legal writings showed a number of inconsistencies of the SDI from the standpoint, first, of the Treaty on the limitation of anti-missile defence systems; second, a number of multilateral treaties and agreements (especially the outer space treaty and the 1963 nuclear test-ban treaty), and third, certain basic principles of international law.[40]

It is useful to dwell briefly on two or three aspects of SDI from the point of view of the ABM treaty, leaving aside the various interpretations of the treaty[41] and modifications of the "strategic defence initiative" itself as beyond the scope of this article.

The "strategic defence initiative" corresponds poorly to the *idea, purposes, and sense of the ABM Treaty*, which is directly expressed in the name of the Treaty and its preamble. The purpose of the ABM treaty is to limit anti-missile defence systems and maxmimally restrain the parties in the creation of such types of armaments. The principal task of the SDI is otherwise, to create a *new system* of anti-missile defence for the United States with space-based elements.

The authors of the "strategic defence initiative" believe that SDI does not represent a danger from the point of view of creating new kinds of weapons and violating strategic military parity since it is purely of a *defensive character* and is directed towards making nuclear weapons ineffective and unnecessary.

As regards nuclear weapons, world public opinion is aware of another much clearer and logical path which does not require the expenditure of trillions – the Soviet proposal concerning the complete elimination of nuclear weapons before the end of the twentieth century.[42] To speak these days of a purely defensive weapon is difficult since technology is constantly erasing the line between offensive and defensive characteristics of arms. Ultimately their possibilities are dependent upon the purposes for using aircraft, missiles, and tanks. In the view of specialists a space strike weapon having a range of 4–5000 kilometres can be used to inflict a first strike on objects in the atmosphere, on earth, and at sea.

However, even if the version that "SDI is a defensive system" is accepted, it should be specially stressed that the ABM treaty is aimed at limiting precisely that kind of weapon. Article 1(1) makes provision for the obligation "... to limit anti-ballistic missile (ABM) systems ..." The paradox of the Treaty at first glance is that it limits means of defence by proceeding from the organic link between strategic offensive and defensive weapons. At the Treaty preamble notes, "... effective measures to limit anti-ballistic missile systems would be a substantial factor in curbing the race in strategic offensive arms and would lead to a decrease in the risk of outbreak of war involving nuclear weapons."

The 1972 Treaty contains *territorial*, quantitative, and qualitative limitations on ABM systems. The Treaty prohibits the deployment of ABM systems on the territory of the countries (Article I(2)). The parties have the right to deploy an ABM system only for an individual region of their territory with a radius of 150 km. Thus, the ultimate task of the SDI, the creation of an "anti-missile shield" covering the entire territory of the United States or several of its most important regions, is not consistent with the provisions of the aforesaid Article.

Of important significance for the correct application of the Treaty is Article II, which defines both the *ABM system itself* and the *components* of the system. This Article, as well as a number of other provisions of the Treaty (for example, Articles III, IV, V(1), Statement E, and others), gave rise to especially sharp disputes in connection with the "new" interpretation of this Agreement.

Article II(1) contains an enumeration of what an ABM consists of. The enumeration is purely illustrative and *is not exhaustive*. Article II subsumes future systems as well and extends together with other provisions of the Treaty not only to the systems mentioned but also to those which may emerge as a result of technological development.

This conclusion is based, first, on the fact that Article II(1) contains the words "currently" before enumerating the components of the ABM system, which means that the enumeration includes only that known to the drafters of the Treaty at the time it was drawn up and concluded. Second, the Treaty, in accordance with Article XV, is perpetual. Therefore, it would simply not be logical to suppose that States, in concluding such an important agreement in perpetuity and connected with the development of technology, would not take into account the prospects of technological progress and undoubted emergence of new technology, and extend the effect of the Treaty merely to those technological systems which existed in 1972. The key to this interpretation is found also in other provisions of the Treaty, as well as in Statement E, which are directly linked with the question of the future or so-called "exotic ABM systems." This Statement supplements Article III of the Treaty, which provides for the possibility of deploying ABM systems only within the limits of mutually agreed limited regions.

The significance of Statement E is that, first, it proceeds from the possibility of the appearance in the future of "exotic ABM systems," and second, extends the effect of the Treaty to them, providing that new technology must not violate the meaning of the Treaty but on the contrary should be inscribed in its limitations. And third, inscribe future systems in the limitations of the Treaty and, in particular, Article III. Consequently, in accordance with the Treaty and Statement E the possibility of stationing ABM systems, both existing and future, is permitted only with respect to limited regions and system deployment areas. In this connection the specific limitations on such systems and their components are subject to discussion and agreement in accordance with Articles XIII and XIV of the Treaty.

Article V(1) of the Treaty contains one of the central provisions, in accordance with which the parties assume the obligation "not to develop, test, or deploy ABM systems or components which are sea-based, air-based, space-based, or mobile land-based." Thus, Article V places a barrier in the path of *space-based* ABM systems or components. However, SDI is directed towards the development of ABM systems with space-based elements.

It is with respect to this Article that the early disagreements were connected under the Treaty. The American side proved in every possible way that the present stage of SDI is of a preliminary, purely research character, and therefore is not a violation of the Treaty, in which "research" is not prohibited. The USSR took another position on this issue; however, wishing to avert the arms race spilling over into outer space, the Soviet Union submitted a proposal under which the parties, besides a joint decision not to withdraw from the perpetual ABM Treaty within a specified period and strictly comply with all of its provisions, would oblige themselves to prohibit the testing of all space elements of anti-missile defence in space except for research and tests done in laboratories.

In essence the Soviet side agreed with the interpretation of Article V of the Treaty prohibiting the creation, testing, and deployment of space-based ABM systems or components under which *reseach and tests within laboratories* (that is, without outer space) do not fall under this prohibition. Later the Soviet side submitted a proposal to negotiate at a high level with a view to determining what work with respect to anti-missile defence is permitted by the ABM Treaty and which is not.

Some allies of the United States gradually were drawn in various forms into the orbit of implementing SDI.[43] In addition to the "individual" participation of a number of Western European countries in SDI, a form of "collective" participation emerged in the guise of the "European defence initiative." Thus, the process of *involving certain countries in SDI* occurred.

For the United States the fact of involving its Allies in the implementation of SDI is not consistent with its obligations under Article IX of the ABM Treaty, which emphasises that the parties are obliged "... not to transfer to other States, and not to deploy outside its national territory, ABM systems or their components limited by this Treaty."

Since the ABM Treaty is a bilateral agreement, one can not speak formally about a direct violation of the provisions of the Treaty by the Allies of the United States. However, this agreement does not merely consolidate bilateral rights and duties of the parties. It treated a complex international situation of global significance. It is the special role of the Treaty for the fate of the world which also predetermines the duty of all States to facilitate compliance with it and not to create any prerequisites for violating it. Illustrative in this respect is one of the resolutions of the Bureau of the Socialist International, which noted that "... while formally a bilateral agreement, this Treaty serves as the basis for control over armaments whose preservation is the subject of legal concern by all peoples."[44]

Notes

1. *U. S. News and World Report*, 17 August 1964, p. 42.
2. Quoted from Iu. M. Kolosov, *Bor'ba za mirnyi kosmos. Kritika burzhuaznykh teorii kosmicheskogo prava* (1968), p. 40.
3. See, for example, International Law Association, Montreal Conference (1982), *Report of the Space Law Committee* (1982).
4. *Pravda*, 6 May 1985.
5. *Argumenty i fakty*, no. 30 (1988), p. 2.
6. See, for example, C. Christol, "The Common Interest in the Exploration, Use, and Exploitation of Outer Space for Peaceful Purposes: the Soviet-American Dilemma," *Revista del CIDA*, no. 10 (1985), 45–56; F. H. Lay, "Space Law: A New Proposal," *Journal of Space Law*, VIII (1980), 44; Iu. M. Kolosov and S. G. Stashevskii, *Bor'ba za mirnyi kosmos. Pravovye voprosy* (1984), pp. 49–57.
7. V. S. Vereshchetin, "Protiv proizvol'nogo tolkovaniia nekotorykh vazhnykh polozhenii mezhdunarodnogo kosmicheskogo prava," *Sovetskoe gosudarstvo i pravo*, no. 5 (1983), p. 81.
8. In English the expression "weaponization" is used.
9. See Kolosov and Stashevskii, note 6 above, p. 28.
10. Doc. DS/SC.I/49.
11. Doc. DC/SC.I/55.
12. See, for example, G. P. Zhukov, *Kosmos i mir* (1985), p. 36; Kolosov and Stashevskii, note 6 above, p. 30.
13. Doc. A/3818.
14. U. N. Doc. A/4219.
15. Doc. ENDC/2.
16. In Soviet literature it is noted that as regards the moon it would be more correct to speak not of demilitarisation, that is, not of the prohibition of military activities previously carried out, but of the inadmissibility of military use, of the prohibition of its militarisation. See, for example, E. G. Vasilevskaia, *Pravovye problemy osvoeniia Luny i planet* (1974), pp. 56–61; *Pravovye problemy poletov cheloveka v kosmos* (1986), p. 205.
17. In accordance with the agreement, the provisions relating to the moon also are applicable to other celestial bodies of the solar system besides the earth except for those instances when specific legal norms with respect to any of those celestial bodies are in force.
18. Note 7 above, p. 80.
19. See, for example, Kolosov and Stashevskii, note 6 above, pp. 47–48; A. I. Rudev, "Programma 'Speis-Shattl': politiko-pravovye problemy," *Sovetskoe gosudarstvo i pravo*, no. 4 (1981), p. 92; S. Gorove, *Studies in Space Law: Its Challenge and Prospects* (1977), p. 87.
20. See, for example, *Pravovye problemy poletov cheloveka v kosmos* (1986), pp.65–77.
21. See, for example, F. Nozari, *Kosmicheskoe pravo* (1979), p. 62.
22. R. Bridge, "International Law and Military Activities in Outer Space," *Akron Law Review*, XIII (1980), 664; A. Butler, "Peaceful Use and Self Defense in Outer Space," *Proceedings of the XXVth Colloquium on the Law of Outer Space* (1983), pp. 77–82; C. Christol, "The Use of Outer Space for Peaceful Purposes: Legal and Political Considerations," *Proceedings of the XXVIIIth Colloquium on tghe Law of Outer Space* (1986), pp. 4–7; J. Fawcett, *International Law and the Use of Outer Space* (1968), pp. 32–34.
23. G. Almond, "Military Activities in Outer Space – The Emerging Law," *Proceedings of*

164

the XXIVth Colloquium on the Law of Outer Space (1982), pp. 149–158.

24. S. March, "The Strategic Defense Initiative Debate: An Interdisciplinary Approach," Proceedings of the XXVIIIth Colloquium on the Law of Outer Space (1986), pp. 83, 91.
25. Doc. CCD/551/Rev.I.
26. Kolosov and Stashevskii, note 6 above, p. 34.
27. See A. I. Ioirysh, "Zapreshchenie voennogo ispol'zovaniia prirodnoi sredy," Sovetskoe gosudarstvo i pravo, no. 12 (1977), pp. 66–70.
28. Mezhdunarodnoe kosmicheskoe pravo (1985), p. 44; also see note 20 above, p. 211.
29. Pravda, 12 August 1981.
30. See for details A. F. Bur'ian, Mezhdunarodno-pravovye aspekty bor'by Sovetskogo Soiuza protiv gonki vooruzhenii v kosmicheskom prostranstve (1987), pp. 42–43; S. Danielson, "Examination of Proposals Relating to the Prevention of an Arms Race in Outer Space," Journal of Space Law, XII (1984), 6.
31. Pravda, 22 August 1983.
32. As regards anti-satellite weapons, see Disarmament: Problems Related to Outer Space (1987), pp. 27, 36, 43–46, 57, 66, 87.
33. See K. Schuttpelz, Statement on the Consideration of the Issue of the Prevention of an Arms Race in Outer Space at the Geneva Conference on Disarmament, InterKosmos Seminar (Berlin, 25–29 September 1988). mimeo. 12 p.
34. Pravda, 17 August 1985.
35. Pravda, 13 June 1986.
36. M. Smith, "Cooperation between the United States and the Soviet Union," Proceedings of the XXXth Colloquium on the Law of Outer Space (1988), pp. 85–91.
37. Izvestiia, 31 March 1988.
38. M. S. Gorbachev, Za beziadernyi mir, za gumanizm mezhdunarodnykh otnoshenii (1987), pp. 19–20.
39. The Memorandum attempted to define a weapon prohibited in outer space. Such a weapon is understood to be "... systems and devices based on any physical principles which from the outset have been created or re-equipped to strike objects in outer space, in the atmosphere of the earth, or on its surface" (a list of such systems and devices is to be agreed in the course of negotiations).
40. V. Vereshchetin, "'Zvezdnye voiny' protiv mezhdunarodnogo prava," Pravda, 4 August 1986. Also see S. A. Zdravomyslov, "Amerikanskie plany militarizatsii kosmosa i mezhdunarodnoe pravo," Pravovedenie, no. 3 (1985), pp. 38–46; A. Natal'in, "Protivopravnost' 'strategicheskoi oboronnoi initsiativy' SShA," Sovetskoe gosudarstvo i pravo, no. 11 (1985), pp.113–119.
41. See Vereshchetin, "Dogovor po PRO iego amerikanskie 'tolkovateli'," Sovetskoe gosudarstvo i pravo, no. 3 (1987), pp. 91–97; Vereshchetin, "Issues Related to Current US and Soviet Views of the Treaty: A Soviet Jurist's Perspective," in The ABM Treaty: To Defend or Not to Defend? (1987), pp. 105–120; S. Nunn, Interpretation of the ABM Treaty. 13 March 1987. mimeo.
42. Zaiavlenie General'nogo sekretaria TsK KPSS M. S. Gorbacheva (1986).
43. B. Docke, "The SDI Agreement and the Deployment of Patriot-Improved Systems: The Contribution of the Federal Republic of Germany Towards the Erosion of the ABM Treaty," International Colloquium on the Militarisation of Outer Space (1988), pp. 257–263.
44. Quoted from A. Bovin, Kosmicheskie fantazii i zemnaia real'nost' (1986), p. 65.

AIR AND SPACE LAW: LAYING THE TRACK AND LEAVING THE RAILS

R. K. GARDINER

A title which refers to "rails" may be thought to present the wrong analogy at the outset of a consideration of restructuring air and space law. Pleading metaphors rather than analogy risks disguising issues confronted when aviation was the subject of the speculation that contributed to the legal régime which was adopted for the infant activity. Nevertheless, the thesis pursued here of restructuring air and space law, when neither has reached an age where this would be thought a priority, is that in each case there has been from the start a tension or paradox which warrants examination.

Inertia makes it harder to change direction once this is established. If the right régime is set initially, there is a fair chance that it will pre-empt the forces that could otherwise prevent a healthy advance.[1] Yet if rules are laid down prematurely, or even simply early in relation to development of the activity which they seek to regulate, they may prove inappropriate. The best way, therefore, seems to be to set the track but be prepared for adjustments or an overhaul if required. In the face of rapid development, the need for such overhaul may arise soon. If no deliberate rearrangement is made, derailment is likely.

Taking air law and space law separately, there are certain aspects of air law which make it a particularly useful area of study if the objective is to inquire into modes of development of the law, into factors favouring cooperative régimes and projections from trends. The relatively recent growth of air law means that much of the necessary material is more accessible than in some other fields, or at least to be found in reasonably well-defined sources. Further, the factors bearing on the development of this body of law are readily identifiable and the areas of common interest strikingly apparent. More important perhaps, much of the relevant law, to the extent that there is a separate field of law specific to aviation, is largely homogeneous in its international aspect and for the most part written.

The present article consists of some observations on the development of air law, making comparisons with the law concerning the sea and its use; a look at defects in air law that have shown up recently; and speculation on lessons to be learnt from air law that might improve its structure and that of space law.

If the development of the law of the sea is taken as a comparison, it seems that some principles were long ago the source of debate and uneasy resolution while other parts of the legal régime remained uncertain at a very late stage in the development of use of the seas. Whether one takes as examples of long established principles the classical (Graeco-Roman) notion of *res communis* or the verbal

W. E. Butler, *Perestroika and International Law*, 165–176.

combat between Grotius and Selden leading to recognition of freedom of the seas, the major codifications of the "public" law of the sea awaited the middle and latter part of the present century. The establishment of an international organisation with a general remit in maritime matters came scarcely any sooner.[2]

Academic debate preceded, and accompanied, the development of air law;[3] but while it could certainly be argued that the influence of Fauchille in the early 1900s on the development of air law was as significant as the contribution of Grotius some three centuries earlier to the law of the sea, the codification of air law followed Fauchille's work much sooner than codification of the law of the sea followed Grotius. Thus the International Convention on Regulation of Aerial Navigation was signed at Paris in 1919. Although not universally accepted, it had a dominant effect on the development of the law on aerial navigation.[4] The Paris Convention laid down the track to be followed by air law, a track little altered by the Chicago Conference in 1944.

The Paris Convention also established an international organisation, the Commission Internationale de Navigation Aérienne ("CINA") which was to be the midwife for necessary new law and regulations at an early stage in the development of aviation and air transport. An important role was also performed by the Comité International Technique d'Experts Juridiques Aériens ("CITEJA") and the International Air Traffic Association.[5]

The rapidity of progress towards a code and an international organisation in the case of aviation may in part be attributable to the state of development of international lawmaking and international organisation prevailing at the relevant time, though other factors probably also contributed. While the sea is laterally adjacent to States, extending inland only by rivers and inland waterways, airspace is not solely or essentially a medium that lies between States' territory but is a pervasive superjacent medium affording possible direct access to the interior, rather than territorially peripheral contact.

Growing realisation of the significance of this difference between the sea and airspace was vividly reinforced by the experience of aviation's military potential in the war years of 1914 to 1918. This led to the demise of hopes of any régime directly analogous to that of the sea. Thus the proposal was rejected that there be "territorial" airspace to a certain height and freedom of navigation beyond that, a proposal which had previously shown some signs of sparking off a debate similar to that centuries before about sea areas and which had once carried hopes of a similar outcome.

Along with the achievement of the technical ability to exploit the air, defence or military considerations can be identified as two major factors influencing development of the law. The third factor was the potential for trade or commerce in the sense of the transport capability of aviation. This, together with the limitations in the range of aircraft during the early development of air law, produced the need for establishment of routes with appropriate supplies and other facilities at frequent intervals. Failure to agree any real multilateral commitment on unrestricted access to these necessities for regular air services marked the final break with any possibility of a direct parallel with freedom of the seas.[6]

It is true that in other aspects of aviation the experience of maritime activity produced comparable principles underlying the actual rules adopted. A good example is the notion of an aircraft as an instrumentality having at once attribution of nationality associated with registration and a legal régime identified thereby, both as regards activities on board and in large measure affecting operation of the craft. Even here, however, there was some advance in that as well as written rules in the Paris Convention itself there were detailed regulations in annexes applicable virtually from the dawn of aviation and capable of systematic amendment through the work of the CINA.[7]

It was, however, in the area of air transport law that the greatest divergence grew up, mainly after the adoption of the Chicago Convention in 1944, which followed the lines set by the Paris Convention, but which established a more comprehensive international organisation.[8] What proved impossible to agree at Chicago was any multilateral exchange of traffic rights, even overflight being left to a separate agreement,[9] with a further associated agreement completing an *à la carte* scheme.[10]

So it was that traffic rights, or "commercial rights," were left for negotiation between pairs of States on a bilateral basis, leading to a network of many hundreds, if not thousands, of agreements. Such agreements, in addition to covering matters specifically left out of the Chicago Convention itself, complement or supplement provisions of the Chicago Convention and other multilateral agreements.

Underlying the rules, bilateral and multilateral, is recognition of the inescapably international character of much aviation and consequently the need for a system of regulation and control which, even if implemented through national agencies for the most part, is nevertheless based on uniform rules and principles prescribed in treaties or the produce of international organisation and benefiting from a degree of acknowledged and structured relationship between various national legal systems and agencies and between them and the international system.

Where has this system been most successful? There have been perhaps two particularly significant successes. One has been in the technical field. Of course, safety requirements have to a large extent mandated a common interest in achieving the highest degree of universality in the rules of the air (the navigation rules equivalent to those which, so differently in various countries, govern use of public roads). Even where there are variations in common rules, the ICAO provides a good clearing house for distribution of information,[11] though it must be noted that there has long been concern that the scheme for notification of departures from standards and recommended practices has not been invariably respected and the Organisation has made efforts to encourage stricter compliance. Also at the technical level the organisation of international airspace has worked reasonably well, with authorities committed to responsibility for particular flight information regions, a system which allows for a high degree of cooperation under a supervisory umbrella provided by the ICAO.[12]

It is the ICAO itself which is the second significant success. Although many issues in which the organisation has a prominent role are politically highly charged, it has managed for the most part to devote its attention to its proper business without the political paralysis which can readily afflict international organisations. There are of course several other international organisations of a specialist and technical character which have largely avoided this pitfall; but few could be cited which combine such comprehensive membership with concern for an activity which involves international contacts occurring throughout the world on a continuous basis.

Where then has the system proved less satisfactory? Taking the three major influences already mentioned (that is technical development, defence or military concerns and commercial requirements) only in coping with technical advances and regulating civil operations to produce the necessary uniformity and cooperation has the system worked at all well; and the inability of the organisation to achieve detailed standards of airworthiness shows up a large gap in the ICAO's achievements even in the technical area. Once military and defence considerations enter the picture, a long trail of disasters with considerable loss of civilian life and equipment is found, culminating in recent years with the destruction of the Korean Airlines' aircraft operating flight KE 007 and the Iran Airbus brought down over the Gulf in July 1988.

Is it the legal régime that has been shown to be inadequate? It would be easy to lay the blame for such disasters at some other door. Further, it might be said that the general rules of public international law have failed to regulate these matters properly. Yet the rules about minimum standards of treatment for aliens, about issuing proper warnings of known hazards and limiting self-defence strictly, are well developed. Can one then say that the ICAO, which has been reasonably successful on the technical side, has failed to secure the safety of civil aviation?

Hamstrung by provisions which exclude any role for the organisation in matters which involve State aircraft (and thus military matters),[13] the Organisation has painfully tried to advance the legitimate interests of civil aviation by framing rules for protection of civil aviation which would, if implemented have consequences for military activities. This approach cannot, and does not, work properly. The constitution of the organisation is inadequate to cope with this. The member States should recognise that cosmetic measures do not provide the necessary régime for safe operations. Equally, as regards security against anarchic and terrorist assaults on civil aviation and its users, an effective legal régime has not emerged.

On the commercial side is an immensely costly and inefficient system for negotiating rights to use airspace for transport. Of course, given the great economic potential of air transport, the cost may be justified by the return achieved by individual States and their enterprises through this system. That it has, however, at times produced situations in which huge amounts of unused capacity (empty seats) are flown with consequent waste of the earth's energy resources, and that different airlines frequently operate between the same points at virtually the same time leaving the users with long intervals between services, seems to follow almost inevitably from a system which has failed to regulate matters on the basis of respect for general interests rather than in a manner which owes its being to the adoption of a legal régime acknowledging the property rights of States in, or their dominion over, superjacent airspace, rights which have only been allowed to interfere in a limited way with use of adjacent waters and the high seas.

Thus while a promising track was laid down in the Paris Convention, the path ahead needs to take account of those matters not foreseen and where the development of air law has gone off the rails. The threats to civil aviation from military action and from terrorist activities have been all too apparent; yet the legal response has been inadequate. Increasingly crowded airspace will also bring together environmental and safety factors to require a stronger role for the ICAO in relation to air transport.

The clear lesson for space law is that it is important for a proper institutional framework to be established from the start, with an organisation which can provide sensible and thorough direction for the development of the legal régime and which will be able to take action when unforeseen developments take place. There are also pointers to approaches which result in the greatest chance of acceptance and effective operation of appropriate rules. The system of Annexes embodying codes of regulations for particular aspects of aviation has much to commend it, though there are some drawbacks in the system. The weakness of the ICAO in dispute resolution is to some extent balanced by its role in investigating and reporting which may have helped, if not in resolving disputes at least in learning lessons from them.

Detailed study of such matters is not possible here. The summary conclusion for air law is that the Organisation needs an extension of its powers; that its efforts should be further concentrated on developing technical regulation of aviation; that it should avoid being dragged into the trap of confusing political statements with effective legal instruments; and that global, and environmental, rather than State interests will mandate a greater role for action with regard to air transport as well as air navigation.

What follows is a brief examination of the constitutional inadequacy of the ICAO to deal with dangers to civil aviation from military activity; some observations on legal measures bearing on protection of aviation against the terrorist threat; and some comments on the legal techniques adopted in some legal instruments concerning aviation.

Examining more closely the relationship of military and civil aviation, one sees that the regulation of military aircraft as well as civil aviation was attempted in the

Paris Convention. True it was regulation of rather limited scope, but that reflected the development of aviation at the time. The relevant provisions also harked back to shipping analogies rather than looking forward to likely developments and potential problems specific to aviation. Here a comparison between the development of the law of the sea and air law tends to favour the former with the progressive codification of certain rules governing merchant ships, State-owned vessels on commercial service, and naval vessels. In contrast, even the limited regulation of military aviation in the Paris Convention was retrogressively eliminated from the Chicago Convention with the blanket exclusion of all State aircraft from its scope.

Yet the very provision which defines State aircraft out of the Convention indicates the inescapable fact that there are points of contact between military and civil aircraft (or rather of the desirability of non-contact) in the requirement that States take account of the safety of civil aviation in framing rules for their State aircraft.[14] Elsewhere in the Convention one might also see signs of military considerations, notably in provisions such as those on prohibited or restricted areas which contain military requirements as one justification for such restrictions.[15]

Looking at the development of the Convention and associated legal regulation one sees:

(1) some activity under Article 3(d);[16]
(2) an amendment to the Chicago Convention itself to add a new Article 3 *Bis* in the wake of one of several instances resulting in the catastrophic destruction of aircraft;
(3) some reaction to the many cases of interception or action against civil aircraft which intrude, stray or otherwise excite a military response, leading to ICAO's adoption of an amendment of Annex 2 in 1986.[17]

As to implementing Article 3(d) of the Chicago Convention, the ICAO can have little strength to its elbow. This is largely left to the mercies of each State. Yet the fulfilment of the obligation to operate military aviation in a way that takes account of the need for civil aviation safety is a matter of continuing importance to the community and the provision is a peg, although a weak one, to support some activity by the ICAO.

That the problem is wider than that of interception is shown by the ICAO Report of its inquiry into the destruction of the Iran Airbus in July 1988.[18] This reveals the desperate lack of coordination between civilian air traffic controllers and the naval forces, even though the latter viewed their activities as intimately affected by aviation. The majority of the warnings given by the warship to the approaching aircraft were on a military frequency which the civil aircraft was not equipped to receive; nor was there a record of receipt of these warnings at the airport of departure such that they could have been relayed to the aircraft even if they could have been identified as directed to it. The civilian identifying code, continuously available from the Airbus' transponder, was not used in any but the last warning, and the warnings given on the civil air distress frequency were incomplete. Military and civil aircraft were using that airport and the airspace around the warships, yet liaison and dissemination of information to ensure safe operation of civil flights seems to have been poor or absent.

While the ICAO Report has great value as an exposition of the facts, and by that act alone performs an important task, the occurrence of this tragedy shows how hollow an achievement is a legal provision such as that provided by Article 3 *Bis* of the Chicago Convention which, even were it in force, would not provide a régime adequate to prevent such a disaster.

With the increasing pressure on airspace, a medium which is limited in extent (even if the upper limit is not yet defined), regulation of all activities in a manner sufficient to ensure safety of civil aircraft is essential. Coordination on an international basis, or following a clear formula established by the ICAO, will become increasingly necessary unless military and civil uses of airspace are to continue their uneasy co-existence with volcano-like eruptions causing violent destruction and loss of life.

In addition to the protection of civil aviation against military threats, measures to thwart the terrorist have long been on the international agenda. The Tokyo, Hague, and Montreal Conventions[19] failed to include obligations of a kind likely to have any significant effect on this problem area. Their provisions are subject to qualifications giving States such a wide margin of appreciation as to allow them virtually as much free reign in responding to security threats as they would have without the Conventions. In requiring States to provide in their criminal law serious penalties for the defined offences, the Conventions may have had some marginal beneficial effect; but there is little evidence that they have influenced the course of events.

The urge to commit to treaty form aspirations unclothed in properly formulated rules has recently been taken further by the adoption by the ICAO Council of a recommendation that States take into account a model clause on aviation security.[20] This model clause shows what may be a developing and unwelcome trend in treaty provisions. For its principal purport is to "re-affirm" existing obligations. Codification of customary international law may have the wholly admirable effect of making certain what was previously unclear and rendering firm obligations hitherto of uncertain value. Re-affirmation of legal commitments without any improvements has the opposite effect, particularly when the obligations reaffirmed were poorly formulated and of doubtful efficacy anyhow. To "re-affirm" an obligation (i.e., an already binding provision) carries with it the connotation that by its repetition a commitment becomes stronger. This suggests that it was less than complete in the first place. How many times does an obligation have to be reaffirmed for it to become binding?[21]

Thus one can foresee a pernicious trend of weak and ill-formulated obligations being repeatedly reaffirmed until such provisions become little more than political statements or propaganda, and thus treaties merely a public relations tool. Only to the extent that the model clause contains new obligations and commitments that are not qualified into non-existence by allowing States a free hand in how they choose to apply them, does the draft Article have any potential value; and that leaves precious little.

A model clause which encourages bilateral statements that as between States already party to the Tokyo, Hague and Montreal Conventions they "shall in particular act in conformity with the provisions" of those instruments, or assertions in relation to the Chicago Convention Annexes that they will "act in conformity with the aviation security provisions ... to the extent that such security provisions are applicable to [them]," make poor reading. More useful is a specific provision that "each party shall ensure that adequate measures are effectively applied within its territory to protect the aircraft and to inspect passengers, crew, carry-on items, baggage, cargo and aircraft stores prior to and during boarding or loading." But this, together with details (kept confidential if necessary) of what the best measures are and how they must be accomplished, should be established in standards applicable to all and not merely included in bilateral agreements among those prepared to include such a provision.

Thus the work of the ICAO in the field of aviation security is a particularly good illustration of the strengths of the organisation when it lays down standards and recommendations with expert advice on their implementation and its weakenesses when it's work is merely on the public relations front. Elaboration of an Annex (Annex 17) requiring States to take effective measures and work in technical bodies capable of assisting in their practical implementation is real action against the danger.

A conclusion one may draw from examining the military and the terrorist threats are that in the former case the ICAO needs a clear mandate to adopt provisions of general application which will ensure that at a minimum there is adequate communication and co-ordination between the civil and military arms to ensure the safety of civil aviation, while as regards aviation security technical standards which States must apply (or publicise their departures from such standards) are better than empty rhetoric.

In the failure to treat military and civil activities on an integrated basis (other than on paper) space law presents a developing parallel to air law. Yet in the context of laying the track and leaving the rails, space law shows many of the symptoms that constitute the syndrome seen in the development of air law, but advanced at an even smarter pace.

Some far-sighted principles have received a push at an early stage. If properly established, principles of non-appropriation, shared use and environmental protection could prevent some of the troubles that lie ahead. Yet many of these are poorly drafted and already fissiparous tendencies are entering the legal régime. The absence of a specialist organisation produces uncertainty over competence to produce a systematic régime. There are, of course, pitfalls in any attempt to carry over existing regulatory mechanisms into a new situation; and reluctance to establish rules where this does not yet seem necessary can be supported by some arguments.

Take, for example, the vexed question of where airspace ends and outer space begins. The three schools identified by Bin Cheng comprise the "functional", the "spatial" and the "wait and see."[22] In favour of the latter could be said to be the experience of air law, (and perhaps the history of the rules relating to the extent of the territorial sea).

While airspace of States was defined in terms of adjacency to sovereign territory, its upper limit remains undefined. Yet there has been little dispute arising from the absence of an upper limit to airspace. Characterisation of overflight without permission as being a violation of sovereignty has posed no apparent difficulty.[23] Probably the closest there has been to a problem analogous to those felt to arise in the case of outer space was the arrival of hovercraft. For this the question was whether the régime of the sea or that of the air should apply. The hovercraft was excluded from the ambit of air law by the addition of a rider to the definition of "aircraft" so as to exclude any vehicle which derived its support from the reaction of the air against the surface of the earth.

This rather lends support to the functional approach as a means for avoiding the difficulty of drawing a line in space where airspace ends and outer space begins. However, to opt out of a decision on the grounds of unpredictability is to ignore the predictable. Space shuttles which already operate are definitional hybrids deriving support from the reaction of the air at a certain stage of their flight while plainly entering the area of outer space and operating as a spacecraft at another stage. Transport craft capable of performing partial orbits are on the drawing-board and cannot be regarded as so futuristic to be ignored. Surface damage by objects returning from space is already an actual hazard.

Thus, the involvement of airspace in each of these examples, the difficulties that may follow from a chameleon-like craft able to change from space object so as to come within the definition of "aircraft," and the uncertain area of application of the developed régime for liability for carriage by air (if with over-multiplied options) as against the elaborated (if untried)[24] régime for liability for damage caused by space objects, all these should be enough to show that an attempt at definitions, even if later requiring refinement or modification, would be appropriate.

In the realm of potential conflict between military and civil uses of outer space a direct parallel with air law is not very far advanced. Already, however, the failure to ensure that adequate information is required to be notified under the Registration Convention[25] has meant that insufficient warning of dangers from nuclear power sources on board satellites is built into the international system. Already the new problem encountered in the oceans of providing for removal of spent production structures and the old problems of dangerous wrecks and environmental degrada-

174

tion from waste products are being repeated in the space orbits around the earth with spent military and civil hardware posing a long-term threat. Plainly it is essential that a sensible régime be established now to restrict the harm before it is too far advanced.

What, then, is required institutionally to achieve this? The ICAO has in large measure managed to provide a single machine for global consideration of aviation matters, not to the exclusion of useful regional work, but without undue functional overlap within universal organisations.[26] Yet for space, the United Nations Committee on the Peaceful Uses of Outer Space while working on several general problems shows signs of leaving some important matters to be treated elsewhere. The International Telecommunications Union has perforce arrogated to itself a role in the use made of the geostationary orbit. Yet if this is to be regarded as a space resource, principles for rights of access and equitable distribution would seem more appropriately the creature of a larger plan so that the ITU's work could be consistent with that. Thus it is not too early to establish a specialised agency to set space activities on the right track and to move from an organ of the United Nations to a specialised institution.[27] Such an institution must have the broadest constitutional remit.

As regards the content of rules, it is not enough merely to develop principles, particularly where (as with the present provisions bearing on risks of contamination of, or harmful changes to, outer space itself) the formulation of such principles is defective. Consultative machinery and development of regulations of a technical character comparable to the system of the Annexes to the Chicago Convention need to be achieved. The lessons learned from the ICAO should be heeded.

Notes

1. This notion emerges very clearly from H. A. Wassenbergh, "Parallels and Differences in the Development of Air, Sea and Space Law in the Light of the Grotius Heritage," *Annals of Air and Space Law*, IX (1984), 163.
2. The treaty establishing the Intergovernmental Maritime Consultative Organisation was signed in 1948 and came into force in 1958. The Organisation changed its name to International Maritime Organisation in 1982.
3. A. Roper, in *La Convention Internationale du 13 Octobre 1919 portant Réglementation de la Navigation Aérienne* (1930), pp. 9–12, notes the extensive literature for the period 1891–1911.
4. Other multilateral Conventions signed between 1919 and 1929 at Madrid (never in force), Havana and Bucharest largely paralleled the Paris Convention.
5. The CITEJA was set up by the International Conference on Private Air Law in Paris, 1925, and first met in the following year. It had an important role in the private air law conventions. The IATA, in its original form, was established on 29 August 1919. Its successor is the now much criticised body the International Air Transport Association. Current criticism is often ill-informed and certainly the Association's early function

was not that of a cartel but a body acting very much in the general interests of aviation, for example, in attempting to ensure that there was uniformity in operation of certain aircraft controls, an important safety measure, and working on problems affecting all aspects of aviation. See J. W. S. Brancker, *IATA and What It Does* (1977).

6. The 1926 amendments to Article 15 of the Paris Convention deprived the provision of its potential for committing States along prospective aviation routes to allow others a free hand in setting up such routes.

7. On nationality, Article 7 set out particular requirements, namely that in the case of a company owning the aircraft the president or chairman and two-thirds of the directors had to be nationals of the state of registration. This is an example of how legal regulation began on the right track by ensuring that there was some real link. The particular provision did not survive to re-appear in the Chicago Convention and the nationality of airlines has perhaps assumed greater significance, particular for regulating commercial rights. Renewed interest in problems of nationality may well arise with increasing mergers and joint operations which may lead to important issues of safety and regulation. See belated (and probably unsuccessful) attempts to make real for ships the notion of a genuine link in the 1986 Convention on Conditions for Registration of Ships, *International Legal Materials*, XXVI (1987), 1229.

8. Work on legal matters became the province of the ICAO's legal committee which took over from CINA and CITEJA.

9. The International Air Services Transit Agreement.

10. The International Air Transport Agreement provided extensive commercial rights on a multilateral basis. The theory underlying the Convention and the two associated agreements was that states would select the instruments embodying the grant of rights which they were prepared to exchange on a multilateral basis. Despite initial American support, however, the broadest option failed to attract wide adherence and the USA soon denounced the Transport Agreement. The Transit Agreement has been more widely accepted but a number of states treat transit rights as a matter for bilateral negotiation, and some effectively put such rights up for sale.

11. See generally B. Cheng, *Law of International Air Transport* (1962) and T. Buergenthal, *Law-Making in the International Civil Aviation Organisation* (1969).

12. This assessment applies only to civil aviation. The failure of the international community to regulate properly the relationship of civil and military aviation in use of airspace is considered below.

13. See Article 3 of the Chicago Convention.

14. Article 3(d) Chicago Convention.

15. *Ibid.*, Article 9.

16. See Repertory-Guide to the Chicago Convention. ICAO Doc. 8900/2.

17. See M. Milde, "Interception of Civil Aviation vs Misuse of Civil Aviation," *Annals of Air and Space Law*, XI (1986), 105, where the constitutional problems of making effective rules for safeguarding civil aircraft in cases of interception are explained.

18. Report of Investigation as Required in the Council Decision of 14 July 1988, ICAO Doc. C-WP/8708, 7 November 1988.

19. 1963 Convention on Offences and Certain Other Acts Committed on Board Aircraft, Tokyo; 1970 Convention for the Suppression of Unlawful Seizure of Aircraft, The Hague; 1971 Convention for the Suppression of Unlawful Acts against the Safety of Civil Aviation, Montreal. See B. Cheng, "Aviation, Criminal Jurisdiction and Terrorism: The Hague Extradition/Prosecution Formula and Attacks at Airports," in *Contemporary Problems in International Law:Essays in honour of Georg Schwarzenberger on His Eightieth Birthday* (1988), pp. 25–52.

20. Resolution of 25 June 1986.
21. There may be good reasons for bilateral repetition if there is a risk of denunciation of a multilateral agreement and a need to continue treaty relations on a bilateral basis. For example, many bilateral Air Services Agreements grant rights which are already provided under the multilateral International Air Services Transit Agreement. If a State denounces the multilateral Agreement in the course of a bilateral dispute, it may nevertheless want transit rights to be granted in its bilateral relations with other States. No such justification is appropriate here where integrity and universality of the provisions (poor as they are) is a key factor.
22. B. Cheng, "The Legal Status of Outer Space and Relevant Issues: Delimitation of Outer Space and Definition of Peaceful Use," *Journal of Space Law*, XI (1983) 89.
23. See O. J. Lissitzyn, "Some Legal Implications of the U-2 and RB–47 Incidents," *American Journal of International Law*, LVI (1962), 135; and *Case Concerning Military Activities (Nicaragua v USA)*, ICJ Reports (1986), p. 14.
24. The Cosmos 954 incident did not put the Convention properly through its paces. The Canadian claim included the Convention as a basis; but it was questionable whether "damage" had occurred within the Convention's definition. The matter was settled without invoking the machinery envisaged by the Convention. See W. M. Reisman and A.R. Willard (eds), *International Incidents* (1988), pp. 68–84.
25. 1975 Convention on Registration of Objects Launched into Outer Space.
26. The sterile application in the 1958 Geneva Convention on the High Seas of maritime notions of piracy to aviation by simple textual addition showed perhaps that it is generally better not to meddle beyond one's own area of competence; but this must be qualified by recognising that the United Nations Conference on the Law of the Sea probably provided the most convenient occasion for regulating the airspace above the new maritime creations.
27. See V. Vereshchetin and E. Kamenetskaia, "On the Way to a World Space Organisation," *Annals of Air and Space Law*, XII (1987) 337.

LEGAL TECHNIQUES OF SETTLING DISPUTES: THE "SOFT SETTLEMENT" APPROACH

P. W. BIRNIE

> A lawyer as a social engineer must produce machinery to resolve
> differences or disputes between states. Where dispute resolution is
> organized, settlement is more likely to be peaceful. The structure
> of soft law assists in this aim.[1]

Traditional methods of settlement of legal disputes: their weaknesses

When lawyers refer to "dispute settlement procedures," it can generally be taken
for granted that they are referring either to establishment of a system of courts or
tribunals, which can give a binding decision in a contentious case, or, as in the case
of the International Court of Justice (ICJ), an authoritative Advisory Opinion on the
legal aspects of a contentious issue. The reference will often comprehend also such
machinery as establishment of a Conciliation Commission, which can only
recommend a solution that does not bind the disputing parties, or even the setting
up of preliminary bodies such as Commissions of Inquiry or Fact Finding Commissions, which can be used in both the political and legal dispute settlement process.
A typical approach is that of D. Harris who states, for example, "This chapter is
limited to the machinery for the settlement of disputes on a basis of law, whether
by arbitration or judicial," partly for reasons of space but also because such bodies
"necessarily apply international law so that their functioning is of particular interest
to lawyers."[2] However, he admits that litigation is very much a matter of last resort
and "in international relations most disputes are settled through negotiation
between parties or by third party assistance …".

It is notable that the Hague Conventions of 1899 and 1907,[3] and the General Act
for the Pacific Settlement of Disputes of 1928,[4] provided only for such machinery.
Most recently, the 1982 Convention on the Law of the Sea,[5] in its Part XV entitled
"Settlement of Disputes,"[6] after providing that States must settle any dispute
between them concerning the interpretation of the Convention by peaceful means in
accordance with Article 2(3) of the UN Charter,[7] and to this end that they must
seek a solution by the means set out in Article 33(1), does institute some innovations in these procedures. As well as providing for the option of using the ICJ, it
institutes in its section on "Compulsory Procedures Entailing Binding Decisions" a
specialist court and specialised tribunals, viz: an International Tribunal for the Law
of the Sea, and specialist as well as traditional arbitration panels, all of which can

W. E. Butler, *Perestroika and International Law,* 177–195.
© 1990 *Kluwer Academic Publishers. Printed in the Netherlands.*

give binding decisions on legal disputes. As an alternative, in some cases, a Conciliation Commission, the formal procedures of which are laid down in the Convention, is established to make recommendations to the disputing parties. The small print (Article 280), however, reserves the rights of parties to settle a dispute concerning application of the UNCLOS "by any peaceful means of their own choice". It is one of these means that is the subject matter of this article.

Article 33 of the United Nations Charter, referred to in the 1982 Convention, covers all disputes threatening international peace and security including not only legal ones but also those of a purely political nature – that is to say, those in which no point of law is in issue – or in which law and politics are mixed; it is thus more comprehensive in its approach. The Charter requires disputants to first of all seek a solution by peaceful means of their own choice and offers them an unlimited choice of means: "negotiation, enquiry, mediation, conciliation, arbitration, judicial settlement, resort to regional agencies or arrangements" or whatever other peaceful means the disputing parties themselves elect to use. Perhaps the reason why commentators so often think only of judicial or quasi-judicial tribunals as the means of resolving legal disputes is because the Charter goes on, in Article 36(3), to emphasise that the Security Council, in making recommendations for "adjustment" of disputes threatening international peace and security, "should ... take into consideration that legal disputes should as a general rule be referred by the parties to the International Court of Justice," but, as is well known, it was only in the case of one of the earliest such disputes to come before it, the *Corfu Channel Case*[8] in 1947, that the Security Council found it appropriate to make such a recommendation and the Court in general, until very recently, has been under-used. It is widely recognised that this is only in part because issues are predominantly political in nature and more because States, except in rare cases where vital national interests are not involved or a binding decision is vital, prefer not to be limited by binding decisions.

Except in commercial matters or in the rare case of a regional economic grouping such as the European Community, it appears that States are not particularly willing to resort to binding procedures and even non-binding procedures; procedures such as conciliation or fact-finding by impartial international commissions are not popular. Disputes over legal obligations occur virtually all the time, particularly in view of the vast changes that have occurred since World War II in the composition of the international community, its values, cultures and legal systems, which must now accommodate not only the aspirations of North and South, East and West, but legal systems based on very different histories and ideologies, both political and religious. Yet it is seldom that such disputes reach the stage of becoming so exacerbated or long-standing that they threaten international peace and security. They must then be being resolved by some other means, but how? It appears that though States are willing collectively to resolve problems they also want to limit the constraints upon them. They do this first by retaining discretion over the definition of the obligations they accept, and second by avoiding crystallizing these as legal obligations, sometimes combining both methods.[9]

How do States achieve the objectives of collective settlement but limited constraint? It is not possible to settle legal disputes simply by political negotiation, good offices, or mediation, since some change or harmonization in the law must result and some vehicle must be found for recording this. It will be the thesis of this paper that settlement of legal disputes is now largely facilitated, evidenced and effected by new developments in the law-making process itself: by increasing resort to new means of promoting and hastening the development of customary international law (including bringing about changes therein), the conclusion of treaties, and identification and application of appropriate principles.

New problems and perceptions concerning traditional methods of law-making

The three traditional methods of law-making referred to above have proved to be wanting in certain respects, given the almost irreconcilable differences between the approaches of different legal systems and the different goals of members of the present international community.[10] For example, customary law, except in rare instances, takes a long time to crystallise or to change; treaties, though useful when parties are sufficiently *ad idem* to accept specific solutions, require unanimity or at least widespread agreement and acceptance among interested parties to be successful. Legal principles, traditionally, have been given a restrictive interpretation by most commentators and courts, confining them to procedural maxims.

Yet one of the wider purposes of the United Nations, of which 159 States are now members, as expressed in Article 1(1) of the Charter, is "to bring about by peaceful means, and in conformity with the principles of justice and international law adjustment or settlement of international disputes or situations which might lead to a breach of the peace.[11] Article 1(3) adds the purpose "to achieve international co-operation in solving problems of an economic, social, cultural or humanitarian character." It must also be borne in mind that environmental problems and disputes are now occurring and would, it is suggested, undoubtedly also have been referred to had they been perceived as a threat in 1945, though as most of the peaceful solutions to these have economic and social implications, they in any case, already come within the purposes of the United Nations. Moreover, we must take account of the fact that in the context of disputes threatening international peace and security, the concept of "ecological" or "environmental security" is now being advanced by some States and writers, taking account of the growing concern of the whole international community for these matters and in the light of the accumulating scientific evidence concerning various potential threats to continuation of human, animal, and vegetable existence on our planet.

180

The mere possibility of such threats, whether or not they are substantiated, requires changes and developments in international law that are highly disputatious because of their economic and ideological implications and the threat that they will further erode the State sovereignty doctrine. It is notable that even in the case of serious environmental threats, disasters, and problems, which involve shared as well as national resources, formal dispute settlement has rarely been used. Such threats include those arising in connection with the *Torrey Canyon* and *Amoco Cadiz* type casualties; or in so-called "acid rain" damage; the "greenhouse effect;" radioactive fall-out from atmospheric nuclear tests and other possible threats from use and disposal of radioactive materials on land and in the sea; the Chernobyl power plant explosion; the destruction of tropical rain forests, and the endangerment from over-exploitation and habitat disturbance of numerous species of animals (including marine mammals and fish and plants). There has been little or no agreed resort to international tribunals in such cases, and such treaties as have been concluded provide only partial and limited solutions, while the customary law concerning the required standards of conduct and on the principles governing state responsibility are confused, uncertain and contentious. Similar problems arise in the related field of international economic law.

Treaties can resolve or avoid conflicts, but there are problems in negotiating treaties that lay down any clear or specific rules and of securing wide ratification, without reservations.[12] They also present problems as vehicles for changing the law as opposed to codifying it.[13] Their relation to customary law is also contentious. There are the further problems in today's multinational, multidoctrinal, international society of identifying customary international law itself and especially the necessary *opinio juris* when there are so many modes for its expression (State practice; resolutions of inter-governmental and non-governmental organizations, and of ad hoc diplomatic conferences; etc.).[14] It is increasingly difficult clearly to distinguish between what is *lege lata* and what *lege ferenda*,[15] and this too represents a conflict situation.

New processes in conflict resolutions: new approaches to law making?

New approaches to lawmaking, or perhaps, to put it more accurately, new *stages* of lawmaking thus are increasingly resorted to as halts, way-stations, or half-way houses on the winding road between no law and settled law. We can call in mind Codes of Practice, Recommendations, Guidelines, Resolutions and Declarations of Principles, promulgation of International Standards, and so-called "umbrella" or "framework" treaties, none of which fit neatly into any of the established sources referred to in Article 38(1) of the Statute of the International Court of Justice.[16] While clearly not being law in the sense required by these sources, nonetheless States expect that these codes etc. will command respect and be adhered to in the long-term as well as, as far as practical and possible given the particular situation of concerned States, in the shorter-term. As Judge Jennings has pointed out, deciding which of these vehicles has crystallised into customary law is in many areas "not just a question of enquiring, but also of policy choice."[17] As he also notes, the old tests are irrelevant since much of the new "law" is not custom: "it is recent, it is innovatory, it involves topical policy decisions, *and it is often the focus of contention*" (emphasis added).[18]

Such instruments are generally riddled with ambiguity, and deliberately so, for in this way they stave off the conflict by papering over the cracks and allow the negotiation to continue within a peaceful framework of reference. Many of these codes, etc. are concluded under the auspices of international organizations, which then provide a continuing forum for their further negotiation, elaboration, interpretation and a mechanism for monitoring their progress and effectiveness including, for example, their rate of and manner of incorporation into national laws and into treaties. Judge Jennings observes that materials which rival contending States put in evidence in cases before courts as State practice in support of their claim is often identical since each party can give such ambiguous provisions its own slant.[19]

This surely is the very point of the approach adopted in these instruments. They are not intended to be legally binding *per se* but to resolve the immediate conflict and gradually to influence practice. Such instruments should not be judged in the context of the familiar and now sterile debate concerning whether or not resolutions of the General Assembly have legal significance if voted for by the affected States or if they are subsequently and strictly observed by them, but by the extent to which they obviate the contention by expecting that participating States will conform their behaviour to them. The International Maritime Organization (IMO), the International Labour Organization (ILO), and the United Nations Environment Programme (UNEP) have done notable work in keeping such expectations live. Whether or not these codes, etc. attract consensus or unanimity or are acted on in practice, and whatever the status of the arguments concerning whether there is evidence of *opinio juris* or the difficulties of interpretation.

As Judge Jennings also recognises, in practice, courts and other judicial fora increasingly rely on and apply such resolutions even though they are *prima facie* merely recommendations since the standards established by international cooperation cannot be ignored;[20] some are so widely given effect as to be almost comparable to laws.[21] Much international law, including these codes, has to be enacted into and enforced by national legal systems and adjudicated in municipal courts. The codes, guidelines, and the like have much of their influence at this domestic level; that States do find them useful in resolving potential conflicts is increasingly obvious as relevant national laws and decisions referring to them proliferate. Moreover, in appropriate instances when they have the necessary powers, regional bodies such as the European Community or federal governments as in the United States or USSR may adopt and apply them.

Foreign ministers nowadays are probably more given to employing their advisers to sift through this mass of materials to find principles "friendly" to their argument to fire as peaceful salvoes – international legal counter-arguments – than they are to sending gunboats. Even if the latter are despatched, it is generally only after the ministries concerned have "softened up" the ground by a continuous barrage of legal opinions concerning the interpretation of instruments left deliberately vague, as in the Libya-USA incidents in the Gulf of Sirte,[22] or the US-USSR incident in the Black Sea.[23] Judge Jennings contends that it is "a mistake to try to force these newer trends and techniques into one or other of the compartments of the 1920 mould"[24] since they relate to all sources and to none. Courts have to take decisions, in his view, when they get a chance to do so, despite this problem; thus they identify the trends concerning the equities and decide as they think best in the circumstances. In evidencing trends and equities such codes contribute, not only to immediate conflict resolution, but to the ultimate binding settlement of legal disputes.

States can reduce tension by beginning to conform their conduct to internationally expected standards of behaviour leaving it to the longer term for other developments to occur that will finally resolve the dispute. Meanwhile States can expect that other States will behave reasonably and act in good faith (as befits their obligations under the United Nations Charter) in endeavouring to put these codes, standards, and the like into operation. They provide the States following them not so much with so-called "soft" laws but with a means of "soft settlement" of legal disputes, a "soft" stick with which to goad slow or recalcitrant States whilst avoiding the diplomatic affront to sovereignty and provocation involved in charges that another State has violated "the law" inevitably imply. The Hague Memorandum of Understanding on Port State Enforcement, referred to below, provides an excellent example of this point.[25]

The 1982 Convention is another example, based as it is on a series of negotiated texts, both the texts and the issues covered having been discussed and negotiated on a basis of consensus[26] for a period of ten years. The final treaty dealt with hard-core disputes by "constructive ambiguity" or subsequent development of "standards," thus postponing the conflict to subsequent negotiations.[27] It has been described as "brilliant invention and a new contribution to the resources of international diplomacy."[28] Certainly the negotiating process, the series of texts, the constructive ambiguities, the associated, and equally opaque, General Assembly Declaration of Principles Governing the Deep Seabed, the Resolutions attached to the Final Act establishing the Preparatory Commission (PrepCom) and Protection of Investment in Pioneer Activities Relating to Polymetallic Nodules (the legal status of which had been and still is disputed) have proved a brilliant device for resolution of conflicts in areas of seas and seabed over which many States had scattered the explosive powder of extended sovereignty and had detonated the fuses of unilateral claims.

Even without the 1982 Convention having come into effect, its provisions have been effective in staving off a violent eruption. The discipline of the negotiation and its approach having instilled, it is submitted, habits of accommodation rather than confrontation as the means of settling disputes, and the very existence of a framework text largely based on consensus having shifted the burden of "disproof" onto the States rejecting it, which encourages conformity. States conversely may rely on such codes to justify behaviour that would otherwise be unlawful, such as the imposition of certain sanctions to force adherence to them. They give a certain character to actions that would otherwise be lacking and serve to internationalize it[29] so that the actions in question can no longer be said to lie exclusively within one State's preserve: human rights, economic and environmental matters, all provide examples of this effect, justifying international intervention and refuting the argument that such action infringes Article 2(7) of the United Nations Charter.

Increasingly, international bodies and conferences are resorting to "framework" treaties and to non-treaty techniques to develop the norms necessary to promote international legal order and stability, particularly in economic and environmental fields which have many inter-relationships. These means are often now referred to as "soft law" and are regarded by many lawyers as a "second best" approach[30] because of their alleged lack of binding capacity and because it is not possible to negotiate a highly specific treaty, but this is perhaps unfair: particular techniques suit particular situations at the given time. Rather the new techniques recognise the differences between different sections of the modern international society, and that society naturally resorts to the most appropriate means of screening or harmonizing these differences and deflecting latent conflicts to the greatest extent possible.

Soft approaches to settlement of disputes

Although, in the present writer's view, the term "soft *law*" is unfortunate, insinuating that the approach is lacking because it is not law, whereas in fact it has great strength as a conflict resolution device and the term "soft settlement" is more accurate and thus preferable; nonetheless, because its use is now so familiar and widespread, the term "soft law" will be used here. So-called "soft law,"[31] which is "by its nature the articulation of a norm," includes both legal and non-legal instruments.[32] The recording in a written instrument of the necessarily abstract norms in issue agreed by States or international organizations is a vital part of this solution (unlike custom and some treaties). Soft law is characterized by allowing a relatively large degree of discretion to the parties.[33] Thus it enables States to take on some obligations that they otherwise would not simply because these can be very vaguely expressed. On the other hand, the converse may be the case since legal form may inhibit States from agreeing to specific obligations; soft law may appeal to them in particular cases and be expressed in a precise and restricting way so far as the obligation's content is concerned. But on the whole, it is the subjective element, the retention of States' discretion and control over the situation, that is its key attraction. At the same time the very existence of a "soft law" instrument stimulates a trend towards the "hardening" of the international order and subsequent use of such instruments enables them to be refined and interpreted.

The use of this technique attracts States in situations where, though they are prepared to tackle a problem collectively, at the same time they do not want too strictly to fetter their freedom of action. By using these means they can avoid immediate legal obligations and retain discretion concerning whatever obligations they do agree to undertake. This makes enforcement difficult, of course, but that is part of the attraction; it does not make all elements of the obligation unenforceable. It has always been difficult for States to agree widely or to agree on universally acceptable rules; it has become even more so in our multicultural world; former colonial territories seek the freedom and equality and the control over their own destinies that their colonial masters had and their emergence as independent States presents numerous, complicated, and seemingly intractable problems[34] so that international law has increasingly to take into account great differences in municipal law, national legal conditions, and cultures. It can only do this by adopting a flexible approach that respects State sovereignty whilst binding it with transparent and elastic threads. Given the subjects in relation to which such techniques have increasingly been used – human rights, economic, and environmental concerns – relations between States are involved both in the subject matter and in the formulations of the behavioural norms[35] which cannot be confined within State boundaries.

Soft law, in its various forms, can be found in resolutions of international organizations and diplomatic conferences, their decisions, their treaties, and other agreements. Its non-legal manifestations are the most diverse and include codes of conduct, generally formulated under the auspices of an international organization. They raise high expectations of conformity in conduct and uniformity in interpretation[36] (even of vague obligations to "co-operate") leading to consistency and thus orderly relations. Some such codes aim to regulate, *inter alia*, the conduct of individuals; they thus require enactment in national law and become enforceable; otherwise they are generally enforceable only by political means. As the codes are negotiated they meet the consensual requirements of dispute settlement between sovereign States as does the fact that they may also provide for exceptions or opting-out.[37] The international nature of the negotiation of such codes may have some influence on new parties to the negotiation; as one writer says, "non-parties may conform to the soft law norm because where there is no other norm, any standard has a certain attractiveness, depending on the number, importance and diversity of States involved."[38] Courts could also be similarly tempted when lacunae in the law occur.

Examples of "soft law"

(a) Trade law

As already pointed out, human rights[39] and economic law[40] have, since the advent of the United Nations, provided many examples of the use of these techniques. As these have been extensively documented elsewhere they will not be discussed here, except to note the marked shift in international trade law away from exclusive reliance upon traditional techniques towards a new approach, based on an "exercise of imagination" coupled with functionalism, which bears in mind the realities of the present international community. UNCITRAL's progress and policies have provided the model for this[41] by promoting harmonization and uniformity of practice, not by mandatory rules but by recommended and, therefore optional, adaptable rules[42] aimed directly at the elimination of the sources of disparities in national legal systems and the practices of private parties, and which are to be enacted by them.[43] These have been welcomed as the ideal mechanism for ordering trade inter-State relations, are often referred to as the rules governing disputes and have provided a model for the arbitration rules of arbitral institutions in many countries. This in itself has stimulated reform of such bodies, ensuring that their procedures are fair and widely acceptable and that their awards will be respected and implemented, thus stimulating recourse to such procedures.

(b) Environmental "soft law" solutions and programmes

(i) UNEP's programme
Developing international environmental law is difficult since it generally requires that States limit their freedom and that of their nationals and companies to conduct certain profitable economic activities. The United Nations Environment Programme (UNEP), following its institution in 1973 by the United Nations Stockholm Conference on the Human Environment (UNCHE) to fulfil a catalytic and coordinating role in developing measures to protect the environment, has taken an initiative in promoting the long term development of environmental law, within a pragmatic approach, following its 1981 "In Depth Review on Environmental Law."[44] Its main long-term programme, the "Montevideo Programme for the Development and Periodic Review of Environmental Law," was based on the report of an Ad Hoc Meeting of Senior Government Officials Expert in Environmental Law. The Programme has been integrated into the broader United Nations System-Wide Medium-term Environment Programme (SWMTEP) for 1984-89. The Montevideo Programme projects three categories of projects: (i) international agreements; (ii) international guidelines, principles, and standards; and (iii) international assistance for national legislation and administration to develop, apply and administer these.

(1) *Normative Conventions*: Much of the results will be embodied, as increasingly is the case in this field, in a "process of norm setting, norm-applying, and norm reviewing" in this field;[45] some norms are found in "framework treaties" such as the 1979 Convention on the Conservation of Migratory Species of Wild Animals,[46] which lays down broad general obligations and principles but leaves detailed regulation to the conclusion of Range State Agreements between States through whose territories and across whose boundaries threatened species migrate. The series of conventions for protection of the seas against pollution, known as UNEP's "Regional Seas Programme,"[47] are another example. In these the main "framework" convention lays down only general obligations to protect the marine environment, detailed protection typically requires optional separate adherence to specific Protocols on Prevention of Pollution from Dumping from Ships, on Co-operation in Combatting Pollution by Oil and other Harmful Substances in Cases of Emergency,[48] on Protection Against Pollution from Land-Based Sources of Pollution[49] (in the Mediterranean only) and concerning Mediterranean Specially Protected Areas.[50] In other fields UNEP has promoted the global framework Convention for the Protection of the Ozone Layer, the general obligations of which recently required to be elaborated by the Montreal Protocol to Protect the Ozone Layer against chlorofluorocarbons,[51] which itself now requires further protection.

(2) *Normative guidelines, principles and standards*: UNEP has now published ten sets of Guidelines and Principles on various aspects of environmental protection: These have stemmed from the generalised Declaration of Principles on the Human Environment adopted by the Stockholm Conference in 1970,[52] and relevant United Nations General Assembly Resolutions.

These include 15 Principles of Conduct in the Field of the Environment for the Guidance of States in the Conservation and Harmonious Utilization of Natural Resources Shared by Two or More States,[53] which were produced by a UNEP Working Group of legal experts; States were asked, in a General Assembly resolution,[54] to use them as guidelines and recommendations in the formulation of bilateral or multilateral conventions; reports to the United Nations on their progress have indicated increasing acceptance of them, for example, in ILC drafts on shared water resources, and in African inter-State practices. Handl, analysing the contents of the principle of "equitable use," hoping thereby "to cast light on its role in the avoidance of international environmental disputes in those potential conflict situations in which no specific norms regarding States' rights and duties are readily applicable,"[55] concludes that even in the absence of specific conduct-related standards, the legitimacy of a stated use of an international shared natural resource is now more extensively circumscribed by more readily available parameters than one might have expected through development of international objectives and standards. He considers that there are now clear and far-reaching procedural restraints – duties to inform and consult – aiming to negate transfrontier impacts by internationalizing the State's decision-making process. Clarity in the interplay of rights and duties in a situation of potentially conflicting uses of common resources will aid a non-disputatious solution whilst enabling maximum utilisation.

Riphagen points to the dispute potential of shared resources and concludes that classic approaches must come to grips with the solidarity imposed by natural conditions, and the "common heritage" and "shared resources" approaches must take account of the differences between States with respect to natural resources, technology, and social systems.[56] This the UNEP guidelines endeavour to do, but by generalisation. Provisions for Co-operation between States in Weather Modification[57] were adopted by UNEP in 1980 and recommended to states "to take into account". In 1982 UNEP endorsed the Conclusions of the Study of Legal Aspects Concerning the Environment Related to Offshore Mining and Drilling within the Limits of National Jurisdiction;[58] these included general requirements for pollution prevention concerning which States "should adopt" legislative and regulatory measures, provide appropriate machinery and ensure that their laws were no less effective than international rules, standards, and recommended practices. They also included provisions on an authorization system for offshore operations and on the need for and form of environmental assessment and monitoring (including of transfrontier impacts), safety and contingency measures and liability and compensations. The United Nations General Assembly recommended that States should consider these guidelines when formulating national legislation or undertaking negotiations for the conclusion of international agreements in this field. Progress has been reported.[59]

In 1984 UNEP adopted proposals for a Provisional Notification Scheme for Banned and Severely Restricted Chemicals[60] in order to provide experience which would assist the work of its Ad Hoc Working Group of Experts for the Exchange of Information on Potentially Harmful Chemicals (in particular pesticides) in International Trade; it included a requirement to notify other countries of the control action taken by a country to ban or severely restrict a chemical so that those other countries can assess the risk and take timely action. "Feedback" reporting to the UNEP Ad Hoc Group is required under the scheme.

In 1985 the Montreal Guidelines for the Protection of the Marine Environment against Pollution from Land-based Sources[61] were recommended to governments by UNEP, which encouraged States and international organizations to take them into account in the process of developing bilateral, regional, and, as appropriate, global agreements in this field. They were based on common elements and principles drawn from relevant existing agreements and the experience gained from their preparation and implementation, including the 1982 Convention and the 1974 Paris Convention on Land-based Sources.[62] They present a broad framework for development of similar agreements in regions where these are required and for preparation, in the long-term, of a global convention on the subject to ensure, *inter alia*, harmonization and application of global and regional rules. They provide a check-list of basic provisions rather than a model agreement, from which governments can select and adapt or elaborate upon as appropriate, to meet specific regional situations.

In 1981 UNEP adopted the Cairo Guidelines and Principles for the Environmentally Sound Management of Hazardous Wastes,[63] which not only made general provision for cooperation, prevention of transfrontier effects and for technology transfer, but covered preventive measures on generation and management of hazardous wastes and control over their disposal, transfrontier transportation, monitoring and safety, *inter alia*. They were addressed to governments with a view to assisting them in the process of developing policies for the environmentally sound management of these substances and were based on the common elements and principles derived from relevant existing bilateral, regional, and global agreements and national regulations and experience gained thereon. The balance contained in the Stockholm Principles (UNCHE) between the rights and duties of States over their natural resources and to the environment was particularly respected.

At present waste management differs greatly in various countries, according mainly to economic development. Though the Cairo Guidelines are not specifically addressed to developing countries, it is hoped that the guidelines will assist them to avoid costly problems of mismanagement. UNEP is currently endeavouring to facilitate negotiation of a Convention on Transport of Hazardous Waste but this is proving difficult because of North/South confrontations over the recent dumping of waste in Third World States.[64] UNEP also, in 1987, adopted a set of very general Goals and Principles of Environmental Impact Assessment and the generalised London Guidelines for the Exchange of Information on Chemicals in International Trade[65] addressed to governments to assist them in the process of increasing chemical safety in all States; again they have been derived from the common elements and principles of relevant existing bilateral, regional and global instruments and national legislation and experience related thereto. The guidelines aim at improving management through information exchanges, including exchanges of legal information and concerning banned and severely restricted chemicals. They complement related WHO and FAO guidelines on pesticides and should again help developing countries avoid expensive mistakes, especially concerning banned substances, without being especially addressed to their situation.

The World Charter for Nature[66] is also worthy of note in the context of this paper. Initiated by Zaire but drafted by the IUCN (International Union for Conservation of Nature)[67] and finalised by UNEP processes, the Charter was finally adopted in 1982 by the United Nations General Assembly, which stated that "the principles set forth in the present Charter *shall be* reflected in the law and practice of each State, as well as at the international level."[68] Its principles, directed at conservation of nature, are very general.

A Convention administered by UNEP but not drafted by it should also be mentioned, the 1973 Convention on Trade in Endangered Species (CITES).[69] Non-binding rules have been developed under it at the bi-ennial conferences of its parties, such as the Guidelines for Transport and Preparation for Shipment of Live Wild Animals and Plants.[70] It is one of the most effective and widely ratified wildlife conventions; the guidelines have had considerable impact since they provided standards which can be monitored and demanded by international and national non-governmental organizations (NGOs).

It will be seen that much of the considerable body of international law pertaining to the environment, often on highly controversial issues on which acceptance of restraints poses serious economic disadvantages, has been first developed through informal instruments of the so-called "soft law" type, despite some criticism.[71] Meanwhile new concepts are also emerging *ad hoc* from this process, such as inter-generational rights, themselves a source of dispute.[72] No doubt further "soft" elaboration of principles will be required here. There is, as the above account reveals, even with UNEP's co-ordinating role, a largely pragmatic approach to development of international environmental law; this is evidenced by the numerous other relevant treaties concluded outside UNEP, many generating other guidelines and standards.[73] Some further systematisation and harmonization seems to be required if conflict over dwindling natural resources, living and non-living, and pollution damage is to be avoided, accompanied ultimately by a hardening of the obligations in the guidelines.

(ii) IMO approach

The IMO has also played a major role in developing international environmental law concerning pollution from vessels and has made considerable use of the "soft law" approach to "soft settlement" of potential disputes. Its many conventions and codes have been outlined elsewhere;[74] the "jewel in its crown," however, is undoubtedly its non-binding International Maritime Dangerous Goods Code (IMDG) produced in cooperation with other United Nations bodies.[75] The Code was introduced by an IMO Assembly Resolution in 1965; it sets out in great detail the provisions and requirements applicable to individual classes of dangerous substances, materials, or articles carried by sea. It is constantly amended, revised, and rearranged to keep pace with and respond to the changing needs of shipping and the chemical industry and relevant developments in maritime transportation facilities and procedures. Its focus is more the safety of the ship and crew than protection of the marine environment, however, though no doubt the former contributes to the latter aim. In its General Introduction, the goods are classified; required marking, labelling, packaging, and documentation is prescribed and also carriage procedures; the remainder of the Code consists of provisions concerning nine specified classes of dangerous goods.

Special procedures have been developed to supplement the Code; they are intended to be the basis of national legislation by governments or act as operational guidelines for ship-owners, seaborne, and port personnel and cover many aspects of safety. Important also are the IMO's 1983 International Code for the Construction and Equipment of Ships Carrying Dangerous Chemicals in Bulk (IBC Code) and 1983 International Code for the Construction and Equipment of Ships Carrying Liquified Gases in Bulk (IGC Code),[76] which set international standards for safe transport by sea of the substances covered therein, including ship design and construction standards.

The IMDG Code's provisions on radioactive materials are based directly on the IAEA's (International Atomic Energy Agency) Regulations for the Safe Transport of Radioactive Material, recommended to governments by the IAEA General Conference as "the basis for national regulations" to be applied to international transport of such materials. Most recently IMO adopted Guidelines on the Decommissioning of Oil Platforms,[77] specifying the circumstances in which they should be totally removed and the standards for partial removal; these supplement Article 63(3) of the 1982 Convention and help to defuse the difficult situation created by the continued existence of the provisions of 1958 Geneva Convention on the Continental Shelf, Article V(6), which required total removal of offshore installations on disuse, and the new 1982 Convention Article which permits partial removal in some cases, subject to safeguards and taking account of any "international standards."

These Codes may not be legally binding *per se*, but they constitute an indispensable part of the current regulatory regime in the carriage of dangerous goods by sea, and supplement certain parts of IMO Conventions (MARPOL; SOLAS) and are essential to their meaningful application. The IMO Assembly recommended the IMDG Code to governments "for adoption as a basis for national regulation;" 45 States have enacted them, including all major shipowning States.[78] The regulatory regime for carriage of dangerous goods by sea includes the codes and recommendations in effect, as well as the relevant treaties; they are the "essential frame of reference" and additionally, therefore, are part of the criteria for determining question of negligence and responsibility, liability, and compensation for damage that will be used by courts before whom such claims can come under the relevant treaties.

The Hague Memorandum of Understanding, an agreement between governmental administrations, providing for inspection of a targeted number of vessels entering the ports of participating States to ascertain the extent to which they comply with certain specified conventions and codes of IMO and the ILO (International Labour Organization) illustrates a "soft" use of their "soft" standards; the port States do not provocatively arrest or detain the offending vessels but report them to their flag States, unless they pose a serious and direct threat to the environment.

Conclusion

The best technique for settlement of disputes concerning issues of law is that best suited to the particular circumstances of the case and the objectives aimed at. Sometimes this will be the conclusion of a treaty, or crystallisation of new customs, or even submission to binding settlement (as recently in many maritime boundary disputes), but increasingly, especially in relation to new issues and fields such as development of international economic or environmental law, which also involve disputatious regulation of the use of complex new technologies that pose serious threats to the environment including living resources, account has to be taken of these considerations with both speed and flexibility. Yet source points are often wholly within areas under national sovereignty, despite their adverse international impacts. "Softer" techniques may be much more appropriate here. Hence the lowering tempers at the Third Session of UNCLOS III (1975) when the negotiating text approach was adopted.

The use of "hard" techniques can exacerbate, not ameliorate disputes, and if these are adopted at the outset they can provoke more extreme and polarised positions than would otherwise be the case. "Soft settlement" by development of "soft law" standards can channel negotiations and lead to peaceful settlement. As one writer concludes,

> The norm will establish new standards of relevance for the negotiations between the parties. Certain arguments will be ruled out. The norm will establish the legal framework within which the dispute about its application may be resolved. It will establish presumptions, indicate the prevailing trend of opinion, provide a guiding principle which may have a certain inherent appeal for the parties and channel negotiation and settlement into legal and ordered paths.

The new techniques play as important a role in appropriate cases in promoting international stability and order as did and do the old, despite the difficulty of defining "soft law," which, in its widest sense, is no more than "a convenient shorthand to include vague legal norms." But the new processes represent the "play dough" out of which flexible mechanisms for conflict resolution from which soft, peaceful settlements can be moulded. As such, as lawyers, we should encourage them, not despise them.

Notes

1. T. Gruchalla-Wesierski, "A Framework for Understanding 'Soft Law'," *Revue de droit de McGill*, XXX (1984), 37–88.
2. D. Harris, *Cases and Materials on International Law* (2d ed., 1979), in the introductory

note to Chapter 12, p. 730. Also see I. Brownlie, *Principles of International Law* (3d ed., 1979), chapter 31.

3. 1899 Hague Convention for the Pacific Settlement of International Disputes, UKTS 9, (1901) Cmnd. 798 [establishing the Permanent Court of Arbitration]; 1907 Hague Convention for the Pacific Settlement of International Disputes, UKTS 6, (1971) Cmnd. 4575.

4. 1928 General Act for the Pacific Settlement of Disputes.

5. *United Nations Convention on the Law of the Sea* (1983).

6. On these provisions, see P. Birnie, "Dispute Settlement Procedures in the 1982 UNCLOS," in W.E. Butler (ed.), *The Law of the Sea and International Shipping: Anglo-Soviet Post-UNCLOS Perspectives* (1985), pp. 39–68.

7. Charter of the United Nations, in I. Brownlie (ed.), *Basic Documents in International Law* (3d ed., 1983), pp. 1–44.

8. *Corfu Channel Case*, ICJ Rep. (1948), p. 15; (1949), p. 4.

9. *Ibid.*

10. Note 2 above, p. 39.

11. See A. Casesse, *International Law in a Divided World* (1987).

12. R. Y. Jennings, "What is International Law and How do we Tell it When We See It?," *Annuaire Suisse de droit international*, XXXVII (1981), 61–65.

13. *Ibid.*, p. 66, where he points out that in the period between the two world wars, it was thought that one of the ways of preventing war was to find procedures of "peaceful change" in international relationships.

14. *Ibid.*, pp. 65–71.

15. *Ibid.*, p. 67.

16. Statute on the International Court of Justice, in note 7 above, p. 397.

17. Note 12 above, p. 67.

18. *Ibid.* (emphasis added).

19. *Ibid.*

20. As in Texaco v Libya: Compensation for Nationalized Property, *International Legal Materials*, XVII (1977), 17 [hereinafter *ILM*].

21. Note 12 above.

22. United States Note to the United Nations, 10 July 1985, on Libyan notices to mariners. *Law of the Sea Bulletin*, no. 6 (October 1985), p. 40.

23. W. E. Butler, "Innocent Passage and the 1982 Convention: The Influence of Soviet Law and Policy," *American Journal of International Law*, LXXXI (1987), 331–347. The United States proclamation of an exclusive economic zone is reproduced in *ILM*, XXII (1983), 461.

24. Note 12 above, p. 71.

25. He adds that courts in making innovatory decisions are "not exactly making new laws, but perceiving that familiar, existing materials form a pattern, when looked at in a right or just novel, perspective, which has not hitherto been fully appreciated." *Ibid.*, p. 75.

26. 1982 Memorandum of Understanding on Port State Control, *ILM*, XXI (1982), 1–30.

27. For a definition of "consensus" in this context, see the 1982 Convention on the Law of the Sea; but also see three other possible meanings outlined in *Annuaire Institut de droit international*, LXI (1986), 155–156.

28. P. Allott, "Power Sharing in the Law of the Sea," *American Journal of International Law*, LXXVII (1983), 1–30.

29. Note 12 above, pp. 87–88, where the author concludes that the 1982 Convention "is only one symptom of a generally new and rapidly changing position in international law, which reflects the major movements in international relations: the emergence of so

many new States into the international society; the aftermath of war and the 'decolonization' process; the realignments of power; military tensions between north and south;" all of which made for radical changes in international society and its methods of adjusting conflicts.

30. Note 1 above, pp. 58, 62.
31. K. Sono, "A Query into the Supremacy of the Traditional Treaty Approach – Experience of UNCITRAL with New Techniques," *Japanese Annual of International Law*, XXVIII (1985), 47.
32. "Soft" as distinct from "hard" law has been defined in various ways, but there is no uniform opinion on definition. Gruchalla-Wisierska uses it to describe provisions which employ the techniques of retaining State discretion over the definition of obligations whilst simultaneously avoiding legal obligations, whilst limiting constraints upon their actions. He identifies a "subjective" element (retention of discretion) and an "objective" element (a residual enforceable element) present when soft law is evidenced in a binding legal instrument or the legally binding decisions of an international organization. Some writers include both legal and non-legal norms; others restrict it to the former, when they are vague or weak. See *Ibid.*, p. 24. Also see M. Virally, "La distinction entre textes internationaux ayant une portee juridique dans leur relations mutuelles entre leur auteurs et textes qui sont depourvus," *Annuaire Just. de droit international*, LX (1983), 166, at 328–330; I. Seidl-Hohenveldern, "International Economic 'Soft Law'," *Recueil des cours*, CLXIII (1979), 173–175.
33. Note 1 above, p. 79.
34. *Ibid.*, p. 73, cited as an example of this the Framework Agreement between Canada and the European Economic Community under which the parties agreed to "take fully into account their respective interests and needs regarding access to and processing of resources" (Article II(1)(c)).
35. Note 1 above, pp. 1-2.
36. Note 12 above, pp. 191, 194, 195.
37. Note 1 above, p. 45. See this article generally for a full discussion of the numerous problems involved in a "soft" law approach; e.g., its legal/non-legal status; effects (direct and indirect); the effect of subsequent State practice; the political effect; interpretation; and the use of sanctions to force compliance; relation to *opinio juris*, and changes therein.
38. *Ibid.*, pp. 46–47.
39. *Ibid.*, pp. 49–50.
40. Note 1 above, p. 68 and n. 133. He refers to the "collective legitimization" and "collective will" effects; which also enhance the use of soft law as a guide to the negotiation and settlement of disputes (p. 69).
41. On Human rights, see Brownlie, note 7 above; on economic law, see Seidl-Hohenveldern, note 32 above and note 1 above.
42. Note 1 above gives many economic law examples and references throughout, including the United Nations Charter of Economic Rights and Duties of States (G.A. Res. 3281 (1974)); the 1976 OECD Guidelines (Declaration) on Multinational Enterprises, *ILM*, XV (1976), 967; and Decision of the Council on National Treatment, *ILM*, XV (1976), 978; the 1976 Framework Agreement between Canada and the EEC, *OJ Eur. Comm.* (1976), no. L/260. also see note 31 above.
43. Note 31 above, p. 48.
44. *Ibid.*, p. 50. Following its establishment in 1966, it moved from promoting rule-making, mostly through treaties, to preparing sets of uniform rules recommended for implementation by national legislatures or private parties, as appropriate. UNCITRAL's measures

194

include the UNCITRA Arbitration Rules, a Model Law on International Commercial Arbitration adopted in 1985, and two legal guides, which have proved popular. *Ibid.*, pp. 53–55. It proved easier to attract consensus on the Model Law than on a treaty, especially as the report on the negotiations thereof reflected all views on its provisions, thus providing a guide to interpretation. The guides on electronic transfer of funds and the drawing up of international contracts for construction of industrial works clarify the new legal issues, establish the common understanding and prevent growth of a legal vacuum on electronic funds. Rules on the legal status of computer records are now under consideration.

45. See generally P. H. Sand, "Environmental Law in the United Nations Environmental Programme," in *The Future of International Law of the Environment Colloque* (1984), pp. 51–88. Also see the UNEP publication of the same title (1985). Both give succinct accounts of the UNEP treaties, guidelines, and the like. Also see P. Contini and P. Sand, "Methods to Expedite Environment Protection: International ECO Standards," *American Journal of International Law*, LXVI (1972), 37–59.

46. Sand, note 45 above, p. 52.

47. *ILM*, XIX (1980), 869.

48. See *UNEP Activities Related to the United Nations Convention on the Law of the Sea* (1984); other regional seas conventions cover the Gulf, West and Central Africa, the South-East Pacific and South Pacific. Also see Sand, note 45 above, pp. 53–54.

49. 1985 Vienna Convention for the Protection of the Ozone Layer, *ILM*, XXVI (1987), 1529–1540; 1979 Geneva Convention on Long-Range Transboundary Air Pollution, *ILM*, XVIII (1979), 1442, the last developed by the U.N. Economic Commission for Europe (ECE) being another example of a framework convention concerning atmospheric pollution, to which specific "conduct" protocols have subsequently been negotiated on the highly controversial issues of sulphur and other chemical emissions.

50. UNEP Series on Environmental Law Guidelines and Principles, *Stockholm Declaration* (1973); Report of the United Nations Conference on the Human Environment, Stockholm, 5–6 June 1972, A/CONF.481/14/Rev.1 (1973).

51. UNEP, *Shared Natural Resources* (n.d.). On this question, see W. Riphagen, "The International Concern for the Environment Expressed in the Concepts of the 'Common Heritage of Mankind' and of 'Shared Natural Resources';" and G. Handl, "The Principles of 'Equitable Use' as Applied to Internationally Shared Natural Resources: Its Role in Resolving International Disputes Over Transfrontier Pollution," *Revue Belge de droit international*, XIV (1976–79), 40–64.

52. G. A. Res. 34/186, 18 December 1979.

53. Handl, note 51 above, p. 40.

54. Riphagen, note 50 above.

55. UNEP, *Weather Modification* (n.d.).

56. UNEP, *Offshore Mining and Drilling* (n.d.).

57. G. A. Res. 37/327, 20 December 1982.

58. UNEP, *Banned and Severely Restricted Chemicals* (n.d.).

59. UNEP, *Marine Pollution from Land-Based Sources* (n.d.).

60. 1974 Paris Convention on the Prevention of Pollution from Land-Based Sources, *UKTS* (1978), 64; K. R. Simmonds, *New Directions in the Law of the Sea*, IV, p. 499.

61. UNEP, *Environmentally Sound Management of Hazardous Waste* (n.d.).

62. It has been reported that the difficulties have been resolved; can one surmise that "soft law" will have been used?

63. UNEP, *Environmental Impact Assessment* (n.d.).

64. UNEP, *Exchange of Information on Chemicals in International Trade* (n.d.).

65. UNEP, *World Charter for Nature* (n.d.).
66. The IUCN World Conservation Strategy, IUCN-UNEP-WWF (1980) makes only very general reference to the development of law but places under its section on Priorities for international action, at 15: International action: Law and assistance. It states "Action should not be restricted to conventions: attention should be paid to some of the other ways in which international law develops, for example the exploration of new concepts and the elaboration of "soft law," such as the UNCHE Declaration since "it provides a set of generally agreed standards of behaviour ...".
67. G. A. Res. 37/7, 28 October 1982.
68. UNTS, DCCCCXCIII, 243–438.
69. Adopted at the CITES Conference in San Jose, Costa Rica, 1979.
70. Sand, note 45 above, pp. 65-66.
71. *Ibid.*, and E. Brown-Weiss, "The Planetary Trust: Conservation and International Equity," *Ecology Law Review*, II (1984), 495–581.
72. For the text of the main ones and comment thereon, see S. Lyster, *International Wildlife Law* (1986).
73. There is a huge literature on the IMO role, but see especially T. Mensah, "International Regulatory Regimes on the Carriage of Dangerous Goods by Sea." Paper presented at the Ninth International Symposium on the Transport and Handling of Dangerous Goods by Sea and Inland Waterways (TDG-9), Rotterdam, Netherlands, 13-17 April 1987; and Carriage of Goods, Status of Adoption and Implementation of the International Maritime Dangerous Goods (IMDG) Code, IMO Doc. MSCCr. 497, 26 July 1988, Ref. T33.06, which evidences its wide implementation.
74. For a succinct outline of its contents, see Mensah, note 73 above.
75. *Ibid.*
76. IMO Doc. MSC/Cir. 490, 4 May 1988.
77. Mensah, note 73 above.
78. Note 1 above, p. 86.

PROTECTION OF WATER RESOURCES UNDER INTERNATIONAL LAW

L. V. KORBUT AND Iu. Ia. BASKIN

The numerous contradictions of the postwar period, encompassing all the principal spheres of human activities, have brought the world community to the edge of a catastrophe. It is now a matter of the very existence of civilisation. A transition has begun under these conditions to a wholly new epoch in which general humanitarian interests will be the basis of progress, when the cooperation of States will have precedence over their implacable rivalries, when the world will pass on to "co-creativity" and "co-development."

Such is the principal idea of the new philosophy of international relations, and consequently, of international law. It was formulated by M. S. Gorbachev in his address to the United Nations General Assembly on 7 December 1988. The priority of general humanitarian interests and values does not mean disregarding the interests of individual States or nations. It acts in unity with them: what is vitally important for the international community in all of its class and national-State diversity also is important for individual members of this community.

International protection of water resources

A central problem of the modern day is finding a way out of the ecological crisis, a major component of which is the catastrophic pollution and contamination of the water environment, the natural reserves of fresh water being in a most tragic state. The protection thereof has become in recent decades the subject of numerous multilateral agreements to which the United Nations, its organs, and other international organisations constantly turn. To be sure, here the urgency of the problem is primarily the reason, but no small role is played by a circumstance noted by the ECOSOC Committee on Natural Resources. It consists in the fact that "the extention of international water resources is a unique opportunity to promote friendly relations among States."[1] But this same diversity has led to the most various approaches in international acts toward defining the essence and the sources of pollution. Consider some most frequently used.

Many treaties and agreements establish a general rule prohibiting anthropogenous water pollution. The sources thereof are not specifically indicated (and consequently all sources are implied). This treatment of the issue is typical of treaties concerning the State boundary and conventions on the regime of frontier waters. As a example take the Treaty between the Government of the USSR and the

W. E. Butler, *Perestroika and International Law*, 197–202.
© 1990 *Kluwer Academic Publishers. Printed in the Netherlands.*

Shahinshah Government of Iran on the Regime of the Soviet-Iranian Frontier and on the Procedure for Settlilng Border Conflicts and Incidents, of 14 May 1957. Article 10(1) of the Treaty provides: "The Contracting Parties shall be concerned that all frontier waters are maintained at proper purity and are not subjected to any artificial pollution and obstruction."[2] Also noteworthy are the provisions of the Canadian-American Convention on Border Waters of 11 January 1909, one of the first on the American continent.[3]

One may also point to the agreement between Yugoslavia and Romania on frontier water systems of 7 April 1955 and between Hungary and Yugoslavia on the creation of a mixed commission on water conservancy of 8 August 1955; the treaty between Belgium and the Federal Republic of Germany of 24 September 1956; the agreement beween Czechoslovakia and Poland on the use of frontier water resources of 21 May 1958;[4] a number of agreements on the Mosel River;[5] as well as the provisions of the Act of Asuncion of 3 June 1971 and the agreement on the State frontier between Finland and Sweden of 16 September 1971.[6]

The second principal form is to separate out pollution connected with industrial activities and the use of water for municipal needs (sometimes they are distinguished, but most often they are combined). Such are the provisions of Article 19 of the Treaty between the Governments of the USSR and Hungary on the regime of the Soviet-Hungarian State Frontier, Cooperation, and Mutual Assistance on Border Questions of 3 October 1961: "The appropriate authorities of the Contracting Parties shall take measures to maintain frontier waters at the proper purity so as not to allow poisoning and pollution with acids and wastes of factories and plants nor obstructing by any other means."[7] The same formulations are contained in the provisions of the Niamey Act of the Basin of the Niger River of 26 October 1963; the Convention on the Senegal River and its basin, signed at Dakar on 7 February 1964; and agreements on the River Chad Basin signed on 21–22 May 1964. One may also point to the multilateral agreement on the use of certain types of detergents signed at Strasbourg on 16 September 1968.[8]

The problem of radioactive contamination requires special attention, for the danger is growing. It is not confined merely to direct discharges of waters. Serious alarm is caused by the burial of radioactive wastes which may under certain circumstances entail first the contamination of subsoil waters and then of rivers and lakes. Such activities are a direct violation of the 1975 United Nations Convention on the Prohibition of Military or Other Hostile Use of Influences on the Natural Environment. Regrettably, the number of international agreements on this question is small. Among them is the Belgian-Dutch Treaty on the Big Terneuzen Canal of 20 June 1960.[9]

Some international acts on navigation, especially multilateral ones, specially prohibit the discharge of oil and oil products into rivers and lakes, and likewise other substances which may cause the pollution of river routes. For example, Article 75bis of the Basic Provisions for Navigation on the Danube, which prohibit the discharge into the water of any oil wastes both during the voyage and in lo anchorages.[10] Such are the provisions of the Belgian-Dutch Treaty on Connectin Water Ways between the Rhine and Scheldt of 13 May 1963, as well as the Agreement between the United States and Canada on the St. Lawrence River of 27 February 1959.[11]

Significant water pollution may ensue as the result of timber rafting. It is therefore not surprising that special formulations are encountered even now directed toward the prevention of similar consequences (although most frequently the general provisions of treaties on the State boundary and regime of frontier waters are applied). Such is basically the practice of the Soviet Union. Note, for example, the Agreement between the USSR and Finland of 20 May 1965.[12]

Somewhat apart stand the issues of polluting international river basins as a result of irrigation and agricultural activities as a whole. This occurs principally as a result of fertilizers and pesticides being washed away from the soil. It is a matter not only of pollution and contamination in the strict sense of the word. Such an agreement was signed by the United States and Mexico on 24 August 1966. India and Pakistan have signed analogous agreements regulating in detail the problems of water use, including irrigation, together with combatting pollution.[13]

Since the struggle against polluting international river basins is of primary importance for fishing, and likewise for the preservation and extraction of other biological resources, a significant number of international acts consider it on this plane. The respective article either directly affects the protection of fish stocks or is of a general character and appertains to all biological resources. The first of these formulations is often used in agreements on frontier waters: between Poland and the German Democratic Republic of 6 February 1952, Hungary and Czechoslovakia of 13 October 1956, Hungary and Yugoslavia of 15 May 1957;[14] and the Soviet Union and Finland of 29 April 1964.[15]

An example of multilateral treaties is the Agreement on Fishing in the Waters of the Danube of 29 January 1958. Article 7 provides: "The Contracting Parties shall work out and implement measures for the prevention of pollution and obstruction of the Danube and its reservoirs specified in Article 3 by untreated sewage waters and other materials of industrial and municipal enterprises which are harmful to fish and other water organisms ..."[16]

The second formulation (relating to all biological resources) is widely utilised in international documents adopted in Africa and South America. It is found in the aforementioned Niamey Act on the Niger River Basin of 26 October 1963, the Convention on the Senegal River of 7 February 1964, and the agreements on the Chad Lake basin signed on 21–22 May 1964. They all have articles making provision for protecting river and lake waters with a view to preserving flora and fauna. This formulation is contained in the Treaty between Argentina and Uruguay of 19 November 1973 on the La Plata River basin.[17]

To this same group should be relegated international conventions devoted

199

protection; for example, the Convention on Water and
ional Importance Mainly as Habitat of Aquatic Birds,
').[18]

..ly given the rapidly growing shortage of surface fresh
..on and protection of subsoil (underground) waters is acquiring
..nce. Matters related thereto already have been considered at the
..nolm Conference. The Declaration on the human environment adopted
. contains a provision that water is one of the natural resources which must be
protected through careful planning and management.[19] The same matter was
discussed at the 1977 Conference in Mar del Plata. There it was specially stressed
that it was a matter not only of surface waters, but of the entire water-collection
basin system. Measures for its protection, among others, were proposed.[20] A
number of international documents make provision for protecting underground
waters against specific pollution sources, most often against oil and oil products.[21]

Principles for protection of international rivers

We turn to the issue of the most material provisions which are common for the
legal protection of international river basins against pollution.

The first is the principle of cooperation of coastal States. It was proclaimed by
the 1970 Declaration on the Principles of International Law Relating to Friendly
Relations and Cooperation of States in Accordance with the Charter of the United
Nations. The application of this principle to the domain of international river law
represents a clarification, the manifestation of both the general and the specific. To
be sure, until the respective international legal acts have been signed and enter into
force, such cooperation does not impose on the interested parties specific legal
obligations. But something else is important: the cooperation of States in the
domain of protecting international river basins. This is not merely their political
and moral duty, but also a legal one. Rejection of such cooperation would mean
evasion of a widely recognised rule according to which "the sovereign rights of
coastal countries on the sectors of international river belonging to them must be
used so as not to violate the interests and sovereign rights of other coastal
countries."[22] We speak here of the political and legal duty to take all possible
measures for cooperation in the protection of international river basins. It seems
that this view is supported by the recommendations of the Montreal (1982)
Conference of the International Law Association, which stresses again the urgent
necessity for international cooperation in the cause of protecting and jointly using
international river basins.[23]

This leads us to the second important principle: ecological security. Although it
is not expressly named in the 1970 Declaration, today it would be more than rash to
deny its existence. As regards rivers, it means that all interested States do not have

the right to evade negotiations and conclusions of respective international legal acts, on the basis of sovereign equality and non-interference, to be sure. And until such agreement is reached, all necessary and possible measures must be taken to prevent pollution which might violate the material interests of other States.

This view is supported, in particular, by the following provisions of the Helsinki Final Act of 1 August 1975:

... the participating States, in accordance with the principles of international law, ought to ensure, in a spirit of co-operation, that activities carried out on its territory do not cause degradation of the environment in another State or in areas lying beyond the limits of national jurisdiction.[24]

This provision means that no State has the right to use its territory for causing harm to the territory or interests of another. This understanding is conditioned by the fact that contemporary international law is based not simply on the principle of State sovereignty, but also on their sovereign equality. With regard to the regime of rivers it means that each interested party has the right to a just share of the use of international waters and the right to demand of others not to create any obstacles whatever in this respect. Such is the approach of the International Law Commission to these issues. Draft Article 8 on the right of non-navigational rights of use of international waterways provides: "Waterway states shall use the international waterway in the manner not to cause appreciable damage to other States."[25]

It should be explained that a material violation of interests should be understood to mean pollution which is of a protracted and persistent nature, preventing and obstructing a reasonable and traditional use of waters.[26] By interested parties is understood above all countries within those limits the particular river basin is located. But other States may be among the interested parties, depending upon the specific circumstances, especially those geographically proximate to the rivers, other waterways, and underground waters, for the pollution thereof may materially influence the climatic conditions of the country, the spreading of epidemics, and the like.

International legal responsibility ensues in those instances the principles and provisions of international acts based thereon are violated. A State must bear responsibility both for the action or the failure to act of its agencies, any institutions and organisations situated within its territory, and likewise individuals. B. M. Klimenko is right that "the presence of guilt in any form is not absolutely essential ... A State in any event is obliged to have regard to the consequences of the use of international rivers and control such use."[27] Therefore, we suggest that the principle of absolute, or objective, responsibility should underlie such responsibility. The need to recognise it has been repeatedly spoken of in the literature and at international conferences.[28] In 1961 at the Geneva Conference on Problems of Water Pollution in Europe it was justly noted that the principle of absolute responsibility is characteristic of the legislation of a number of States.

With respect to the pollution of international river basins a State bears direct responsibility for the actions or failure to act of not merely its organs, but also of institutions, organisations, and individuals who are within its jurisdiction. This view is the most appropriate for doctrine and practice in the realm of international law relating to responsibility today.[29] It is another matter what measures a State will take with respect to the guilty. This is, of course, a question of its domestic jurisdiction. An exception from the general rule is possible only in those instances when the responsibility of individual persons or organisations is specially stipulated.

Notes

1. U.N. Doc. E/C. 7/2/Add. 6.
2. *Sbornik deistvuiushchikh dogovorov, soglashenii i konventsii, zakliuchennykh SSSR s inostrannymi gosudarstvami* (1967), XXII, p. 80.
3. W. M. Mallory, *Treaties, Conventions, International Acts, Protocols, and Agreements between the United States of America and Other Powers* (1923), III, p. 2607.
4. See U. N. Doc. ST/LEG/Ser. B/12, pp. 928, 831,and 534; U. N.Doc. A/CN.4/274, I, p.122.
5. See U. N. Doc. A/5409, p. 250; A/CN.4/274, II, p. 275.
6. U. N. Doc. A/CN.4/274, I, pp. 176, 167.
7. Note 2 above, XXII, p. 48.
8. See U. N. Doc. A/CN.4/274, II, pp. 80, 82, 84; I, p. 118.
9. See U. N. Doc. ST/LEG/Ser.B/12, p. 556.
10. See *Protokoly Dunaiskoi komissii* (1961), pp. 1, 68.
11. See U. N. Doc. A/CN.4/274, I, p. 139; U. N. Doc. ST/LEG/Ser.B/12, p. 206.
12. Note 2 above, XXIV, p. 48.
13. See the Treaty on the Indus River of 19 September 1960 and Annex thereto.U. N. Doc. ST/LEG/Ser.B/12, pp. 300–365.
14. See U. N. Doc. ST/LEG/Ser.B/12, pp. 766, 572, 836.
15. Note 2 above, XXIV, p. 48.
16. See note 2 above, XX, p. 533.
17. See U. N. Doc. A/CN.4/274, I, p. 106.
18. Note 2 above, XXXIII, p. 463.
19. U. N. Doc. E.73.II.A.14.1972, p. 4.
20. U. N. Doc. E.77.II.A.12.1977, p. 12.
21. U. N. Doc. A/CN.4/274, II, pp. 207. 262.
22. A. D. Keilin, "Aktual'nye voprosy sovremennogo mezhdunarodnogo morskogo i rechnogo prava," in *Sovetskii ezhegodnik mezhdunarodnogo prava 1962* (1963), p. 100.
23. See International Law Association, Montreal Conference (1982), *Report of the Committee on International Water Resources Law* (1982), p. 11.
24. Note 2 above, XXXI, pp. 562–563.
25. U. N. Doc. A/CN.4/412/Add.2,1988, p. 64.
26. International Law Association, *Report of the Fifty Second Conference*, p. 500.
27. B. M. Klimenko, *Mezhdunarodnye reki* (1969), p. 145.
28. See U. N. Doc. S/T/ESA/5, p. 196.
29. See P. M. Kuris, *Mezhdunarodnye pravonarusheniia i otvetstvennost' gosudarstv* (1973), pp. 196–198.

CHERNOBYL AND THE DEVELOPMENT OF INTERNATIONAL ENVIRONMENTAL LAW

ALAN E. BOYLE

The accident which occured at the Chernobyl nuclear power plant in April 1986 is the most serious incident the nuclear industry has experienced. The reactor itself was destroyed, some thirty people were killed, three hundred required treatment, and 135,000 had to be evacuated from the vicinity. Agricultural land, foodstuffs, and drinking water were contaminated by radioactive substances over a wide area. Extensive decontamination and precautionary measures had to be taken in the Soviet Union itself, while in the rest of Europe various restrictions were introduced on the sale and distribution of livestock and agricultural produce. Radioactive particles transported at high altitude may have reached countries as far as the Pacific. While long term health consequences cannot be determined accurately, some 7,500 fatal cancers have been predicted for the European part of the USSR. Even in the United Kingdom, 35 cancer fatalities are thought possible. Effects on wildlife and ecosystems beyond the immediate area of the accident are also speculative, but is is known that contamination was sufficient to make some meat from Scandinavian reindeer herds unfit to eat, and for their food chains to be affected.[1]

Like the *Torrey Canyon* tanker disaster of 1967, the Chernobyl accident has revealed the limitations of international policy for containing catastrophic risks from beneficial but potentially hazardous activities. It has exposed disagreement on the applicable principles of international law for the protection of other States and the global environment and cast doubt on the adequacy of national and international regulation of the nuclear industry and on the role of the International Atomic Energy Agency. These matters have become the subject of urgent review following the accident, and lead to the adoption of a number of measures intended to remedy some of the evident failings of the existing system.[2]

The legal implications of the accident have to be seen against a background of seventeen years of development in international environmental law since the United Nations Conference on the Human Environment at Stockholm in 1972.[3] International concern with environmental issues had not diminished; indeed the problems of the environment have become sharper and more pressing. Efforts have been made to build on the Stockholm Declaration. The 1982 United Nations Law of the Sea Convention contains for the first time comprehensive provisions for the protection of the marine environment.[4] The world Commission of Environment and Development has proposed legal principles on which a general codification of environmental law might be based.[5] UNEP has sponsored a series of treaties and

W. E. Butler, *Perestroika and International Law*, 203–219.
© 1990 *Kluwer Academic Publishers. Printed in the Netherlands.*

recommendations dealing with marine pollution, shared natural resources, and the ozone layer.[6] With IUCN it has also secured United Nations endorsement of a World Charter for Nature[7] and helped foster wider acceptance of principles of conservation, wildlife protection, and rational use of living resources.[8] The international Law Commission has also become involved with topics of environmental concern, and matters on its agenda now include the pollution of watercourses, liability for environmental harm, and pollution as an international crime.[9]

Despite this evidence of agreement on principles of environmental protection, the experience of Chernobyl indicates that the present international legal system is not yet able to supply clear answers to many of the issues of responsibility and international cooperation raised by the accident.

State responsibility for environmental harm

The role of any system of tort liability is to determine how the losses occasioned by human activity, or inactivity, should be distributed. The international legal system has demonstrated some capacity for fulfilling this role in cases where harm is occasioned to the territory of environment of other States.[10] In the *Trail Smelter Arbitration*,[11] the tribunal, in awarding damages to the United States and prescribing a regime for the regulation of a Canadian Smelter which had caused air pollution damage, concluded that no State had the right to use or permit the use of its territory in such a manner as to cause serious injury to other States. Jurisprudence of the ICJ supports a similar principle. In the *Corfu Channel* case,[12] the Court held Albania responsible for damage to British warships caused by failure to notify them of the danger of mines in territorial waters, and indicated that it was "every state's obligation not to allow knowingly its territory to be used for facts contrary to the rights of other states."

Continued international support for this broad principle that States must control sources of harm to others or to the global environment is reflected in United Nations resolutions, [13] in Principle 21 of the Stockholm Declaration of 1972, [14] in Articles 192 and 194 of the 1982 Law of the Sea Convention, and in the work of the International Law Commission.[15] These instruments indicate also that the narrower form, which protected only States, has been rejected in favour of a wider principle which seeks to include the protection of common spaces, the high seas, deep seabed, outer space, and international airspace.[16]

But if there is agreement on the desirability and existence of such a general principle of law,[17] evidence of consensus on its content is lacking. Without such consensus, State responsibility cannot fulfil the role of providing a principled system of loss distribution. The Chernobyl accident merely illustrates the problem which this causes. There are three main obstacles:

(1) The standard of responsibility. It remains unclear whether States are responsible for the fact that damage has been caused by pollution emanating activities or sources within their territory – that is, a standard of absolute or objective responsibility – or whether they are responsible only for a failure to use due diligence in the control and regulation of the sources of harm.[18] Discussion of the role of fault in the law of State responsibility is unhelpful in answering this question, because it does not tell us what is meant by fault, and assumes that a single answer is possible.[19] A more useful approach is afforded by consideration of specific obligations and how they are defined.[20] However, on this point the *Trail Smelter* and *Corfu Channel* cases do not permit definitive conclusions. At most they indicate that knowledge of a source of risk is essential, but not whether the obligation itself is broken wherever harm occurs regardless of the diligence of States in seeking to control it. Nor does resort to academic commentary resolve the issue, because commentators are divided in their interpretation of these cases, and on the inferences which can be drawn from national legal systems or civil liability treaties by way of general principles of law.[21] Principle 21 of the Stockholm Declaration on the Human Environment is open to equally ambiguous interpretation.[22]

Although a few treaties do support a strict or absolute standard of liability,[23] most tend to adopt a due diligence form of basic obligation. Thus Article 194 of the 1982 Law of the Sea Convention requires States to take "all measures necessary" to ensure protection of other States, and the Convention goes on to specify what these measures consist of in some detail, incorporating by reference other treaties, such as the 1973 Convention on Marine Pollution from Ships.[24] This approach has the advantage that it may help to clarify what is meant by due diligence in specific contexts,[25] but other treaties are less helpful. Thus the 1979 Long Range Transboundary Air Pollution Convention requires only that States "endeavour to limit and as far as possible gradually reduce and prevent air pollution," but it indicates no specific measures.[26] As we shall see, international regulation of the nuclear industry conforms more closely to this looser standard and makes it harder to define due diligence when applied to nuclear activities.

There is much force in Dupuy's conclusion that due diligence reflects the actual practice of States and the present state of customary law in environmental matters,[27] but it is evident that this view is not universally shared. Nor, even if it is correct, does it follow that due diligence is the right standard in all cases; the arguments for using a strict or absolute standard of responsibility to redistribute more of the loss back to the polluter are strong, particularly where the source constitutes an ultra-hazardous activity capable of widespread and serious harm.[28] But faced with the inherent difficulty either of proving lack of due diligence, or of establishing an absolute standard of responsibility, it is not surprising that no inter-State claims have been made arising out of the Chernobyl disaster.[29]

(2) The threshold of harm. A second problem is to determine the appropriate threshold of harm for which States may be responsible. Here too there are competing possibilities. The *Trail Smelter* case talks of "serious injury," General Assembly Resolution 2995 refers to "significant harmful effects," the International Law Commission has used the term "appreciable injury," which is thought to mean more than perceptible, but less than serious,[30] while Principle 21 of the Stockholm Declaration and formulations derived from it omit any qualification of the scale of harm.[31]

A more serious difficulty is that any threshold may be essentailly relative and dependant on its factual context, taking into account the relative social utility of the activity in question. Some academic commentary, and the work of the International Law Commission on international watercourses and international liability, has taken this approach, which links responsibility to a threshold of unreasonable and inequitable use.[32]

The principle of reasonable and equitable use has been employed by international tribunals and the ILC as a basis for allocating rights in international watercourses,[33] and UNEP has endorsed its application to other shared resources.[34] The doctrine of abuse of rights, with which it has much in common, has been similarly employed in the *Icelandic Fisheries* case.[35] But it is less clear that this principle has received endorsement as a test of responsibility for transboundary pollution damage. Relevant UN declarations,[36] UNEP's Principles concerning shared natural resources, and the pollution provisions of the 1982 Law of the Sea Convention[37] all speak of preventing harm to other States or the environment, or of liability for damage; they do not indicate that this is conditional on equitable considerations or a balance of interests.

It is not easy to link nuclear power to any concept of shared resources,[38] or to see that responsibility for damage based on a failure or due diligence should be dependent on prior assessment of competing equities. Failure to use such diligence might itself indicate that the use was unreasonable and inequitable.[39] But the notion of a balance of interests commands more support in prescribing remedies for the future conduct of harmful activities, as in the *Trail Smelter* award,[40] or in allocating the burden of strict or absolute liability for damage. The latter can be observed in the nuclear civil liability conventions where the common risk for all European States arising from their collective use of nuclear power dictated a solution which spreads the burden of loss equitably across all States.[41]

(3) The type of harm. The final problem is to consider what sort of intersts are protected by the obligation to protect others from harm. The *Trail Smelter* case took a narrow view. Its concentration on property loss places no significance on wider environmental interests such as wildlife, aesthetic values, or the unity of ecosystems.[42] More modern treaty definitions of "pollution" are much broader than this, and usually include harm to living resources or ecosystems, interference with

amenities and legitimate uses of the environment or the sea.[43] But treaties dealing specifically with civil liability for nuclear pollution continue to adhere to the *Trail Smelter Arbitration's* concentration on property loss and human health.[44] Only the 1984 Protocol to the Convention on Civil Liability for Oil Pollution Damage adopts the broader perspective and allows recovery of the cost of environmental clean-up and reinstatement. A similar claim brought by Canada in respect of clean-up costs following the crash of a nuclear satellite was succesful;[46] this precedent may indicate that reparation for a breach of obligation is not limited to property damage or human health but extends to consequential environmental costs. Nevertheless, it is notable that the Soviet Union has contested the need for many of the precaution- ary costs incurred in Western Europe following Chernobyl, and it maintains that the issue of "material, moral and political damage" caused by nuclear accidents has not yet been sufficiently studied.[47] Hence it cannot readily be assumed that reparation will cover the whole of any damage resulting from serious accidents.

International Liability

"International Liability" as used by the International Law Commission in its current work on "Liability for Injurious Consequences of Acts not Prohibited by Interna- tional Law"[48] means the liability of States for harm caused without breach of obligation. This is the main sense in which the ILC has distinguished it from State responsibility for wrongful acts.[49] The primary element of the topic is the duty to provide reparation for appreciable injury by activities involving risk to others.[50]

Although the precise terms of this reparation are open to negotiation between the parties, and are subject to a balance of interests based on criteria still to be elaborated by the ILC,[51] the strict liability of the State, over and above any obligation of due diligence, is the essential feature of liability in this form.[52] The intention behind the topic is to provide a basis for the continuation of socially beneficial but harmful activities while at the same time providing for States likely to be affected the assurance of compensation, albeit not full compensation, and of other procedural protections, such as notification and consultation on safety matters. The International Atomic Energy Agency has identified the ILC work as offering a possible framework for special rules intended to regulate international liability for nuclear damage.[53]

There are important objections to the ILC work on this topic however. First, its scope has been conceived in narrow terms, applying only to cases of foreseeable, higher than normal risk.[54] Thus activities not known to be potentially harmful are excluded, as are those where the risk is small, even though the possible harm may be extensive. Since this typifies the risks of nuclear power, the ILC topic may not apply to Chernobyl-type accidents.

Secondly, the conceptual basis of the topic and its separation from State responsibility has been questioned, and described by one commentor as "misconceived."[55] At issue here is not the use of strict liability, but the need for a new basis for such a principle.

Third, it is questionable whether in this form the topic can be said to codify existing law. The relevant case law, such as the *Trail Smelter Arbitration* and the *Corfu Channel* case, is based on the responsibility of States for their wrongful acts, not on the ILC concept of liability. A few treaties do make States strictly or absolutely liable for damage caused by their activities,[56] but as we have already seen there is no consensus on whether this represents a general principle in international law, or applies only to those cases provided for by treaty.[57] Attempts to bolster international acceptance of the principle by reliance on inference from general principles of law or civil liability conventions are unconvincing because these schemes are normally conditioned on limited liability, compulsory insurance, and channelling of liability which cannot be replicated easily at the level of customary international law.[58] As a principle for redistributing environmental costs, international liability is thus even more uncertain than state responsibility.

Civil liability schemes

An alternative method for dealing with the transboundary costs of accidents such as Chernobyl is to facilitate transboundary civil liability proceedings by individual victims. This requires the removal of jurisdictional obstacles which may confront the foreign plaintiff;[59] and places the burden of liability on private parties responsible for the harm, not on the State, unless it acts as the operator of the industry concerned. An important advantage of this approach is that it moves the issue away from State responsibility in international law and frees the injured party from reliance on diplomatic claims pursued by his government.[60]

One form of this civil liability model of loss distribution is the principle of equal access and non-discrimination. This principle allows the foreign plaintiff access to judicial and administrative remedies on the same terms as nationals, and requires transboundary nuisances to be treated like those within national boundaries. The OECD has endorsed the equal access and non-discrimination principle as an important policy for dealing with transboundary environmental harm in Western Europe.[61] It has also been adopted in a number of treaties. The 1974 Nordic Convention on the Protection of the Environment, a few boundary waters treaties,[62] and at least two bilateral agreements on nuclear risks[63] employ the principle, which is also found in some legal systems, notably within the EEC and in North America.[64]

Equal access has one major disadvantage however. It provides access to whatever national law States choose to adopt; it does not guarantee the existence of appropriate legislation or require harmonisation of laws in different countries. In practice, therefore, it assumes the existence of relevant laws and works best where these are based on a common legal system, as in Scandinavia.[65] Where the relevant legal systems are as diverse as those of Western Europe, on one hand, and Eastern Europe on the other, equal access is not a productive principle on which to rely. Crucially, the Soviet Union has no legislation dealing specifically with liability for nuclear accidents, and it is unclear that proceedings brought there would be successful.[66]

A more sophisticated model is offered by international conventions on civil liability for nuclear incidents. These conventions, of which there are now four,[67] seek to harmonise national laws around a common pattern, which compromises strict liability, channelled to the operator of the installation, (whether or not this is a State), limited in total amount and supported by compulsory insurance. There are also agreed rules on which the court has jurisdiction; usually this will be where the installation is located, or in the case of ships, where the harm occurs. The same basic elements are also found in the 1969 Convention on Civil Liability for Oil Pollution Damage from Ships.

None of these conventions guarantees injured plaintiffs recovery in full for their losses; one major drawback of the Vienna Convention in particular is that the liability limit is much lower than the likely cost of a major accident, and in that event most of the loss would still fall on third parties.[68] The Paris Convention is more successful in this respect, because a supplementary scheme involves the source State and all other western European nuclear States in providing substantial additional compensation from public funds.[69] In effect this treaty creates a scheme for the equitable distribution of burdens shared among all participating States who use nuclear energy. The Oil Pollution Damage Convention achieved a similar result by involving oil companies in funding extra compensation beyond what the operator could bear.[70]

A more radical defect of the global nuclear liability conventions is their failure to attract widespread support.[71] Major nuclear States outside Western Europe have not become parties, and the Conventions are thus inapplicable in cases such as Chernobyl or Three Mile Island. Although the IAEA has sponsored a joint protocol to link the Paris and Vienna Conventions,[72] this will only be successful if it encourages wider participation. Another problem faced by all of the nuclear conventions is their limited environmental focus; unlike the 1984 version of the Oil Pollution Liability Convention they do not provide for the costs of environmental clean-up and reinstatement.[73]

Nevertheless, the scheme provided by such treaties has important benefits. It makes access to legal remedies much easier, minimises difficult issues of proof or liability, and ensures availability of compensation funds regardless of the defendant's solvency. The provision of public funds under the Paris Convention offers a precedent for exceptional provision for wider loss distribution in cases of ultra-hazardous activities, based only in part on absolute or strict liability of the operator.

But there is no evidence that outside Western Europe this precedent has found any support, and it is therefore difficult to generalise from the experience.

International regulation of serious risks

A developing feature of the international legal system is the use of internationally agreed standards for the regulation of potentially hazardous activities.[74] This form of international cooperation is seen at its most developed in the standards which now control the design, construction, equipment, and operation of ships, especially oil tankers. These international standards, such as in the 1973 Marine Pollution Convention,[75] can be used to ensure comprehensive and uniform regulation of sources of pollution.

This approach has the particular advantage of setting minimum criteria which States must meet in fulfilment of their obligations as flag States or as territorial powers bound to protect others from harm. In the case of marine pollution, international standards established by treaty are given additional force by the 1982 Law of the Sea Convention;[76] and a relatively strong scheme of enforcement exists.

No similar choice has been made for nuclear installations. Here national sovereignty, and the freedom to set national standards, by and large prevails.[77] International bodies, including IAEA, OECD, and the EEC, do have a responsibility for formulating international standards of health and safety regulation,[78] but although these standards are often adopted into national law, in the case of IAEA and OECD they are not binding on States in most instances, and lack the force of treaties such as the MARPOL Convention. The result is that international regulation of nuclear energy is unsatisfactorily weak. It fails to offer the assurance of minimum standards of environmental protection which apply to other sources of transboundary risk.

IAEA's Nuclear Safety Standards Programme, revised in 1988, sets basic minimum requirements and guiding principles for the design, construction, siting, and operation of nuclear power plants. Its work has coverd a wide range of health and safety issues relating to all aspects of the use of nuclear energy.[79] But nothing in its statute confers any obligatory force on such standards, or gives the agency any compulsory power of inspection and enforcement.[80] Although it does conduct safety inspections, these are by request only, and while it may recommend, it cannot require changes to be made.[81] Only where it provides assistance to States for their nuclear programmes does it have stronger power to insist on adequate safety standards.[82]

Thus although IAEA has had an important influence on State practice in health and safety matters, its standards are by no means universally adhered to, and the Agency is in no position to insist on compliance. For these reasons it is also difficult to regard them as "international standards," or to use them to define the content of due diligence. At its 1986 Conference, no agreement could be reached on the adoption of obligatory minimum safety standards for reactors. Instead the Conference affirmed the responsibility of each State engaged in nuclear energy activity to ensure adequate safety and environmental compatibility.[83] With over 400 nuclear reactors in operation, it may be too late to move significantly towards stronger international regulation.

International co-operation

The most important and positive feature of international action in response to the Chernobyl disaster has been the widespread agreement on principles of notification and cooperation in cases of nuclear emergencies. The existence of a customary obligation to warn other States likely to be affected by known risks of harm had already formed the basis of the ICS findings against Albania in the *Corfu Channel* case,[84] and had also received recognition in treaties dealing with maritime casualties,[85] in UNEP recommendations[86] and in the 1982 Law of the Sea Convention.[87]

The application of this principle to circumstances such as the Chernobyl accident has now been acknowledged by the rapid adoption of a Convention on Early Notification of Nuclear Accidents, which requires States to notify others likely to be affected by transboundary releases of radiological safety significance, and to give appropriate information to enable precautionary measures to be taken.

Several States, including the USSR and United Kingdom, have declared that they will apply the Convention pending entry into force, and although it does not cover military installations, the Soviet Union has given notification in one case when a nuclear submarine was in difficulty.[88] A large number of States in Eastern and Western Europe have also concluded bilateral agreements implementing the Convention's requirements.[89] Although it will only be effective if States possess a radiological monitoring and assessment capability, this treaty does represent a significant recognition of the basic customary principle derived from the *Corfu Channel* case.

The Notification Convention has been complemented by a Convention on Assistance in Cases of Nuclear Emergency,[90] which provides a framework for requesting assistance, and gives IAEA a coordinating role. No explicit obligation to request help, or to render it if asked, is placed on States however, and responsibility for taking or directing appropriate action within its territory remains with the requesting State. It is thus sharply different from the principle of intervention recognised by State practice and multilateral treaty in respect of maritime casualties.[91]

The Chernobyl accident has not prompted comparable action to clarify the responsibilities of States in consulting their neighbours about the siting and safety

212

of installations which may pose transboundary risks, or in making environmental impact assessments.[92] State practice and the jurisprudence of international tribunals, such as the *Lac Lanoux Arbitration*,[93] have supported an obligation to inform, consult, and take account of the representations of other States with regard to watercourses,[94]. and the principle has received more general recognition. The Long Range Transboundary Air Pollution Convention requires States contributing to such pollution to consult others likely to be exposed to a significant risk,[95] and a few continental shelf exploitation agreements make similar provision.[96] OECD's regime of equal access,[97] the ILA's Montreal Rules on Transfrontier Pollution, and relevant UNEP recommendations[98] also require communication of information and consultation with other States.

Such requirements are now complemented by an emerging principle which obliges States to undertake environmental impact assessment where activities are likely to have significant environmental effects. UNEP has developed guidelines on this subject,[99] and the principle is adopted in the 1982 Law of the Sea Convention and a number of regional seas treaties.[100]

The evidence of bilateral agreements among a number of European States confirms the application of these general principles to the siting of nuclear power installations.[101] Such treaties mainly apply to facilities within 30km. of an international border, but all require a full exchange of information on the proposed installation to enable the other State to review the decision-making process and offer appropriate views in health and safety protection. Although this does not represent an extensive body of State practice, it does suggest that obligations of notification and consultation now extend to planned nuclear activities which pose a serious risk of transboundary harm.

International organisations

The International Atomic Energy Agency, created in 1956, was not conceived at the outset as an emergency with environmental responsibilities. Rather its main tasks were to encourage and facilitate the development and dissemination of nuclear power, and to ensure through non-proliferation safeguards that it was used for peaceful purposes only.[102] Setting standards of health and safety in collaboration with other international agencies was very much an incidental or secondary responsibility, where the weakness of its powers contrasted with the authority it was given under the 1968 Non-Proliferation Treaty to police obligatory safeguards against diversion of materials for military use.

The Chernobyl accident has had the effect of recasting the Agency's priorities. Providing the main forum for consideration of measures made necessary by that accident, member States confirmed its central role in encouraging and facilitating cooperation on safety and radiological protection.[104] Among the recommendations of a review group[105] were that the agency should promote better exchanges of information among States on Safety and accident experience, develop additional safety guidelines, and enhance its capacity to perform safety evaluations and inspections on request. States were urged to make more use of it for this purpose. The Convention on Assistance in Cases of Nuclear Emergency, as we have seen, also gave it the task of coordinating assistance and responding to requests for help.[106]

Thus the agency has emerged from the accident with nuclear safety as one of its major priorities, and with a clear mandate to develop additional standards for the guidance of States on a wide range of issues. Despite its very different objectives in 1956, it has, rather like IMO after the *Torrey Canyon* disaster, acquired a new environmental perspective. This at least may prove a further positive result of the Chernobyl accident. But without stronger powers of inspection and oversight, the Agency can only continue to exhort and encourage States to follow its practices. It remains a weak guarantor of the safety of nuclear power.[107]

Conclusions

The Chernobyl accident has encouraged significant consensus on principles of notification and cooperation in cases of nuclear emergency, it has enhanced the role of the IAEA as an environmental agency, and it has renewed interest in wider acceptance of the Vienna and Paris Conventions by means of a joint protocol. While raising important issues concerning State responsibility, strict liability, and the usefulness of equal access and civil liability regimes, progress has been less satisfactory in providing answers to these questions. Nor have the rights and responsibilities of States when creating transboundary nuclear risks been clarified. There has thus been some progress in the development of legal principles relevant to the problems posed by nuclear accidents, but much uncertainty remains.

Notes

1. See IAEA, *Summary Report on the Post Accident Review Meeting on the Chernobyl Accident* (1986); U.K.A.E.A., *The Chernobyl Accident and its Consequences* (1987); NEA/OECD, *The Radiological Impact of the Chernobyl Accident in O.E.C.D. Countries* (1988).
2. See IAEA General Conference, Special Session, 1986, IAEA Doc. GC(SPL.1)/4 and GC (SPL.1)/15/rev.1, *International Legal Materials*, XXV (1986), 1387 [hereinafter *ILM*]; Council of Europe Parliamentary Assembly Rec. 1068 (1988); OECD, *NEA Activities in 1986*; EEC, *20th General Report*, 1986, paras. 759–762.
3. *Report of the UN Conference on the Human Environment*, Stockholm, 1972, U.N. Doc. A/CONF/48/14/Rev.1; L. B. Sohn, "The Stockholm Declaration on the Human

Environment," *Harvard International Law Journal*, XIV (1973), 423.

4. Articles 192–235; See A. E. Boyle, "Marine Pollution Under the Law of the Sea Convention," *American Journal of International Law*, LXXIX (1985). 347; J. Schneider, "Codification and Progressive Development of International Environmental Law and the 3rd U.N. Conference on the Law of the Sea," *Colombia Journal of Transnational Law*, XX (1981), 243.

5. WCED, *Our Common Future* (1987); R. D. Munro and J. G. Lammers (eds.), *Environmental Protection and Sustainable Development* (1986).

6. See treaties in the Regional Seas Series (collected in K. R. Simmonds (ed.), *New Directions in Law of the Sea* (1983–); 1985 UNEP Montreal Guidelines on Pollution from Land-based Sources of Marine Pollution, *Environmental Policy and Law*, XIV (1985), 77; 1985 Vienna Convention for the Protection of the Ozone Layer, *Environmental Policy and Law*, XIV (1985), 71, with 1987 Montreal Protocol, *ILM*, XXVI (1987), 1541; 1978 UNEP Principles of Conduct in the Conservation and Harmonious Utilisation of Natural Resources shared by Two or more States, *ILM*, XVII (1978), 1091.

7. *ILM*, XXII (1982), 455; See Wood, "The U.N. World Charter for Nature," *Environmental Law Quarterly*, XII (1984), 977.

8. See for example, 1973 Convention of International Trade in Endangered Species, *ILM*, XII (1978), 1085; 1979 Convention on the Conservation of Migratory Species of Wild Animals, *ILM*, XIX (1980), 15; S. Lyster, *International Wildlife Law* (1985).

9. See draft articles on International Watercourses, 1984 *Yearbook of the International Law Commission 1984*, II(I), p. 101 [Hereinafter "yearbook"]; draft articles on International Liability, 1988, UN Doc. A/CN.4/413; draft articles on State Responsibility, Article 19, Yearbook 1980, II(2), p. 30.

10. P. M. Dupuy, *La Responsabilité Internationale Des États Pour Les Dommages D'Origine Technologique et Industrielle* (1976); Dupuy, in M. Bothe (ed.), *Trends in Environmental Policy and Law* (1980), p. 363; G. Handl, "State Liability for Accidental Transnational Environmental Damage by Private Persons," *American Journal of International Law*, LXXIV (1980), 525; J. Schneider, *World Public Order of the Environment* (1979), chapter 6.

11. *American Journal of International Law*, XXXIII (1939), 182; XXXV (1941), 684.

12. ICJ Rep. (1949), 4. See also *Nuclear Tests Cases*, ICJ Rep. (1973), 99 and ICJ Rep. (1974), 253.

13. G. A. Res. 2849 (1971); G. A. 2995 (1972); G. A. Res. 2996 (1972); G. A. Res. 3281 (1974); G. A. Res. 34/186 (1979).

14. Note 3 above.

15. Note 9 above.

16. A. L. Springer, "United States Environmental Policy and International Law: Principle 21 Revisited," in J. E. Carroll (ed.), *International Environmental Diplomacy* (1988); L. B. Sohn, note 3 above. See also 1985 Vienna Convention for the Protection of the Ozone Layer; Article 145, 1982 Convention on the Law of the Sea; 1967 Outer Space Treaty, *ILM* VI (1967), 386; 1979 Moon Treaty, *ILM*, XVIII (1979), 1434; the 1988 Convention on Antarctic Mineral Resource Activities; and C. A. Fleischer, "The International Concern for the Environment: The Concept of Common Heritage," in Bothe, note 10 above, p. 321.

17. G. A. Res. 2996 (1972) asserts that Principles 21 and 22 of the Stockholm Declaration "Lay down the basic rules governing the matter." 112 States voted for this resolution, none opposed. Several States made declarations during the Stockholm Conference affirming that Principle 21 accorded with existing international law: see Canadian and

215

United States comments in U.N. Doc. A/CONF. 48/14 Rev. 1 at 64 and 66. Eastern bloc States did not attend the Stockholm Conference and abstained on Res. 2996, but have supported subsequent treaties recognising the normative character of Principle 21: see 1979 Geneva Convention on Long Range Transboundary and 1985 Vienna Convention for the Protection of the Ozone Layer.

18. See generally I. Brownlie, *State Responsibility* (1983), pp. 40ff and compare C. W. Jenks, "Liability for Ultra-Hazardous Activities in International Law," *Recueil des Cours*, CXVII (1966), 105; L. F. E. Goldie, "International Principles of Responsibility for Pollution," *Colombia Journal of Transnational Law*, IX (1970), 283; A. L. Springer, note above 16; B. D. Smith, *State Responsibility and the Marine Environment* (1988); Dupuy, note 10 above; M. J. L. Hardy, "International Protection Against Nuclear Risks," *International and Comparative Law Quarterly*, X (1961), 739; G. Handl, note 10 above; E. J. de Arechaga, "International Responsibility," in M. Sorensen (ed.), *Manual of Public International Law* (1968) p. 539; P. Reuter, "Principles de Droit International Public," *Recueil des Cours*, CIII (1961), 590; Handl, "Balancing of Interests and International Liability for Pollution of International Watercourses: Customary Principles Revisited," *Canadian Yearbook of International Law* (1975), 156; L. Oppenheim, *International Law* (8th ed., 1955), I, 343; de Arechaga, "General Course on Public International Law," *Recueil des Cours*, CLIX (1978), 267. Note also opposition to the concept of strict liability expressed by members of the U.N. General Assembly 6th Committee at *Yearbook 1986*, II (1), p. 157, para. 52.
19. See Arechaga, Reuter, and Handl, note 18 above.
20. Brownlie, note 18 above, pp. 40–48.
21. See note 18 above.
22. Compare Handl, note 10 above, pp. 535–536, and note 18, pp. 160–161, and Springer, in Carroll, note 18 above.
23. See 1972 Convention on International Liability for Damage Caused by Space Objects; Canadian Claim for Damage Caused by the Cosmos 954 Satellite, *ILM*, XVIII (1979), 902.
24. Simmonds, note 6 above, IV, p. 345, and 1978 Protocol, *ibid.*, X, p. 32. On this point see W. Van Reenen, "Rules of Reference in the New Law of the Sea," *Netherlands Yearbook of International Law*, XII (1981), 5; D. Vignes "La Valeur Juridique de Certaines Regles et Normes ou Pratiques Mentionées au TNCO Comme Généralement Acceptées," *Annuaire Français de Droit International* (1979), 712; Boyle, note 4 above; P. Contini and P. H. Sand, "Methods to Expedite Environment Protection: International Eco-Standards," *American Journal of International Law*, LXVI (1972), 37. Other "international standards" include those on construction and design, seabed pollution, and pollution from dumping: see generally 1982 Convention on the Law of the Sea, Articles 208, 210, 211.
25. See generally Dupuy, in Bothe, note 10 above, p. 369.
26. Article 2. See now the 1985 Sulphur Protocol to the Convention however.
27. *Ibid.*, p. 363. See also note 18 above.
28. For consideration of these arguments, see references by Jenks, Goldie, Reuter, and Dupuy at note 18 above.
29. P. Sands, *Chernobyl: Law and Communication* (1988), pp. 26 ff.
30. Draft Articles on International Liability, Articles 1, 2, U.N. Doc. A/CN.4/413 (1988); Draft Articles on International Watercourses, 1982 *Yearbook 1982* II(1), pp. 98–99, paras. 130–141, and draft Article 9, *Yearbook 1984*, II(1), p. 112.
31. See also 1982 Convention on the Law of the Sea, Article 194(2); G. A. Res. 3281

(1974), Article 30; United Nations Environment Programme, Principles of Co-operation in the Field of the Environment Shared by Two or More States, 1978, Principle 3; United Nations Environment Programme, Montreal Guidelines for the Protection of the Marine Environment against Pollution from Land based Sources, 1985, Article 17. See Munro Lammers, note 5 above, pp. 75–78; Handl, "National Uses of Transboundary Air Resources: The International Entitlement Issue," *Natural Resources Journal*, XXVI (1986), 405, 512; Springer, in Carol, note 18 above, p. 51, for analysis of conflicting interpretations of these thresholds.

32. See Handl, notes 18 and 31; R. Q. Quentin-Baxter, *Yearbook 1981* II(1), pp. 112–119; S. McCaffrey, *Yearbook 1986* II(1), pp. 133–134.

33. *Territorial Jurisdiction of the International Commission of the River Oder*, PCIJ Series A, No. 23 (1929), *Lac Lanoux Arbitration, Reports of International Arbitration Awards*, XII (1957), 281; ILC Draft Articles on International Watercourses, Articles 6-9, *Yearbook 1984*, II(1), p.101.

34. Principles of Co-operation in the Field of the Environment Shared by Two or More States, 1978. See generally L. F. E. Goldie, "Equity and the International Management of Transboundary Resources,", in A. E. Utton and L. A. Teclaff (eds.), *Transboundary Resources Law* (1987), p. 103.

35. ICJ Rep. (1974), 3; 1958 Geneva Convention on the High Seas, Article 2.

36. Stockholm Declaration on the Human Environment, Principle 21; G. A. Res. 3281 (1974), Article 30; G. A. Res. 2995 (1972).

37. Articles 139, 194.

38. The term "shared resource" is not defined in UNEP's Principles. The Executive Director reported that it included river systems, air sheds, enclosed and semi enclosed seas; mountain chains, forests and areas of conservation interest, migratory species: U.N. Doc./GC/44, (1975), para 86. The views of States differed; see the Report of the Intergovernmental Working Group, U.N. Doc. U.N.E.P./IG. 12/2 (1978), and the Executive Director's Report. For differing views of the relevance of this concept to transfrontier pollution, see Handl, note 31 above; W. Riphagen, "The International Concern for the Environment as Expressed in the Concepts of the Common Heritage of Mankind and of Shared Natural Resources," in Bothe, note 10 above; Handl, "The Principle of Equitable Use as Applied to Internationally Shared Natural Resources," *Revue Belge de Droit International*, XIV (1978), 40.

39. Handl, note 31 above, p. 426.

40. J. E. Read, "The Trail Smelter Dispute," *Canadian Yearbook of International Law* (1963), 213; A. P. Rubin, "Pollution by Analogy: The Trail Smelter Arbitration," *Oregon Law Review*, L (1971), 259.

41. See below, section 4.

42. Rubin note 40 above, pp. 272–274.

43. See 1982 Convention on the Law of the Sea, Article 1(4); 1974 Paris Convention on Prevention of Marine Pollution from Land-Based Sources, Article 1; 1979 Geneva Convention on Long Range Transboundary Air Pollution, Article 1; 1977 OECD Recommendation C(77) 28 on Implementing a Regime of Equal Right of Access and Non-Discrimination. See A. L. Springer, "Towards a Meaningful Concept of Pollution in International Law," *International and Comparative Law Quarterly*, XXVI, (1977), 531; M. Tomczak, "Defining Marine Pollution, a Comparison of Definitions Used by International Conventions," *Marine Policy*, VIII (1984), 311.

44. 1960 Paris Convention on Third Party Liability in the Field of Nuclear Energy, Article 1; 1962 Brussels Convention on the Liability of Operators of Nuclear Ships, Article 1(7); 1963 Vienna Convention on Civil Liability for Nuclear Damage, Article 1(1).

45. Article 1(6). See M. Jacobsson and N. Trotz, "The Definition of Pollution Damage in the 1984 Protocols to the 1969 Civil Liability Convention," *Journal of Maritime Law and Commerce*, XVII (1986), 467.
46. Claim for Damage Caused by Soviet Cosmos 954, *ILM*, XVIII (1978), 902.
47. *Proposed Programme for Establishing an International Regime for the Safe Development of Nuclear Energy* (1986) reprinted in Sands, note 29 above, p. 227.
48. Draft Articles, 1988 U.N. Doc. A/CN. 4/413 and Rapporteur's 4th Report. For earlier reports and commentary see *Yearbook 1980* and following years.
49. *Yearbook 1969*, II, pp. 229 ff; *Yearbook 1973*, I, pp. 7–14, and compare draft Article 3 on State Responsibility, *Yearbook 1980* II(2), pp. 30 ff.
50. 1988 draft Article 10, U.N. Doc. A/CN. 4/413.
51. (1987) UN Doc. A/CN. 4/405, paras. 55–57; (1988) UN Doc. A/CN. 4/413, paras. 112–116; *Yearbook 1986* II(1), p. 147.
52. *Yearbook 1986*, II(1), pp. 154–161; (1987) UN Doc. A/CN. 4/405, paras. 60–69; (1988) UN Doc. A/CN. 4/413, para. 113.
53. IAEA Doc. GOV/INF/509, Annex 2.
54. U.N. Doc. A/CN. 4/413, para. 30; Draft Article 1 uses the term "appreciable risk."
55. Brownlie, note 18 above, p. 50. See also M. Akehurst, "International Liability for Injurious Consequences Arising out of Acts Not Prohibited by International Law," *Netherlands Yearbook of International Law*, XVI (1985), 3; D. B. Magraw, "Transboundary Harm: The I.L.C. Study," *American Journal of International Law*, LXXX (1986), 305.
56. 1972 Convention on International Liability for Damage Caused by Space Objects, Article 2; 1967 Outer Space Treaty, Article 7.
57. Above, part 2(1).
58. See below, part. 4.
59. See McCaffrey "Transboundary Pollution Injuries: Jurisdictional Considerations in Private Litigation Between Canada and the United States," *California Western International Law Journal*, III (1973), 191; R. W. Lanni, "International and Private Actions in Transboundary Pollution," *Canadian Yearbook of International Law*, XI (1973), 258.
60. On diplomatic claims, see *Barcelona Traction Case*, ICJ Reps. (1970), 3; *Nottebohm Case*, ICJ Reps. (1955), 4; *Ambatielos Arbitration, Reports of International Arbitration Awards*, XII (1956), 83.
61. Recommendations C(74) 224, C(76) 55; C(77) 28, reprinted in *O.E.C.D. and the Environment* (1986); H. Smets, "Legal Principles Adopted by the O.E.C.D. Council," *Environmental Policy and Law*, IX (1982), 110.
62. For example, 1909 U.S.-Canada Boundary Waters Treaty.
63. 1986 Switzerland-F.R.G. Agreement on Third Party Liability in the Nuclear Field, *Nuclear Law Bulletin*, XXXIX (1986), 51; 1976 Canada-U.S. Nuclear Liability Rules.
64. See 1968 and 1978 EEC Conventions on Jurisdiction and the Enforcement of Judgments; E.C.J. Case 21/76 *Handelswerkerig Bier v Mines de Pottase D'Alsace*, E.C.J. Repts. II (1976), p. 1735; 1982 U.S.-Canada Uniform Transboundary Pollution Reciprocal Access Act, implemented by legislation in New Jersey, Colorado, Montana, and see also *Michie v Great Lakes Steel Div.*, 495 F. 2d. 213 (1974).
65. A.C. Kiss, "La Convention Nordique Sur L'Environment," *Annuaire Français de Droit International*, XX (1974), 808. For other criticisms see E. Willheim, "Private Remedies for Transfrontier Environmental Damage: A Critique of O.E.C.D.'s Doctrine of Equal Right of Access," *Australian Yearbook of International Law* (1976), 174.

66. Soviet Civil Legislation allows for strict liability in cases of damage caused by sources of "heightened danger": W. E. Butler, *Soviet Law* (2d ed., 1988), p. 192. Enterprises engaged in economic activity have no immunity from civil actions in the USSR.

67. See note 44 above, and the 1971 Brussels Convention on Civil Liability in the Field of Maritime Carriage of Nuclear Materials. See generally N. Pelzer, "Concepts of Nuclear Liability Revisited," in P. Cameron et al. (eds) *Nuclear Energy Law After Chernobyl* (1988), p. 97.

68. Article V provides for U.S. $5 million at 1963 values, worth approx. $58 million in 1988. $29 million was paid out by insurers after the Three Mile Island Accident; the USSR is estimated by OECD to have paid compensation of $1.2 billion after Chernobyl.

69. 1963 Supplementary Convention on Third Party Liability in the Field of Nuclear Energy.

70. 1971 International Convention for the Establishment of an International Fund for Compensation for Oil Pollution, with 1984 Protocol.

71. The 1963 Vienna Convention has ten parties. Onlu two Argentina and Yugoslavia) possess nuclear facilities. The United States and the USSR are not parties. The 1960 Paris Convention has fourteen parties, with 120 of the world's 400 (approx.) nuclear reactors.

72. Joint Protocol Relating to the Application of the Paris Convention and the Vienna Convention, 1988.

73. See note 44 above.

74. See Contini and Sand, note 24 above; L. K. Caldwell, *International Environmental Policy* (1984).

75. See also 1974 Safety of Life at Sea Convention, and generally R. M. M'Gonigle and M. W. Zacher, *Pollution, Politics and International Law* (1979).

76. Articles 192–220. See note 4 above.

77. J. Barkenbus, "Nuclear Power Safety and the Role of International Organisation," *International Organisation*, XXXXI (1987), 475.

78. IAEA Statute, 1956; Euratom Treaty 1957. OECD is involved through its Nuclear Energy Agency. See generally P. Szasz, *Law and Practices of the I.A.E.A.* (1970), chapter 22; J. Grunwald, "The Role of Euratom," and P. Reyners and L. Lellouche, "Regulation and Control by International Organisations in the Context of a Nuclear Accident," in Cameron, note 63 above, pp. 33 and 1.

79. The 1981 Basic Safety Standards for Radiation Protection; 1984 Regulations on Safe Transport of Radioactive Materials; 1985 Code of Practice for Management of Radioactive Waste.

80. Article III of the Statute requires the Agency to establish "standards" for the protection of health and minimising danger to life and property, but places no obligation on States to adopt them. The 1968 Nuclear Non-Proliferation Treaty deals only with non-proliferation safeguards against military use, not with operational safety.

81. Barkenbus, note 77 above.

82. Statute, Articles III, XI, XII.

83. IAEA, 30th Conference Special Session. G. A. Res. 41/36 (1986) calls for the highest standards of safety in the design and operation of nuclear plants.

84. ICJ Rep. (1949), 3.

85. 1973 Marine Pollution Convention, Article 8 and Protocol 1.

86. 1978 Principles of Co-operation in the Field of the Environment shared by Two or

More States; 1985 Montreal Guidelines for the protection of the Marine Environment Against Pollution from Land-Based Sources.

87. Articles 198, 211(7).
88. See *ILM* XXV (1986), 1370.
89. For example, Belgium-Netherlands, 1987; Norway-Sweden, 1987; U.K.-Norway, 1987; Finland-U.S.S.R., 1987; F.R.G.-G.D.R. 1987; Denmark-Sweden, 1986; Denmark-Poland, 1987; Denmark-U.S.S.R., 1987 Brazil and Argentina are also parties to a similar agreement, 1987. Several earlier treaties provide for notification: Spain-Portugal, 1980; France-Switzerland, 1979; U.K.-France, 1983; F.R.G.-Switzerland, 1978; France-F.R.G. 1981; France-Luxembourg, 1983.
90. *ILM*, XXV (1986), 1377. See Cameron, note 67 above, p. 19.
91. 1982 Convention on the Law of the Sea, Article 221; 1969 Convention on Intervention in Cases of Maritime Casualties.
92. See generally Handl, "An International Legal Perspective on the Conduct of Abnormally Dangerous Activities in Frontier Areas: Nuclear Power Plant Siting," *Ecology Law Quarterly*, VII (1978), 1; Cameron, note 67 above, pp. 49–96.
93. *Reports of International Arbitration Awards*, XII (1957), 281.
94. ILC Draft Articles on International Watercourses, Articles 11–14 *Yearbook 1984*, II(1), p. 103.
95. Articles 5, 8(b).
96. 1983 Canada-Denmark Agreement for Co-operation Relating to the Marine Environment, *ILM*, XXIII (1984), 269. See also 1981 UNEP Recommendations concerning the Environment Related to Offshore Drilling and Mining within the Limits of National Jurisdiction, *Environmental Policy and Law*, VII (1982), 50.
97. See note 61 above.
98. See note 86 above, and Bothe, note 10 above, p. 391; A. E. Utton, "International Law and Consultation Mechanisms," *Columbia Journal of Transnational Law*, XII (1975), 56.
99. 1987 Principles of Environmental Impact Assessment, *Environmental Policy and Law*, XVII (1988), 36. See also the 1982 ILA Montreal Rules on Transfrontier Pollution, *Environmental Policy and Law*, X. 27.
100. 1982 Convention on Law of the Sea, Articles 204–206; 1983 Cartagena Convention for the Protection of the Marine Environment of the Caribbean, Article 12.
101. Spain-Portugal, 1980; Netherlands-FRG, 1977; Denmark-FRG, 1977; Belgium-France, 1966; Switzerland-FRG, 1982.
102. 1956 Statute, Article III.
103. See above, part 5.
104. IAEA, 30th Conference, Special Session, GC/SPL.1/Res.1. See also the statement of the Group of Seven on the Implications of the Chernobyl Accident, *ILM*, XXV (1986), 1005.
105. IAEA, *Summary Report on the Post Accident Review Meeting on the Chernobyl Accident* (1986).
106. Above, part 6.
107. Barkenbus, note 77 above.

INTERNATIONAL ORGANISATIONS AND NEW ASPECTS OF INTERNATIONAL RESPONSIBILITY

N. B. KRYLOV

Ensuring peace and international security, strengthening the peaceful coexistence of States with different social systems, and the struggle to end the arms race and for disarmament are among the global problems of the modern era. Their successful resolution depends to a great extent on the effectiveness of international legal regulation of international relations.[1] The growing requirement for the maintenance of international legal order objectively enhances the attention given to the institute of State responsibility. Accordingly, the scholarly working out of problems of responsibility is taking on special practical and theoretical importance.

States are the principal subjects of international relations and international law. Therefore, the question of responsibility under international law arises first as an issue of State responsibility.[2] But in addition to States there are other subjects of international law. Above all there are international inter-State organisations, whose quantitative increase and enhanced significance in doctrine is akin to an explosion.

Responsibility of international organisations

The diverse and vast activities of international organisations raise the question of the grounds, prerequisites and forms of their responsibility as subjects of international law. Beyond doubt this is one of the most recent and under-studied phenomena in the theory of international law, for two reasons. First, international organisations are a comparatively new phenomenon and relatively recently began actively to take part in international relations. In addition, there are no general norms in contemporary international law regulating the responsibility of those organisations.[3] Nonetheless, life itself requires a profound working out of these issues.

It is essential to draw attention to the different nature of their responsibility and the responsibility of States.[4] The last are the primary, basic subjects of international law. They act as bearers and the practical realizers of extensive sovereign powers without restriction. This finds concrete expression in the institute of responsibility. In the Draft Articles on State Responsibility prepared by the International Law Commission it is noted that "Any State may be regarded as having committed an act contrary to international law which entails international responsibility" (Article 2).

Unlike States, international organisations are derivative, secondary subjects of

W. E. Butler, Perestroika and International Law, 221–226.

international law. They are distinctive in that they lack such features as sovereignty. The international legal personality of international organisations "is a quality recognised for them by contemporary international law; contemporary international law proceeds in principle by recognising that any institution which is an international (inter-State) organisation has this quality."[5]

Naturally this is not to say that States and international organisations enjoy equality as subjects of international law. "The diversity of paths when a State and an international organisation become a subject of international law predetermine that States have and an international organisation lacks the properties of sovereignty and determine the distinctiveness of an international organisation as a subject of international law."[6]

As regards the issues being considered here, this finds concrete expression in the fact that "unlike the institute of State responsibility which exists ipso facto, the responsibility of international organisations arises only ipso jure."[7] Being based on an international treaty as the constitutive act, various international organisations are endowed with dissimilar amounts of rights and duties, and therefore naturally have varying amounts and limits of responsibility.

The institute of responsibility divides subjects of international law into two groups: subjects bearing responsibility, and subjects having the right to demand responsibility be borne. A fully-fledged subject of responsibility must be in a position to act in one or the other capacity.[8] Do international organisations, having regard to the specific features of their legal personality, meet these propositions?

Various utterances, sometimes contrasting ones, exist in international legal doctrine on these issues. Therefore it is advisable to turn to the factual aspect of the matter.

Responsibility and international practice

The Advisory Opinion of the International Court of Justice of 11 April 1949 on the compensation of harm incurred in the service of the United Nations has played a significant role in the theoretical treatment of the issues of the responsibility of international organisations. According to this Opinion, the United Nations as a bearer of international rights and duties may exercise its rights by filing international claims. The competence to bring claims represents the capacity of the organisation to have recourse to methods deemed to be customary in international law for establishing, filing, and settling claims. Among those methods are protest, negotiations, demanding an investigation, and referring the case to an arbitration tribunal or a court.[9]

The ICJ Advisory Opinion recognised the right of the United Nations to bring claims against governments. Relying on this opinion, the General Assembly at its fourth session adopted on 1 December 1949 Resolution 365(IV) empowering the

United Nations Secretary General to conduct negotiations with States to recover the damage sustained by the United Nations and its employees.

International practice knows a number of examples of when the United Nations acted as a plaintiff. In connection with the murder in 1948 of the United Nations mediator, Count Bernadotte, the United Nations demanded compensation for the damage sustained. In a letter of 21 April 1950 addressed to the Israeli Minister of Foreign Affairs, the United Nations Secretary-General demanded: (1) that Israel make formal changes and continue to search for and punish the criminals; (2) compensation of the damage sustained by the United Nations in the amount of $54,628. In September 1952 the United Nations Secretary-General made a second claim against Israel for compensation of damage in the amount of $23,233 in connection with the murder of a U. N. military observer.[10]

At the present time the conclusion is clear that it is possible for claims to be brought by an international organisation itself, pursuant to the Advisory Opinion of the ICJ of 11 April 1949, whether a universal or a regional inter-State international organisation. As Schermers has noted in this connection, if the right to bring claims directly is not prohibited in the Charter of the organisation or in some other document, it has the right to do so.[11]

More complex is the issue of the possiblity of bringing suit against a State which is not a member of the organisation. The ICJ has answered this question positively with respect to the United Nations.[12] But one important circumstances must be taken into account. The United Nations is an organisation of a universal character whose members consist of practically all the States of the world. Therefore, its bringing a suit against a non-member States is well-founded. As regards regional international organisations, the situation is different. In the present writer's view, a regional organisation bringing suit against a non-member State is possible only if that State was in a treaty relationship with the organisation, since otherwise it is difficult to imagine who norm of international law may be violated as the basis for responsibility.

In characterising the specific features of an international organisation it is important to dwell on its capacity to bear responsibility. As already noted, there are no general norms in contemporary international law which regulate these questions. Nonetheless a number of treaties have emerged in recent decades which speak directly of these organisations as subjects of inter-national legal State responsibility. Their conclusion is linked first with the effectuation by international organisations of activities relating to the use of material objects, among which are means relating to so-called sources of increased danger (space rockets and sputniks, nuclear installations, and so forth).[13]

This was reflected for the first time in the Declaration of Legal Principles Governing the Activities of States in the Exploration and Use of Outer Space of 13 December 1963. Point 5 of that Resolution noted that "When activities are carried on in outer space by an international organisation, responsibility for compliance with the principles set forth in this Declaration shall be borne by the international organisation and by the States participating in it" (G.A. Res. 1962 (XVIII).

Subsequently this provision was consolidated in the 1967 Treaty on Principles Governing the Activities of States in the Exploration and Use of Outer Space, Including the Moon and Other Celestial Bodies. Article VI of the Treaty provides: "When activities are carried on in outer space, including the moon and other celestial bodies, by an international organization, responsibility for compliance with this Treaty shall be borne both by the international organization and by the States Parties to the Treaty participating in such organization." And Article XIII stipulates that: "Any practical questions arising in connection with activities carried on by international inter-governmental organizations in the exploration and use of outer space, including the moon and other celestial bodies, shall be resolved by the States Parties to the Treaty either with the appropriate international organization or with one or more States members of that international organization, which are Parties to this Treaty."[14]

Article 6 of the 1968 Agreement on the Rescue of Astronauts, the Return of Astronauts and the Return of Objects Launched into Outer Space establishes:

> For the purposes of this Agreement, the term "launching authority" shall refer to the State responsible for launching, or, where an international intergovernmental organization is responsible for launching, that organization, provided that that organization declares its acceptance of the rights and obligations provided for in this Agreement and a majority of the States members of that organization are Contracting Parties to this Agreement and to the Treaty on Principles Governing the Activities of States in the Exploration and Use of Outer Space, including the Moon and Other Celestial Bodies.[15]

Thus at present there are quite a sufficient number of examples of consolidating the responsibility of international organisations in respective international legal documents. Can one consider, however, that the mere violation of these treaties is grounds for the responsibility of the organisations to arise? In all likelilhood the grounds for responsibility are significantly broader.

The responsibility of an international organisation may arise when its organs violate norms of general international law or norms contained in the constitutive act or internal law of that organization. Hypothetically, moreover, an international organization must bear responsibility for such actions as war propaganda, racism, acts of aggression, and the like, that is, for actions which are classified by international law as an international crime and represent a threat to international peace and security.[16]

Types of responsibility

However, what types of responsibility are applicable to international organisations?

It is wholly evident that they may bear material responsibility. Two variants are possible in this event: first, joint and several responsibility with member States; and second, through establishing the responsibility of the organisation itself and then of the States who are members. This follows since one cannot exclude a situation in which an international organisation is not in a state to itself compensate for material harm caused by its actions. Moreover, and most importantly, the organisation is not a sovereign entity and its actions in the overwhelming majority of instances are determined by the actions of its member countries, and this in turn makes it possible to carry over responsibility in some measure to the member States.

An example of resolving the issue of joint and several responsibility of an international organisation and States-parties is the 1972 Convention on International Liability for Damage Caused by Space Objects (Article XXII(3):

> If an international intergovernmental organization is liable for damage by virtue of the provisions of this Convention, that organization and those of its members which are States Parties to this Convention shall be jointly and severally liable; provided, however, that: (a) Any claim for compensation in respect of such damage shall be first presented to the organization; (b) Only where the organization has not paid, within a period of six months, any sum agreed or determined to be due as compensation for such damage, may the claimant State invoke the liability of the members which are States Parties to this Convention for the payment of that sum.[17]

To be sure, this does not preclude the possibility of an international organisation being exclusively responsible. This could arise, for example, in the case of specific activities of officials of an organization undertaken inviolation of its constitutive act and damaging the prestige of the organisation.

Together with material responsibility there exists political responsibility. As G. I. Tunkin notes, all forms of State responsibility except financial responsibility, from so-called moral satisfaction to the various measures connected with limiting a State's sovereignty, and so forth, are treated as political responsibility: "... all types of the responsibility of a State as a political entity have to a certain extent a political character. Nonetheless, one can hardly object to isolating financial responsibility as an independent type of responsibility. At the same time, there are forms of responsibility not linked to financial compensation. It is more correct to treat all these forms of nonmaterial responsibility as political responsibility."[18]

The application of material responsibility to international organisations has, as we have noted, a certain specific nature. However, the political responsibility of international organisations must be even more particular because the organization lacks both sovereignty and territory. Therefore, with respect to an international organisation the application of such types of political responsibility as temporary limitation of sovereignty, occupation of territory, and the like are precluded.

226

At the present time this issue has been treated only to the slightest extent not merely in doctrine, but in practice there are few precedents. Nonetheless, one can point to a number of possible forms of political responsibility which in one way or another have been considered in Soviet international legal literature.[19]

Above all, an international organisation may make official apologies. The conflict in 1959 in IMCO could have been resolved in this way if the chairman of the Assembly of that organisation had made appropriate apologies to Panama and Liberia on the basis of the advisory opinion of the International Court of Justice of 8 June 1960.[20]

An international organisation can be deprived of certain rights and privileges. It would be admissible, for example, when an official performs actions outside the scope of the constitutive act of the organisation. In this event the official might be deprived of diplomatic privileges.

This examination of the problems appertaining to the international responsibility of international organisations shows how little they have been worked out. International practice requires that a profound and comprehensive theoretical consideration commence.

Notes

1. See Iu. T. Barsegov, *Mirovoi okean: pravo, politika, diplomatiia* (1983), p. 7.
2. N. A. Ushakov, *Osnovaniia mezhdunarodnoi otvetstvennosti gosudarstv* (1983), p. 3.
3. *Yearbook of the International Law Commission 1963*, I, pp. 299–305.
4. R. Bernhardt, et al. (eds.), *Encyclopedia of Public International Law*, V, p. 162.
5. E. T. Usenko, "Sovet Ekonomicheskoi Vzaimopomoshchi – subekt mezhdunarodnogo prava," in *Sovetskii ezhegodnik mezhdu-narodnogo prava 1979* (1980), p. 42.
6. E. A. Shibaeva and M. Potochnyi, *Pravovye voprosy struktury i deiatel'nosti mezhdunarodnykh organizatsii* (1980), p. 47.
7. Iu. M. Kolosov, *Otvetstvennost' v mezhdunarodnom prave* (1975), pp. 242–243.
8. *Ibid.*, p. 243.
9. *ICJ Reports* (1949), p. 177.
10. *Everyman's United Nations 1945–1958* (1959), pp. 428–429.
11. H. Schermers, *International Institutional Law* (1980), p. 937.
12. Note 9 above, p. 184.
13. Note 9 above, p. 249.
14. *Vedomosti verkhovnogo soveta SSSR* (1967), no. 44, item 588.
15. *Vedomosti SSSR* (1969), no. 4, item 31.
16. See note 6 above, p. 63.
17. *Mezhdunarodnaia zhizn'*, no. 5 (1972), p. 157.
18. G. I. Tunkin, *Theory of International Law*, transl. W. E. Butler (1974), p. 424.
19. See Note 6 above, p. 64; E. M. Krivchikova, "Nekotorye teoreticheskie aspekty problemy otvetstvennosti mezhdunarodnykh organizatsii," *Uchenye zapiski MGIMO*, vyp. 3 (1972), pp. 4–12.
20. See E. A. Shibaeva, *Pravovoi status mezhpravitel'stvennykh organizatsii* (1972), p. 134.

THE LAW OF INTERNATIONAL ECONOMIC INSTITUTIONS AND THE PRINCIPLE OF UNIVERSALITY IN THE CONTEMPORARY INTERNATIONAL LEGAL ORDER

KABIR-UR-RAHMAN KHAN

Salient features of international economic institutions

International institutions may be, and generally are, studied in terms of their functions and structures, that is, largely on the basis of their constitutive texts and the decisions made under those provisions.[1] This in itself, though valid, is at best a partial approach. In a pioneering work on international organisation, Inis Claude has rightly established that in addition to structures and functions, international organisations also essentially involve a *process* of regulation.[2] This observation is particularly valid in relation to international economic institutions. As a process of international regulation, an international organisation, for example the GATT, has to be examined not only by its text but by its economic principles and precepts and assumptions which nurture that text. And in assessing the compatability of an international economic institution with the contemporary international legal order, it is necessary to examine that institution in all its relevant dimensions. Thus, an international economic institution may be universalist in its text; that is, it is open to all States, and yet may operate on economic precepts and principles which are very parochial and restrictive. The operative norms of the GATT, for example, stem from the liberal free market economy, and consequently State intervention or direction is very much frowned upon.[3] The principle of substantive universality requires that modern international institutions are not only comprehensive in membership but they function on broadly-based and generally shared precepts and norms.

The international legal order, which originates from the Treaty of Westphalia (1648), has certain hall-marks set by that treaty: equality of States, law-making through consent of States, and States being the direct and initially the sole instruments of international action. This system, which is appropriately described as the Westphalia model, has been supplemented by the Charter of the United Nations. The salient characteristics designed or instituted by the Charter are: in the sphere of maintenance of international peace, it attempted to institute an authoritative system. Building on the balance of power technique,[4] the Concert of Europe of the

W. E. Butler, *Perestroika and International Law*, 227–243.
© 1990 *Kluwer Academic Publishers. Printed in the Netherlands.*

nineteenth century,[5] gradual containment of the recourse to war, and the Pact of Paris 1928,[6] the Charter (Chapter VII) provides for effective machinery for international measures for the maintenance of peace, with legal power to the Security Council to declare a threat to peace and to institute a permanent UN force.[7] This authoritative model proved largely an aberration; in practice, a coordinative model has become the norm.

Secondly, the material scope of the Charter system is much broader than that of any of its preceding systems. In addition to the maintenance of international peace it deals with the conditions which are recognised as prerequisites to the establishment of international peace, such as elimination of colonisation or to put it in positive terms, with securing self-determination of peoples, human rights, and social and economic development.[9]

Third, since the measures needed for the achievements of the above positive objectives cannot be confined to some prescriptive rules, but process has to be institutionalised and pursued through stages. While organs of States retain, as in the past, the ultimate say, the quasi-legislative system first utilised in the International Labour Organisation,[10] or its variations are increasingly used.[11]

Fourth, the Charter provides a machinery for coordination with international organisations dealing with specific social and economic areas, the so-called specialised agencies.[12] Thus the Charter system extends to the UN and the related organisations, combinedly described as the United Nations System.[13]

Fifth, the Charter system is firmly rooted in the principle of universality.[14] The Charter system is not the Concert of Europe to which only the European and Christian nations had access, and the Ottoman Empire, a Muslim nation, was not admitted until 1856.[15] The universality of the Charter system extends not only to the sphere of membership of the international community, but necessitates a recognition of major legal systems of the world, as demonstrated in the Statute of the International Court of Justice,[16] and the right of nations to choose their own economic and political system, as recognised by the Covenant on Economic Social and Cultural Rights.[17]

In 1969 Richard A. Falk, in a study of the two systems, observed: In the contemporary international system the Charter conception is far from fully realised, the Westphalia conception is far from fully displaced.[18] One could perhaps add that far from replacing the Westphalia system, the Charter System has added some ad ediface to that system, particularly by providing new instruments of coordination, and these new instruments, interestingly enough, have come largely through international economic institutions of the UN System.

Salient characteristics of GATT

With all its complexities, the GATT utilizes simple, and in legal terms primitive, modes of regulation. Part I, comprising only two articles, provides a framework for negotiated reduction of tariffs on the principles of reciprocity and non-discrimination. The latter is more formally described as Most-Favoured-Nation treatment.[19] The two principles serve interrelated, but distinct functions. Reciprocity provides the basis on which tariff concessions are negotiated and exchanged among principal suppliers and buyers of particular products; and the MFN principle prescribes how the negotiated concessions are shared among the GATT members. In this sense, the MFN principle serves a distributive function.

Reciprocity

The principle of reciprocity is of cardinal value in bilateral or regional trade relationships among States of relatively homogeneous economic standards. At global level, however, this principle suffers from serious limitations. The GATT, with respect to Part I, is based on the sanguine, though unsustainable, assumption that all members of the GATT enjoy an equal bargaining position, that in the framework of multilateral trade negotiations of the GATT all members will emerge with "reciprocal and mutually advantageous benefits;"[20] that all members of GATT operate and have a more or less uniform tariff policy. This assumption presented serious difficulties when some socialist countries began to negotiate accession to the GATT.[21] Further, one operational rule of the principle of reciprocity initially was that negotiations for tariff concessions should be on an item-by-item basis. This mode of negotiation, which may be described as single-track reciprocity, is very restrictive.

Most of these assumptions relating to reciprocity have now been modified. The item-by-item tariff negotiations worked reasonably well in the early years of the GATT when the items in world trade were within manageable limits and the number of GATT members was not large. With the multiplicity of trading items and the expansion in the membership of GATT, this process of negotiations has proved to be cumbersome and counterproductive. Thus since the Kennedy Round of the multilateral trade negotiations, the sectoral approach has been adopted.[22]

That every country operates tariffs is generally but not universally true. Since the GATT is open to accession by all States – and is universalist in its membership – this assumption, as was shown in the example of Poland's membership, has to be modified. In that case, an innovative approach was taken under which dual-track reciprocity was instituted, that is, in exchange for tariff concessions by GATT members Poland offered guaranteed access to her markets for the imports from the GATT parties, with prescribed annual increase.[23]

Perhaps the only other instance of this type of dual-track reciprocity was that relating to wheat during the Kennedy Round. Several European countries, including the United Kingdom, undertook to import specified quantities of wheat from North America under the multilateral contract system of the International Wheat

Agreement and in exchange received tariff concessions from the United States.[24]

Despite these two rather unsuccessful experiments in extending the scope of reciprocity, there is an independent and perhaps more cogent case for operating dual-track reciprocity in the multilateral trade negotiations of GATT. Such an extension of reciprocity is particularly called for in relation to the current negotiations under the Uruguay Round on services and intellectual property. In these negotiations only the capital-surplus and capital exporting countries are likely to benefit from a new regime, as a capital-importing country has very little to gain from the vacuous exchange of reciprocal rights.[25] Interestingly, in the recently-negotiated Protocol on Global System of Tariff Preferences among Developing Countries provision for broad-based reciprocity is made, and the reciprocal benefits are construed more widely.[26]

Another assumption underlying the principle of reciprocity – that all participating members of GATT are more or less equal and thus capable of benefiting in tariff negotiations – has long been jettisoned and replaced by a recognition that in the original multilateral trade negotiations system of the GATT, further prejudiced by the protectionist practice of major trading nations, the developing countries, now comprising majority in GATT, have failed to, and in the normal working of that system are unlikely to, benefit from the world trading system, and that a special, albeit temporary, regime was needed. This recognition was first officially stated in the famous Haberler Report on GATT in 1958.[27] This led to the adoption of Part IV and in pursuance of its provisions the Generalised System of Preferences has been accorded.[28] The need to give special concessions to developing countries on non-reciprocal and differential basis was placed legally on firmer ground in 1979, by the Enabling Clause.[29] The GSP does not now need specific exemption under the waiver clause of Article XXV(5) but receives general recognition under the Enabling Clause of 1979. But the GSPs however remain unilateral, selective, with a total control of donor countries on material scope, and as to selection of the beneficiaries. Attempts to place these schemes on firmer and negotiated regimes, something on the lines of the Lomé Convention between the EEC and ACP countries, have remained unsuccessful.[30]

Non-tariff barriers

Part II of GATT, comprising over twenty articles, deals with various forms of non-tariff barriers. The mode of regulating these barriers varies according to the hierarchy of disapproval or acquiescence by GATT. Dumping, for example, is condemned in GATT; hence the measure to deal with this transgression is legitimised self-help on the part of the complaint party. In the original provisions of GATT, the corrective measures of self-help was susceptible to "auto-determinism" and carries few restraints.[31] Subsequently, the anti-dumping code has attempted to rectify the imbalance resulting from unrestrained measures of self-help.[32]

In relation to subsidies, the GATT has an ambivalent attitude. It largely acquiesces to production subsidies attempting to regulate export subsidies through the reporting technique and by giving an aggrieved member the right to seek remedies against alleged impairment or nullification of benefits and concessions otherwise received.[33]

Dealing with State-trading enterprises, GATT construes such enterprises in terms of exclusive and special privileges and requires the members to apply the principle of non-discrimination, which is elaborated to mean that decisions in relation to buying and selling of products by such enterprises are required to be made strictly on commercial considerations.[34] In contrast, special measures for the development of new industries in developing countries are made subject to special scrutiny and approval. Each such case requires special approval by the GATT and needs to be prefaced by an agreement for compensation to a member who felt aggrieved by such a plan.[35] Not surprisingly, these cumbersome provisions have been very sparingly used.[36]

The general pattern in GATT relating to non-tariff barriers, with the exception of dumping, is that of a weak form of coordination. These barriers are loosely defined, the general attitude of GATT being expressly or implicitly indicated and according to that attitude, a certain standard of behaviour is prescribed for members – which may be that of national treatment, equitability, or non-discrimination. The GATT exercises general surveillance, and the members may seek remedy under consultation and complaint machinery.[37] This original approach of regulation by reference to specific standards soon was supplemented by a developed regime with more specifically defined objectives and greater accountability through reporting or complaint procedures.[38]

Regionalism versus global regime

As in the fields of collective security and human rights, the original design of the global system has been largely replaced by regional regimes. In the original design of the Havana Charter, the global system of world trade was envisaged in terms of a gradual elimination of tariff barriers through Most-Favoured-Nation Treatment and reciprocity, and only as a minor alternative, was voluntary association among some member States through regional arrangements recognised as a desirable route to the expansion to world trade.[39] It is difficult to imagine that the drafters of Article XXIV, which deals with regional arrangements through customs unions and free trade areas, could have foreseen the multiple-tier complex of the EEC: a customs union of twelve members, a network of about sixty free trade areas under the Lomé Convention, further layers of preferential arrangements with numerous countries,[40] and the prospects of forming a customs union with EFTA countries.[41]

The total membership of GATT at present is just over 90, and the States involved with the EEC complex approaches 70. Not surprisingly, MFN is no longer considerd to be the best possible treatment in world trade. This raises a fundamental question as to the future role of GATT in the legal regulation of world trade. With the upsurge of the regional complex such as the EEC and with the possible growth of the Global System of Tariff Preferences among Developing Countries, the Most-Favoured-Nation treatment – a cardinal benefit under GATT – has obviously lost its original attraction; but GATT is more than the mere sharing of tariff concessions on the MFN principle. The original coordination role of GATT is perhaps more reinforced by recent changes, particularly in relation to providing specific rules for the containment of non-tariff barriers and for mediating between different trading groups and parties.

The GATT will also need to develop measures concerning the new phenomenon of counter-trade. Several developing countries, having failed to secure for their products access to the markets in the developed countries, are increasingly linking the purchase of manufactured products from developed countries with the disposal of their products. Strictly, it may involve an infringement of the principle of non-discrimination as it offers benefits only to specific customers, but with the limited opportunities open to developing countries, this is one means available to them for promoting their trade.[42]

Settlement of disputes

A major flaw of the contemporary international legal order is that most legal regulations are either truncated from an effective machinery for the settlement of disputes or are at best only linked with a nebulous provision for the peaceful resolution of conflicts. As an exception to this trend, the correct position was stated in the 1928 Declaration of Paris, which linked inextricably the renunciation of war with the unqualified and comprehensive obligation to settle all disputes of whatever origin by peaceful means.[43]

In GATT the machinery of peaceful settlement is further enfeebled by the fact that in the original provisions there was little, if any, room for third party adjudication.[44] The main form of resolution of conflicts in GATT is consultation, which essentially is an element of negotiation. A significant contribution of GATT, however, is that it has given a legal connotation to the term consultation which it otherwise did not have. There is an obligation to consult; consultation is conducted in accordance with the provisions, and within the parameters of, the General Agreement. Consultation initially is between the parties or perhaps with the mediation of GATT, a minor element of third-party involvement. In the event of a failure to consult, if the GATT so adjudges, corrective action may be prescribed against a recalcitrant or offending party, which is in the form of withdrawal of concessions or obligations under the agreement.[45]

The consultation machinery of the GATT, based on the good faith and "best endeavour" model, is open to abuse and has serious flaws. The provision of Article XXII "Each contracting party shall accord sympathetic consideration ... to representations ... by another contracting party ..." gives a semblance of a firm obligation, but in practice has proved to be a device of protraction.

Second, consultation, being a species of negotiation, is more suited to the parties which are more or less equal economic strength and where each has extra-legal means to persuade the other, for example, the United States and EEC. Between two unequal contracting parties, such as Botswana and the EEC, consultation is less likely to produce fair results. The ultimate corrective measure – the withdrawal of concessions or other obligations – in itself assumes that such a measure would be effective. But such an assumption is only valid in relation to more or less equal partners. An attempt to institutionalise the settlement of dispute machinery in 1955 was rejected at the Review Session mainly on the ground that the parties preferred to preserve the then existing situation and that to establish judicial procedure might put excessive strain on the GATT.[46]

Some of the deficiences of the consultation machinery have been mitigated by the institution of Working Parties and Panels and by the provisions reducing the possibility of protraction by a recalcitrant or transgressing contracting party. These improvements were consolidated in the Understanding of 28 November 1979.[47] A major improvement in this repect is the institution of Panels which in their constitution and function have certain recognised elements of judicial organs, for example third party composition, the requirement of impartiality, and application of the provisions of the General Agreement.

In relation to disputes between developing and developed countries, the good offices of the Director-General of GATT may be requested.[48] In the current Uruguay Round of the Multilateral Trade Negotiations, the Ministers committed themselves to improve "and strengthen the rules and procedures of dispute settlement process" with a view to ensuring "prompt and effective resolution of disputes to the benefit of all contracting parties." Negotiations shall also include the development of surveillance machinery over compliance of decisions and recommendations.[49]

A provisional agreement has also been reached, which improves certain aspects of the settlement of dispute machinery. The general objective of the settlement of disputes has been succinctly stated:

Contracting parties recognize that the dispute settlement of GATT serves to preserve the rights and obligations of contracting parties under the General Agreement and to clarify the existing provisions of the General Agreement. It is a central element in providing security and predictability to the multilateral trading system.[50]

234

The process of consultation is expedited by requiring a contracting party to whom request for consultation is made to respond within ten days and to enter into consultation within thirty days of that request. If no response is made within that period, request for the institution of a panel shall be made within sixty days.

These are but minor changes, and an effective machinery needs to be supplemented by other measures. One major difficulty relating to the settlement of disputes in GATT stems from its own provisions which contain loosely-defined precepts, for example subsidies or dumping, or contains deceptively simple and attractive criteria: for example, that of "trade-creating" in relation to a customs union or free trade area in Article XXIV, or the requirement application of equitable shares in the world market in relation to subsidies for export.[51] These matters can be better resolved by the clarification of law and not by mere strengthening of the institutional machinery of the Panel System, conciliation, and arbitration. This is gradually being done by the so-called transparency in the national provisions in the related areas, and the improvement of surveillance machinery for those national domestic provisions. The various codes adopted in the Tokyo Round illustrate this approach substantively.[52] Interestingly, a similar approach to the harmonisation of laws is adopted in the field of promotion and protection of investments.[53]

International monetary fund

The international monetary order, designed at the Bretton Woods conference in 1944 and a prerequisite to fair and secure world trading system, has three elements. Two relate to national currencies, that is, fixed par value system and convertibility; the third element relates to the provision of resources in foreign currencies to member countries facing temporary disquilibrium in their balance of payments.[54] The fixed parity system had now been replaced by flexible provisions[55] – it would be an exaggeration to call it a system – and the lending by the IMF has changed beyond recognition. Some characteristics of these two major functions are worth noting.

The fixed parity system, untypically for international organisations, was a perfect legal regime. The obligation to have one's currency fixed at an agreed level was clearly stated and rigorously applied, for such an arrangement was a prerequisite to membership. Any change in the agreed par value could only be made for specific reasons and within prescribed margins and by consultation with the IMF. A violation of these obligations entailed the sanction of being declared ineligible for Fund's resources.[56]

But that legal regime had the Achilles' heel of unrealistic and transient assumptions, for example, that a monetary regime of the fixed parity system of a region could be sustained without any corresponding coordination of national economies, particularly those factors which created pressures on the world monetary system; or that the United States dollar, which was the effective reference currency for the operation of the fixed parity system, would continue to be backed by a thriving and surplus economy in the United States. As the depression in the Western economies began to set in during the early 1970's and the American economy came under strain, the fixed parity system collapsed.[57] That collapse left in its wake perhaps two salutary lessons: One, that a single-track regulation of the parity system without supporting coordination in the national economies of the member countries cannot operate, let alone be successful, for long; and second, that it is hazardous to pivot the international monetary system on a single particular reference currency.

The Jamaica accord, which gave formal recognition to that demise of the old regime and formally amended Article IV of the IMF, now has a more flexible regime. Each member may adopt exchange arrangements of its choice, but should notify the IMF of its choice and any subsequent changes. In the distant horizon the goal of a stable but adjustable exchange rate is kept alive. This flexible arrangement is supported by the old-style "best-endeavour" method of coordination, as the members are enjoined to pursue the objective of economic growth and reasonable price stability and to seek orderly and economic financial conditions. The Fund has been given the much-heralded function of surveillance over the exchange rate arrangements and in general over the compliance of each member with its obligations. Among the latter, there is a specific and prescriptive obligation that the members must avoid manipulation of exchange rates with a view to gaining unfair competitive advantage.[58] The IMF is mandated to exercise "firm surveillance" and to that end develop specific principles and guidelines.[59] There are three essential elements of surveillance: first, an obligation on the part of the members to notify the initial decision and to provide additional relevant information; second, an obligation to consult on a regular basis or on specific request by the Managing Director of the IMF; and third, and perhaps most importantly, the development by the IMF of the standards by which the obligations of the members are to be adjudged. The 1977 principles evolved by the IMF, it has been rightly observed, provide minimal guidance in the way of explicit norms. Since the obligations under that article are indeterminate, there is no machinery for implementing the norms contained in the guidelines. An obvious shortcoming of the present surveillance system is that its reach is somewhat restricted. The shortcoming is in the translation of generally agreed recommendations and norms into effective decisions and policies at national level.[60] As the Managing Director of the IMF has observed:

What is needed now is the political will on the part of the membership to carry forward their commitments into policy decisions and concrete action. This applies, of course, with particular force to the major industrial countries who have been outside the reach of conditionality, yet whose policy actions have such a decisive influence in shaping the world economic environment.[61]

This is the nub of the problem. Another flaw, which a discerning commentator has observed, is that the operation of surveillance has largely been bilateral. Instead of concentrating on the situation of the individual country, the interaction of the policies of major countries should also be taken into substantive consideration.[62]

In relation to the lending functions of the IMF, one major element is the unsymmetrical relationship that obtains between the IMF and its borrowing members. The stand-by arrangements, which are the bases for borrowing from the Fund, are not treated, unlike the loan agreements between the World Bank and its members, as an international agreement:

> Stand-by arrangements are not international agreements and therefore language having a contractual connotation will be avoided in stand-by arrangements and letters of intent.[63]

While the IMF has full authority to take appropriate corrective measures in the event of non-fulfilment of the terms of the stand-by arrangement, a member has little or no remedy in relation to those arrangements.

Another instance of unsymmetrical relationship, which has become more pronounced, relates to the present debt crisis. While the full force of conditionality and surveillance by the IMF is brought to bear on a borrowing country, the private creditors, the major financial institutions are not subject to any surveillance as to their policies relating to their increased role in the world economy. They, who perhaps contributed to the aggravation of the debt crisis in the first place, should be subject to some advanced surveillance by the IMF.[64]

World intellectual property organisation

The international patent system, now administerd by the WIPO, was created by, and is essentially based on, the 1863 Paris Convention for the Protection of Industrial Property.[65] The high ideal of constituting a Union for the protection of industrial property among the member States with uniform international standards implemented through national legislation was jettisoned at the early stage of negotiations of the Paris Convention.[66] The diversity of provisions and economic precepts in national legislation of the member countries was too wide to be bridged by a single international convention. The minimalist approach was thus prudently adopted. The international patent system of the Paris Convention has three main strands. First, the objective and scope of the protection of industrial property is stated. Article 1 gives very wide meaning to that protection:

(3)   Industrial property shall be understood in the broadest sense and shall apply not only to industrial and commerce proper, but likewise to agricultural and

extractive industries and to all manufactured or natural products ...

(4)   Patents shall include the various kinds of industrial patents recognized by the laws of the countries of the Union, such as patents of importation, patents of improvements, patents and certificates of addition, etc.[67]

In securing this protection, the Paris Convention set two international standards: the right of priority[68] and independence of patents.[69] The right of priority gives a patentee who has registered his application in one country of the Union a priority of claim for one year in all members of the Union to enable him to have his claim registerd in those countries. The principle of independence of patents gives each patent an independent legal existence; thus, nullification of that patent in one country does not entail an automatic nullification in other member countries.

The second strand of the international patent system is the requirement of national treatment as a standard for securing the protection of industrial property. An effective protection of industrial property as envisaged by the Paris Convention can only be accorded if national legislation provides the range of protection envisaged by the Paris Convention.[70] This could, however, be a vacuous exercise if States retained an unfettered freedom as to the content of their legislation. Thus, as a corollary of constituting a "Union for the protection of industrial property,"[71] Article 25 of the Paris Convention sets an obligation of the contracting parties "to adopt, in accordance with its constitution, the measures necessary to ensure the application of this Convention."[72] It is further assumed that by the deposit of its accession, a new member has expressed its readiness to implement the Convention.[73]

There is considerable divergence as to the scope of national legislation. It is, on one hand, contended that States remain free, subject to the minimum constraints of the Paris Convention, to adopt measures, and give scope, to protection of industrial property. A member of the Paris Union is thus free to determine what sectors are or are not patentable. Some Western industrialised nations, in particular the United States, is of the view that the question of what is patentable is in itself determined by the international convention.[74] The United States has threatened to deny Brazil certain benefits under the GATT because Brazil has refused to grant patents to certain American applicants in the field of pharmaceutical products.[75]

Third, the international patent system sets certain minimum standards of protection. These, it is significant to note, are largely to curb the power of the patent-giving States in taking corrective measures against a foreign patentee. For example, it is stated that the mere importation of patented goods in itself does not entail forfeiture.[76] While it is somewhat grudgingly recognised that the non-working of a patent may constitute an abuse of the patent system, an action for compulsory licence in the case of such an abuse cannot be taken in the first three years of the grant of that patent, and even then the patentee is given a good and broad defence, that is "if a patentee justifies his inaction by legitimate reasons."[77] The legitimate reason may cover any commercial, technical, and market reasons. A patent can be revoked only in exceptional cases.

With this rather heavy emphasis on the protection of industrial property and with only a half-hearted recognition that the patent system may be abused, the international patent system gives little recognition to the call from developing countries for the reform of the international patent system so as to eliminate its obvious abuses, nor does it recognise that the international patent system can profitably be used as an instrument of transfer of technology.[78] The international regime is also based on the old precept, and reward for an invention is envisaged in the form of the exclusive and monopolistic right entrusted to the patent over the commercial exploitation of their inventions. In 1967, when the USSR declared its intention at the Stockholm Conference to accede to the Paris Convention, it put forward a case for the recognition of the Inventor's Certificate, which gives full recognition of the right over and reward for an invention on fair and equitable basis and separates the right of the State to appropriately exploit that invention for the public interest.[79] One obstacle to bringing about appropriate changes in the Paris Convention is that, being a product of the nineteenth century, it leaves the States-parties as the chief and direct arbiters of change. It does not have any provision for amending the substantive provisions of the convention through the organs of the Union; such a change can only be brought about by the old-style diplomatic conference, that is, by unanimity.[80]

Thus the substantive provisions of the international patent system fall short of the goals of universality. In the current Uruguay Round of the multilateral trade negotiations of GATT, proposals put forward by the United States for the trade-related provisions of intellectual property are being considered. The Ministerial declaration sets the agenda on this issue:

> In order to reduce the distortion and impediments to international trade, and taking into account the need to promote effective and adequate protection of intellectual property rights, and to ensure that measures and procedures to enforce intellectual rights do not themselves become barriers to legitimate trade, the negotiation shall aim to clarify GATT provisions and elaborate as appropriate new rules and disciplines.[80]

The United States, the main proponent of this proposal, has more specifically declared its aim "to conclude, in the new GATT round of multilateral trade negotiations, an enforceable multilateral trade agreement against trade-distorting practices arising from inadequate protection of intellecual property."[82] Among the proposals being considered is the United States Proposal which should provide adequate and substantial standards for the protection of intellectual property, effective international enforcement measures, and the utilisation of improved machinery for the settlement of the disputes in GATT. Brazil, who with other major developing countries has been against this extension, has proposed that the discussion on this issue should be in the broader context of growth and development, bearing in mind the impediments that the present international patent system causes for the transfer and technology for developing countries.[83]

It is more than likely that the superior bargaining power of the major Western industrialised nations would, in this case as in others, prevail and some new code or standards relating to the strengthening of the present intellectual property regime would emerge from the current negotiations. But it may be noted that GATT negotiations have virtually bypassed the normal machinery of the WIPO and Paris Convention, and unless there are some preferential and differential treatments for developing countries, as in relation to trade, such provisions are less likely to be of much benefit for the majority of GATT members, the developing countries.

Conclusions

The criteria for establishing the need for reform, it is suggested, are effectiveness, the principle of universality, and equal or equitable bases of economic relationship.

The principle of reciprocity – a cardinal principle governing economic transactions – with its accompanying assumption of equal bargaining positions of the participants and more or less equal economic standard, is unsuited for a general organisation such as GATT. It has been replaced, temporarily at least, in relation to developing countries. Reciprocity, as operated in GATT, has hitherto been largely a single-track phenomenon; this could be made more effective by introducing wider tracks. The replacement of item-by-item negotiations by sector-based negotiations is a step in the right direction.

The authoritative model of legal regime, such as operated in the IMF in relation to a fixed parity system, is unusual in the international legal system, as it was based on unrealistic and ephemeral assumptions. This in due course has been replaced by a more traditional "endeavour" model.

In the legal regimes examined above, three models of coordination are identified. The "best endeavour" model now utilised in the new Article IV of the IMF, the good-faith coupled with the prescribed standards of behaviour, such as national treatment and non-discrimination and some surveillance, as used originally in the GATT, and lastly the model used in the Paris Convention on the protection of industrial property: international standards fused with national treatment, and a prescribed threshold of minimum standard of protection with little international accountability.

The "best endeavour" model is at best a transitory device; it needs to be strengthened by more specific obligations and measures of international accountability. The surveillance provisions of the IMF at present fall short considerably in their effectiviness. National policies need to be more specific and conducive to the achievement of the objectives set for the international monetary system.

The experience in GATT has shown that the good-faith model in itself does not enable the parties to contain, let alone eliminate, non-tariff barriers. This was soon supplemented by specific definitions of the various relevant barriers, reducing the rampant use of "auto-determinism," and introducing greater accountability.

The pattern of regulation utilized in the field of intellectual property is an interesting fusion of the so-called Union Standard, national treatment, and the threshold of minimum standards; but being the product of the phase of the unorganised stage of the international legal system, it lacks the element of international accountability. Concentrating on the protection of the patentee, it falls short in conforming to the principle of substantive universality.

The principle of universality historically has been an integral part of public international law, originally as a rule of reason, and in the post-Charter phase, empirically, by the universal membership of the international community. This universality in relation to international economic institutions, however, requires that the diversity of economic precepts and systems prevalent in the major regional groups of the international community comprising the United Nations System are given full recognition in the working of these institutions. In this respect, in varying degrees, all the three organisations examined above call for reform. The GATT has made remarkable strides meeting the special needs of the developing countries and also in accomodating the centrally-planned economy countries. The Paris Convention has given recognition to the Inventor's Certificate, but still falls short of giving substantive recognition to public interest and of eliminating the abuse of patent system as an instrument of monopoly.

The IMF falls perhaps by a wide margin in the implementation of the principle of substantive universality. In its lending functions, it operates on an authoritative unsymmetrical model; and the unequal relationship between the Fund and its borrowing members is further aggravated by the fact that the Fund allows its effective tool of conditionality to be used in transactions – loan facilities – which involve non-governmental organisations who in themselves are not subject to IMF discipline.

The settlement of disputes, as originally provided in GATT, was largely a part of the process of negotiation. The essential nature of that machinery has not changed by the institutionalisation of the Panel System or by the recent improvements agreed at the Uruguay Round. The difficulty perhaps lies in the ambivalence of objectives and interdeterminate nature of some concepts used in GATT.

On the issue of regionalism versus global system, one need not be pessimistic. While the role of the Most-Favoured-Nation treatment as an instrument of gaining the best possible treatment no doubt has diminished, the role of GATT in ensuring non-discrimination, in providing machinery for tackling non-tariff barriers, in mediating in controversies among different units and States has increased.

On the membership of international institutions, in particular GATT, while one can see good reason for the membership-by-negotiation rule, such negotiations should perhaps conform to some objective rules and have some time-limits. In the coordination model, national legislation and system, as has been noted, has an important role. At present, however, the international system and national systems are seen as distinct, perhaps even opposed to each other. An effective international system can only be built on more effective links with the national systems.

Notes

1. See, for example, D. W. Bowett, *The Law of International Institutions* (4th ed., 1982); M. A. G. Van Meerhaeghe, *International Economic Institutions* (1985); and H. G. Schermers, *International Institutional Law* (1972).
2. I. L. Claude, *Swords into Ploughshares* (1965), p. 8: "International organizations may come and go, but international organization is here to stay" (p. 5).
3. See Article VII (State trading enterprises) and Article XVIII (governmental assistance for economic development).
4. F. H. Hinsley, *Sovereignty* (2d ed., 1986), pp. 199–200.
5. R. B. Mowat, *The Concept of Europe* (1930).
6. Article I provides: "The High Contracting Parties declare in the names of their respective peoples that they condemn recourse to war for the solution of international controversies, and renounce it as an instrument of national policy in their relations with one another." Article 2 stipulates: "The High Contracting Parties agree that the settlement or solution of all disputes or conflicts of whatever nature or of whatever origin they may be, which may arise among them, shall never be sought except by specific means." *LNTS*, XCIV, 57.
7. H. Kelsen, *The Law of the United Nations* (1951), Chapters 10 and 18.
8. R. Higgins, *United Nations Peacekeeping 1946–1967* (1980); see volume 3 on Africa, for example.
9. Kelsen, note 7 above, chapter 16.
10. *LNTS*, XV, 40; also see S. M. Schwebel (ed.), *The Effectiveness of International Decisions* (1971), pp. 134–155.
11. O. Y. Asamoah, *The Legal Significance of the Declarations of the General Assembly of the United Nations* (1966).
12. Kelsen, note 7 above. The Charter provisions are based on Article 24 of the League of Nations Covenant.
13. See United Nations, *A Study of the Capacity of the United Nations Development System* (1969).
14. G. Schwarzenberger, *International Law and Order* (1971), pp. 5–6.
15. Note 5 above.
16. Article 9 of the ICJ Statute provides that in electing judges the electors shall bear in mind "... that in the body as a whole the representation of the main forms of civilisation and of the principle legal systems of the world shall be assured."
17. Article I provides that all "peoples have the right of self-determination. By virtue of that right they freely determine their political status and freely pursue their economic, social, and cultural development."
18. "The Interplay of Westphalia and Charter Conceptions of International Legal Order," in

R. A. Falk and C. E. Black (eds.), *The Future of International Legal Order* (1969), I, pp. 32–33.

19. On these two principles of GATT, see J. H. Jackson, *World Trade and the Law of the GATT* (1969), chapters 11 and 12.

20. Preamble to GATT. Also see *ibid.*, chapter 10.

21. See K. R. Khan, "The Law of the GATT, Aspects of East-West Trade and Expanding Principles of Reciprocity," *Anglo-Polish Legal Essays*, II (1986), pp. 113–148; F. Yu-Shu, "China Membership of the GATT: A Practical Proposal," *Journal of World Trade Law*, XXII (1988).

22. Note 19 above.

23. GATT, *Basic Instruments and Selected Decisions*, Supp. [hereinafter *BISD*]; Khan note 21 above.

24. Khan, *The Law and Organisation of International Commodity Agreements* (1982), chapter 5 and pp. 229–230; also see UNCTAD, TD/5Add.1, cited in note 19 above, p. 729.

25. J. M. Finger and A. Olechowski (eds.), *The Uruguay Round* (1987), pp. 239–240.

26. See Kahn, "International Law of Development and the Law of GATT,", in F. Snyder and P. Slinn (eds.), *International Law of Development: Comparative Perspectives* (1987), pp. 175–214; and for further developments, *UNCTAD Bulletin*, no. 223 (June 1986).

27. GATT, *Trends in International Trade* (1958).

28. For the development and salient provisions of Part IV entitled "Trade and Development," see A. Yusuff, *Legal Aspects of Trade Preferences for Developing Countries* (1982).

29. *BISD* 265/203 (1980).

30. UNCTAD, General Report on Generalised System of Preferences, TD/B/C.5/9, 22, 41, 53, 67/Corr.1, 73, 81/Corr.1, 90, 96, 105 and 111/Add.1.

31. Article VI.

32. *BISD* 26/56 (1980).

33. E. McGowan, *The Law of the GATT* (19), Chapter 6.

34. *Ibid.*

35. *Ibid.*, Chapter 9; GATT, Article XVIII.

36. By 1980 only four cases were listed under this heading. See *BISD*, II/21 (1949); II/20 (1949); II/27 (1949); Sri Lanka, Cuba, Haiti, and India.

37. McGowan, note 33 above, Chapters 6 and 7.

38. *BISD* 265/8, 56, 116, 171 (1980).

39. K. W. Dam, *The GATT, Law and International Organization* (1969), Chapter 7.

40. *BISD*, 26/371–72 (1982) Index lists the various arrangements of the EEC.

41. *Financial Times*, 15 March 1989 and 17 March 1989.

42. R. F. Bertrams, "Countertrade and the Third World," in P. De Waart et al., *International Law and Development* (1988), Chapter 4.4.

43. Note 6 above.

44. Articles XXII and XXIII, GATT; also E. McGowan, "GATT, Adjudication and Negotiation," in M. Helf et al., *The EEC and GATT* (1986).

45. Articles XXII and XXIII, GATT; Note 33 above.

46. *BISD*, 26/203 (1980), p. 215, fn. 2.

47. Understanding Regarding Notification, Consultation Dispute Settlement and Surveillance, *BISD*, 26/210 (1980).

48. *Ibid.*, p. 211; note 33 above, Chapter 1, section 16.

49. See the Ministerial Declaration in note 25 above, p. 219.

50. GATT, MTN.TNC/7 (MIN), p. 26.
51. Article XVI, GATT, Sec. B(3).
52. *BISD*, 26 (1980), pp. 3–189.
53. ICSID, *Annual Report* (1988).
54. Article I, IMF; see note 1 above (Meerhaeghe)
55. See new Article IV, IMF.
56. Meerhaeghe, note 1 above, Chapter 1.
57. J. Williamson, *The Failure of World Monetary Reform 1971–74* (1977).
58. Article IV, IMF.
59. IMF, *Selected Decisions of the International Monetary Fund and Selected Decisions* (1981), pp. 8–16.
60. W. E. Holder, in *Proceedings of the American Society of International Law 1986*, p. 33.
61. IMF Survey, 10 December 1984, p. 379, cited in *ibid.*
62. E. Brau, "Surveillance of National Economy and Financial Policies," in *Proceedings*, note 60 above, pp. 35–38; also see G. G. Johnson, "Enhancing the Effective Surveillance," *Finance and Development*, XXII (1985), 2–6.
63. Guidelines on Conditionality, 2 March 1979, note 59 above, p. 20.
64. World Bank, IMF, BIS, and OECD, *External Debt Definition: Statistical Coverage and Methodology* (1988), Table I. See also *The Independent*, 18 March 1989.
65. WIPO, *Paris Convention for the Protection of Industrial Property 1883* (1986); *id.*, *Background Reading Material on Intellectual Property* (1988), Chapters 4 and 5.
66. S. P. Ladas, *The International Protection of Industrial Property* (1930), pp. 73–99.
67. *Paris Convention*, note 65 above, p. 6.
68. Article 4, *ibid.*; *Background*, note 65 above, p. 88.
69. Article 4bis, *ibid.; Background*, note 65 above, p. 111.
70. Article 2, *ibid.*
71. Article 1, *ibid.*
72. *Ibid.*, p. 40.
73. *Ibid.* (Article 25, para. 2).
74. See Khan, "The International Patent System: A Cass for its Reform from Developing Countries," in *Science Technology and Development*, V (1987), 3–10.
75. *Financial Times*, note 41 above.
76. Article 5, *Paris Convention*, note 65 above.
77. Article 5(a) (4), *ibid.*; *Background*, note 65 above, Chapter 4, Section 14.4.
78. United Nations, *The Role of Patents in the Transfer of Technology to Developing Countries* (TD/B/AC.11/19) (1975).
79. WIPO, *Records of the Intellectual Property Conference of Stockholm* (1967), II, para. 2549; *Background*, note 65 above, pp. 110–111.
80. Article 18, *Paris Convention*, note 65 above.
81. Note 25 above, p. 239.
82. *Ibid.*, p. 206, fn. 1. Also see R. Stern, "Intellectual Property," *ibid.*, pp. 198–206.
83. Note 50 above.

INTERNATIONAL ADJUDICATION TODAY IN THE VIEW OF A SOVIET INTERNATIONAL LAWYER

G. G. SHINKARETSKAIA

The negative attitude on the part of the Soviet Union toward international adjudication has for many years been mentioned in the Western literature on the peaceful settlement of disputes. In recent years, however, the position of the Soviet Union on this issue has changed. The beginning was laid in the course of the Third United Nations Conference on the Law of the Sea, when it was proposed to include as one of the elements of the "package" the compulsory settlement of disputes in the future comprehensive Convention with regard to its interpretation and application, without recourse to any other procedures. The Soviet delegation at the Conference did not express great enthusiasm on this occasion, stressing the need to draft as carefully as possible the substantive needs so as to minimise future disagreements concerning their significance.[1]

When signing the 1982 Convention on the Law of the Sea, the Soviet delegation made a Statement concerning the choice of compulsory procedures for the settlement of disputes under Article 287(1) with the participation of the USSR. The Soviet Union chose arbitration as provided for by Annex VII and special arbitration for disputes concerning fisheries, the protection and preservation of the marine environment, marine scientific research, or navigation, including pollution from vessels and by dumping as provided for in Annex VIII. Also recognised was the International Tribunal for the Law of the Sea on questions connected with the prompt release of vessels and their crew under Article 292.

The extent of the jurisdiction of compulsory organs was greatly reduced by reservations made in accordance with Article 298: the Soviet delegation declared that the USSR does not recognise any compulsory procedures with respect to disputes concerning the delimitation of boundaries and military activities, nor disputes with respect to which the United Nations Security Council exercises functions entrusted to it by the United Nations Charter.[2]

Remarkable turnabouts began after perestroika commenced. Soviet international legal thinking began to turn to the compulsory jurisdiction of the ICJ. New publications emerged in the literature. One of M. S. Gorbachev's articles favoured recognising the compulsory jurisdiction of the ICJ on mutually acceptable conditions.[3] Later, speaking at the United Nations, Gorbachev proposed that all States accept such jurisdiction with respect to the interpretation and application of human rights agreements.

We now confront the enormous task of analysing the experience of international courts and arbitration tribunals. To date the literature on the means of the peaceful

W. E. Butler, Perestroika and International Law, 245–258.
© 1990 *Kluwer Academic Publishers. Printed in the Netherlands.*

settlement of disputes generally and on the ICJ in particular was a literature for the "dilettante," or expressed more officially, for specialists. All the books written on this subject throughout the entire history of the Soviet State can be placed on one little shelf. We shall use the experience of jurists from other countries.

International adjudication is a proceeding in an international court. International agreements do not define an international court: this is the task of doctrine. The *Encyclopedia of Public International Law* states, for example:

> International courts and tribunals are permanent judicial bodies, composed of independent judges, whose tasks are to adjudicate international disputes on the basis of international law according to a pre-determined set of rules of procedure, and to render decisions which are binding upon the parties.[4]

Although the author refers only to courts and tribunals, it is not limited to these, but also may apply to permanent arbitration tribunals, particularly to those provided for by Part XV of the 1982 Convention on the Law of the Sea. Such a general approach is not contrary to the Convention. Together with the words "court or tribunal"[5] in Part XV is used the general expression "procedures specified in this Part."[6] The same provisions define the use of courts and tribunals, their jurisdiction, provisional measures, access, applicable law, preliminary proceedings, and others.

The difference consists solely in that the composition of the courts is permanent, whereas the membership of arbitration tribunals is determined anew in each instance of recourse. A special procedure is described in Annex VII, Article 3, for this purpose. However, it is appropriate to recall here that any international court also commences a proceeding by establishing the bench. Respective prescriptions are also in the 1982 Convention. For example, Article 13(2) of the Statute of the Tribunal for the Law of the Sea provides that the Tribunal shall determine which members are available to constitute the Tribunal for the consideration of a particular dispute, having regard to the effective functioning of the chambers.

Not every judge may be a member of the bench. According to the Statute of the Tribunal, his previous participation in the proceedings in a particular case in a national or international court (Article 8[1]) prevents his being a member of the bench. Tribunal members resolve doubts which arise with respect to any judge (Article 8[4]).

The difference between the means for forming an arbitration tribunal and a judicial bench consists in the fact that the court itself decides the question of the bench, whereas with respect to the arbitration tribunal, the last word belongs to the chairman of the Tribunal (Annex VII, Article 3[e]) or to the United Nations Secretary General (Annex VIII, Article 3[e] on Special Arbitration).

Even greater similarity exists in the means of forming an arbitration tribunal and the special chambers of international courts created at the request of the parties to consider a specific case and formed "with the approval of the parties" (Article

15(2) of the Statute of the Tribunal for the Law of the Sea).

Such similarity between the arbitration tribunal and the international court is no accident. Being the result of the development of arbitration tribunals, modern international courts have preserved a rather solid tie. Lady Fox writes: "In many respects ... the Permanent Court was – and its successor, the International Court, even more so, remains – an institutionalised arbitration tribunal rather than a court."[7]

Therefore, in speaking of international arbitration one may have in view a proceeding in both an international court or in arbitration tribunals; the more so, if one is speaking of means of settling disputes under Part XV of the Convention, where provision is made for permanent arbitration tribunals having, just as courts, compulsory jurisdiction.

All the elements of the concept of international adjudication are simultaneously precise and diffuse. Consider one element: "judicial organs." In international courts there is a judicial bench, the litigating parties, witness testimony, experts, and most importantly, the decisions of the courts are binding, which brings them close to national courts. However, the absence of means to enforce this decision gives international courts a very different character than national courts. The international court renders a decision, but there is no power by which it can compel a sovereign State to fulfil it.[8] For example, the usual request to the ICJ is to give judgment on whether particular actions of a State are consistent with international law. But if the Court believes that actions do violate international law, it may not specify measures to terminate the violation. This means that a sovereign State may never be "punished" as a result of a judicial proceeding. The court declares the inconsistency with law, and only that. The State itself whose actions are deemed to depart from international law must not only concur with the Court's opinion but also decide what measures should be taken to eliminate the violation as well as implement those measures.

The independence of judges is not a self-contained concept. Independence just as in national legal systems is a means of ensuring impartiality in rendering decisions. No one should exert pressure on a judge, and a judge should be subordinate to no one except to international law, and he should be guided by nothing other than international law.

There are two aspects to this problem: the independence of an individual judge and of the court as a whole. No person grows up in a vacuum, and every judge is shaped within the framework of a particular system and carried the ideas of that system with him to an international court. Hence the idea to assemble as members of a universal judicial institution the citizens of various States, or in more polished form, through the representation of various people to ensure the representation of different schools of law, legal trends, and even world outlooks. Thus, in the Statute of the International Court there is a provision on the need to ensure the representation of the principal forms of civilisation and legal systems of the world.

T. O. Elias explains that the two expressions "civilisation" and "legal system" ... are intended to represent the divergent ways of political thought and social action as well as the diverse juridical ideas in the world of today."[9] In his view it would be appropriate to replace these terms with the word "cultures."

The idea of the "personification" of legal systems at one time was widely shared in world literature in general and in Soviet literature, especially as it seemed a way to alter the membership of the ICJ sufficiently so that the Court could never take doubtful decisions. In the treatise on international law published in 1968, after concluding that "one can not pass over many decisions of the Court which to a significant extent discredited it in the eyes of peaceloving peoples," said: "All the facts cited testify to the urgent need to materially change the membership of the Court."[10]

In fact, it is not so simple. A multicultural composition of the Court, to be sure, is consistent with the prestige and authority of such a universal international organisation as the ICJ; however, an honest man elected to the Court must be capable of discarding narrow egoistic interests of his nation. The position of Lord McNair in deciding a whole series of cases is a worthy example.[11]

Ensuring a diverse membership of the Tribunal for the Law of the Sea differs from the traditional approach. Article 2(2) of its Statute says that in the Tribunal as a whole must be assured the "representation of the principal legal systems of the world" and "equitable geographic distribution." These two conditions are quite different. Whereas the "representation of the principal legal systems" is a traditional requirement, "equitable geographic distribution" leans to the side of having regard to the political and ideological unity of the world.

The essence of the requirement becomes understandable when it is viewed in the larger context of the 1982 Convention on the Law of the Sea and especially the Third UNCLOS: a characteristic feature of the Conference was not only representing the requirements and interests of individual States, but bringing them together in "interest groups," the geographic position of a particular State sometimes becoming the criterion for entry into a particular group (for example, landlocked States). The influence of the ideas of regionalism, strongly manifested in the Conference, were felt here.

The requirement of diversity with respect to arbitration was strengthened in Annex VII, Article 2(1) on the right of every State Party to nominate in a list maintained by the Secretary-General four arbitrators. Thus, the representation of various schools of law or cultural systems is ensured here more consistently than in the case of the Tribunal for the Law of the Sea, for here each State has a full equal right when necessary to form an arbitration tribunal and appoint arbitrators who are not only not its own citizens but and not even on the list.[12]

The independence of a court as a unified organ is determined by its character as a legal institution working on the basis of law, with the assistance of law, and for law. From the formal point of view, any dispute may be referred for international adjudication. In Article 36 of the Statute of the ICJ the definition of a "legal dispute" relates only to disputes referred to the Court unilaterally (para. 2), the general provision being that the "jurisdiction of the Court comprises all cases which the parties refer to it" (para. 1). However, Article 38(1) provides that "the Court ... is to decide in accordance with international law such disputes as are submitted to it," which deprives the Court of the possibility of submitting facts from the political, military, or other advantageous viewpoint. The Court itself has repeatedly emphasised that its task is purely a legal one. Recently the Court once again affirmed this position. In the judgment in the case of Nicaragua and Honduras,[13] one of the objections against the acceptability of the Nicaraguan suit made by Honduras was that the suit was imbued with politics and therefore the ICJ as a judicial body could not consider it.[14]

The Court rejected this objection, declaring that "The Court is concerned to establish ... that the dispute before it is a legal dispute, in the sense of a dispute capable of being settled by the application of principles and rules of international law ... The Court's judgment is a legal pronouncement, and it cannot concern itself with the political motivation which may lead a State ... to choose judicial settlement."[15]

It is precisely this, the evaluation of events from the standpoint of international law, that ensures the impartiality of the Court. Otherwise it would be impossible for the Court not to favour one of the litigants before all the data had been elicited and evaluated. The balance of interests of individual States, a balance whose maintenance guarantees observance of the common interests of all States and the preservation of general humanitarian values, is expressed only in norms of international law. Only norms of international law offer a standard against which events and facts can be measured to demonstrate whether they conform or not to the lawful interests of all.

A category such as a "previously determined selection of procedural norms" is relative in nature. To be sure, the ICJ and the Tribunal for the Law of the Sea each operate in accordance with rules of procedure. These rules are purely of a formal nature and seemingly deprive the parties in dispute of their autonomy of will. In fact this is not so, and States retain a great degree of freedom. Here perhaps is one of the paradoxes of international adjudication, the most striking one. Judge Manfred Lachs wrote that international adjudication is generally like a two-faced Janus.[16]

Rules of procedure have developed in waves. Historically, they were not formalised when first used: organs settling a dispute were not bound by any rules. Formalisation commenced with the 1899 and 1907 Hague Conventions. Next the rules of procedure were clarified. Perhaps the 1982 Convention on the Law of the Sea represents the highest peak of detail. The Reglament of the Tribunal for the Law of the Sea under preparation it appears will continue this line of development. Moreover, there is an evident growth in popularity of the ad hoc chambers of the

ICJ, which shows that States prefer to influence the organisation and course of the proceedings.

One characteristic of an international court – the most "judicial" feature – is that the decision is binding upon the parties to the dispute. But the completely different basis for this binding nature in comparison with national courts must be stressed. Within a State the binding character of judicial decisions is created by law and maintained by the authority of State power and secured by coercive force. This is wholly absent in the international arena. Agreement underlies the binding nature of decisions of an international court or arbitration tribunal. Only the common will of sovereign States serves as the source of the imperative force of a decision and guarantees its fulfilment.

The treaty nature of the binding character of a decision explains why States not participating in the dispute are formally indifferent to it. The treaty does not create either rights or duties for third countries, and therefore the decision has no direct legal force for non-parties to the dispute. However, third countries are bound to respect it, as they respect any other international obligations of parties to any agreement. Obviously, third countries are bound to behave so as not to create obstacles to execution of the decision. Moreover, in accordance with general principles of the international law of treaties, third countries may assume obligations to take part in effecting the decision or assisting the parties to the dispute to do so.

The functions of international courts and arbitration tribunals

Soviet scholars, just as jurists the world over, evaluate the role of international courts and arbitration tribunals in the modern world from the standpoint of the three functions they perform: peaceful settlement of international disputes, the maintenance of legal order, and the development of international law. To be sure, this classification is conditional: the settlement of disputes leads to legal order; without the development of law, in turn, it is impossible to maintain legal order and to settle disputes.

The primary function of international adjudication is the settlement of international disputes, that is, as defined by the Permanent Court of International Justice: "disagreement on a point of law or fact, a conflict of legal views or interests between two persons."[17]

What does "settle a dispute" mean for an international court or arbitration tribunal? Can we say that as a result of the decision made by a court the "conflict of legal views" ceases to exist? The practice of international courts is already rather rich and diverse enough to say that the ultimate outcome of a dispute depends upon the task which the parties to the dispute have entrusted to it.

This task can be divided into two categories: (a) to assess legislative or other actions from the standpoint of their conformity to international law (for example, the *Anglo-Norwegian Fisheries* case); (b) to suggest what principles and norms of international law should be applied to settle the situation in dispute between the parties (the best example is the application of the Netherlands, Federal Republic of Germany, and Denmark to delimit the continental shelf). The difference between these two is, as Judge H. Mosler writes, that in the second instance the Court "only settles part of the dispute, e.g. a preliminary question of law, leaving the parties free to resolve the matter on the basis of the preliminary ruling."[18]

But when the Court does not simply say what principles and norms are applicable to a resolution of the dispute, and renders judgment on the lawfulness of specific activities, the implementation of this judgment appertains, as already noted, to the parties themselves. Changing the situation so that the relations between the parties are restored, that is, a de facto true resolution of the dispute, is done by the parties themselves. Having determined the legal position of the parties, the court may not control their future conduct and relations, and is not competent to settle issues which arise in connection with the execution of its decision.

As regards the law-creation function of international courts and arbitration tribunals, Soviet literature, unlike Western, has not discussed the issue. In a country where the decisions of national courts have no significance as precedent, the notion of courts creating law is alien to jurists. Soviet doctrine has accepted the thesis formulated by G. I. Tunkin: "... decisions of the International Court enter the process of norm-formation as part of international practice in that they relate to the declaration of the existence of norms of international law or their interpretation."[19]

For a long time, when the ICJ had only academic significance for the Soviet Union, this thesis was adequate. Now, with enlivened interest in international adjudication, the appearance of new studies should be expected analysing in more detail the role of international courts and arbitration tribunals in the development of international law.

An international court does not create international law, but makes its contribution to the development thereof through the judicial resolution of specific legal problems. First, the court explains the law; second, it formulates the norm which should operate between those States who believed its content to be ambiguous and applied to the court for an explanation. One of the parties may deny the existence of the norm in general. For this part the norm formulated by the court is a new one, and with respect to the State concerned, direct law-creation of the Court. In relations between the parties in dispute, this newly formulated norm replaces the effect of previous ambiguous or disputed norms. To be sure, the introduction of this norm into bilateral or multilateral but local agreements is possible only thanks to the agreement of the parties in dispute that the Court formulate a new norm for them. The court itself has no right to formulate new norms, that right being delegated to it by sovereign States. The combined will of the parties in dispute is the source of the new norm. However, there is the role of the court as a highly qualified organ giving such formulations of norms which reflect the true content of the right directly. The court so to speak assists this norm, which exists covertly, to emerge.

The experience of the modern progressive development of international law leaves no doubt on this score. Whatever realm of international relations we take, we cannot avoid seeing that the decisions of the ICJ have played the role of preparatory materials when drafting important international documents, including universal documents. The international law of the sea and the 1982 Convention on the Law of the Sea are a perfect illustration. Sir Robert Jennings cited the *Anglo-Norwegian Fisheries* case as having been "of the very greatest importance in giving a new direction to legal development in a particularly important and sensitive area of international law."[20]

Soon after the entry into force of the 1982 Convention on the Law of the Sea an interesting process will begin: the settlement of disputes concerning its interpretation and application in organs of international justice. Since the drafters of the Convention in an effort to balance often completely opposed interests widely used compromise, and since its norms regulate a number of new phenomena of international life, many Convention provisions require clarification. The Convention still has not entered into force, but some of its provisions already have become the object of judicial interpretation. In the decision to refer to the ICJ a dispute on the continental shelf Tunisia and Libya requested the Court, in particular, to have regard to equitable principles as well as the recent trends admitted at the Third Conference on the Law of the Sea."[21]

As John Collier has correctly noted, the ICJ had "to take into account factors which may become part of the law, but are not yet such."[22] Although the judgment of the ICJ has been much criticised for neglecting the criterion of equidistance, it has become part of the jurisprudence. In fairness we should note that we have read the criticisms of this judgment but possibly there are supporters of it whom we simply have not read. Without commenting on the problem before the ICJ in particular, the present writer was impressed in this judgment by the fact that Judge Gros criticised it in his dissenting opinion in the *Gulf of Maine* case for the significance placed on the equation of international law plus equity in deciding problems of delimitation. The indefiniteness of the legal concept of equity and the various meanings attached to it in different systems of thought make it possible to have regard to the views of the parties to the utmost extent: equitable is that which the parties have agreed to regard as equitable. It is the combination of these two things will enables the settlement of a conflict to be achieved in relations between parties. The framework of international law serves as a guarantee that this decision is not an abuse or the result of coercion by one party. The conflict will end, the dispute is resolved, and that is what is required.

Another example of peaceful settlement after the Third Conference on the Law of the Sea is the arbitration award in the Canadian-French dispute concerning the

St. Lawrence Bay,[23] which touched upon the legal status and regime of the exclusive economic zone – a new category of marine expanses introduced by the United Nations Convention on the Law of the Sea. The matter concerned the right of French trawlers to process their catch in St. Lawrence Bay within the Canadian exclusive economic zone. Although the arbitration tribunal based its award on an interpretation, first of all, of the 1972 Canadian-French agreement on fishing, it had regard to the events which had occurred in international law since the conclusion of the 1972 agreement, having studied a number of 1982 Convention provisions and used them in its argumentation.

This is a noteworthy event: it may serve as a pattern for the possible use of means of dispute settlement under the 1982 Convention after it enters into force by third countries. In this writer's view, the access of non-parties to the arbitration tribunals provided for in the 1982 Convention is possible only by agreement and not with regard to disputes concerning the interpretation and application of the Convention but only disputes concerning the interpretation and application of "agreements connected with the purposes of the Convention."

An agreement such as the 1972 Canadian-French agreement may be classified as an "agreement connected with the purposes of the Convention," and Canada and France are non-parties (since it is not yet in force, and Canada and France have any obligations under it). Application of the norms of the 1982 Convention is unavoidable in interpreting this agreement, and since the decision is binding upon the parties, conditions are created for extending if not the letter than the spirit of the 1982 Convention to the relations of non-parties. Thus, the court or arbitration tribunal in this instance is clearly developing the law prevailing between the parties in dispute, bringing it closer to the Convention.

The consistency and successiveness of decisions are important for the development of law, and therefore the proponents of the concept of developing law through the courts usually stress the usefulness of permanent judicial organs. Yet another peculiarity of the effect of the Convention will be the fulfilment of this role not only by the ICJ or International Tribunal for the Law of the Sea, but also by arbitral and special arbitral tribunals.

The provisions of Part XV of the 1982 Convention and the Annexes are so structured that the arbitration tribunals are something very close to an ad hoc chamber of an international court. Although the number of arbitrators in the list may be rather large (each State-Party may appoint 4 persons), it all the same is limited; the applicable law is determined; and to a rather large extent, also the procedural framework. It is difficult to imagine that the arbitrators, in commencing to examine a new case, are not informed of how their colleagues acted in preceding cases. And since arbitration is accorded a place of priority among the compulsory procedures (Article 287), one may suppose that no fewer cases will pass through than through the courts.

For a long time the functions and role of compulsory means of peaceful dispute settlement have been evaluated in Soviet literature from the standpoint of an approach to the world divided into hostile camps. Since the principal task under this approach was to preserve peace, the ICJ was regarded as an instrument for preserving the peace. Was indeed that not the position of those who created the United Nations and the ICJ?

Placing the peace-creating mission of the ICJ as the top priority began even in the preparatory materials at the San Francisco Conference. Quoting from the Report of the First Committee of the Fourth Commission: "In establishing the International Court of Justice, the United Nations hold before a war-stricken world the beacons of Justice and Law and offer the possibilities of substituting orderly judicial processes for the vicissitudes of war and the reign of brutal force," Steinberger noted that these words expressed the hopes and expectations of the majority of countries.[24] And truly every Article of Chapter VI of the United Nations Charter on the "Pacific Settlement of Disputes" refers to disputes "the continuance of which is likely to endanger the maintenance of international peace and security," although in Chapter XIV on "The International Court of Justice" there is no such narrow orientation. In Chapter VI there is no preference for judicial settlement; the entire Chapter points towards political proceedings within the framework of the Security Council if the parties to a dispute threatening the peace do not settle it by one of the methods specified in Article 33.

Inclusion of the ICJ in the machinery for the maintenance of peace was a somewhat naive exaggeration of the possibilities of a judicial organ, as subsequent practice has affirmed. Although theoretically one could imagine a situation when recourse by the parties to a court would avert or terminate an armed conflict, there has not been a single instance in practice.

Oscar Schachter analysed all the instances when States had recourse to the ICJ in disputes connected with the use of force.[25] He included in his analysis an extensive range, from individual overflights of ships and aircraft to large-scale military operations, taking as the criterion the involvement of armed forces. Although the instances of the use of force in international relations since 1945 have been numerous (Schachter counted them in the hundreds), only 13 instances were referred to the Court, and only in one instance did the defendant (Albania in the Corfu Channel dispute) agree to take part in the proceedings.

From his analysis it is evident that the peace-creating role of the ICJ was only latent. Conflicts as such were not settled by decision of the Court, but yielded only to interference of the Security Council. But where the purely legal aspects were separated out and there was a jurisdictional basis to accept the case for proceedings, the ICJ could play a role. Schachter's general conclusion was that "cases involving the use of force may be suitable for adjudication by the Court." However, "cases involving current hostilities on a large scale present special difficulties for adjudication."[26]

His prediction was confirmed by the ICJ when Nicaragua appealed to it in connection with activities by armed groups on the frontier with Honduras. Although Honduras disputed the Court's jurisdiction to hear the case, he agreed to take part in the proceedings. The ICJ is not the only means of peaceful settlement used in this case. The active and persistent participation of other Central American States in lessening the conflict played an important role. When direct negotiations between Nicaragua and Honduras became impossible in 1983 because of increased tension, the neighbouring States formed the so-called "Contadora Group," as it was first called, and then the "Support Group." The Contadora procedure lasted for several years and was described by the ICJ as mediation; it undoubtedly facilitated bringing the relations of the parties in conflict to the level where it became possible to apply to the ICJ. But even afterwards multilateral negotiations continued with the framework of a procedure called "Contadora-Esquipulas P."

Now the situation in the world has changed. That which seemed so terrifying in 1945 – the flaring up of war and the death of people and loss of valuables – remains no less terrible. But things have emerged which are perhaps even more dangerous because they threaten with extinction not merely whole peoples but all mankind. Only the combined efforts of all people on this planet can confront these dangers. This new reality forces us to evaluate certain phenomena anew. International adjudication needs to find its place in this changing world.

Expressed in terms of international law, this new situation in the world presupposes the establishment of a unified legal order in the entire world that will accord to each sovereign State the freedom of action within the framework of generally recognised legal principles and norms. International courts and arbitration tribunals as organs settling disputes and explaining the law may be useful here. A closed circle needs to be created: international judicial procedures must facilitate the establishment of a climate of cooperation and good-neighbourliness. At the same time, they themselves can successfully work only in such a climate. The more developed is the legal order, the more effective are the legal means (carried over to the political as well) for settling disputes. Perhaps it is precisely because in the law of the sea that we have succeeded in agreeing a universal convention, that there also have emerged far-reaching and significant provisions on the settlement of disputes as included in Part XV.

At a time when the peaceful settlement of conflicts which arise is absolutely necessary in order to maintain the legal order, the legal order is indifferent as to which methods are used. Richard Bilder has noted that "effective international legal order can be, and in fact has been, maintained even in the absence" of adjudication.[27] But the modern international legal order can not be regarded as perfected, nor even simply satisfactory; the perfection of the legal order requires judicial procedures of great effectiveness.

True, sometimes compulsory procedures in this context are unpleasant, smack of an instrument of coercion. This phenomenon is especially to be noted in many works in connection with drafting norms on the settlement of disputes for the

Convention on the Law of the Sea.[28] These are echoes of the role which courts play within States. Although one may concur with those who believe that the existence of an international law and the probability of being brought before one will move States to settle their disputes without a judicial proceeding, it is doubtful whether a sovereign State will be guided in doing so by this type of apprehension.

The attitude of States towards international adjudication is traditionally described as "guarded." Virtually every study devoted to the ICJ ends with reflections on the topic: why is it not more popular and how can it be made more popular. A great deal of attention has been devoted to this problem by American scholars after the unfortunate refusal of the United States to recognise the compulsory jurisdiction of the ICJ under Article 36(2). Several analyses have been done and brilliant reckonings made. The conclusions are various. Widely known is the tragic phrase that the bell tolls for the compulsory jurisdiction of the ICJ, although some believe that these rumours are greatly exaggerated.

Is there hope that international adjudication will be used more extensively and become popular? The present writer proposes to answer this question affirmatively. Yes, there is hope, and it is well-founded.

The criteria for predicting the future the present writer, as a Marxist, derives from the past. Usually when assessing the popularity or effectiveness of compulsory procedures one takes the most obvious: the number of acceptances of the jurisdiction of the ICJ under Article 36(2) or the frequency with which the formula on referring disputes under a treaty to the ICJ is included in treaties. These criteria are too narrow; a sociological assessment is somewhat more attractive: an important role is played by the milieu about the Court and in which it functions, that is, the general world situation. The more favourable the atmosphere, the more effective is the Court. During the "cold war," the Court could not be a democratic institution. Only with the development of genuine good-neighbourly relations could one expect relations of confidence to be established between judicial organs and States.

Several phenomena are in sight now which will lead to the creation of a favourable situation for the activities of courts and arbitration tribunals:

[1]. The development of international law is proceeding rapidly. Its principles and norms are being clarified. The share of relations regulated by conventional norms is growing, together with customary norms. The norms are increasingly detailed.

[2]. There is a growth in international legal consciousness. Enormous masses of people previously indifferent to world politics and to the life of their neighbours on the planet are becoming active, people's movements being more distinctly shaped by categories of international law.

[3]. The role of international organisations is growing. Again we turn to the 1982

Convention on the Law of the Sea. Often we see in it provisions which oblige States not to undertake unilateral actions without the agreement of or at least without consulting international organisations. This affects many aspects of the struggle against pollution, determining the outer boundary of the continental shelf, establishing sea corridors and traffic movement schemes, and others.

[4]. The use of law enforcement procedures is expanding. In bilateral and multilateral treaties provisions are encountered more frequently concerning mixed commissions for the execution of the treaty, control machinery, sanctions.

All these are merely prerequisites for the creation of a true universal legal order, for a transition to the rule-of-law in international relations. But it is a beginning, a favourable trend.

These theoretical notions are confirmed by the practical steps of States.

Conclusion

In conclusion it is appropriate to quote the words uttered by the Prime Minister of Great Britain in an interview with the Editor in Chief of the popular weekly magazine *Ogonek*. Concisely formulating the multitude of problems confronting Britain and the Soviet Union, Mrs. Thatcher recalled the words of Winston Churchill: "Our difficulties, our problems are enormous, but sometimes before our gaze open the sunlit summits."

On 10 February 1989 the Presidium of the USSR Supreme Soviet adopted a decision to remove reservations concerning the non-recognition of the compulsory jurisdiction of the ICJ entered with regard to the 1948 genocide convention, the 1952 convention on the political rights of women, the 1949 convention on slavery and prostitution, the 1965 convention on the elimination of all forms of racial discrimination, the 1979 convention on the elimination of all forms of discrimination against women, and the 1984 convention against torture.

Commenting on the Edict, the chief of the international law division of the USSR Ministry of Foreign Affairs, Iu. M. Rybakov, used the following title-head: "We Give Priority to Law."

Notes

1. See the remarks of the head of the delegation of the USSR at the plenary session of the Conference, 5 April 1976. U. N. Doc. A/Conf.62/SR.68
2. *Law of the Sea Bulletin*, no. 1 (April 1986).
3. *Pravda*, 17 September 1987.

258

4. Ch. Tomuschat, "International Courts and Tribunals," in R. Bernhardt, et al. (eds.), *Encyclopedia of Public International Law*, I (1981), 92–93.
5. Articles 286, 288, 289, 290, 292, 293, 294, 296.
6. Articles 291, 295.
7. H. Fox, "States and the Undertaking to Arbitrate," *International and Comparative Law Quarterly*, XXXVII (1988), 6.
8. This is a simplified statement and does not take into account such powerful forces as world public opinion or enforcement under the United Nations Charter.
9. T. O. Elias, "Does the International Court of Justice, as it is Presently Shaped, Correspond to the Requirements which Follow from its Functions as the Central Judicial Body of the International Community?," in *Judicial Settlement of International Disputes* (1974), p. 23.
10. *Kurs mezhdunarodnogo prava v shesti tomakh*, IV, p. 384.
11. For example, in the *Corfu Channel* case and in the Anglo-Iranian case.
12. According to Annex VII, Article 3(b), members of the arbitration tribunal are appointed "preferably" from the list.
13. Case Concerning Border and Transborder Armed Actions (Nicaragua v. Honduras), Judgment of 20 December 1988.
14. *Ibid.*, p. 25.
15. *Ibid.*
16. M. Lachs, "Proces miedzynarodowy," *Panstwo i prawo*, XXXVII, no. 9 (1982), p. 16.
17. PCIJ (1924), Ser. A., No. 2, pp. 11–12.
18. H. Mosler, "Problems and Tasks of International Judicial and Arbitral Settlement of Disputes Fifty Years After the Founding of the World Court," in *Judicial Settlement of International Disputes*, p. 6.
19. G. I. Tunkin, *Theory of International Law*, transl. W. E. Butler (1974), p. 183.
20. R. Y. Jennings, "International Court of Justice," in *Judicial Settlement of International Disputes*, p. 37.
21. Case Concerning the Continental Shelf (Tunisia/Libyan Arab Jamahiriya), Judgment of 24 February 1982, p. 7.
22. J. G. Collier, "The International Court of Justice and the Law of the Sea," Paper delivered to the V Anglo-Soviet Symposium on the Law of the Sea, 17–23 July 1988, Moscow. Forthcoming.
23. See U. N. Doc. A/41/742. 20 October 1986.
24. H. Steinberger, "The International Court of Justice," in *Judicial Settlement of Disputes*, pp. 194–195.
25. O. Schachter, "Disputes Involving the Use of Force," in L. Damrosch (ed.), *The International Court of Justice at a Crossroads* (1986), pp. 223–241.
26. *Ibid.*, p. 241.
27. R. B. Bilder, "International Dispute Settlement and the Role of International Adjudication," in Damrosch, note 25 above, p. 162.
28. For example, L. Sohn, "Problems of Dispute Settlement," in *Law of the Sea: Conference Outcomes and Problems of Implementation* (1977), p. 227; J. K. Gamble, "The Law of the Sea Conference: Dispute Settlement in Perspective," *Vanderbilt Journal of Transnational Law*, IX (1976), 323.

NEW DEVELOPMENTS IN TECHNIQUES OF DISPUTE RESOLUTION: THE CANADIAN-AMERICAN FREE TRADE AGREEMENT

CATHERINE J. REDGWELL

On 1 January 1989 the Canada-United States Free Trade Agreement ("FTA") entered into force.[1] Despite several previous free trade initiatives between the two countries, it was not until negotiations commenced in the autumn of 1985 that the possibility of a free trade arrangement from the process appeared likely.[2] The United States was able to draw upon recent experience gained from the negotiation of a free trade area with Israel, which came into effect in September 1985.[3] At one stage the United States had promoted a regional free trade area for the whole of North America, a concept rejected by both Canada and Mexico. Nonetheless, the logic of a bilateral free trade agreement between Canada and the United States seemed inescapable. Over 80% of Canada's export trade is with the United States, notwithstanding the promotion in certain quarters of the "third option" – increased trade with the EEC. Rising protectionism in the United States in the 1980s had led many Canadian firms to fear that access to the larger American market was uncertain: indeed, the "single major condition" sought by Canada in the FTA was "that firms should be enabled to escape from both the old problem of limited market size and, what is a more recent variation on the same theme, uncertain access."[4]

But the FTA is more than simply an example of bilateral cooperation between close neighbours already tied economically and culturally. Both parties maintain that the agreement is consistent with Article XXIV of the GATT (which permits the establishment of free trade area arrangements) and there are frequent references to the GATT throughout the provisions of the FTA which is both consistent with and built upon GATT principles.[5] Not only has the GATT influenced the parameters and substance of the FTA, but the provisions of the FTA are arguably of great significance to the GATT during the Uruguay Round for at least two reasons: (1) the FTA is the first international agreement to be concluded that contains binding rules applicable to a wide range of trade in services;[6] and (2) it contains new methods of dispute settlement. These comprise two subject-areas of the fifteen which have been under consideration by Negotiating Groups during the Uruguay Round.[7]

The FTA does not diminish either parties GATT rights or obligations which are expressly preserved in Article 1205. Furthermore, both parties may avail themselves of either the FTA or GATT dispute settlement procedures in relation to trade

W. E. Butler, *Perestroika and International Law,* 259–274.

disputes – hence the FTA's appellation as the "GATT-plus system." It goes beyond the GATT in providing for, inter alia, a binding dispute settlement mechanism, which will be discussed below. In fact the FTA dispute settlement provisions cover two kinds of trade dispute: those which already arise in trade relations between Canada and the United States; and those which will arise in the future out of the FTA itself.

The purpose of this article will be to examine the dispute resolution mechanisms of the FTA in order to ascertain whether they are indeed of significance in the debate surrounding reform of existing GATT mechanisms of dispute resolution. This will neccessarily entail some discussion of the current dispute mechanisms of the GATT, its perceived failings, and the proposals for reform. Consideration of these matters is timely as the Negotiating Groups of the GATT reported in April 1989, and the dispute settlement mechanism of the FTA is already being put to the test by Canada through the reference of two disputes to it.[8]

Dispute settlement in the FTA

As mentioned above, the FTA adresses two different kinds of disputes: those arising from the interpretation of the Agreement itself, the provisions for which are located in Chapter Eighteen, entitled "Institutional Provisions"; and trade remedy procedures found in Chapter Nineteen of the Agreement, entitled "Binational Panel Dispute Settlement in Antidumping and Countervailing Duty Cases."

(1) Institutional provisions

The institutional provisions for joint management of the Agreement and the prevention and resolution of disputes arising from it are found in Chapter 18, the main provision of which establishes a Canada-United States Trade Commission (Article 1802). Disputes arising under the FTA and the GATT may be settled in either forum, according to the choice of the aggrieved party, but once the choice is made that dispute resolution procedure "shall be used to the exclusion of any other" (Article 1801.3). Should a dispute arise regarding the interpretation or application of the FTA,[9] or "whenever a Party considers that an actual or proposed measure of the other Party is or would be inconsistent with the obligations of this Agreement or cause nullification or impairment in the sense of Article 2011" (Article 1801.1), the steps to be followed in its resolution under the FTA are as follows:
- *mandatory notification* of any measure which a Party considers might materially affect the operation of FTA must be given; any information regarding an actual or proposed measure must be provided if requested by the other Party (Articles 1803.1 & 1803.3).
- either Party may request *consultations* regarding actual or proposed measures or

any matter affecting the operation of the FTA, in order to arrive at a mutually satisfactory resolution (Article 1804).
- if consultations fail the Parties may request a meeting of the *Canada-United States Trade Commission* within 30 days of the request for consultations under Article 1804; the Commission must meet within 10 days unless otherwise agreed and "shall endeavour to resolve the dispute promptly". In so doing the Commission may call upon technical advisors or on the assistance of a *mediator* acceptable to both Parties.
- should the Commission fail to resolve the dispute the additional dispute settlement procedures of the FTA apply, which are:

(1) *Arbitration* (Article 1806)
If the Commission has not resolved the dispute within 30 days of referral, it may refer the dispute to "binding arbitration". With the exception of safeguard actions under Article 1103, where arbitration is compulsory, each country exercises a veto through the Commission over the creation of a binding arbitration panel.[10] Moreover, by requesting binding arbitration the aggrieved party waives its rights to a GATT panel. As regards enforcement, "[If] a Party fails to implement in a timely fashion the findings of a binding arbitral panel and the Parties are unable to agree on appropriate compensation or remedial action, then the other Party shall have the right to suspend the application of equivalent benefits of this Agreement to the non-complying Party." (Article 1806.3)

(2) *Panel procedures* (Article 1807)
If the matter is not referred to arbitration either Party may request the Commission to establish a panel of experts to consider the matter; such a request requires waiver of GATT panel rights. Unless otherwise agreed the panel is to present its initial report to the Parties within 3 months of the appointment of the chairman; where feasible the Parties will be provided the opportunity to respond to the initial findings of fact of the panel before its final report is referred to the Commission.[11] If the Commission fails to reach agreement upon receipt of the panel recommendation, then as was the case with respect to non-compliance with arbitral awards the aggrieved Party may suspend the application of equivalent benefits under the FTA until the issue is resolved.

Regular annual review of the FTA is carried out by the Commission, which is composed of equal members of both parties and has the ability to appoint binding arbitration panels from the roster of experts it is obliged to develop and maintain (Article 1807.1). The panel may establish their own rules of procedure unless the Commission decides otherwise. In establishing panels each party is entitled to choose two national members with the fifth selected by the Commission. To prevent deadlock occurring with repect to the choice of panelists, and hence delay

262

in the establishment of the panel, the Agreement further provides that if the Commission is unable to select the fifth member, the other four members of the panel will choose, failing which the fifth member is to be selected by lot. (Article 1807.3) This is a clear attempt to avoid the problem of delays with the respect to the composition of panels encountered within the GATT. Furthermore, the parties are given strict time limits: within 15 days of the establishment of the panel a party must choose his members, failing which they will be drawn by lot from the roster of experts (Article 1807.3). One criticism of the GATT mechanism is that no such time limit exists. A point in favour of the GATT is the multinational character of the panel; under the FTA only nationals of the disputants will sit on the panel, which may lead to problems of political pressure being brought to bear on members as well as the possibility of conflicts of interest. Whilst such abuse is not unknown within the GATT, the potential for such abuse in the bilateral context appears much greater.

The general dispute settlement provisions described above have been called the "GATT-plus system" and their function was described to the House of Commons Standing Committee on External Affairs and International Trade as follows:

> In the event that either country feels the other country has taken some action that is inimical to their interest under this Agreement, it will be open to them to require the other country to notify them of such actions, to consult about it and to raise hob about it. If they are unable politically to resolve the dispute, then there would be a panel review of the matter and the panel would make its recommendations. *If both parties agree to be bound by the decision of the panel, then it would indeed be a binding form of dispute settlement.*
>
> However, I must say in honesty that where for example we have such a provision under the International Joint Commission, it is never used. The reason is that *if you think you have a weak case, you do not agree to be bound by a panel decision.* This is for the general purposes under the Agreement. It gives us a sort of GATT-plus set of rights.[12]

Evaluation of the institutional provisions of the FTA. Prior to the FTA, there were no formal mechanisms for the resolution of trade dispute between the two countries apart from the GATT. Dissatisfaction with the dispute settlement procedures of the GATT was one motivation for the inclusion of detailed provisions regarding such within the FTA, whilst at the same time ensuring conformity with rights and obligations arising under the GATT. The institutional provisions of the FTA may be said to improve upon the current system in the following ways:

– mandatory notification and consultation procedures are required in a broader range of areas than under the GATT;
– time limits are imposed at every stage of the dispute settlement process;

– in some cases, decisions are binding.

These improve upon the GATT mechanism, which is frequently subject to lengthy delays in, inter alia, the establishment of panels. To the extent that the decisions of panels under the FTA may be binding, this is an improvement over GATT panels whose decisions are not binding.

On the negative side, the possibility of a veto over binding arbitration raises the spectre of serious cases involving political considerations simply not proceeding by this route. Should such a route be pursued and the resulting decision ignored by the offending party, then it is open to the aggrieved party to take trade-weighted compensation. Not only is this frequently ineffective from the Canadian viewpoint given its weaker economic position vis-à-vis the United States, but it is already available to both parties under the GATT. Furthermore, the binational panel of experts may find itself under great political pressure in controversial cases with the attendant temptation to tailor its judgments to ensure their acceptance by the Commission.[13]

(2) Binational dispute settlement in antidumping and countervailing duty cases

The major achievement of Chapter 19 of the FTA is to replace judicial review of trade remedy procedures by the municipal courts of Canada and the United States with final orders by a binational panel. It also provides for continuing negotiations addressing the problems of dumping and subsidisation with a view to implementing a new regime within five to seven years which will obviate the need for border remedies.[14] Article 1902 provides for the retention of existing antidumping and countervailing duty laws BUT requires notification of changes in or modification to such laws. To avoid "sideswipe" problems such laws apply to the other party "only if such application is specified in the amending statute."[15] Following notification, consultation may be requested prior to the enactment of the amending statute. Article 1902.2(d) stipulates that the amendment must be consistent with the provisions of the GATT, particularly, the Antidumping Code and the Subsidies Code, and with the provisions of the FTA.[16] Review of statutory amendments by a panel under the FTA is provided for in Article 1903, which may issue a declaratory opinion as to whether the amendment is inconsistent with Article 1902.2(d) (i.e. the GATT and the FTA) OR with a previous decision of the binational review panel under Article 1904. If the amendment is found to be inconsistent, then a 90-day consultation period commences from the date of the final declaratory opinion in order to achieve "a mutually satisfactory solution to the matter." Such solution may include remedial legislation, in which case the amending party has nine months from the conclusion of the consultation to enact it, failing which the aggrieved party may take comparable legislative or executive action OR, upon 60-days written notice, terminate the Agreement.

Article 1904 establishes the binational review panel, which is a unique feature of the FTA, designed to ensure the impartial application of the antidumping and countervailing laws of the respective parties. Either party may request the panel to review the application of a final antidumping or countervailing duty determination; the findings of the panel are binding on both governments. If the panel finds that the administering author[17] has erred on the basis of the same standards which would apply to a domestic court, the matter will be returned to that authority for re-determination. Hence producers who in the past complained of political pressures disposing officials to side with their own nationals will now be able to appeal such a decision to the binational review panel.

Chapter 19 contains a number of stringent time limitations in order to expedite resolution of the dispute,[18] in contradistinction to lengthy domestic court proceedings which had been utilised in the past as a deliberate tactic in the litigation of trade disputes. The efficacy of this delaying tactic was enhanced by the requirement under United States law that the duty complained of be paid pending the outcome of the litigation, which could last anywhere from two to five years.

Panelists are selected from a roster of individuals who have previously agreed to act; the majority are to be lawyers in recognition of the judicial nature of the review carried out by the panel. Each party selects two panelists with the fifth selected jointly or, failing agreement, the four panelists will choose the fifth from the roster; if they too fail to reach agreement, then the fifth panelist will be selected by lot. Impartiality and fairness are preserved through the requirement that panelists disclose a conflict of interest,[19] although he or she is not required to step down as a consequence. This pragmatic solution is a result of the recognition of the fact that those most suitably qualified to act as panelists are also those most likely to have conflict of interest problems. In any event each party may exercise two preemptory challenges of panelists chosen by the other side, with an additional safeguard provided through the mechanism of the extraordinary challenge procedure whereby a panel of three former judges determine whether an allegation of conflict of interest or serious miscarriage of justice is valid and whether a new panel will be required to examine the issues.

Evaluation of the binational dispute settlement procedure. The binational review panel performs the dual function of legislative watchdog and "panel of last resort" with respect to certain trade disputes. The Canadian Legal Adviser to the Trade Negotiations Office has stated the advantages of the binational dispute settlement mechanism over the status quo as three-fold: (1) decisions of the panel are binding; (2) "these decisions would be framed against the provisions of the FTA, which fully incorporates but substantially goes beyond the provisions of the GATT;" and (3) the panel process is more expeditious and expert.[20] Unlike the United States Court of International Trade, where judicial review of a case could take from two to five years, the binational panel is required to arrive at a decision within a maximum of 300 to 315 days. Furthermore, the use of a five-member panel AND the requirement that subsequent trade legislation be consistent with its decisions, suggests that more consistent and predictable decisions will be forthcoming. In testimony before a Canadian House of Commons Standing Committee, the Legal Advisor to the Trade Negotiations Office was asked whether the 1986 Softwood Lumber ruling would have been decided differently had the dispute settlement mechanism on countervailing duties been in place. He explained

> that this case was based on the decision by one judge in 1985 and that the loose language of the judge's decision "gave a signal to the U.S. Lumber industry to file their second lumber petition, and the U.S. Department of Commerce used that to justify the preliminary application of duties ... In May and June of this year [1988], three other Court of International Trade judges ruled on the same basic issue. They all came down with a very different set of principles, a set of principles under which you probably would not have seen the second lumber case. What that means basically is that if you get a five-judge panel then you are more likely to get a statistically averaged, smoothed-out variation than if you just have one judge. That is a sobering history."[21]

It has been suggested that in late 1987 a group of energy companies in the United States dropped plans for a countervailing duty case against Canadian exports of electricity to the United States "because the Agreement's provision for binding binational panel review of countervailing duty decisions removed the opportunity from [sic] a politically based U.S. decisions against Candian imports."

The binational panel considers appeals from the Governments of the parties, whilst past practice had been for the firm or firms affected to take action before the courts of the offending party. The question must be asked whether a government will decide not to invoke the binational panel procedure for broader bilateral political considerations notwithstanding the legitimate nature of the complaint by one of its firms. Indeed the joint committees of the United States and Canadian Chambers of Commerce, amongst others, argued for a mechanism open to business to resolve trade disputes expeditiously and inexpensively without the necessity of recourse to the full formal administrative and appeal procedures in the respective countries. Clearly it would be necessary to distinguish betwen normal contractual disputes between firms, which would follow the usual domestic channels of dispute resolution, and those disputes where firms are involved in wider issues of a trade dispute between the parties involving countervailing or antidumping duties.

Lessons for the Uruguay Round of the GATT

Does the FTA establish a useful model for the negotiation of, inter alia, dispute settlement, in the current Uruguay Round of the GATT? Before such an evaluation may be made, it is first necessary to outline briefly the existing dispute settlement provisions of the GATT, the major criticisms of them, and what changes have been suggested. Consideration of these issues is timely: although the Negotiating Group considering dispute resolution was ready to report at the GATT Ministers' Conference in Montreal in December 1988, the presentation of final reports was delayed until April 1989 in order that four of the remaining fifteen Negotiating Groups may achieve consensus.

(1) The dispute settlement procedures. It is frequently stated that there is no single dispute settlement procedure within the GATT system which is of general application;[23] it is as frequently stated that there are over 30 such procedures within the GATT.[24] Within this fragmented system three elements may be isolated: (1) Articles XXII and XXIII; (2) the specific dispute settlement procedures provided for in most of the Tokyo Round agreements; and (3) the special procedures for developing countries (e.g. BISD 14S/18 (1966)). Further, if the parties to the dispute agree, the good offices of the Director-General may be called upon (BISC 29S/14 (1983)). To the extent that a central dispute settlement procedure exists within the GATT, it is contained in Articles XXII and XXIII, which have three aims: (1) the realisation of GATT's purpose; (2) the protection of benefits accruing under the Agreement; and (3) dispute settlement.[25] Article XXII concerns any matter affecting the operation of the GATT, whereas Article XXIII provides protection against nullification or impairment of any benefit under the Agreement. Both articles call for bilateral consultations followed by a working party (Article XXII) or investigation by the contracting parties (Article XXIII), where the practice of establishing a panel has emerged. There have been approximately 10 disputes under Article XXII, mainly in the 1950s and 1960s, whilst there have been over 100 complaints pursuant to Article XXIII.[26] In addition to these provisions, the extensive customary practice in dispute settlement which had developed within the GATT system was codified in 1979 after the Tokyo Round negotiations – the "Understanding regarding Notification, Consultations, Dispute Settlement and Surveillance" ("the 1979 Understanding").[27]

As the title of the 1979 Understanding suggests, there are four stages to dispute settlement within the GATT system: (1) notification of measures which may lead to disputes; (2) consultation on a bilateral and multilateral basis to reach settlement; (3) settlement of disputes through recommendations, which is "more conducive to re-establishment of a balance of concessions and advantage between the parties to the dispute";[28] and (4) surveillance by the Contracting Parties of matters on which they have made recommendations or given rulings to ensure compliance through "collective moral pressure." If bilateral contact between the contracting parties under (1) and (2) fails to achieve resolution of the dispute, recourse may be had to the Contracting Parties to settle the dispute through the use of a working party or a panel of experts, well-established procedures in GATT practice yet neither mentioned in the GATT Agreement. Nonetheless, the GATT panel has been described as "the most original feature of the GATT dispute settlement procedure and, at the same time, the most useful."[29] When a panel is requested the Director-General of GATT is reponsible for proposing the composition of the panel of three or five members, after consultation with the contracting parties, who have seven days to respond and should not reject the Director-General's choice "except for compelling reasons." Nationality would not be such a "compelling reason" for, unlike under the FTA, in the GATT system citizens of the parties to the dispute may not serve on the panel. The nominations are then submitted to the Contracting Parties for approval, with the requirement that the panel be constituted within 30 days of the decision of the Contracting Parties as to its composition. Delays may thus be caused if there is disagreement amongst the Contracting Parties as to the composition of the panel. The Director-General maintains an informal list of possible panel members who are to act independently and represent a wide spectrum of experience and diverse backgrounds.

The function of the panel is to assist the Contracting Parties in discharging their function under Article XXIII: 2, and it will make such enquiries as are requested of it, most commonly an objective assessment of the facts and their applicability to and compatibility with the GATT Agreement. The panel establishes its own procedure. Throughout there are consultations with the contracting parties and the opportunity for them to present their case, including those contracting parties having a substantial interest in the matter. The purpose of such consultations is to assist the parties in arriving at a "mutually satisfactory solution." If it fails, the panel submits a written report to the Contracting Parties which is first circulated to the contracting parties in two parts: first, the findings of fact, and second, their conclusions. There is no time limit regarding the work of the panel save for urgent cases where it is three months from the time the panel was established.[30] If resolution of the dispute has not been achieved prior to the formal submission to the Contracting Parties of the written panel report, it will be released as a GATT document and put on the agenda of the next Council meeting. This is consonant with the Contracting Parties' obligation to give the report their prompt consideration and take appropriate action within a reasonable time. Although ostensibly an advisory opinion, the Council generally adopts the report as submitted. However, because adoption is on the basis of consensus, the "losing party" may refuse to accept the recommendations, in which case adoption of the Report will be prevented. If adopted and recommendations or rulings are made, the failure to implement them within a reasonable time enables the contracting party to request the Contracting Parties "to make suitable efforts with a view to finding an appropriate solution." Article XXIII contemplates the possibility of the aggrieved party suspending the application of concessions or other obligations on a discriminatory basis against the offending party, with the authorisation of the Contracting Parties. This procedure has only been implemented once.[31]

(2) Deficiences of the great dispute settlement procedure.[32] One of the fifteen subjects for discussion in the new round of multilateral trade negotiations in the GATT – the Uruguay Round – is dispute settlement. In the Ministerial Declaration launching the new round the following statement on reform of the GATT dispute settlement procedure is found:

> In order to ensure prompt and effective resolution of disputes to the benefit of all parties, negotiations shall aim to improve and strengthen the rules and procedures of the dispute settlement process, while recognizing the contribution that would be made by more effective and enforceable GATT rules and disciplines. Negotiations shall include the development of adequate arrangements for overseeing and monitoring the procedures that would facilitate compliance with adopted recommendations.[33]

Some of the most frequently occurring criticisms of the GATT dispute settlement procedure are:

1. Initiation of procedure only by a contracting party having a direct interest in the matter constrains weaker States from bringing complaints as submission of a claim is often viewed as an unfriendly act and they lack an effective sanction for non-compliance;
2. Composition of panels (frequently officials working at the delegations of Contracting Parties in Geneva);[34]
3. Inordinate time delays and "foot dragging;"
4. Ability of the losing party to block action on the panel report;
5. Ambiguous findings in panel reports, reflecting to some extent the ambiguity of certain GATT concepts such as "nullification or impairment;"[35]
6. Legal or precedent-setting effect of reports not always clear;
7. Leaks and interference by national officials with panel members;
8. Inplementation phases are too loose and ill-defined;
9. No effective compliance procedure.

Some of the suggestions for reform suggested in Negotiating Group No. 13 include:[36]

1. Enhancement of the consultation process;
2. An increased mediation role for the Director General;
3. Some form of binding arbitration, at least regarding factual matters, so long as the interests of third parties are protected;
4. Meetings of the Council under a different chairman in "dispute resolution

mode" to enhance compliance and surveillance;
5. Exclude disputants from Council during discussion of their dispute to prevent blocking OR abolish requirement of consensus, e.g. with the contracting party either joining the consensus or abstaining;
6. Accelerate time period for the establishment of a panel and impose time-limits on the identifiable stages of their work;
7. Tighten rules on confidentiality;
8. Use standard terms of reference and standardize panel procedures;
9. Define interests and role of third parties in disputes.

The FTA: any lessons for the GATT?

Has the FTA established a useful model for the negotiation of dispute settlement procedures in the Uruguay Round? Certainly the FTA provisions address at least two major criticisms of the existing GATT framework, namely time delays and, to some extent, the binding force of decisions. Both the provisions of the FTA and the suggested reforms of the GATT dispute settlement procedures reflect a growing trend towards "legalism" in the settlement of international trade disputes – the "formalisation of due process." However, if this is the model the FTA is providing, is it one the GATT should adopt? It must be remembered that the GATT grew out of the abortive attempt to establish an international trade organisation and was not itself originally intended as an international institution – hence the "constitutional infirmity" frequently alluded to by commentators on the GATT system. The cohesive force behind the GATT has been the general consensus amongst Contracting Parties as to desirability of liberalising trade and the undesirability of protectionist barriers to it. The purpose of the GATT's dispute settlement procedures is therefore not solely to determine the rights and obligations of the parties:

> the primary objective of dispute settlement procedures is not to decide who is right and who is wrong, or to determine a State's responsibility in the matter, but to proceed in such a way that even important violations are only temporary and are terminated as quickly as possible.[37]

The dispute settlement process is designed to preserve a balance of concessions and obligations – therefore its procedures are not primarily concerned with strict compliance with GATT provisions. Thus action may be taken in the absence of a formal contravention of a GATT provision where the purpose of spirit of the GATT has been violated in a way not expressly foreseen in the Agreement itself.

In part the shift in attitude from "consensus" to "legalism" may be explained historically by the change in composition of the membership of the GATT since

1960, and in particular the transformation of the developed country membership into a "triad of economic superpowers," i.e. Japan, the EEC, and the United States. This led to a decrease in consensus and a move to a more power-oriented than rule-oriented approach.[38] Nowhere is the tension between these approaches better illustrated than in the attitudes of the EEC and the United States towards the dispute settlement procedures under the GATT: the EEC adopts a more power-oriented approach of emphasising settlement based on conciliation, negotiation, and consensus, whereas the United States clearly adopts a rule-oriented approach which "has its basis in the American tradition of adversarial proceedings, strict statutory interpretation and adherence to common law precedent."[39]

Given the origins of the GATT and the dominant role of consensus therein, it is clear that whilst its dispute settlement procedures clearly require reform, for which the FTA may provide a useful technical reference, "[t]o increase the effectiveness of the procedure there has to be consensus concerning the means to realise the purposes of the GATT in the first place."[40] Such consensus on the international level is not to be derived from a bilateral free trade agreement which reflects a growing trend towards regionalism and the "formalisation of due process" in international economic affairs. Indeed, it may be that the purposes of the GATT itself will need to re-examined and modified in light of arrangements such as the FTA.

Notes

1. The full text of the Agreement is found in *International Legal Materials*, XXVII (1988), 281–402.
2. The Canadian Prime Minister, Brian Mulroney, staked his political reputation and the life of his Conservative government on free trade with the United States which emerged as the major issue of the autumn 1988 federal elections.
3. *International Legal Materials*, XXV (1984), 653.
4. D. L. McLachlan, A. Apuzzo, and W. A. Kerr, "The Canada-U.S. Free Trade Agreement: A Canadian Perspective," *Journal of World Trade*, XXII (1988), 10. The authors point out that reducing the impact of U.S. contingency protection policies was a strong motivator for Canada in entering into the agreement. They cite the fact that Canada has taken actions against imports from the United States totalling Cdn$ 403 million whilst being on the receiving end of U.S. actions affecting Canadian exports totalling Cdn$ 6,225 million (p. 14).
5. In a Canadian Government publication promoting the FTA the relationship with the GATT was described as follows:

   Many articles in the FTA are based on the GATT (e.g. the provisions on national treatment, on import and export restrictions, on technical standards, on procurement and on exceptions). The FTA builds on and extends these GATT provisions in a manner that better reflects our specific bilateral trading interests. In other areas, such as dispute settlement, services, and investment, the FTA goes significantly beyond existing GATT agreements and establishes useful models for the negotiation of these issues in the current Uruguay Round.

"The Canada-United States Free Trade Agreement;" Department of External Affairs, Canada, 1988, p. 3.

During the December 1988 GATT ministerial meeting in Montreal Canada's International Trade Minister "reaffirmed the Government's commitment to a two-track policy of liberalized trade on a bilateral basis with the United States, Canada's largest trading partner, while seeking to liberalize global trade on a multilateral basis through the GATT." (*Ibid.*, p. 30)

It is interesting to note that, although the FTA between Canada and the United States is sui generis, a Working Group established by the GATT to examine the conformity of the Israel-United States Free Trade Agreement with Article XXIV was unable to achieve consensus. *GATT Focus*, no. 56, p. 7.

6. In November 1987 the United States presented the GATT Negotiating Group on Trade in Services with a proposal for liberalising trade in this area.
7. In December 1988 11 of the 15 Negotiating Groups had achieved consensus, including Negotiating Group 13 which was considering dispute settlement.
8. Two bilateral trade disagreements have been submitted for settlement. The first regards the equality of low-grade plywood from the United States which for two decades Canadian officials have refused to approve, arguing that the knotholes are too large and closely spaced; this was met with a 20% tariff on the imports of Canadian plywood into the United States. The second dispute relates to the problem of measuring the wool content in garments for tariff purposes. Both disputes involve technical standards and are perceived as relatively straightforward to settle; it has been suggested that they were a deliberate choice to demonstrate that the dispute settlement machinery of the FTA functions: *McCleans's*, 16 January 1989, p. 15.
9. Except for disputes regarding Financial Services (Chapter Seventeen) or those covered by Chapter Nineteen, "Binational Dispute Settlement in Antidumping and Countervailing Duty Cases," discussed below.
10. The Commission operates on the basis of consensus which in effect provides each party with a de facto veto over its decisions.
11. To ensure fair and prompt resolution of disputes Article 1807 further provides that: each Party shall have at least one hearing before the panel and the opportunity to make written submissions and rebuttal arguments (1807.4); panelists may furnish separate opinions if matters are not unanimously agreed (1807.5); a Party disagreeing in whole or in part with the initial report of the panel may indicate such to the Commission and panel; the panel may on its own motion, or at the request of the either Party or the Commission, reconsider its report, with the final report in any event issuing within 30 days of the intial report (1807.6); the Commission will normally agree on the resolution of the dispute in conformity with the recommendations of the panel (1807.8); failing such agreement within 30 days of receiving the final report of the panel, the aggrieved Party who considers its fundamental rights or benefits under the FTA affect may suspend the application to the other Party of benefits of equivalent effect until the dispute is resolved (1807.9).
12. "The Canada-United States Free Trade Agreement," A Report of the House of Commons Standing Committee on External Affairs and International Trade on The Elements of the Agreement Tabled in the House of Commons on October 5, 1987 (December, 1987), per the Honourable Pat Carney, Minister of Trade (emphasis added).
13. See Fisher, "Politics of FTA trade disputes" *International Perspectives* (1988), 18 and

the C. D. Howe Institute *Trade Monitor*, No, 6 (October 1988) which contains "Two Views on Dispute Settlement and Trade Laws in the Canada-U.S. Free Trade Agreement" – "A View from the United States" by Gary Horlick and Debra Valentine, and "A view from Canada" by Debra Steger.

14. During the Free Trade negotiations the parties were unable to agree a definition of "subsidy," long a bone of contention between them. Canada has committed itself to negotiating such a definition, with the prospect that federal schemes aimed at reducing regional disparities will be caught within it.

15. In the past Canadian exporters had been adversely affected by U.S. trade laws not expressly directed at Canadian imports into the United States. Horlick and Valentine give the following example:

> In 1980, one Canadian food processor appealed a U.S. safeguard decision to impose tariffs on South Korean and Taiwanese mushrooms that, in a classical example of the "sideswipe" effect, also hit frozen breaded mushrooms from Canada. After a lengthy appeal process in the U.S. courts, all the Canadian company got was a court opinion that the U.S. safeguard decision could be challenged only it if were procedurally invalid. (note 13 above, p.4).

16. Article 1902.2(d)(ii) states that "the object and purpose of this Agreement and this Chapter, which is to establish fair and predictable conditions for the progressive liberalization of trade between the two countries while maintaining effective disciplines on unfair trade practices, such object and purpose is to be ascertained from the provisions of this Agreement, its preamble and objectives, and the practices of the Parties." This appears sufficiently broad to incorporate the concept of violations of the spirit, rather than merely the letter, of the FTA and would be consonant with the approach taken to the GATT. Whether this is indeed the approach taken remains to be seen.

17. The Department of Commerce and the International Trade Commission in the United States; the Department of National Revenue and the Canadian Import Tribunal in Canada.

18. For example, Article 1904.14 provides that the parties shall adopt rules of procedure by 1 January 1989 which "shall be designed to result in final decisions within 315 days of the date on which a request for a panel is made, and shall allow:

a) 30 days for the filing of the complaint;
b) 30 days for designation or certification of the administrative record and its filing with the panel;
c) 60 days for the complainant to file its brief;
d) 60 days for the respondent to file its brief;
e) 15 days for the filing of reply briefs;
f) 15 to 30 days for the panel to convene and hear oral argument and;
g) 90 days for the panel to issue its written decision."

19. *The Globe and Mail*, 13 January 1989.
20. Note 12 above, p. 36.
21. *Ibid*, p. 37.
22. Horlick and Valentine, "A View from the United States", note 13 above, p. 3.
23. See K. R. Simmonds and B. H. W. Hill, *Law and Practice under the GATT* (1988), p. 11; O. Long, *Law and Its Limitations in the GATT Multilateral Trade System* (1985), p. 71.
24. See J. H. Jackson, "GATT as an instrument for the Settlement of Trade Disputes,"

Proceedings of the American Society of International Law (1963), p. 144.

25. Jackson has suggested that the drafters of the GATT had at least three objectives in mind in drafting Article XXIII; objectives of doubtful consistency:

> The first objective was that Articles XXII and XXIII were to be the framework of a dispute settlement procedure, stressing the general obligation to consult on any matter relating to GATT. The second objective was that Article XXIII would play an important role in obtaining compliance with the GATT obligations. The customary international law analogy of *retorsion* was used. A third goal for these provisions of GATT was to establish a means for ensuring continued "reciprocity and balance of concessions" in the face of possibly changing circumstances. This third goal is more in the nature of an "escape clause" or "changed circumstances" provision.

J. H. Jackson, "Gatt Machinery and the Tokyo Round Agreements", excerpt in J. H. Jackson and W. J. Davey, *International Economic Relations* (2d ed., 1986), p. 346.

26. I. Van Bael, "The GATT Dispute Settlement Procedure" *Journal of World Trade*, XXII (1988), 68. Of the 100 complaints brought pursuant to Article XXIII: 2 during the period 1948–1986, 48 were settled without a report and 52 resulted in the submission of report to Council. Out of these 52, 50 were adopted by the Council or a "mutually satisfactory solution" achieved: *GATT Focus* (May 1987), p. 2.
27. BISD 265/210 (1980).
28. See I. H. Courage-van Lier, "Supervision within the GATT," in P. van Dijk (ed.), *Supervisory Mechanisms in International Economic Organisations* (1984) p. 76.
29. Note 23 above, p. 77.
30. Paragraph (ix) of the Annex to the 1979 Understanding states:

> Although the CONTRACTING PARTIES have never established precise deadlines for the different phases of the procedure, probably because the matters submitted to panels differ as to their complexity and their urgency, in most cases the proceedings of the panels have been completed within a reasonable period of time, extending from three to nine months.

31. When in 1953 the Netherlands were authorised by the Contracting Parties to suspend obligations they owed the United States: Cf. BISD 1S/32 and BISD 1S/62 (1953).
32. Long, note 23 above; J. H. Jackson, "Role of Supervisory Mechanisms in the Restructuring of the International Economic Order," in P. van Dijk, (ed.), *Restructuring the International Economic Order: The Role of Law and Lawyers* (1986); Van Bael, note 26 above.
33. BISD 33S/19, at 25 (1986).
34. R. Plank, "An Unofficial Description of How a GATT Panel Works and Does Not," *Journal of International Arbitration*, IV (1987), 4; see also I. H. Courage-van Lier, "Supervision within the GATT," note 28 above, pp. 96–97.
35. In this regard it may be asked whether an issue is an appropriate one for the GATT dispute settlement process, i.e. "when is a disputed issue so inextricably bound up in the need for "rule making" as opposed to "rule applying" that the dispute settlement mechanism of the GATT ought not to be the technique for resolving the differences?:" J. H. Jackson, "The Juisprudence of International Trade: The DISC Case in GATT," *American Journal of International Law*, LXXII (1978), 781.
36. See Van Bael, note 26 above, pp. 73–74; *GATT Focus* has also been running summaries of the proposals within the Negotiating Groups.

274

37. G. Malinverni, *Le règlement des différends dans les organisations internationales économiques* (1974) cited in O. Long, note 23 above, p. 71.
38. Cf. Courage-van Lier, note 34 above, Van Bael, note 26 above, and Long, *ibid.*
39. P. D. Ehrenhaft, "The U.S. View of the GATT," (1986) *International Business Lawyer* (1986) 149; See R. Phan van Phi, "A European View of the GATT," *ibid.*, at p. 152.
40. Courage-van Lier, note 28 above, p. 97.

ARMED CONFLICT: POLITICAL AND LEGAL ASPECTS

I. V. KHAMENEV

In order to demonstrate the importance and urgency of the problem, consider the following statistics. Armed conflicts and local wars since 1945 have killed more than twenty million persons and brought enormous material losses.[1] According to the International Institute for Comparative Studies of Social Systems (West Berlin), since 1946 on average there have been twelve local wars and international conflicts each year.[2] For example, the United States alone between 1945 and 1983 used its armed forces more than 260 times in order to achieve foreign policy objectives.[3]

How can contemporary international law be used so that armed conflicts do not become the norm for deciding issues in dispute between States and that it can eliminate conflicts already in existence? One of the fundamental international legal documents in this domain is the United Nations Charter, which contains a number of principles directed towards the maintenance and preservation of friendly relations between States. In this writer's view the significance of those principles is such that they may be relegated to the category of generally-binding (imperative) norms of international law since they are directed toward preserving peace between nations and averting war.

There exist a series of other international legal documents whose object is to prevent armed conflicts between States and settle peacefully conflicts already existing. The subject of regulation of such international legal agreements is the relations of States involved in an armed conflict. By way of illustration it is sufficient to recall the long history of the conflict between Israel, the Arab countries, and the Palestine Liberation Organisation. The Middle East conflict has two levels of measurement: on one hand, it is a regional conflict, and on the other, it is a global conflict between modern imperialism headed by the United States, whose interests Israel expresses, and a national-liberation movement represented by the Arab countries. The heart of the conflict is the problem of Palestine, connected with the Israeli occupation of territories captured in 1967 and the refusal to recognise the right of self-determination and the right to create an independent State for the Arab peoples.

The 1979 Camp David agreements did not resolve the problem since they completely ignored the right of the Palestinian people to their own independent State. Israel's subsequent aggression against the Palestine arabs in the camps of Sabra and Shatila in Lebanon proved once again the inappropriateness of the Camp David agreements for a settlement of the Middle Eastern conflict and was condemend by the international community, particularly by the Human Rights Commission and other organisations of the United Nations system. Precisely

W. E. Butler, Perestroika and International Law, 275–280.

because the measures taken were ineffective, the Soviet Union insisted and insists on holding a large-scale international conference on the settlement of the Middle East conflict with all the interested parties being involved. The USSR Minister of Foreign Affairs, E. Shevardnadze, so declared to the leaders of the Arab countries and Israel during his visit to the region in 1988.

Forms of armed interference

Armed interference – one of the most dangerous manifestations of aggressiveness of a State for international peace and security and the freedom and independence of peoples – frequently leads to armed conflicts. According to international law, armed interference is a violation of the norms and principles of the mutual relations of States consolidated in the United Nations Charter and other international legal documents. Armed interference is the most flagrant form of interference in the internal affairs of countries and peoples. The use of armed force with a view to interference is equivalent to aggression, which according to a United Nations resolution (1979) is a crime against international peace and entails international responsibility.

Among the forms of armed interference which fall within the definition of aggression are, in particular, the intrusion or attack of armed forces of one State into the territory of another, the sending of armed bands, groups, irregular forces, or mercenaries which use force against another State by a State or on its behalf. Armed interference with the use of such methods, being equivalent to aggression, creates grounds for the victim State to use its right to individual or collective self-defence in accordance with Article 51 of the United Nations Charter. The term "undeclared war" is used in recent years in international political vocabulary with respect to armed interference of this type. As example is the actions of a number of capitalist States and their accessories against Afghanistan, Nicaragua, and Angola.

Great efforts within the framework of the United Nations with regard to working out international documents with a view to preventing armed conflicts from arising were undertaken by countries of the socialist commonwealth and non-aligned movement. Thanks to the joint activities of these two groups of States, the United Nations has approved a number of decisions specially aimed at strengthening and clarifying the principle of non-interference, in particular the 1965 Resolution on the Inadmissibility of Intervention in the Domestic Affairs of States and the Protection of their Independence and Sovereignty and the 1981 Declaration on the Inadmissibility of Intervention and Interference in the Internal Affairs of States. They stress in particular the duty of States to refrain in their international relations from the threat or use of force in any form for the purpose of violating internationally-recognised boundaries of any State, the political, social, or political order of other States, to overthrow or change the political system of another State or its government, to cause tension between two or more States, or to deprive peoples of their national identity or cultural heritage.

Armed conflicts may also arise as a consequence of a policy of State terrorism. In order to eliminate this dangerous phenomenon from inter-State life, the United Nations General Assembly in 1984 adopted an appropriate Resolution in which it resolutely condemned the policy and practice of terrorism in inter-State relations and required all States not to undertake any actions directed at armed interference and occupation, coerced changes and subversion of the socio-political system of States, destabilisation and overthrow of their governments, in particular, not to begin under any pretext military actions for this purpose and immediately to cease such operations underway. "Undeclared wars" (Afghanistan, Nicaragua, Angola) are being waged with the aid of armed bands and direct armed aggression is being committed (Grenada) in order to impose their will on peoples who have chosen a free path of development.

In response to ceaseless aggressive actions by the United States against it, Nicaragua was forced to have recourse to the International Court of Justice, requesting judgment on the following: (a) violation by the United States of its international obligations, in particular, those arising from Article 2(4) of the United Nations Charter and Articles 18 and 20 of the Charter of the Organisation of American States; (b) cessation of the use of force and violations of its sovereignty, territorial integrity, and political independence; (c) payment of a certain amount of reparations for harm caused to individuals, property, and the economy of Nicaragua; (d) the taking of provisional measures by the court for the purpose of protecting its rights. The judgment issued by the ICJ on 27 June 1986, first, classified the actions of the United States against Nicaragua as a violation of norms of international law and, second, directly condemned the aggressive policy of the United States with respect to Nicaragua.

Several words need to be said about the Iranian-Iraqi conflict. It arose as a result of a protracted dispute over frontier questions, and also as a result of disagreements of a political, religious, and national character. Eight years of a sanguinary war not only has not resolved the problems, but on the contrary the problems have become greater. For the moment the war has stopped. To a considerable extent this has been promoted by the efforts of the Security Council, which adopted Resolution 598. Thus, we are speaking of the direct participation of the United Nations, whose role in suspending the conflict is difficult to overestimate. Without the active involvement of the members of the Security Council, it would have been difficult to bring the parties to the conflict to the negotiating table.[4] A cease-fire is operative, but there is no settlement. But it is important that the parties in dispute have agreed to the mediation mission of the United Nations Secretary-General and are negotiating to resolve the conflict.

Consideration of the aforesaid examples of armed conflicts is a classical, traditional, and rather well-studied variant. However, in recent studies of inter-State conflicts there is a new orientation stressing the link between the exhaustion of natural resources and the exacerbation of armed conflicts. Many scholars draw the conclusion that such conflicts will occur principally in the developing countries.[5] An important prerequisite for the constantly expanding regeneration of capital as the basis for the existence of capitalist means of production is the access of imperialist States to the raw materials resources of the "third world."

The role of natural resources

The use of inexpensive raw materials from developing countries has led to close dependence between the well-being of industrially developed capitalist countries and the quantity and quality of resources accessible on the world market. "Many 'third world' countries have an abundance of natural resources (and on this level it is difficult to classify them as 'poor'), but the developed capitalist countries exploit them ruthlessly in order to maintain their prosperity and economic growth."[6]

The industrially developed States use every possible means to keep developing countries in their sphere of influence. International monopolies in the domain of producing raw materials enjoy control not only over the production and sale of raw materials, but also over the prices; also the indebtedness of developing countries, and, finally, the sale of arms to them – in the mid-1980s more than 75% of arms sales on the world market were to countries of Asia, Africa, and Latin America.

The "vicious circle" in which liberated countries are entangled consists in the fact that the further import of arms is linked directly with the export of raw materials. The basic part of so-called "development assistance" also is aimed at countries exporting natural resources. If one of these means "does not work," conflicts arise. The enormous dependence of industrially developed countries is the more evident as the question of natural resources becomes a central issue of international politics. "Natural resources became a principal cause of conflicts in the 1970s."[7] Thus, the dependence of industrially developed capitalist States on the natural resources of developing countries has led to any changes in the developing countries being taken by the leaders of industrial States as a threat to the security of the industrially developed countries. Hence the reaction to such a "threat" is frequently expressed in military actions. The military conflicts also promote the delivery of weapons to those countries of the "third world" which aspire to reduce their dependence on the world system of capitalism.

Among the most probable reasons for armed conflicts to arise in the long-term experts in this area call the struggle for energy and mineral resources. The "development of mankind and each individual State depend on natural wealth extracted from the natural environment. One of the ways opening access to such resources traditionally was war."[8]

The protection and rational use of natural resources today is becoming a strategic task. There are virtually no States who can completely provide themselves with all necessary resources and raw materials. Dependence upon external sources influences the foreign policy of many States; for imperialist States, this is linked with economic neo-colonialism and expansion. Some consider that the United States must protect its economic interests "throughout the whole world" by maintaining stable access to energy raw materials and the strategic resources of other countries, including foreign markets for goods and agricultural raw materials. This view of a representative of the United States administration is used by Western authors to support a theoretical concept of global ecological dependence, of the need for freedom to penetrate to the raw materials markets of other countries.[9]

The problem lies in the unequal distribution on this planet of the most important natural resources. This, in turn, leads to the fact that the majority of modern wars occurred "in essence because of natural resources, irrespective of whether the belligerent States took this into account or not."[10] Modern civilisation has turned out to be in a curious position, in which natural resources might play a more important role as a pretext for future armed conflicts and military operations than in any preceding periods of human history. It is evident that ecological problems today are being transformed into a more serious and difficult to resolve task touching the interests of many countries. In this situation only one path to resolving the ecological problems leads to reducing the military danger – the realisation of the concept of natural resources as the world heritage of mankind, in accordance with which "earth men must rationally and zealously use these resources in the interests of all inhabitants of the planet."[11]

This proposition merits attention and might be supported from a general humanitarian position, but from the international legal point of view, at least today, it is doubtful for the simple reason that States, international organisations, and nations struggling for their independence were the traditional subjects of international law in the classical variant. The rational use of natural resources by "earth men," that is, by all humanity, places before international law an unusual and untraditional question: can human civilisation act as a subject of international law? The answer to the question for the moment is a negative one.

Returning to the problems of interdependence between armed conflicts and the worsening ecological situation, the conclusion should be drawn that in order to bring armed conflicts which arise on an ecological basis to an end, it is essential above all to eliminate the reason for the emergence of such conflicts. In this event we speak of the need to resolve the ecological problem on a global scale. Three suggested variants of the solution seem most evident.

Pursuant to the first, it is necessary to create an all-embracing convention which would regulate the entire complex of relations between man and nature. This notion, it seems, has little chance of success since it took ten years to draft merely the 1982 United Nations Convention on the Law of the Sea. And if we add to this the protracted and difficult preparatory work of the respective United Nations

280

committee on these matters, the prospects for concluding an all-embracing international convention on environmental problems seems unlikely, if not unrealistic.

The second position comes down to drafting individual conventions on very specific issues of nature use. The process of codifying nature protection measures of an international legal character is moving in this direction. And this position is appropriate; however, under conditions of a colossal growth in the technical might and energy provision of mankind, the influence of man on nature is becoming ever greater in scale. This influence has led more than once to catastrophic consequences. Therefore the need has arisen for developing a third position: to draft fundamental principles for the international legal protection of the environment, to give them a generally-recognised and generally-binding character, to formulate them so as to preclude the possibility of diverse interpretations. One is speaking, therefore, of creating an international legal ecological imperative for mankind.

Conclusion

The age requires decisive transformations in connection with the problems of a global character confronting mankind. It is time to cease mutual recriminations and reproaches and pass on to a creative, constructive dialogue. It is evident that powerful political and legal machinery for regulating international relations must be created and function, which ultimately will lead to a system of universal legal order ensuring the primacy of international law in politics.[12] Each State must manifest a sincere interest in being self-restrained by international law. In this state of affairs there should not only disappear armed conflicts which arise on an ecological basis, but also armed conflicts as such. In any event, one would wish to believe this to be true.

Notes

1. See *Gosudarstva NATO i voennye konflikty* (1987), p.4.
2. See *Chto est' chto v mirovoi politike* (1986), p. 210.
3. *U.S. News and World Report*, 11 April 1983, p. 70.
4. See *Pravda*, 2 March 1989.
5. W. J. Taylor (ed.), *The Future of Conflict in the 1980s* (1982), p. 4.
6. J. Kakonen, *Natural Resources and Conflicts in the Changing International System* (1988), p. 78.
7. *Ibid.*, p. 147.
8. A. H. Westing (ed.), *Global Resources and International Conflicts: Environmental Factors in Strategic Policy and Action* (1986), p. 3.
9. *Ibid.*, p. 5.
10. *Ibid.*, p. 183.
11. *Ibid.*, p. 193.
12. *Pravda*, 17 September 1987.

PEACE WITHOUT JUSTICE: RECONSIDERING THE LAW ON THE USE OF FORCE

A. V. LOWE

On 18 November 1987 the United Nations General Assembly adopted by consensus the Declaration on the Enhancement of the Effectiveness of the Principle of Refraining from the Threat or Use of Force in International Relations.[1] The title of the Declaration reflects a widely held view that the threat or use of force in international relations, except in the exercise of the right of self defence, is always undesirable; and the major part of the text of the Declaration is devoted to the articulation of various aspects of the duty to settle disputes by peaceful means and not to resort to force. In the words of the Declaration,

> No consideration of whatever nature may be invoked to warrant resorting to the threat or use of force in violation of the Charter.

The central arguments advanced in this article are: it is wrong to suppose that the use of force in international relations is always undesirable, that the notion that it is only States which can properly be defended by the use of force should be re-examined, and that the rules of law concerning the threat or use of force are in some respects an obstacle, rather than a means, to the achievement of the ends towards which the international community is or should be working.

No particular originality is claimed for this argument.[2] The case will be put, as others has been done before, for a fundamental re-examination of the law concerning the use of force, of the values which underlie it, and of its effects in the real world. That re-examination will not necessarily indicate a need for change. Even the most radical reform may consist as much in retaining old rules, albeit often for reasons different from those which led to their creation, as in the making of new rules. Indeed, when it is recalled that all of the modern formulations of the laws of war, from the Lieber Code onwards, were forged from direct experience of the sheer horror and suffering of war, we should exercise the utmost caution in seeking to upset the system in any way. These are rules concerned with issues of ultimate importance. They purport to decide when, where, and how one human being may kill another. They dispose, in abstract statements of law, of concrete questions of life and death – and one is tempted to say, not merely with questions of life and death, but with the avoidance of suffering and misery on a scale and of an intensity that must make death seem a welcome release. But it is precisely because of the ultimacy of the importance of these issues that we must ensure that the laws of war are the right laws.

W. E. Butler, Perestroika and International Law, 281–295.
© 1990 *Kluwer Academic Publishers. Printed in the Netherlands.*

The purpose here is only to identify the main considerations pointing to a need for a revision of the law, and not to propose simple solutions to the problems which exist. These problems demand the most painstaking examination and the serious moral reflection.

This article addresses principally the rules on the use of force set out in the United Nations Charter, and primarily in Articles 2(4) and 51, as supplemented by other instruments such as the 1949 Geneva Conventions and by customary law. These rules are meant by the term "Laws of War." This is not to imply that all of those rules are necessarily binding today in all conflicts in all their detail, either as a matter of customary law or of treaty obligation. Although the legal status of these detailed rules, and of the very notion of a distinct state of "war" in contemporary international law are important and controversial questions,[3] they are not the questions addressed here. There is, however, a consistency in the principles upon which the great majority, if not all, of those rules are based, and the validity of these underlying principles is examined here.

An obvious and important characteristic of the laws of war is that, humanitarian law apart, they are designed to protect States from attacks made by other States. Article 2(4) of the United Nations Charter stipulates that

> All members shall refrain in their international relations from the threat or use of force against the territorial integrity or political independence of any State, or in any other manner imcompatible with the Purposes of the United Nations.

While the Purposes of the United Nations, which are set out in Article 1 of the Charter, include references to the self-determination of peoples and to humanitarian cooperation, it is evident that those Purposes are themselves perceived within a framework in which nation-States are the actors. The nation-State is central to the system, and the vehicle for the advancement of objectives such as self-determination and humanitarian cooperation. Similarly, the second pillar of the Charter regime on the use of force, Article 51, is focused upon the State: it refers to the "... inherent right of individual or collective self-defence if an armed attack occurs against a Member of the United Nations ... ." The right is vested in States, and exercisable in the event of attacks upon States.

The centrality of the concept of the sovereign, independent State is evident also in the principle of non-intervention. This principle, inextricably linked to the prohibition on the threat or use of force and to the principle of self-determination, is spelled out in the 1970 Declaration on Principles of International Law Concerning Friendly Relations and Co-operation Among States, which stipulated that

> No State or group of States has the right to intervene, directly or indirectly, for any reason whatsoever, in the internal or external affairs of any other State. Consequently, armed intervention and all other forms of interference or

attempted threats against the personality of the State or against its political, economic and cultural elements, are in violation of international law.[4]

The breadth of the prohibition, which mirrors the broad meaning intended to be given to the phrase "against the territorial integrity or political independence of any State"[5] in Article 2(4), is such as to rule out any intervention in the domestic affairs of another State.

The principle of non-intervention, or fundamental importance in international law, seeks to ensure that as the people of one State exercise their right to self-determination, their choices are not thwarted by the intervention of other States. It is the expression of the division of the community of mankind into independent, geographically-delimited communities, each of which is entitled to choose its own destiny independently (so far as possible in practice in this increasingly interdependent world) of the choices made by other communities. It is that principle which expresses, for instance, the right of one community to maintain in its internal dealings a centrally planned economy while its neighbours choose to organize their dealings on the basis of a free-market economy, or to choose a democratic, aristocratic, theocratic or other form of government. And one essential element of self-determination is that it includes the right for the people to make their own mistakes. Neighbouring countries may see only too clearly the failings of capitalism or communism, and the hardship and suffering which it causes to some or all of the citizens of another State. But neighbouring States have no right to intervene: the right to choose includes the right to make what others may see as an unwise choice.

The maintenance of the principle of non-intervention is vital if self-determination is to have any meaning, and self-determination is itself vital if democracy within a State is to have any substance. But there comes a point where this principle must surely yield to another. The principle of non-intervention can be and is deployed to ward off foreign intervention when governments deliberately and systematically butcher large numbers of their subjects in the repression of internal opposition. To take but one example from the long, sad litany of repression in the post-war world, the representative of a government faced with imminent armed intervention by a neighbouring State referred in the United Nations to the undermining of his State's sovereignty and disruption of its territorial integrity which any such intervention would cause, and to the need for the United Nations not to encroach upon its domestic jurisdiction, because such moves would be contrary to the United Nations Charter.[6] The problem was seen as one within its domestic jurisdiction in which neither the United Nations nor any other State could intervene. Forceful intervention was regarded as being prohibited by international law. At around the same time, the *Guardian* reported that troops belonging to that government had burned a village to the ground and murderd most of its 7,000 inhabitants, many being thrown into the flames of their own houses; and the

Washington Post reported that in another month.[7]

The examples could be multiplied; but the point is clear. What begins as an attempt to guarantee freedom from foreign oppression is perverted into a veil to be drawn over domestic oppression. To the extent that the prohibition or intervention and the threat or use of force against another State forbids armed intervention to end or forestall such atrocities, its protects the abstract values of the sovereignty and independence of a State at the expense of more important values implicit in the Rule of Law. A State which appeals to international law to prevent intervention aimed at preventing massive violations of basic human rights either has no coherent concept of what Law is, or is acting with a degree of cynicism and hypocrisy which almost defies belief. Can it seriously be argued that the rules on the use of force and non-intervention require that States must stand by and watch the systematic slaughter by a State of its own citizens? States are not attacked. States are not the victims of war. States do not suffer. They are abstract conceptions. People are the victims of war, and a system which preserves peace between States while allowing such atrocities to continue may secure "peace" in a limited and utterly abstract sense between States, but it is a peace which exists only in a paper world, a worthless peace, without justice or moral value. There is an overwhelming case for a radical revision of any rule which leads to such absurdly repugnant effects, and a strong moral argument for allowing the use of force in such circumstances.

This much is familiar. Many jurists are prepared to admit an exception to the principles of non-intervention and the prohibition on the use of force, in order to allow interventions intended to bring an end to large scale violations of human rights; and there are signs of a limited acceptance of this view in State practice.[8] To take two of the least controversial examples, the interventions of the Indian army in Bangladesh in 1971 and of the Tanzanian army in Uganda in 1978,[9] whatever the precise nature of the motives which led to them, are widely regarded as having made a significant and valuable contribution to the ending of massacres in those countries and were widely tolerated, if not expressly approved.[10] But while there may be a measure of an agreement in support of the view that "[i]t is idle to argue in such cases that the duty of the neighbouring people is to look on quietly,"[11] it is far from clear how far this principle extends or should extend. What scale of violation, and of what kinds of rights, has to occur before the exceptional right to intervene arises?

The traditional approach to these questions is to argue that there is a right to intervene to defend people in certain circumstances, as an exception to the principle that States are the only institutions which may be forcibly defended under international law, and to argue the point out within the confines of human rights law.[12] But why should the State be the only institution which may be protected by the use of force, even as a matter of principle to which exceptions are admitted? Perhaps States ought not to occupy that privileged position. The State is merely one of many social and political institutions around which we organise our lives, and in many cases it is by no means the most important. Perhaps there are institutions and values of equal or greater importance than the independence of States and the preservation of peace between nations.

We should consider whether we do not have things the wrong way around in seeking to establish rights of intervention as exceptions to the rule limiting the use of force to the self defence of the State. The need for an exception arises because of the central role which we give to the sovereignty and independence of States and to the desire to preserve international peace. But the mere absence of war between nations is of no value as an objective if it simply allows governments to go unhindered about the business of domestic repression. There must surely be some connection between the legitimacy of a government on the international plane, which qualifies its actions for protection from forcible intervention by other States, and the internal legitimacy of that government. To rank Hitler's Final Solution and the privatisation of the water industry as governmental policies equally deserving of respect and demanding non-intervention by the international community is as absurd as it is offensive. Of course, the definition of those limits is the crucial issue, but its complexity ought not to lead us to persist in defending an institution which regularly treads the international stage in a role that is utterly indefensible.

Progress is being made in this direction by the acceptance of a right of humanitarian intervention. But is is arguable that humanitarian interventions are merely the clearest and most acceptable instances of a wider category of cases in which principles more important than respect for State sovereignty and the prohibition on the use of force are at stake: cases where, to put it another way, international law ought to allow the protection of institutions and values other than those of the State. It is true that, at present, those other institutions could, at least in general, only be protected *by* States, because States control most of the military forces capable of acting across national frontiers.[13] But that does not detract from the point raised here, which is that such forces might be used in or against other States in circumstances where there is no attack on the defending State – that they might be used to defend other interests.

It is noteworthy that the very conception of the State as an appropriate object of protection (let alone as the *only* appropriate of protection) is neither self-evident nor universally held. For example, Islamic law, according to one distinguished Muslim lawyer,

... knows neither nationality nor frontiers. Neither the Koran nor the Sunna contain any rules concerning the form of the State. God is the head of the community. All people are equal before him; the most respected is the most pious.

Under this conception, the state has no power to legislate. The state exists not because of a prerogative of legislation, but in order to protect and apply the *Shari'a* which may not be changed or restricted.[14]

Implicit in this approach is a view of the whole of Islam as a seamless entity, in which the divisions established by political frontiers are of little relevance. Such a view exists in the Islamic concept of the *umma*, the community of all who profess the Islamic faith.[15] And it would be logical to include within this community believers in non-Muslim countries. It is then a sort step to the argument that the State as such has no claim to protection under the law, but that an attack on Islam in one Islamic (or even non-Islamic) State is an attack on Islam in all States. Indeed, in the case of an attack which is seen as a direct challenge to the sovereignty of God, it might be thought that Muslims in all countries are under a positive duty to join in opposition to that challenge. This view has not been expressly advanced by the governments of Islamic States, although something of the kind appears to underlie the response of certain Islamic groups to the alleged apostasy of Salman Rushdie, exhibited in his book *The Satanic Verses*.[16] There is here, as in the case of humanitarian intervention, a set of values independent of the sovereignty of nation-States, which might be considered to prevail in certain circumstances over the limitation of the use of force to situations of self defence against attacks upon the State, and to justify the use of force in the defence of Islam as much.

Similar concepts appear in a number of guises in State practice. The references in the Declaration of Independence, made by the Palestinian National Council on 15 November 1988, to "the Arab nation" of which the Arab State of Palestine is but a part, is one example.[17] The importance attached in the *Eichmann* case to the right to protect Jews, in the discussion of the Israel's jurisdiction over crimes against Jews committed by non-Israelis outside Israel and before the establishment of the State of Israel, is another.[18] In both cases an underlying community, transcending the limitations of State and nationality, is affirmed in contexts where the existence of the community is capable of bearing legal significance.

There are persuasive arguments to support such views. For example, if a person, or property, is attacked *because* that person adheres to the Jewish or Muslim faith or is a member of some other group, rather than because he or she is national of, say, Israel or Jordan or wherever, the attacker defines the community which he attacks, and that attack ought not to be characterized simply as an attack upon the State to which the victim belongs.[19] Why should the community to which the victim belongs, membership of which actually qualifies him or her as a target for attack, not be entitled to respond to the attack? Why should international law recognize only States as entitled to use force in their defence against attacks from other States? Why should even protection not involving the use of force depend on the nationality of a victim, who might feel that he has closer links with some other community?

There are other instances, albeit isolated, in State practice of a reluctance to accept that force can only lawfully be used by States to defend themselves against attack. Such a view underlay the "Brezhnev Doctrine," according to which, in the words of A. A. Gromyko at the time of the Warsaw Pact intervention in Csechoslovakia,

> The countries of the socialist commonwealth have their own vital interests, their own obligations including those of safeguarding their mutual security ... This commonwealth constitutes an inseparable entity cemented by unbreakable ties such as history has never known.[20]

On this view, a threat to Socialism in one State within that commonwealth was a threat to Socialism in them all. A somewhat similar view might be argued to lie behind the Monroe Doctrine, according to which, it was said, the United States "would consider any attempt on the part [of the European powers] to extend their system to any part of this hemisphere as dangerous to our peace and safety."[21] There were fundamental interests transcending the borders of the United States and shared with other States in the hemisphere which the United States would act to protect.[22] Something of the same approach may be thought to underlie the responses of the western States to the Rushdie affair, in which the existence of a community committed to the preservation of freedom of speech (at least in this instance) appears to be an unstated premise.

In fact, two distinct situations must be envisaged. The first is where one State uses force to protect interests, such as Islam or Socialism under attack in another State by a third State. The second is where it uses force against another State in which those interests are under attack by the government or groups within that State. Both possibilities should be examined in consideration of the restructuring of international law on the use of force. Furthermore, it may be that, whether or not such a move is desirable, political developments will lead to an increase in the practice of using force for purposes other than defending the State against an armed attack.

Quite apart from the possible adverse consequences for international relations of the acceptance of this view, it may seem as a matter of pure doctrine to be an extreme extension of the proper limits of the right to use force against other States for defensive purposes. But is it any less rational than extending the right of "self" defence to include a right of collective self-defence for States which possess no significant geographical, political economic or cultural links?[23] Yet Article 51 of the Charter does not appear to limit the "inherent" right of collective self defence in any such way. Why should, for example, the United States be entitled to use force in response to an attack on South Vietnam merely because it has a collective defence treaty with that country (assuming. for the sake of argument, that South Vietnam was a State for the purposes of Article 51), but Syria not be entitled to respond to an Attack on Lebanon or Libya unless it has such treaty relations with them?

Are we not so completely blinded by the magic of the treaty, so that we can no longer look for any rational principle underlying the rule? The question of the right of States to invoke outside assistance involving the use of armed force in dealing with international or external threats serves only to complicate, not to resolve, the problem. Why *should* an invitation to a State to intervene be legally material, where the State is invited in simply because it is powerful and despite the fact that it has no real links with the inviting State? Why, to take another example, should a State be entitled to use force to protect ships which have been "re-flagged" under its flag, when neither the ship nor its owners or former flag State have any real connection with it?

Are the links established by the casuistry of collective defence treaties or by re-flagging any more deserving of respect by the law than the links between the members of the *umma* or the Socialist commonwealth? Why should States, but not other interests or institutions, be protected from attack? Why should States not be explicitly permitted, or even expected, to respond with force to genocide committed in neighbouring States? Is there a rational answer to these questions, which does not consist either in the repetition of the very premise which is being challenged, that rules of international law must always give expression to the fact that the world is made up of independent nation States, or in the assertion that the world is divided into spheres of influence in which the right of the major powers to intervene under the cloak of legality must be conceded? We are hypnotized by the concept of the State, and are prepared to protect its abstract interests regardless of concrete questions of justice and injustice which are involved.

It is a task of the greatest difficulty to say where the line should be drawn between protectable and non-protectable interests. It is difficult enough even where there is a measure of agreement on the existence of a right such as self-determination. Should there have been a right to use forcible intervention to assist in securing the fulfillment of the right of self-determination in Algeria, or Bangladesh, or Biafra? Should there be such a right in respect of South Africa, or Kurdistan? Much as one might suspect the operation of double standards in the response of States to these situations, there is no easy answer to these questions. There is even greater difficulty in deciding what other values or institutions might be admitted to justify intervention. Should the defence of socialism, or capitalism, or religion, be added to human rights? Should a community have the right to define itself, in the way that the Socialist commonwealth did in 1968, or must the community receive the imprimatur of the international community before it be regarded as a defendable community? There is an obvious and significant danger that an extension of the right to use force will lead inexorably to unconscionable interventions by powerful States in the affairs of the weak. But that does not mean that the line which is drawn at present is better than any other line which could be drawn. The threat to the stability of the system of Nation-States might be a price we should be prepared to pay, if equally or more important interests are thereby advanced.

We have concentrated up to this point on that aspect of the current law which singles out the State as the proper object of protection against the use of force in the context of situations where there is no attack upon a State, but rather an attack on some other social or political institution. There is another aspect to the issue. States do not have a monopoly in relation to the use of force.While wars have raged throughout the world, the developed States have largely remained immune to inter-State attacks. But they are vulnerable to terrorism. Some terrorism may be State-sponsored. It may be an attractive option to a State which knows that it has no chance whatsoever of winning an outright military conflict with, say, a Super-power. Other terrorists may be purely "unofficial," in the sense that their acts are not imputable to any State (a characterisation which itself raises important questions as to where we should draw the line defining State responsibility).

It might be argued that there is an issue here similar to that discussed above. Might it not be said that if terrorist groups are based in another State which cannot or does not control or restrain their activities to the extent required by international law, we might in some circumstances admit a right of forcible intervention in defence against attacks launched by those groups? Is there not a case for allowing force to be used defensively against "unofficial" groups which threaten to use it, without such defensive action being deemed to be *ipso facto* a use of force against the State in which the group is located. Is there not a case for linking the duty not to violate the sovereignty of other States to their willingness and ability to discharge international responsibilities through the exercise of that sovereignty?[24] If a State is genuinely incapable of extending its sovereign power so as to exercise control over, say, terrorist groups operating from within its borders, is there any real sense in which an action against those terrorists can be said to violate its sovereignty? If it were possible to release the hostages held in Beirut by military action of a kind of which the Lebanese government is incapable, would the harm done to Lebanon outweigh the benefits of a third State intervening to release them?

It will no doubt be said that to allow such developments – or rather, to cloak with the authority of law the occasions when States assume the right to take such steps, is a recipe for anarchy or for the arbitrary use of force by strong States against weak States. The United Nations Charter envisaged the avoidance of this danger by allowing States only a temporary right to take action unilaterally, in pursuit of the right of self defence, pending action by the Security Council. It is well known that the United Nations peace-keeping system envisaged the maintenance of military forces at the disposal of the Security Council and the Military Staff Committee consisting of the Chiefs of Staff of the permanent members of the Security Council.[25] That system failed because of political tensions, and the use of the veto power, in the Security Council. Sceptics may doubt whether it was genuinely believed by the governments represented at the 1945 San Fransisco Conference that the United Nations enforcement actions would ever become a routine possibility, given the existence of the veto power and the signs of the "cold war" which were apparent even then.[26] Whatever the true position was, it is evident that the United

Nations cannot be relied on routinely to engage in military action, or even to give an unequivocal determination of situations of aggression entitling the victim State to use force in self defence. Far from being a temporary stop-gap, to be relied upon pending the activation of UN measures, the right of individual or collective self defence embodied in Article 51 of the Charter has become the primary basis for the protection of States' interests in the normal course of events.[27]

Despite signs of a growing *rapprochement* between the United States and the USSR, it is unlikely that the United Nations will be transformed in the foreseeable future into an effective guarantor of peace and justice. In these circumstances it seems inevitable that a wide interpretation will be given to Article 51 whenever a State feels it necessary to do so. The arguments are familiar. Use of the Article to justify action taken in anticipation of an armed attack is one major extension of the strict wording of the Article, which was foreseen at a very early stage. It was noted that the Charter was written before the first use of the atomic bomb, and that in its first report to the Security Council the United Nations Atomic Energy Commission suggested that a violation of an atomic energy convention "might be of so grave a character as to give rise to the inherent right of self-defence recognized in Article 51."[28] Given the nature of nuclear weapons, it is doubtful if any other approach makes sense in the post-atomic world, and it should not be claimed that States are doing anything extraordinary in claiming such a right. Similarly, the well-known arguments over the requirement of proportionality grafted on to Article 51 from the *Caroline* case, over the right to act against a continuing series of minor cross-border raids, and over the right to use force to protect nationals abroad, all signal the demise of Article 51 as an accurate statement of the circumstances in which the international community claims or tolererates claims to use force.

Given the probability that decisions on the use of force will normally be taken unilaterally by States or groups of States, and not by the United Nations, is it not time that Article 2(4) and 51 were redrafted so as to meet more fully the exigencies of modern life and protect more adequately the values which ought to be protected? It might be said that in practice the world is coping, and that the Charter articles remain useful precisely because they are more narrowly drawn than many States would wish; that their very narrowness helps to ensure that action which goes beyond their limits will always be the exception and not the rule. There is certainly a plausible argument to be made out here. But it is not obvious that the contorted interpretations of Article 51 offered as justifications for actions such as the raids on Entebbe by Israel and on Tripoli by the United States actually do reinforce what has been called the "pull of compliance" in Article 51.[29] It may be that, if Article 51 is increasingly seen as being too restrictive, it will be disregarded and become discredited *in toto*, and that we will be left without any rule which States regard as a real constraint on their actions. This is not a question to be answered in the abstract. We need hard evidence of how States do respond to written rules.

Similar considerations apply to the *jus in bello*. There is plainly a need for such rules: it is difficult to construct a coherent moral argument for using barbaric methods of warfare in order to preserve what the State in question regards as civilization. But here again, it is unwise to draft rules without determining what their practical effect is likely to be. Do rules requiring, for example, that arms be carried openly encourage that practice in circumstances where it might not otherwise be adopted, or do they rather establish an expectation which forces are likely to exploit by disregarding it in order to obtain the advantage of surprise? Do rules forbidding attacks on places of religious worship avert attacks on such places more often than they lead to the siting of military facilities near or in them? Making the rule may actually encourage the conduct which it seeks to proscribe.

It is necessary to discover in what circumstances a rule is and is not likely to be effective in advancing the interests which it is designed to protect. There is no point in, say, banning biological weapons if the effect is to give a decisive military advantage to a State or group unscrupulous enough to disregard the ban. And it is necessary to discover what form of rule is likely to be the most effective. Are precise and detailed rules more likely to secure compliance than vague and general ones around which a body of interpretative State practice can build up? Is it more expedient to seek international agreement on the drafting of a comprehensive body of rules, or to seek agreement on a re-vitalization of the system for the centralised determination of the existence of states of aggression and entitlement to use force, under the auspices of the United Nations or of other organizations? Nonetheless, there is at least a presumption that a rule which no longer correspondends to reality should be changed.

We must also consider the role of disarmament. International law is frequently criticised, with more force than insight, for its inability effectively to contain and regulate conflict. Such criticism must be taken particularly seriously when they are made by those directly responsible for the use of force. Experience in teaching on courses for the British armed forces over the last decade suggests that the generalizations of Articles 2(4) and 51 of the Charter are widely regarded as unhelpful in concrete situations (except to set the broad lines of policy) and ill-adapted to the constraints imposed on decision-making by modern weaponry. The difficulty of determining the existence or imminence of an "armed attack," and of reconciling the concept of proportionality in the use of forced in self-defence with the need to ensure that defensive action achieves its aims, are the two most common criticisms. But the criticisms are addressed to the wrong people.

It is not the law which is the root cause of these inadequacies. It is the arms procurement policies of countries throughout the world. Immense resources are employed in the development of weapons whose precise aim is to circumvent the very restraints to which governments pay lip service in international negotiations. What is the point in limiting the right of self-defence to circumstances where an armed attack occurs, if governments are commissioning bomber aircraft and missiles designed to elude detection by the target State's radar and other defensive facilities, so that they cannot know, but only guess, when they are under attack? What is the point in establishing rules setting out the duty to respect the distinction between combatants and non-combatants, if governments are developing nuclear and other weapons whose primary military value lies in the fact that they can inflict death and destruction on a scale which makes it utterly impossible to respect that distinction?

It may be said that it is idle to pretend that such weapons cannot be made or that the bomb can be un-invented. Whether that be true or not, it does not excuse the hypocrisy of negotiating legal and moral constraints on the conduct of war which are systematically undermined by the procurement of such weapons. Even less can it excuse the enthusiasm with which government-backed arms salesmen peddle such weapons among potential buyers in other States. Is there not a case for saying that the time has come when, instead of demanding that law and morality adapt to new methods or warfare, those methods must adapt to the legal and moral constraints which alone can justify their use? Is it not time that those seriously concerned to limit violence – be it international or domestic – in the world turned their attention to the flourishing arms trade which sustains it.

Finally, it must be said that the search for effective Laws of War is not a task to be conducted in isolation. Weapons are bought and wars fought at the expense of other, more valuable contributions to the welfare of the men, women, and children with whom we share this planet. In a sense, the search for peace is a preoccupation of the rich, or rich States and of ruling élites in poorer States. The poor themselves are too busy trying, and often failing, to survive. The question of when, where, and how it is legally and morally justifiable for us to kill one another cannot ignore the fact that the expenditure of resources on waging or preparing for war always involves a choice not to invest those resources in other areas, such as bringing food and medicine to the starving or the sick, or developing the economy of the State; and that that choice itself involves more issues every bit as important as the establishment of restraints on war. Fashionable as it is to regard those who assert a link between disarmament and development as naive, there is such a link, and it must be addressed.

Conclusion

The limitation of the law to the protection of States may come increasingly to be challenged, and contemporary international law appears to be breaking down because of its lack of internal choices. In conclusion, the essential point can be summarised briefly. It is that there is no point in severing the rule of law between States from the rule of law and maintenance of justice between individuals. Max Huber said, in his classic award in the *Island of Palmas* arbitration, that "International law, like law in general, has the object of assuring the co-existence of different interests which are worthy of legal protection."[30] If that object is to be achieved, and international law to retain a role not merely in the maintenance of peace but also in the maintenance of justice, we need to have a hard look at the Laws of War.

Notes

1. GAOR, 42d session, Supp. No.41 (A/42/41); reprinted in *International Legal Materials*, XXVII (1988), 1672 [hereinafter *ILM*].
2. The exchanges between Brownlie and Lillich remain one of the best discussions of the issue. See R. B. Lillich, "Forcible Self-Help by States to Protect Human Rights," *Iowa Law Review*, LIII (1967), 325; *id*, "Intervention to Protect Human Rights," *McGill Law Journal*, XV (1969), 205; I. Brownlie, "Humanitarian Intervention," in J. N. Moore (ed.), *Law and Civil War in the Modern World* (1974), pp. 217–228; Lillich, "Humanitarian Intervention: A Reply to Ian Brownlie and a Plea for Constructive Alternatives," *ibid.*, pp. 229–251.
3. See, for example, C. Greenwood, "The Concept of War in Modern International Law," *International and Comparative Law Quarterly*, XXXVI (1986), 283–306; A. V. Lowe, "The Laws of War at Sea and the 1958 and 1982 Conventions," *Marine Policy*, XII (1988), 286–296.
4. G. A. Res. 2625 (XXV), 24 October 1970. Similar provisions appear in the 1987 Declaration.
5. See Brownlie, *International Law and the Use of Force by States* (1963), p. 638.
6. U. N. General Assembly, Third Comm., 1879th meeting, 22 November 1971.
7. *Keesing's Contemporary Archives*, p. 25109 (19–26 February 1972).
8. See Lillich, *Humanitarian Intervention* (1973). Practice does not, as yet, indicate support for the legality of humanitarian intervention with the clarity which would be necessary for such intervention to be an established right in international law. The practice demonstrates growing toleration of the practice, rather than acceptance of the right as such. For instance, after the Entebbe raid, the United Kingdom and the United States proposed a resolution which condemned hijacking but not the rescue mission, and another draft resolution condemning Israel was not put to the vote. See *ILM*, XV (1976), 1226–27. After United States intervention in Grenada, the United Kingdom did "not dispute that a State has the right in international law to take appropriate action to safeguard the lives of its citizens where there has been a breakdown in the Charter of the United [Nations] that makes it unlawful to take such action." See *House of Commons Debates*, XLVII, cols. 329–330, 26 October 1983. But the furthest that the United Kingdom has gone towards accepting a right to protect non-nationals is to admit the "undoubted benefits" of the interventions in Bangladesh and Uganda and to say that such use of force "cannot be said to be unambiguously illegal." See *Foreign & Commonwealth Office Policy Document*, no. 148, pp. 2–9; reproduced in *British Yearbook of International Law*, LVII (1986), 618–620. Perhaps the fairest summary is to say that there is a tendency to refrain from condemning States for the intervention itself in such circumstances, although their motives, their claim to a right to intervene, and their subsequent conduct may well be questioned.
9. See M. Walzer, *Just and Unjust Wars* (1980), pp. 105–107; S. K. Chatterjee, "Some Legal Problems of Support Role in International Law: Tanzania and Uganda,"

International and Comparative Law Quarterly, XXX (1981), 755–768; K. P. Misra, *The Role of the United Nations in the Indo-Pakistan Conflict, 1971* (1973).

10. On the other hand, the reaction of Western States to the intervention in Kampuchea by the Vietnamese Army does not fit this pattern. See C. Warbrick, "Kampuchea: Representation and Recognition," *International and Comparative Law Quarterly*, XXX (1981), 234–246. Also see the United Kingdom statement in the U. N. General Assembly, where it said that the atrocities of the Pol Pot regime provided "no justification for Vietnam's illegal occupation and imposition of an illegal regime." Quoted in *British Yearbook of International Law*, LVIII (1987), 630. It will be noted that it is the *subsequent occupation*, and not the actual intervention, which is singled out for condemnation; a different view might have been taken had Vietnam withdrawn immediately after displacing the Pol Pot regime.

11. J. Westlake, *International Law* (2d ed., 1910), I, pp. 319–320.

12. See, for example, W. M. Reisman, "Article 2(4): The Use of Force in Contemporary International Law," *Proceedings of the American Society of International Law* (1984), pp. 74–87, where he writes that "Humanitarian intervention ... is an extraordinary remedy, an exception to the postulates of State sovereignty and territorial inviolability that are fundamental to traditional theory" (p. 79). Reisman presents an outstandingly compelling argument for a view similar to that advanced here.

13. There are exceptions, such as the military wings of national liberation movements. These are a good example of the use of force to protect a non-State interest. It is notable that the 1987 Declaration singles out peoples forcibly deprived of the right of self-determination and reaffirms their right "to struggle to that end and to seek and receive support." This is plainly inconsistent with any intention to prohibit absolutely the threat or use of force in international relations.

14. H. Afchar, "The Muslim Conception of Law," in R. David (ed.), *International Encyclopedia of Comparative Law*, II (1975), chap. 1, para. 146.

15. See M. Khadduri, *The Islamic Law of Nations: Shaybani's Siyar* (1966), pp. 10–14, 60–70. By analogy, it might be said that humanitarian intervention amounts to a protection of the international community of humankind. It is, perhaps, a measure of the distance that international law has departed from moral principle that such a phrase should seem odd to the lawyer.

16. See, for example, "Islam's Arrow of Death," *The Economist*, 11 March 1989, pp. 61–62.

17. Palestine National Council, Political Communique and Declaration of Independence, 15 November 1988, *ILM*, XXVII (1988), 1670–71.

18. Attorney-General of the Government of Israel v Eichmann, District Court of Jerusalem, *ILM*, XXXVI (1961), 5. The idea of a "Greater Israel," extending beyond the boundaries of the secular State of Israel, is another aspect of this phenomenon.

19. In the case of an attack on persons or property in another State, the attack might be both an attack on the "host" State and on the wider community to which the person or property belongs. But this does not detract from the point made here, which is that the attack can be interpreted as an attack on the wider community. It might also be noted that this view offers an answer to the otherwise troublesome question of the basis of the claim to use force to protect foreign ships under attack from a third State on the high seas, where such ships are operated by nationals of the defending State. This point was discussed in the present writer's paper delivered to the II Anglo-Soviet Symposium on Public International Law at Moscow in May 1988. See A. V. Lowe, "Self-Defence at Sea," in W. E. Butler (ed.), *The Non-Use of Force in International Law* (1989), pp. 185–202.

20. Quoted in R. R. James (ed.), *The Czechoslovak Crisis 1968* (1969), p.114, citing *Pravda*, 25 September 1968 and G. A. Record A/PV 1679, pp. 28–31.

21. Quoted in T. D. Woolsey, *Introduction to the Study of International Law* (1908), p. 53. Note, too, the Polk Corollary of the Doctrine, according to which the right to take all necessary steps to prevent any non-American power from obtaining control over territory in the hemisphere is claimed regardless of whether the foreign intervention occurs with the consent of the inhabitants of the area affected. See Memorandum for the Attorney General re: Legality Under International Law of Remedial Action Against Use of Cuba as a Missile Base by the Soviet Union, reprinted in A. Chayes, *The Cuban Missile Crisis* (1974), p. 111.

22. Although arguable, this view is not entirely persuasive. As the Polk corollary cited in the previous footnote makes plain, there is rather more of the self-interest of the United States than of an appeal to shared values as the basis of the Monroe Doctrine.

23. See note 5 above, pp. 328–331. The question of what links *are* "significant" gives rise to substantial difficulties, which mirror the problem discussed here.

24. To draw an example from the jurisprudence of the ICJ, is it obvious that we should regard "Operation Retail" as a violation of Albanian sovereignty, as it was characterised in the *Corfu Channel* case. ICJ Reports (1949), p. 4. Was not the British argument that it was a limited measure, confined to the safeguarding of the legal right of passage through the strait, equally, if not more, plausible?

25. Articles 47 and 47, United Nations Charter.

26. See D. Horowitz, *From Yalta to Vietnam* (1967), chaps. 1–2.

27. It is informative to speculate on the idea that the principle of *rebus sic stantibus* might operate in relation to Articles 2(4) and 51 of the Charter, in the light of the failure of the United Nations to achieve its intended role as the international guarantor of peace and justice. Note Reisman's view that "[i]t was in the context of the Organization envisaged by the charter and not as a moral postulate that Article 2(4) acquired its cogency." Reisman, note 12 above, p. 76.

28. U. N. Atomic Energy Commission, Doc. AEC/18/Rev.1, p. 24.

29. T. M. Franck, "Legitimacy in the International System," *American Journal of International Law*, LXXXII (1988), 705–759.

30. Netherlands v U.S., *RIAA*, II (1928), 829.

PERESTROIKA AND THE TEACHING OF HUMAN RIGHTS LAW IN THE USSR

W. E. BUTLER

Although the subject of human rights has generated a substantial scholarly literature in the Soviet Union – a body of writings which awaits a proper bibliography – the teaching of the subject as a cohesive body of legal principles or branch of law has apparently been confined to ad hoc lectures and not found a niche in the law curriculum. In January 1988 the decision was taken by the All-Union Legal Correspondence Institute to introduce a special course for law students on the history, theory, and practice of human rights under the direction of Professor Boris Nazarov.

Teaching of the course commenced in September 1989 with an enrolment in excess of 300 students and is believed to be the first course of its kind not merely in the Soviet Union, but also in the socialist legal systems of Eastern Europe and Mongolia. This alone makes the concept of the subject, as set out in its syllabus, of considerable interest. But the syllabus as an institution of higher education also plays a powerful role in nurturing the rising generation in the doctrinal underpinnings of each discipline, a role which goes far beyond the particular institution where the subject is offered.[1]

The syllabus translated below is novel in at least three respects. In addition to being a first in the socialist legal systems, it also is the product principally of a single individual rather than a committee of law teachers. Further, in substance Western specialists may be surprised by the great stress placed upon what broadly speaking can be classified as matters of legal theory rather than the nuts and bolts of the international law of human rights. This perception is reinforced by the guiding, special, and further readings offered under each topic of the syllabus. Enormous attention is given to the classics of Marxism-Leninism rather than to the contemporary literature on the subject. And even within the special readings devoted expressly to modern human rights the literature will be unfamiliar to even Soviet international lawyers.

Although the syllabus was published by the State Committee of the USSR for Public Education, it carries no formal indicia of official approval. Authorship is collective – the Chair of Human Rights of the VIuZI under the editorship of Professor B. L. Nazarov. The syllabus is described as the "first instructional course on human rights problems within the system of higher education of the country. Without claiming to exhaustively set out all the multifarious peculiarities of the subject, the Chair hopes that the 'History, Theory, and Practice of Human Rights' is a contribution towards inculcating the knowledge which the revolutionary

W. E. Butler, Perestroika and International Law, 297–328.

restructuring of society requires. The Chair thanks all the jurists and philosophers whose advice and wishes assisted it in its work."[2] Although the number of lecture-hours in the course is not prescribed in the syllabus, the scope of the syllabus is comparable to the 140 hours required for the basic course on public international law.

Notes

1. See W. E. Butler, "The Syllabus on Public International Law in the USSR," in *id* (ed.), *International Law and the International System* (1987), pp. 185–208.
2. Gosudarstvennyi komitet SSSR po narodnomu obrazovaniiu, Vsesoiuznyi iuridicheskii zaochnyi institut, *Programma kursa istoriia, teoriia, i praktika prav cheloveka dlia studentov VIuZI*. Moscow, 1988. 32 p. 2000 ptd. Signed to press on 28 November 1988.

SYLLABUS FOR THE COURSE ON THE HISTORY, THEORY AND PRACTICE OF HUMAN RIGHTS OFFERED TO STUDENTS OF THE ALL-UNION JURIDICAL CORRESPONDENCE INSTITUTE

Section I. Introduction to the theory of human rights

Topic 1. Significance of the course

The course on human rights as an independent branch of knowledge essential for a comprehensive consideration of the social being of man and for the development of new political-legal thinking and a fundamental change towards improving the professional training of jurists under conditions of revolutionary perestroika and democratisation of society.

The urgent requirement for knowledge about the socio-political and moral legal status of man in the system of contemporary national and international relations and growing general humanitarian needs, interests, and values.

The role of scholarly approaches to socio-political activities when resolving contemporary humanitarian national and international problems in the process of the cognition and selection of the most effective human rights institutions on the basis of long-term theories for their constant perfection.

Orientation of the course towards the unity of history, theory, and contemporary practice of human rights.

Significance of tendency of the course in the system of higher legal education for a renaissance of Leninist principles and norms of life and for nurturing the active social position of man in the struggle for social justice and the rights and legal interests of citizens in the practical resolution of the task of providing the legal reform with cadres and forming a socialist rule-of-law State.

The importance of the theoretical working out and implementation of optimal principles and conceptions of socio-legal protection of man and a system of guarantees in all spheres of social relations.

Theoretical and practical significance of the doctrine of human rights in the struggle for peace, democracy, and progress.

Topic 2. Subject, method, and system of the course

Logic of shaping the subject and system of the course. History of the question.

Concept of the subject, revealing of its essential indicia.

Doctrine of human rights as generalisation of theoretical knowledge, historical experience, and the practice of the struggle of working people against exploitation and lawlessness, for their liberation. Social revolutions, political power, and human rights.

The historical approach to the problems and concept of human rights. Study of the laws of the process of the origin and development of: (a) the struggle of the working people for freedom, social justice, and human rights; (b) conceptions and theories of human rights; (c) normative forms determining the status of man in the social structure of society, his rights and duties.

The place of bourgeois revolutions in the history of the struggle of the working people for freedom, social justice, human rights, and their normative-legal expression and consolidation.

Awareness by the people's masses, classes, and social strata of economic, political, and spiritual requirements – prerequisite for the development of human rights. Human rights as an expression of the legal views of the individual and class, of man and society, of citizen and individual.

Marxism-Leninism – a qualitatively new level in the theory of human rights. Socialism – universal historical revolution in the development of human rights. Leninist period of origin and development of human rights.

Achievements in construction of socialism and its deformation after V.I. Lenin. Major documents of the Party and its activities regarding the mobilisation of the people for a renaissance of Leninist principles and approaches in resolving practical tasks in the revolutionary perestroika of society. Cleansing socialism of crisis phenomena in the economy and politics, from the practices of dual morality alien to it, double standards, flagrant and mass violations of legality, arbitrariness, and the flouting of the dignity of man in the periods of the personality cult and stagnation.

Use of potential possibilities of socialism for the purpose of strengthening the protection of human rights within the country and in the international arena. Interaction of norms of socialist and international law in the protection of human rights.

The search, in the context of new thinking, for optimal solutions in theory, legislation, and practice regarding the use of the objective and spiritual possibilities of society in the interest of mankind.

Principal orientations in evaluating the social value of human rights. Need for cognition thereof in the dynamics of the historical process, in ways to ensure the comprehensive development of the individual. Contradictory nature of conceptions and of practice itself in resolving problem of human rights guarantees. Modern theories and practice of human rights. Conceptual distinctions of class positions in domain of human rights. Basic features and comparative analysis of socialist and non-Marxist theories of human rights.

Ideological struggle and international cooperation regarding human rights, its laws of development and influence on regional and national normative regulators of social relations.

Theory of human rights as a social science. Its connection with other social sciences and legal disciplines. Integrating role of course in ensuring comprehensive legal education.

Dialectical materialist methodology of cognition of the essence, internal links, contradictions, and laws of development of human rights. Significance of principles and categories of materialist dialectics in studying subject of the course.

Unity of the historical and logical, abstract and concrete in the cognition of human rights.

Historicism and class in the dialectical-materialist theory of human rights.

Correlation of a Party approach [partiinost'] and objectivity in theoretical studies of contemporary problems of the course.

Materialist dialectics and quasi-scientific methods of cognition. Their interaction in the process of studying human rights.

Content and structure of course on the theory of human rights.

Topic 3. Concept of human rights

Multiple meanings of definitions of human rights. Eliciting the concept of human rights through definitions contained in official documents and scholarly studies. Analysis of these definitions.

Link of concept of human rights with major State-law phenomena and concepts.

Significance of philosophical categories for cognition of human rights concepts. Their peculiarities as expression of individual and collective claims and social possibilities in various spheres of the life of society.

Enrichment of concept of human rights in process of historical development of the freedom of society and the individual.

Topic 4. Man and his rights in the system of social links of the modern day

Inextricable link of human rights with economic structure of society and ideological relations.

Human rights, socio-political system, and interaction of two world systems. Man, society, and historical progress. Man, power, and the State. Dependence of extent and content of human rights on level of social development of society in concrete historical conditions. Scientific-technical revolution (STR) and possibilities of ensuring the life and dignity of man.

Freedom, human rights, and objective laws of development. Class and general humanitarian values in their correlation with moral and legal principles in the light of contemporary human rights problems.

Dialectic of the correlation of the interests of the individual, class, and world community at the contemporary stage. Trend toward expanding and enriching human rights as a result of resolving contradictions between man, State, and society.

Humanism, freedom, equality, and equality of rights – basic principles of human rights.

Topic 5. Man, individual, citizen. Correlation of equality and equality of rights

Legal status of the citizen as basis for legal expression of human rights. Conceptual categories of "mankind" (world community), "people," "nation," "national population group," "class," "man," "individual," "citizen," "person." Awareness of differentiation of legal status. Social status as actual status of citizen and individual in society. Dialectic of social equality and equality of rights. Degree (extent) of social equality and effectiveness of functioning of human rights in various types of society. Dynamic of the development of equality, equality of rights, and human rights. Correlation of social and legal status of citizen and individual. Satisfaction of requirements of society and the individual – indication of effectiveness of social institutes in the realisation of human rights. Interconnection of social equality, social justness, and human rights.

Topic 6. Democracy and human rights

Concept of democracy in its link with human rights. Basic laws of development of democracy and human rights. Dependence of content, extent, and provision of human rights on type of democratic system and character of production relations.

Objective and subjective conditions and possibilities of society in historical progress of democracy and human rights.

Sovereignty of the people – expression of its political and legal power. The people as a subject of power and decisive guarantor of human rights.

Contemporary general-democratic movements in the struggle for the development and protection of human rights.

Topic 7. System of human rights

Correlation of concepts of human rights and the system of human rights in historical development. Objective and subjective criteria for shaping the system of human rights. Subjects of human rights. Theory of three generations of human rights. Contemporary national and international (regional and universal) systems of human rights and their correlation. Socio-economic and cultural, civil, and political rights and freedoms, their nature, essence, and interaction. Controversial issues on the interconnections of humanitarian law and the system of human rights as an independent branch of law. Practical significance of system of human rights.

Peculiarities and diversity of classifications of human rights and approaches to shaping the system thereof in socialist theory and practice.

The structure of constitutional rights and freedoms of the citizen under conditions of an all-people's rule-of-law State.

The influence of new historical conditions and new thinking on the development of the system of human rights. Multi-aspect nature of the content of the right to life as the principal one in the system of human rights. The level achieved, basic trends, and contradictions in the development of the right to life in universal and regional international normative standards. Development of content of right to life in its correlation with the right to peace and other human rights.

Section II. History of human rights

Topic 8. History of struggle of working people against oppression of their rights in precapitalist formations

Commencement of history of human rights.

Schism of society into antagonistic classes and struggle of man for freedom and justness against oppression and lawlessness.

Human rights through the medium of class struggle.

Social progress and its contradictory nature. Laws of development of origin and emergence of views, conceptions, and theories of human rights and their normative expression in the history of society before the appearance of bourgeois democracy.

Topic 9. Human rights in epoch of first bourgeois revolutions and industrial capitalism

Basic laws of the origin and development of ideas of human rights under conditions of the decay of feudalism.

First bourgeois revolutions, conceptions of human rights, and the merits of their normative proclamation in the period of victorious capitalism. Historical progressiveness and limited nature of bourgeois theory and practice of human rights.

Revolutionary theory of human rights and struggle for them in Russia.

Representatives of utopian socialism on human rights.

Topic 10. Marxism-Leninism – Qualitatively new stage in the comprehension, scientific substantiation and practice of human rights

K. Marx and F. Engels on human rights in the period of ideological development from revolutionary democratism to scientific communism.

Shaping of dialectical-materialist doctrine on man. Marxist humanism and comprehensive study of problems of man (man, social individual, class individual).

Inextricable link of maturing of socialist approaches to human rights problems with the revolutionary practice of the struggle of the proletariat. Paris Commune and human rights.

The working class – expression of general humanitarian ideas, interests, and values.

Defence and creative development by V. I. Lenin of Marx and Engels' doctrine on human rights. Leninist ideas on the correlation of the interests of society and the individual, of class and the individual.

V. I. Lenin on the dialectical dependence of the status of the individual in society on his social activeness in the struggle for the reality of rights and freedoms. Civilisation, culture, and man in the works of V. I. Lenin. Methodological significance of Leninist critique of contradictory reality of human rights under conditions of bourgeois democracy.

Programmatic documents of RSPRD(b) on the liberation of "oppressed mankind" as a result of proletarian revolution.

Leninist ideas of the use of bourgeois-democratic rights and freedoms in the struggle for the victory of socialist revolution. Marxist-Leninist conception of human rights in the system of ideologically ensuring socialist revolution.

Section III. Basic orientations of the theory and practice of twentieth century human rights

Topic 11. Socialist revolutions and human rights

Great October – commencement of new age in the theory and practice of human rights. Fundamental changes in the socio-economic and politico-legal status of the working people.

Laws of development of socialist revolutions and human rights. Confirmation of basic principles of social justness.

Struggle for peace and peaceful coexistence – major source of the enrichment, content, and new means of protecting the human right to life. Declaration of imperialist war to be a crime against humanity. Leninist programme for ensuring security and peaceful cooperation of peoples and States and the modern day. Significance of Leninist nationality policy for new understanding and practical effectuation of human rights.

Humanism of Leninist programme of socialist transformations on the basis of the power of producers of material wealth themselves and national sovereignty. Use of historical experience of Paris Commune.

Mass law-creation –legislative embodiment of revolutionary energy and revolutionary legal consciousness of the working people. Early Soviet decrees, Declaration, Constitution, and codes – basic normative legal acts regarding human rights.

Struggle against bureaucratism as essential condition for development of creative initiative of the individual and masses. Leninist demand to teach man "to fight for" his own rights and the interests of society. Commencement of process of practical maturing of socialist priorities in domain of human rights.

Eradication of exploitation of man by man – decisive guarantee of rights and freedoms of working people. Constant enrichment and expansion of human rights through the construction, development, and perfection of society – one of the basic laws of development of socialism.

Socialist criteria for the effectiveness of human rights. Influence of October on the socialist revolutions of the second half of the twentieth century. Contribution of countries of the socialist commonwealth in the development of the world revolutionary process "of the liberation of oppressed mankind" in the theory and practice of human rights.

Topic 12. Human rights under conditions of deformation of socialism and democracy

Deviation from Leninist norms of life and principles of democracy and social justness in domain of human rights in the periods of personality cult and stagnation, and of alienation of working people from the authorities. Undermining of socialist priorities in the system of objective and subjective factors of the development and protection of human rights. Gap between theory, normative expression, and practice of human rights.

Coming of crisis phenomena in Soviet society as consequence of criminal, antipeople policy of braking the development of democracy and potential of socialism in the entire system of social relations and in strengthening the social protection of man.

Discrediting in the theory and practice of socialism. Analysis of the reasons for anti-socialist phenomena born in the process of the development of socialist revolution. Natural, objective, and subjective grounds for and requirements of a revolutionary renewal of society by purging socialism of its distortions, ensuring the reliable protection of the individual against any arbitrariness and lawlessness, and confirming genuine guarantees for its free, comprehensive, and worthy development.

Topic 13. Development of socialist conception and practice of human rights under conditions of revolutionary perestroika

Human rights in the restructuring processes of socialist countries.

The activities of the Party and people in overcoming the negative consequences of the personality cult and stagnation through the revolutionary perestroika of society, democratisation, and glasnost, expanding and enriching human rights, and enhancing the effectiveness of their guarantees. The creation of conditions excluding the repetition of arbritrariness and lawlessness. The shaping of a socialist rule-of-law State.

Significance of the Materials of the XXVII Congress of the CPSU, subsequent plenums of the Central Committee of the CPSU, and the XIX Party Conference for effectuation of the legal reform and perestroika in the domain of human rights.

Renaissance of socialist self-government of the people as a decisive condition in ensuring the right of each to take part in deciding questions of State and social life.

The social programme of the CPSU - basis of the real embodiment of human rights in the USSR. Shaping a socially homogeneous society and overcoming economic inequality and negative phenomena in inter-nationality relations.

The social structure of society and contradictions in the process of its restructuring and democratisation. Contribution of mass media to the development and strengthened protection of the rights of citizens.

Socialist conception of human rights. Significance of Marxist-Leninist theory of human rights in new historical conditions of revolutionary perestroika and democratisation of society in socialist countries and in international relations. Influence of these processes on the development of the socialist conception of human rights. Historical and practical need for a Declaration of socialist countries on human rights and the creation of respective regional institutions for their cooperation.

Topic 14. Human rights in the system of social relations of contemporary capitalism

Principal features of bourgeois theory and practice of human rights. Objective and subjective factors of their correlation with institutes of bourgeois democracy and general humanitarian values.

Rise of mass democratic movements, their role in the struggle for human rights, the juxtaposition of neo-conservative trends.

Correlation of the principle of social justness with the legal regulation of distributive relations under capitalism. Concept of legal and actual equality.

Constitutional rights of citizen and the practice of effectuating them under capitalism.

Problems of guarantees of human rights for the working people. Democracy, legality, and problems of social protection of man under conditions of capitalist society.

Topic 15. Contemporary non-Marxist conceptions of human rights

Reasons for the activisation of bourgeois thinking in the sphere of human rights. Philosophical, formal-legal, sociological, biological, and religious conceptions of man and his rights.

Theory of natural and inalienable human rights at the present time. Need for dialogue of different theories on human rights in the modern age.

Topic 16. Shaping of system of human rights in developing countries

National-liberation and democratic movements of the modern day as allies of world socialism in the struggle for human rights.

Problem of human rights and choice of paths of development of liberated countries. Differences of principle in approaches to conceptions of human rights in developing countries of a socialist and capitalist orientation. Struggle in the world for the right to freedom from exploitation comprising the basis of all other rights of the individual. Human rights, shaping of the system thereof in the constitutions of two groups of developing countries (of socialist and capitalist orientation).

Regional organisations and institutions for human rights.

Role of customs, traditions, and religious norms in human rights systems and peculiarities of their realisation in liberated countries.

Supra-class and nationalistic views of human rights in those countries.

Section IV. Contemporary problems of guaranteeing human rights

Topic 17. Theory of machinery of human rights guarantees and the formation thereof – vital requirement of progressive mankind

Concept of guarantees of human rights and correlation of their social and legal provision. Interaction of social and political machinery for human rights guarantees. Place and role of legal guarantees in the system of social machinery for ensuring human rights.

Socio-economic, political, and moral sources of contradictions in the development and embodiment of the ideas of human rights in the theories and conceptions (in political decisions and books), in official legal documents (in norms of law), and in practice (in life itself).

Gap between human rights in legal norms (in international and national legal systems) and the practice of realising them. Overcoming this gap – a major general humanitarian problem. Objective and subjective prerequisites for their optimal resolution under conditions of different socio-economic and political systems. Significance in this process of enhancing the effectiveness of existing and the formation of new social and legal guarantees for the development and protection of human rights.

Theoretical outfitting of system of human rights guarantees. Relationships of various conceptions to the idea of the rule-of-law State, to the principle of the presumption of innocence, to the theory of separation of powers. The criteria of their effectiveness – practice under various social formations. Search for new proposals to improve the human rights situation and strengthen the securing thereof.

Definitive significance of types of ownership and respective relationships in order to secure the reality of guarantees and conditions for exercising human rights and their social protection. The link between strengthening social guarantees and the humanity thereof and the intensiveness and quality of labour activities. Possibilities of expanding and strengthening the socio-economic, political, moral, and legal guarantees of human rights.

Political systems and their role in developing the content, extent, and gurantees of human rights. Power and the protection of its freedom and legal interests.

Socio-psychological and moral stimulators and generators of the machinery for human rights guarantees in contemporary social relations of different socio-economic formations.

Topic 18. Concept of integral and universal machinery for human rights guarantees. Its structure and sphere of activities

Concept of machinery for human rights guarantees as an integral and universal system. Objective and subjective factors of its formation. Structure of the machinery. Concept and types of social guarantees. Principal internal and external links of the system of special legal connections and levers in the structure of a universal and integral machinery for human rights guarantees. Active awareness-of-will activities of man as source of the real integrating activities in the machinery of guarantees of its rights.

All-embracing character of the machinery of legal guarantees. Diversity of basic forms, means, and methods of protecting the legal interests and freedoms of man

308

depending on the peculiarities regulated by the law of social relations. The general and the particular in human rights guarantees embodied in various branches, institutes, and norms of law.

The specific nature of legal guarantees in legal relations embracing various spheres: (a) lawful behaviour; (b) unlawful act; (c) procedural activities; (d) endurance of punishment; (e) reinstatement of full rights.

Universalisation of guarantees of human rights on basis of requirements of legality, legal order, and rule-of-law State.

Topic 19. Political parties, mass social organisations, and movements in the human rights protection machinery

Peculiarities, social roles, and interaction of political parties, mass social organisations, and movements in the sphere of developing and protecting human rights under conditions of different socio-economic and political systems, as well as in contemporary international relations. Evaluation of their activities from the standpoint of the principles of social justness and humanism. Special responsibility of ruling political parties and their leaders for the fate of human rights in their countries and international relations. Influence of political parties, mass social organisations, and movements on the activities of the State in the person of its legislative, executive, judicial, and other law enforcment agencies.

Growth of the role of the Soviet Communist Party in enriching the content and strengthening the guarantees of human rights within the country and in relations between peoples. Analysis of major Party documents of revolutionary perestroika and the democratic renewal of society regarding humanitarian problems and human rights.

The Party as the guarantor of the successive expansion of the rights and freedoms of the individual through the fulfilment of programmes for the socio-economic and cultural development of society, democratisation, and confirmation of glasnost. Reforms of the political system of Soviet society and legal reform. Contradictions in the process of the realisation of Party decisions in the domain of human rights. Overcoming the effect of braking mechanisms.

Contribution of Party to the development of a socialist and international conception of human rights.

New positive features and difficulties in the work of trade unions, the Komsomol, and other social organisations regarding the democratisation of society and protection of human rights. Multifarious forms of manifesting the social activeness of youth. Various means and forms of participation of numerous amateur, including informal, organisations in resolving the problems of ensuring human rights.

Legal and non-legal means of struggle against bureaucratisation and formalism in the activities of State and social organisations. Well-foundedness of need for independent social control over work of these organisations as condition of effective work of all links of machinery for protection of human rights.

Topic 20. Institute of social responsibility – major universal means of securing human rights

Democracy of social responsibility, its universal integrating nature.

Concept and types of social responsibility. Structure thereof. Place, role, and character of interaction of moral, political, and legal responsibility in all their diverse aspects in the integral and all-embracing machinery of human rights guarantees. Growing practical significance of positive responsibility in diverse social relations. Need for introducing into effect all structural subdivisions of institute of social responsibility for enhancing the effectiveness and providing constant energy for machinery of human rights guarantees. Subjects of responsibility for ensuring rights, freedoms, and legal interests of citizens. Mutual responsibility of the individual and the State.

Topic 21. Legislation as basis for legal machinery for ensuring human rights

Role of legislation in system of human rights guarantees. Norm of law – basic link in structure of legal means of social protection of man.

Theoretical bases for working out and introducing into legislation optimal structures of legal norms for the protection of human rights on basis of concept of indestructible unity of law, duties, and responsibility as constant source of legal energy for ensuring human rights.

Basic orientations of renewal and improvement of Soviet legislation under conditions of revolutionary perestroika. Legislative securing of formation of socialist rule-of-law State. Development of constitutional bases of guarantees of rights and freedoms of man. Analysis of new legislation and improvement of legal means for protection of man, his rights and legal interests.

Topic 22. Peculiarities of protecting human rights in various spheres of social relations

Social protection of lawful pretensions of participants of regulatory legal relations.

Principle of "everything is permitted that has not been prohibited by law" – legal basis for development of initiative and activeness of man regarding the realisation of his rights and duties. Significance of his political, moral, and legal culture.

Activities of officials and their responsibility for ensuring the unobstructed exercise of human rights. Intensifying control over the activities of leaders on the part of the masses as condition of creativity of masses themselves and every separate individual as means of eradicating bureaucratism.

Interest of a democratic society in protecting man in the sphere of enforcement legal relations.

Social problems of human rights guarantees for person suspected of committing a violation of law, accused, person on trial, or person sentenced to punishment. Protection of legal interests of man in places of confinement. Peculiarities of ensuring rights of person relieved from punishment and newly restored to full rights.

Significance of analysis of the general and the special in human rights guarantees assumed in the diversity of existing legal relations for working out and creating optimal machinery for social protection.

Topic 23. Law enforcement agencies in the machinery of human rights guarantees

Peculiarities of activities of system of law enforcement agencies in the integral machinery of human rights guarantees.

Forms of interaction of law enforcement agencies with soviets of people's deputies, labour collectives, and the general public regarding the defence and protection of human rights, legal nurturing, and prevention of violations.

Perestroika, glasnost, and democratisation of all spheres of social life – condition of overcoming accusatory bias in activities of law enforcement agencies. Procedural principle of objectivity, completeness, and thoroughness of investigation of all circumstances of unlawful acts as guarantee of legal protection of the individual against unfounded accusations.

Topic 24. Peculiarities of machinery of human rights guarantees in socialist, bourgeois, and developing countries

Constitutions and legislation of foreign socialist countries on human rights and the rights of a citizen.

Peculiarities of procedural forms of protecting human rights. Constitutional control over securing of human rights.

Characteristic features of new institutional forms for guarantees of human rights in countries of socialism.

Activities of communist and workers' parties regarding improvement of human rights guarantees.

Forms of participation of public in securing rights and freedoms of working people.

Individual as subject of activities of legal guarantees machinery.

Positive and negative aspects of work of machinery for protecting rights of citizens under conditions of capitalist Statehood.

Attitude of developing countries towards experience of protecting human rights in socialist and capitalist countries and use thereof in their legal structures.

Comparative analysis of effectiveness of existing machinery for human rights guarantees in their correlation with objective and subjective possibilities for their long-term improvement in different socio-economic and political systems.

Section V. International cooperation in domain of human rights

Topic 25. Internationalisation of human rights

League of Nations. Its efforts to create international institutions for the protection of human rights.

Liberation of peoples from threat of fascist enslavement and lawlessness and rise of favourable historical conditions for beginning of international cooperation in the domain of human rights.

Role of USSR and other countries of socialist commonwealth in forming and improving international standards (norms) and other international documents for development and protection of human rights.

Comparative analysis of existing universal and regional normative acts and institutions relating to human rights.

Historical necessity for creation of official international document containing socialist conception of human rights, and respective declarations and conventions of countries of the socialist commonwealth. Advisability of socialist regional institutions for human rights (Commission, Committee, organisation with control functions and right of norm-creative initiative, functions relating to coordination of research work, etc). Diversity of forms and methods of cooperation, including through international and national institutions for human rights.

Topic 26. Principal contradiction of modern day, ideological struggle, and cooperation in the domain of human rights

Contradictory world-outlook approaches to problems of human rights. Speculation in domain of human rights as means of achieving political purposes. Objective and subjective sources of ideological dispute on priorities in domain of developing and protecting human rights.

Activities of USSR and other countries of socialist commonwealth regarding restructuring of international relations in spirit of development of constructive cooperation in the humanitarian sphere.

Topic 27. Role of international organisations regarding cooperation in the domain of human rights

United Nations and its specialised agencies for human rights – major instrument of cooperation of peoples for the settlement of international global and regional, as well as national problems for the development and protection of human rights. Significance in this process of other international organisations.

Legal and non-legal forms of international cooperation and competence of States. Subjects of international cooperation in domain of human rights. The State – principal subject of moral, political, and legal responsibility for securing material and socio-political conditions and legal guarantees of human rights in the sphere of both municipal and inter-State relations. Significance of international and national, governmental and non-governmental, bilateral and multilateral institutions for cooperation in the domain of human rights.

Problems of peace and war, nuclear disarmament, and the struggle of peoples for the right to life in its contemporary understanding and the formation of a new international humanitarian order. Recognition by international community of conception of all-inclusive system of international security, as well as general-European process. Their significance for development of cooperation of all countries in protecting the right of peoples to life.

Transformation of international human rights standards into national legal systems. Analysis of Soviet legislation in comparison with norms of Universal Declaration and international covenants of human rights.

Significance of direct contacts of contemporary special national and international formations for the development of the theory and improvement of the practice of human rights, dissemination and propaganda of knowledge, legal nurturing, and training at the University level pursuant to special instructional syllabi for human rights.

Role of social organisations, creative unions, churches, and amateur entities in realising the rights of the individual.

LITERATURE

Section I

Topics 1, 2

Guiding

Marx, K., Engels, F. "Sviatoe semeistvo ili kritika kriticheskoi kritiki," *Sochineniia* (2d ed.), II, pp. 124–128.

Marx, K. "Tezisy o Feierbakhe," *Sochineniia* (2d ed.), III, p. 3.

Marx, K. "Kapital," *Sochineniia* (2d ed.), XXXIII, pp. 8–10, 140–144, 188–192.

Engels, F. "Dialektika priroda," *Sochineniia* (2d ed.), XX, pp. 362–363, 482–488, 514–520.

Engels, F. "Liudvig Feierbakh i konets klassicheskoi nemetskoi filosofii," *Sochineniia* (2d ed.), XXI, pp. 295–299, 305–312.

Lenin, V. I. "Chto takoe 'druz'ia naroda' i kak oni voiuiut protiv sotsial-demok-ratov," *Polnoe sobranie sochinenii*, I, pp. 133–141, 146–150.

Lenin, V. I. "Ekonomicheskoe soderzhanie narodnichestva i kritika ego v knige g. Struve," *Polnoe sobranie sochinenii*, I, pp. 423–430, 453–456.

Lenin, V. I. "O znachenii voinstvuiushchego materializma," *Polnoe sobranie sochinenii*, XLV, pp. 23–27, 29–30.

Materialy XXVII s"ezda KPSS. M., Politizdat, 1986, pp. 8–10, 38–41.

Materialy XIX Vsesoiuznoi konferentsii KPSS. M., Politizdat, 1988, pp. 39–43.

Gorbachev, M. S. *Perestroika i novoe myshlenie dlia nashei strany i dlia vsego mira*. M., 1988, pp. 20–33.

Special

Frolov, I. T. *Perspektivy cheloveka*. M., 1983, pp. 9–39.

Further reading

Lenin, V. I. "Filosofskie tetradi," *Polnoe sobranie sochinenii*, XXIX, pp. 316–322.

Iaroshevskii, T. M. *Razmyshleniia o cheloveke*. M., 1984, pp. 5–43.

Andreev, I. L. *Proiskhozhdenie cheloveka i obshchestva*. 2d ed., M., 1988, pp. 10–28.

Topic 3

Guiding

Marx, K. "K kritike gegelevskoi filosofii prava," *Sochineniia* (2d ed.), I, pp. 223–226, 341–344, 261–262.

314

Marx, K., Engels, F. "Manifest Kommunisticheskoi partii," *Sochineniia* (2d ed.), IV, pp. 438–440, 445–447, 452.

Marx, K. "O pol'skom voprose," *Sochineniia* (2d ed.), IV, pp. 488–491.

Marx, K. "Kapital," *Sochineniia* (2d ed.), XXIII, pp. 140–143, 187–189, 192–196, 470–476.

Marx, K. "Kritika Gotskoi programmy," *Sochineniia* (2d ed.), XIX, pp. 13–15, 16–21, 24–25, 30–32.

Engels, F. "Anti-Diuring," *Sochineniia* (2d ed.), XX, pp. 104–109.

Engels, F. "K kritike proekta sotsial-demokraticheskoi programmy," *Sochineniia* (2d ed.), XXII, p. 235.

Lenin, V. I. "Rech' ob obmane naroda lozungami svobody i ravenstva," *Polnoe sobranie sochinenii*, XXXVIII, pp. 347–348.

Lenin, V. I. "Proekt programmy RKP(b)," *Polnoe sobranie sochinenii*, XXXVIII, pp. 90–96.

Lenin, V. I. "Vstavka k politicheskoi chasti programmy," *Polnoe sobranie sochinenii*, XXXVIII, p. 109.

Lenin, V. I. "Velikii pochin,"_*Polnoe sobranie sochinenii*, XXXIX, pp. 22–23.

Lenin, V. I. "K voprosu o natsional'nostiakh ili ob 'avtonomizatsii'," *Polnoe sobranie sochinenii*, XLV, pp. 350–360.

Materialy XXVII s"ezda KPSS. M., Politizdat, 1986, pp. 21, 29, 61, 76, 100, 109–110, 127, 158.

Materialy XIX Vsesoiuznoi konferentsii KPSS. M., 1988, pp. 33–35, 39–42.

Gorbachev, M. S. *Perestroika i novoe myshlenie dlia nashei strany i dlia vsego mira.* M., 1988, pp. 24–26.

"Otvety M. S. Gorbacheva na voprosy gazety 'Vashington post' i zhurnala 'N'iusuik'," *Pravda*, 22 May 1988.

Special
Kuchinskii, Iu. *Prava cheloveka i klassovye prava.* M., 1981, pp. 23–43.
Sotsialisticheskaia kontseptsiia prav cheloveka. M., 1986, pp. 7–28.

Further reading
Lenin, V. I. "O karikature na marksizm i ob 'imperialisticheskom ekonomizme'," *Polnoe sobranie sochinenii*, XXX, pp. 108–112, 125–127.

Lenin, V. I. "Materialy k broshiure o derevenskoi bednote," *Polnoe sobranie sochinenii*, VII, p. 370.

Lenin, V. I. "Rech' po voprosu o pechati," *Polnoe sobranie sochinenii*, XXXV, pp. 54–55.

Lenin, V. I. "Proletarskaia revoliutsiia i renegat Kautskii," *Polnoe sobranie sochinenii*, XXXVII, pp. 265–267.

Topic 4

Guiding
Marx, K., Engels, F. "Manifest Kommunisticheskoi partii," *Sochineniia* (2d ed.), IV, pp. 434–435, 438–448, 447–452.
Marx, K. "Klassovaia voina vo Frantsii," *Sochineniia* (2d ed.), VII, pp. 39–42.
Marx, K. "Kapital," *Sochineniia* (2d ed.), XXIII, pp. 85–90, 140–144, 181–187, 261–267.
Marx, K. "Kritika Gotskoi programmy," *Sochineniia* (2d ed.), XIX, pp. 13–15, 16–21, 24–25, 30–32.
Engels, F. "Ob avtoritete," *Sochineniia* (2d ed.), XVIII, pp. 302–305.
Engels, F. "Iuridicheskii sotsializm," *Sochineniia* (2d ed.), XXI, pp. 503–505, 507–509, 514–516.
Lenin, V. I. "Dekret o mire. Dekret o zemle," *Polnoe sobranie sochinenii*, XXXV, pp. 23–24.
Lenin, V. I. "Sovetskaia vlast' i polozhenie zhenshchiny," *Polnoe sobranie sochinenii*, XXXIX, pp. 285–288.
Lenin, V. I. "Detskaia bolezn' 'levizny' v kommunizme," *Polnoe sobranie sochinenii*, XLI, pp. 30–34.
Lenin, V. I. "Zadachi soiuza molodezhi," *Polnoe sobranie sochinenii*, XLI, pp. 303–306.
Lenin, V. I. "O kooperatsii," *Polnoe sobranie sochinenii*, XLV, pp. 376–377.
Materialy XXVII s"ezda KPSS. M., Politizdat, 1986, pp. 44–53, 150–156, 158.
Materialy XIX Vsesoiuznoi konferentsii KPSS. M., 1988, pp. 11–13, 17, 19–21, 33, 35–43, 60–61, 67–69, 131, 145–148.
Gorbachev, M. S., "O prakticheskoi rabote po realizatsii reshenii XIX Vsesoiuznoi partiinoi konferentsii. Doklad na Plenume TsK KPSS 29 iiulia 1988 g.," *Pravda*, 30 July 1988.

Special
Nazarov, B. L., *Pravo v sisteme sotsial'nykh sviazei*. M., 1978. Chap. 1.
Kuchinskii, Iu. *Prava cheloveka i klassovye prava*. M., 1981, pp. 68–76, 166–175.
Szabo, I. *Ideologicheskaia bor'ba i prava cheloveka*. M., 1986, pp. 17–56.
Sotsialisticheskaia kontseptsiia prav cheloveka. M., 1986, Chaps. I-II.
Matuzov, N. I. *Pravovaia sistema i lichnost'*. Saratov, 1987, pp. 71–110.

Further reading
Marx, K. "Opravdanie mozel'skogo korrespondenta," *Sochineniia* (2d ed.), I, p. 209.
Engels, F. "Proiskhozhdenie sem'i, chastnoi sobstvennosti i gosudarstva," *Sochineniia* (2d ed.), XXI, pp. 83–84, 76–77.

316

Lenin, V. I. "Sotsializm i religiia," *Polnoe sobranie sochinenii*, XII, pp. 142–145.

Lenin, V. I. "Proekt rezoliutsii o svobode pechati (1917)," *Polnoe sobranie sochinenii*, XXXV, p. 51.

Lenin, V. I. "Rech' na zakrytii s"ezda 5 aprelia [IX s"ezd RKP(b)] 29 marta–5 aprelia 1920 g.," *Polnoe sobranie sochinenii*, XL, pp. 285–286.

Topic 5

Guiding

Marx, K. "Kritika Gotskoi programmy," *Sochineniia* (2d ed.), XIX, pp. 18–20.

Marx, K. "Kapital," *Sochineniia* (2d ed.), XXIII, pp. 187–189.

Engels, F. "Anti-Diuring," *Sochineniia* (2d ed.), XX, pp. 100–109.

Lenin, V. I. "Liberal'nyi professor o ravenstve," *Polnoe sobranie sochinenii*, XXIV, pp. 362–364.

Lenin, V. I. "Gosudarstvo i revoliutsiia," *Polnoe sobranie sochinenii*, XXXIII, pp. 83–102, 115–118.

Lenin, V. I. "Rech' ob obmane naroda lozungami svobody i ravenstva," *Polnoe sobranie sochinenii*, XXXVIII, pp. 346–350, 352–354.

Materialy XXVII s"ezda KPSS. M., Politizdat, 1986, pp. 39–40, 44–54, 152–156, 158–159, 162.

Materialy XIX Vsesoiuznoi konferentsii KPSS. M., 1988, pp. 35–43, 62, 66–70, 75–76, 111–112, 127, 135, 138, 149, 144–147, 158.

Gorbachev, M. S. "O prakticheskoi rabote po realizatsii reshenii XIX Vsesoiuznoi partiinoi konferentsii. Doklad na Plenume TsK KPSS ot 20 iiulia 1988 g.," *Pravda*, 30 July 1988.

Gorbachev, M. S. *Perestroika i novoe myshlenie dlia nashei strany i dlia vsego mira*. M., 1988, pp. 99–101, 113–122.

Normative acts

Konstitutsiia SSSR. Section II.

Konstitutsii sotsialisticheskikh gosudarstv. M., 1987, I, pp. 98–102, 104–108 (People's Republic of Albania), 129, 132, 135, 137–141 (People's Republic of Bulgaria), 168–170, 180–183 (Hungarian People's Republic), 207–212 (People's Republic of Vietnam), 240, 245–251 (German Democratic Republic), 274–275, 283–286 (Chinese People's Republic), 283–286 (Korean People's Democratic Republic); II, pp. 15–16, 18, 27–32 (Republic of Cuba), 73–77 (Mongolian People's Republic), 103–109 (Polish People's Republic), 117–124 (Romanian Socialist Republic), 160–163 (Czechoslovak Socialist Soviet Republic), 247–248, 275–278, 306–316 (Socialist Federated Republic of Yugoslavia).

Mezhdunarodnoe pravo v dokumentakh. M., 1982. See the Chapter on Human Rights in International Documents.

Prava cheloveka. Sbornik mezhdunarodnykh dokumentov. M., MGU, 1986, pp. 21–78 (Compiler and author of introduction, L. N. Shestakov)

Special
Chkhikvadze, V. M. *Sotsialisticheskii gumanizm i prava cheloveka.* M., 1978. Chap. II.
Serkova, V. V. "K voprosu o sootnoshenii poniatii ravenstva i ravnopraviia," *XXVII s"ezd KPSS i teoreticheskie voprosy gosudarstva i prava: sbornik nauchnykh trudov.* M., VIuZI, 1984, pp. 70–79.
Problema svobody i prav cheloveka v sovremennoi ideologicheskoi bor'be. ed. D. A. Kerimov and V. M. Chkhikvadze. M., 1986, pp. 67–103.

Topic 6

Guiding
Marx, K., Engels, F. "Manifest Kommunisticheskoi partii," *Sochineniia* (2d ed.), IV, pp. 435, 437–452, 459.
Marx, K. "Grazhdanskaia voina vo Frantsii," *Sochineniia* (2d ed.), XVII, pp. 342–352.
Engels, F., "K kritike proekta sotsial-demokraticheskoi programmy 1891 g.," *Sochineniia* (2d ed.), XXII, pp. 236–238.
Lenin, V. I. "Chto takoe 'druz'ia naroda' i kak oni voiuiut protiv sotsial-demokratov," *Polnoe sobranie sochinenii*, I, pp. 300–302, 311–312.
Lenin, V. I. "Gosudarstvo i revoliutsiia," *Polnoe sobranie sochinenii*, XXXIII, pp. 98–102, 115–118.
Lenin, V. I. "Uderzhat li bol'sheviki gosudarstvennuiu vlast'?" *Polnoe sobranie sochinenii*, XXXIV, pp. 313–317.
Lenin, V. I. "Tezisy i doklad o burzhuaznoi demokratii i diktature proletariata 4 marta (I Kongress Kommunisticheskogo Internatsionala 2–6 mart 1919 g.)," *Polnoe sobranie sochinenii*, XXXVII, pp. 498–501.
Lenin, V. I. "Doklad o partiinoi programme 19 marta [VIII s"ezd RKP(b)] 18–23 marta 1919 g.," *Polnoe sobranie sochinenii*, XXXVIII, pp. 169–171.
Lenin, V. I. "Detskaia bolezn' 'levizny' v kommunizme," *Polnoe sobranie sochinenii*, XLI, pp. 25–26, 30–34, 40–48, 89–90, 101–102.
Materialy XXVII s"ezda KPSS. M., Politizdat, 1986, pp. 54–61.
Gorbachev, M. S. *Velikii Oktiabr': revoliutsiia prodolzhaetsia.* M., 1987.
Materialy XIX Vsesoiuznoi konferentsii KPSS. M., 1988, pp. 35–48, 62, 110–114, 123–124, 128–148.
Gorbachev, M. S. "O prakticheskoi rabote po realizatsii reshnii XIX Vsesoiuznoi partiinoi konferentsii," *Pravda*, 30 July 1988.
Gorbachev, M. S. *Perestroika i novoe myshlenie dlia nashei strany i dlia vsego mira.* M., 1988, pp. 28–33, 71–78, 101–122.

318

Further reading
Marx, K. "Konspekt knigi Bakunina 'Gosudarstvennost' i anarkhiia'," *Sochineniia* (2d ed.), XVIII, pp. 615–618.
Engels, F. "Polozhenie Anglii Tomas Karleil'. 'Proshloe i nastoiashchee'," *Sochineniia* (2d ed.), I, p. 595.
Lenin, V. I. "Novaia ekonomicheskaia politika i zadachi politprosvetov," *Polnoe sobranie sochinenii*, XLIV, pp. 165–166.
Lenin, V. I. "Materialy k broshiure 'K derevenskoi bednote' (1903)," *Polnoe sobranie sochinenii*,VII, p. 370
Lenin, V. I. "Tri konspekta doklada o Parizhskoi Kommune (1904)," *Polnoe sobranie sochinenii*, VIII, p. 490.

Topic 7

Guiding
Materialy XXVII s"ezda KPSS. M., Politizdat, 1986, pp. 44–54, 61, 76, 109–110, 127, 150–159, 162.
Materialy XIX Vsesoiznoi konferentsii KPSS. M., 1988, pp. 35, 37, 39–43, 62, 68–69, 110,123–124, 128–129, 134–138, 140, 142–143.
Gorbachev, M. S. "O prakticheskoi rabote po realizatsii reshenii XIX Vsesoiuznoi partiinoi konferentsii. Doklad na Plenume TsK KPSS ot 29 iiulia 1988 g.," *Pravda*, 30 July 1988.

Special
Problema svobody i prav cheloveka v sovremennoi ideologicheskoi bor'be. M., 1986, pp. 243–284.
Movchan, A. P. *Prava cheloveka i mezhdunarodnye otnosheniia*. M., 1982, pp. 9–19, 54–75.
Szabo, I. *Ideologicheskaia bor'ba i prava cheloveka*. M., 1981, pp. 57–81.
Tuzmukhamedov, R. "Tret'e pokolenie prav cheloveka i prava narodov," *Sovetskoe gosudarstvo i pravo*, no. 11 (1986), pp. 106–113.

Normative material
"Deklaratsiia prav narodov Rossii," *Dekrety Sovetskoi vlasti* (M., 1957), I, pp. 39–41.
"Deklaratisiia prav trudiashchegosia i ekspluatiruemogo naroda," *Dekrety Sovetskoi vlasti* (M., 1957), I, pp. 315–322.
Konstitutsiia SSSR. Section II.
Konstitutsii sotsialisticheskikh gosudarstv (M., 1987), I-II (see Reading in Topic 5).
Mezhdunarodnoe pravo v dokumentakh. M., 1982 (see chapter: Human Rights in International Documents)

Prava cheloveka. Sbornik mezhdunarodnykh dokumentov. M., MGU, 1986, pp. 21–78 (Compiler and author of introduction, L. N. Shestakov).
"Aziatsko-tikhookeanskaia deklaratsiia chelovecheskikh prav individov i narodov," *Sovetskoe gosudarstvo i pravo,* no. 7 (1988), pp. 111–113.

SECTION II

Topic 8

Guiding
Marx, K., Engels, F. "Manifest Kommunisticheskoi partii," *Sochineniia* (2d ed.), IV, Chap. 1.
Engels, F. "Krest'ianskaia voina v Germanii," *Sochineniia* (2d ed.), VII, pp. 350–361.
Engels, F. "Kniga otkroveniia," *Sochineniia* (2d ed.), XXI, pp. 7–13.
Lenin, V. I. "O gosudarstve," *Polnoe sobranie sochinenii,* XXXIX, pp. 66–67, 74–84.

Special
Klibanov, A. I. *Narodnaia sotsial'naia utopiia v Rossii.* M., 1977, pp. 141–164.
Ushakov, A. M. *Utopicheskaia mysl' v stranakh Vostoka: traditsii i sovremennost'.* M., 1982, pp. 71–82.
Paulsen, Ch. *Angliiskie buntari.* M., 1987, pp. 21–26, 37–75.

Further reading
Vosstanie Bolotnikova: dokumenty i materialy. M., 1959, pp. 196–197.
Kuchinskii, Iu. *Prava cheloveka i klassovye prava.* M., 1981, pp. 23–29.
Uder, V. B. *Prava cheloveka: utopiia ili real'nost'.* M., 1985, pp. 22–59.

Topic 9

Guiding
Marx, K. "K kritike gegelevskoi filosofii prava," *Sochineniia* (2d ed.), I, pp. 223–226, 341–344, 261–262.
Marx, K. "Vosemnadtsatoe briumera Lui Bonaparta," *Sochineniia* (2d ed.), VIII, pp. 119–120, 145, 148.
Engels, F. "Anti-Diuring," *Sochineniia* (2d ed.), XX, pp. 107–109, 270.
Lenin, V. I. "O znachenii voinstvuiushchego materializma," *Polnoe sobranie sochinenii,* XLV, pp. 24–27, 29–31.
Lenin, V. I. "Pamiati Gertsena," *Polnoe sobranie sochinenii,* XXI, pp. 255–256.

Special

Rousseau, J. J. "Rassuzhdenie o proiskhozhdenii neravenstva," *Traktaty*. M., 1969, pp. 45–47, 80–81, 85.

—. "Ob obshchestvennom dogovore," *Traktaty*. M., 1969, pp. 152, 154–156, 160–162, 188–191.

Kant, I. "Osnovy metafiziki nravstvennosti," *Sochineniia*. M., 1965, IV(1), pp. 259–262.

—. "Metafizicheskie nachala ucheniia o prave," *Sochineniia*. M., 1965, IV(2), pp. 231–237.

Hegel, F. *Filosofiia prava*. M-L., 1934. Preface, pp. 18–19; Introduction, Sections 1–2, 11, 29; Division, Sections 47, 45, 57; chast' 1, Sections 94, 100; chast' 2, Sections 127, chast' 3, Sections 182, 215, 218, 221, 238, 308, 309.

Smith, Adam. *Issledovanie o prirode i prichinakh bogatstva narodov*. M., 1962, pp. 15–21, 301–309, 557–561.

Saint-Simon, J. *Izlozhenie ucheniia Sen-Simona*. M., 1961, pp. 132–133, 267–279.

Herzen, A. I. *Pis'ma izdaleka*. M., 1984, pp. 178, 287–290, 315–320, 349–350, 355–361, 399–400.

Chernyshevskii, N. G. "Pis'ma bez adresa," *Polnoe sobranie sochinenii*, VII, pp. 102–105, 109–112.

Normative material

England

Akt o luchshem obespechenii svobody podannogo i o preduprezhdenii zatochenii za moriami (6 maia 1679 g.).
Bill' o pravakh, 13 fevralia 1689 g.

United States of America

Deklaratsiia nezavisimosti Soedinennykh Shtatov Ameriki 4 iiulia 1776 g.
Bill' o pravakh 1789–1791 gg. (first 10 amendments to the Constitution)
Popravki k Konstitutsii SShA, priniatye v sviazi s grazhdanskoi voinoi. Popravka XIII, 1865 g. Popravka XIV, 1868 g. Popravka XV, 1870 g.

Legislation of the Great French Bourgeois Revolution

Deklaratsiia prav cheloveka i grazhdanina 1789 g.
Istochniki po istorii gosudarstva i prava. Burzhuaznye revoliutsii xvii-xviii vv. Uchebnoe posobie. ed. Z. M. Chernilovskii. M., VIuZI, 1981, pp. 12–16, 17–20, 33–35, 41–44.

Further reading

Marx, K. "Kapital," *Sochinenii* (2d ed.), XXIII, pp. 628–629.

Lenin, V. I. "O starykh i vechno novykh istinakh," *Polnoe sobranie sochinenii*, XX, p. 283.

Locke, J. *Izbrannye filosofskie proizvedeniia v 2-x tomakh*. M., 1960, II, pp. 18–21, 228–31.

Montesquieu, Ch. "O dukhe zakonov," *Izbrannye proizvedeniia*. M., 1955, pp. 288–289, 553, 572–573.

Pestel', P. "Russkaia pravda," *Izbrannye sotsial'no-politicheskie i filosofskie proizvedeniia dekabritsov*. M., 1951, II, pp. 126–127, 144–155.

Aksakov, K. S., Aksakov, I. S. *Literaturnaia kritika*. M., 1982, pp. 252–254, 306–310.

Topic 10

Guiding

Marx, K. "Zametki o noveishei prusskoi tsenzurnoi instruktsii," *Sochineniia* (2d ed.), I, pp. 14–15.

Marx, K. "K kritike gegelevskoi filosofii prava," *Sochineniia* (2d ed.), I, pp. 223–226, 341–344, 261–262.

Marx, K., Engels, F. "Sviatoe semeistvo ili kritika kriticheskoi kritiki," *Sochineniia* (2d ed.), II, pp. 124–126.

Marx, K., Engels, F. "Manifest Kommunisticheskoi partii," *Sochineniia* (2d ed.), IV, pp. 431–435, 438–448, 447–452.

Marx, K. "O pol'skom voprose," *Sochineniia* (2d ed.), IV, pp. 488–491.

Marx, K. "Klassovaia bor'ba vo Frantsii," *Sochineniia* (2d ed.), VIII, pp. 39–42.

Marx, K. "Konstitutsiia Frantsuzskoi respubliki, priniataia 4 noiabria 1848 g.," *Sochineniia* (2d ed.), VII, pp. 525–529.

Marx, K. "Vosemnadtsatoe briumera Lui Bonaparta," *Sochineniia* (2d ed.), VIII, pp. 124, 131–132, 147–148, 155–158.

Marx, K. "Kapital," *Sochineniia* (2d ed.), XXIII, pp. 82–90, 140–143, 186–192, 406–409.

Marx, K. "Kritika Gotskoi programmy," *Sochineniia* (2d ed.), XIX, pp. 13–15, 16–21, 24–25, 30–32.

Engels, F. "Anti-Diuring," *Sochineniia* (2d ed.), XX, pp. 104–109.

Engels, F. "Iuridicheskii sotsializm," *Sochineniia* (2d ed.), XXI, pp. 495–503, 506–508, 514–516.

Engels, F. "K kritike proekta sotsial-demokratichesoi programmy 1891 g.," *Sochineniia* (2d ed.), XXII, p. 235.

Lenin, V. I. "Chto takoe 'druz'ia naroda' i kak oni voiuiut protiv sotsial-demokratov," *Polnoe sobranie sochinenii*, I, pp. 133–141, 146–150.

322

Lenin, V. I. "Ekonomicheskoe soderzhanie narodnichestva i kritika ego v knige g. Struve." *Polnoe sobranie sochinenii*, I, pp. 423–430, 453–456.

Lenin, V. I. "Dve taktiki sotsial-demokratii v demokraticheskoi revoliutsii," *Polnoe sobranie sochinenii*, XI, pp. 37–40, 70–74, 101–104.

Lenin, V. I. "Proekt rechi po agrarnomu voprosu vo vtoroi gosudarstvennoi dume," *Polnoe sobranie sochinenii*, XV, pp. 139–140, 149–150.

Lenin, V. I. "Liberal'nyi professor o ravenstve," *Polnoe sobranie sochinenii*, XXIV, pp. 362–364.

Lenin, V. I. "Gosudarstvo i revoliutsiia," *Polnoe sobranie sochinenii*, XXXIII, pp. 83–102, 115–118.

Lenin, V. I. "Dekret o zemle. Dekret o mire," *Polnoe sobranie sochinenii*, XXXV, pp. 23–24.

Lenin, V. I. "Deklaratsiia prav trudiashchikhsia i ekspluatiruemogo naroda," *Polnoe sobranie sochinenii*, XXXV, pp. 221–223.

Lenin, V. I. "Rech' ob obmane naroda lozungami svobody i ravenstva (Rech' na 1-m Vserossiiskom s"ezde rabotnikov prosveshcheniia)," *Polnoe sobranie sochinenii*, XXXVIII, pp. 346–360, 367–368, 371–372.

Lenin, V. I. "Velikii pochin," *Polnoe sobranie sochinenii*, XXXIX, pp. 22–23.

Lenin, V. I. "O gosudarstve," *Polnoe sobranie sochinenii*, XXXIX, p. 82.

Lenin, V. I. "Sovetskaia vlast' i polozhenie zhenshchiny," *Polnoe sobranie sochinenii*, XXXIX, pp. 285–288.

Lenin, V. I. "Zadachi soiuza molodezhi," *Polnoe sobranie sochinenii*, XLI, pp. 303–306.

Lenin, V. I. "K voprosu o natsional'nostiakh ili ob 'avtonomizatsii'," *Polnoe sobranie sochinenii*, XLV, pp. 358–362.

Lenin, V. I. "Stranichki iz dnevnika," *Polnoe sobranie sochinenii*, XLV, pp. 364–366.

Lenin, V. I. "O kooperatsii," *Polnoe Sobranie sochinenii*, XLV, pp. 376–377.

Lenin, V. I. "O nashei revoliutsii," *Polnoe sobranie sochinenii*, XLV, pp. 379–380.

Materialy XXVII s"ezda KPSS. M., Politizdat, 1986, pp. 21, 29, 61, 109–110, 127, 158.

Gorbachev, M. S. *Perestroika i novoe myshlenie dlia nashei strany i dlia vsego mira*. M., 1988, pp. 20–21, 24, 26, 28, 41–42, 45–50, 94–95, 105, 153–155.

Special
Sotsialisticheskaia kontseptsiia prav cheloveka. M., 1986, Chap. 1.

Further reading
Marx, K. "K evreiskomu voprosu," *Sochineniia* (2d ed.), I, pp. 386–406.

Engels, F. "Proiskhozhdenie sem'i, chastnoi sobstvennosti i gosudarstva," *Sochineniia* (2d ed.), XXI, pp. 82–84.

Lenin, V. I. "Rech' na I Vserossiiskom s"ezde rabotnits 19 noiabria 1918 g.," *Polnoe sobranie sochinenii,* XXXVII, pp. 185–186.

Lenin, V. I. "Proletarskaia revoliutsiia i renegat Kautskii," *Polnoe sobranie sochinenii,* XXXVII, pp. 277–278, 256–259, 265–267, 311–312.

Lenin, V. I. "Popravki i zamechaniia k proektu zaiavleniia sovetskoi delegatsii na Genuezskoi konferentsii," *Polnoe sobranie sochinenii,* XLV, pp. 63–64.

Kuchinskii, Iu. *Prava cheloveka i klassovye prava.* M., 1981. Chap. 1.

Sotsialisticheskaia kontseptsiia prav cheloveka. M., 1986, Chap. 1.

SECTION III

Topic 11

Guiding

Lenin, V. I. "Doklad o peresmotre programmy i izmeneniia nazvaniia partii," *Polnoe sobranie sochinenii,* XXXVI, pp. 50–53.

Lenin, V. I. "Proletarskaia revoliutsiia i renegat Kautskii," *Polnoe sobranie sochinenii,* XXXVII, pp. 256–259, 265–266, 311–312.

Lenin, V. I. "Doklad o partiinoi programme 19 marta (VIII s"ezd RKP(b) 1919 g.)," *Polnoe sobranie sochinenii,* XXXVIII, p. 159.

Lenin, V. I. "O zadachakh III Internatsionala," *Polnoe sobranie sochinenii,* XXXIX, pp. 108–109.

Lenin, V. I. "Politicheskii otchet Tsentral'nogo Komiteta RKP(b) 27 marta," *Polnoe sobranie sochinenii,* XLV, pp. 108–112.

Lenin, V. I. "Pis'mo k Vserossiiskomu s"ezdu profsoiuzov," *Polnoe sobranie sochinenii,* XLV, pp. 209–210.

Lenin, V. I. "Ob obrazovanii SSSR," *Polnoe sobranie sochinenii,* XLV, pp. 211–213.

Lenin, V. I. "Materialy k XI s"ezdu RKP(b)," *Polnoe sobranie sochinenii,* XLV, p. 414.

Lenin, V. I. "O kooperatsii," *Polnoe sobranie sochinenii,* XLV, pp. 376–377.

Lenin, V. I. "O nashei revoliutsii," *Polnoe sobranie sochinenii,* XLV, pp. 379–380.

Materialy XXVII s"ezda KPSS. M., Politizdat, 1986, pp. 7, 8, 10–11, 121–126, 327–329.

Gorbachev, M. S. *Velikii Oktiabr': revoliutsiia prodolzhaetsia.* M., 1987.

Materialy XIX Vsesoiuznoi konferentsii KPSS. M., 1988, pp. 3, 29, 35–36, 39, 42, 50–51, 54, 59, 100, 134.

Gorbachev, M. S. *Perestroika i novoe myshlenie dlia nashei strany i dlia vsego mira.* M., 1988, pp. 20–21, 34–35, 45–47.

324

Special
Il'inskii, I. P., Strashun, B. A., Iastrebov, V. I. *Politicheskaia sistema zarubezhnykh stran sotsializma.* M., 1981, pp. 87–107, 157–169, 182–204.

Normative acts
"Dekret o zemle. Dekret o mire," *Dekrety Sovetskoi vlasti.* M., 1957, I, pp. 12–16, 17–20.
"Deklaratsiia prav narodov Rossii," *ibid.*, pp. 39–41.
"Deklaratsiia prav trudiashchegosia i ekspluatiruemogo naroda," *ibid.*, pp. 315–322.
Istoriia Sovetskoi Konstitutsii (v dokumentakh) 1917–1956 gg. M., 1958.
Konstitutsii sotsialisticheskikh gosudarstv. M., 1987, vols. 1–2. Preambles.

Further reading
Lenin, V. I. "Detskaia bolezn' 'levizny' v kommunizme," *Polnoe sobranie sochinenii*, XLI, pp. 31–32, 40–48, 73–74, 82–84, 89–90.
Lenin, V. I. "Pis'mo k G. Miasnikovu. 5 avgusta 1921 g.," *Polnoe sobranie sochinenii*, XLIV, pp. 78–83.
Iaruzel'skii, V. "Sotsializm – ne dar istorii trudiashchikhsia," *Problemy mira i sotsializma*, no. 7 (1988), pp. 3–12.

Topic 12

Guiding
Lenin, V. I. "Pis'mo k s"ezdu," *Polnoe sobranie sochinenii*, XLV, pp. 343–348.
Postanovlenie TsK KPSS ot 30 iiunia 1956 g. 'O preodolenii kul'ta lichnosti i ego posledstvii'. M., Politizdat, 1956.
Materialy XXVII s"ezda KPSS. M., Politizdat, 1986, pp. 7–8, 22, 44, 53, 125–127, 128.
Gorbachev, M. S. *Velikii Oktiabr' : resoliutsiia prodolzhaetsia.* M., 1987.
Gorbachev, M. S. *Perestroika i novoe myshlenie dlia nashei strany i dlia vsego mira.* M., 1988, pp. 12, 20–21, 29, 34–36, 38, 42, 43, 47–48, 106, 110–112, 118, 153–155, 200–203.

Normative materials
Konstitutsiia SSSR (1936).

Further reading
Plekhanov, G. V. "K voprosu o roli lichnosti v istorii," *Izbrannye filosofskie proizvedeniia.* M., 1956, vol. 2.

Topic 13

Guiding
Materialy XXVII s"ezda KPSS. M., Politizdat, 1986, pp. 11–12, 18–21, 62–70, 75–76, 150–162, 166–170.
Materialy XIX Vsesoiuznoi konferentsii KPSS. M., Politizdat, 1988.
Gorbachev, M. S. *Velikii Oktiabr' : revoliutsiia prodolzhaetsia*. M., 1987.
Gorbachev, M. s. *Perestroika i novoe myshlenie dlia nashei strany i dlia vsego mira*. M., 1988, pp. 24–28, 33–34, 41–44, 72–80, 110–119, 113–121, 128–131.
Materialy fevral' skogo Plenuma TsK KPSS. M., Politizdat, 1988.
Materialy iiul' skogo Plenuma TsK KPSS. M., Politizdat, 1988.
"Otvety M. S. Gorbacheva na voprosy gazety 'Vashington post' i zhurnala 'N'iusuik'," *Pravda*, 23 May 1988.

Topic 14

Guiding
Materialy XXVII s"ezda KPSS. M., Politizdat, 1986, pp. 8–21, 62–70, 75–76, 99–100, 123, 128–137.
Materialy XIX Vsesoiuznoi konferentsii KPSS. M., Politizdat, 1988, pp. 28–34, 38–41, 116–117.
Gorbachev, M. S. *Velikii Oktiabr' : revoliutsiia prodolzhaetsia*. M., 1987.
Gorbachev, M. S. *Perestroika i novoe myshlenie dlia nashei strany i dlia vsego mira*. M., 1988, Section I, Chap. 2; Section 2, Chaps. 3, 6, 7.
"Otvety M. S. Gorbacheva na voprosy gazety 'Vashington post' i zhurnala 'N'iusuik'," *Pravda*, 23 May 1988.

Normative materials
Burzhuaznye konstitutsii. M., VIUzI, 1982.

Special
Gosudarstvennoe pravo burzhuaznykh i osvobodivshikhsia stran, ed. B. A. Starodubtsev and I. I. Chirkin. M., 1986.

Topic 15

Guiding
Materialy XXVII s"ezda KPSS. M., Politizdat, 1986, pp. 5, 14, 19–21, 74, 75–76, 99–100, 131, 168, 183, 283.
Materialy XIX Vsesoiuznoi partiinoi konferentsii KPSS. M., Politizdat, 1988, pp. 28–34, 38–43, 116–117

Gorbachev, M. S. *Velikii Oktiabr': revoliutsiia prodolzhaetsia.* M., 1987.
Gorbachev, M. S. *Perestroika i novoe myshlenie dlia nashei strany i dlia vsego mira.* M., 1988, pp. 125–134, 137–162, 206–208, 215–216.
"Otvety M. S. Gorbacheva na voprosy gazety 'Vashington post' i zhurnala 'N'iusuik'," *Pravda*, 23 May 1988.

Special
Szabo, I. *Ideologicheskaia bor'ba i prava cheloveka.* M., 1981, pp. 33–56, 57–81.
Burzhuaznaia sotsiologiia na iskhode XX veka. Kritika noveishikh tendentsii, ed. V. N. Ivanov. M., 1986, pp. 246–258.
Kepetsi, B. *Neokonservatizm i novye prava.* M., 1986, pp. 8–12, 31–36, 41–52, 77–79, 88–97.
Grigor'ian, B. T. *Filosofskie kontseptsii katolicheskogo modernizma.* Vilnius, 1982, Chap. 1.

Further reading
Problema svobody i prav cheloveka v sovremennoi ideologicheskoi bor'be. M., 1986, pp. 285–317.

Topic 16

Guiding
Materialy XXVII s"ezda KPSS. M., Politizdat, 1986, pp. 8–9, 16–18, 20–21, 74, 75–76, 99–100, 132–137.
Materialy XIX Vsesoiuznoi konferentsii KPSS. M., 1988, pp. 29–33, 43, 116–117.
Gorbachev, M. S. *Velikii Oktiabr': revoliutsiia prodolzhaetsia.* M., 1987.
Gorbachev, M. S. *Perestroika i novoe myshlenie dlia nashei strany i dlia vsego mira.* M., 1988, Section 2, chap. 5.

Special
Pravovoe polozhenie lichnosti, ed. B. E. Chirkin. M., 1987, pp. 6–27, 73–118, 104–133, 396–400.
Gosudarstvennoe pravo burzhuaznykh i osvobodivshikhsia stran. M., 1986.
Akhmetov, A. *Sotsial'naia doktrina islama.* M., 1982, pp. 9–13, 22–34.

Normative acts
"Deklaratsiia o predostavlenii nezavisimosti kolonial'nym stranam i narodam," in *Prava cheloveka: mezhdunarodnye dokumenty.* M., MGU, 1986, or *Mezhdunarodnoe pravo v dokumentakh.* M., 1982.
"Aziatsko-tikhookeanskaia deklaratsiia chelovecheskikh prav individov i narodov," *Sovetskoe gosudarstvo i pravo*, no. 7 (1988), pp. 111–113.

SECTION IV

Topics 17, 18, 19, 20, 21, 22, 23, 24

Guiding
Lenin, V. I. "Nakaz ot STO," *Polnoe sobranie sochinenii*, XLIII, pp. 273–275.
Lenin, V. I. "Novaia ekonomicheskaia politika i zadachi politprosvetov," *Polnoe sobranie sochinenii*, XLIV, pp. 173–175.
Lenin, V. I. "Pis'mo k D. I. Kurskomu s zamechaniiami na proekt grazhdanskogo kodeksa," *Polnoe sobranie sochinenii*, XLIV, pp. 411–412.
Lenin, V. I. "O 'dvoinom' podchinenii i zakonnosti," *Polnoe sobranie sochinenii*, XLV, pp. 197–201.
Lenin, V. I. "V. V. Adoratskomu," *Polnoe sobranie sochinenii*, LIII, p. 149.
Materialy XXVII s"ezda KPSS. M., Politizdat, 1986, pp. 61–62, 109–110, 158–162, 182–186, 224, 253.
Materialy XIX Vsesoiuznoi konferentsii KPSS. M., Politizdat, 1988, pp. 16, 37–43, 45, 47, 50–54, 56–58, 69–70, 78–81, 99–103, 127, 148.
Materialy iiul'skogo Plenuma TsK KPSS. M., Politizdat, 1988.
Gorbachev, M. S. *Velikii Oktiabr': revoliutsiia prodolzhaetsia*. M., 1987.

Special
Nazarov, B. L. *Pravo v sisteme sotsial'nykh sviazei*. M., 1978.
Sotsialisticheskaia kontseptsiia pravo cheloveka. M., 1986, pp. 113–138.
Matuzov, N. I. *Pravovaia sistema i lichnost'*, pp. 191–215.
Tumanov, V. A. "Sudebnyi kontrol' za konstitutsionnost'iu aktov," *Sovetskoe gosudarstvo i pravo*, no. 3 (1988), pp. 10–19.

Further reading
"Perestroika v pravovoi sisteme, iuridicheskoi nauke i praktike. Materialy konferentsii v Zvenigorode. 18–20 maia 1987 g.," *Sovetskoe gosudarstvo i pravo*, no. 9 (1987), pp. 17–43; no. 10 (1987), pp. 66–87; no.12 (1987), pp. 62–64.
Current newspapers, journals, and periodicals.

SECTION V

Topics 25, 26, 27

Guiding
Materialy XXVII s"ezda KPSS. M., Politizdat, 1986, pp. 3–6, 11–12, 16–21, 62–72, 74–76.

328

Materialy XIX Vsesoiuznoi konferentsii KPSS. M., Politizdat, 1988, pp. 28–34, 43, 115–116.

Gorbachev, M. S. *Velikii Oktiabr': revoliutsiia prodolzhaetsia*. M., 1987.

Gorbachev, M. S. *Perestroika i novoe myshlenie dlia nashei strany i dlia vsego mira*. M., 1988, Section 2, chaps. 3–7.

Special

Problema svobody i prav cheloveka v sovremennoi ideologicheskoi bor'be. M., 1986, pp. 243–284.

Movchan, A. P. *Prava cheloveka i mezhdunarodnye otnosheniia*. M., 1982, pp. 9–19, 54–75.

Sotsialisticheskaia kontseptsiia prav cheloveka. M., 1986, pp. 190–219.

Normative acts

Prava cheloveka: sbornik mezhdunarodnykh dokumentov. M., MGU, 1986.

Mezhdunarodnoe pravo v dokumentakh. M., 1982.

NOTES ON CONTRIBUTORS

BASKIN, Iu. Ia., doktor iurid. nauk, professor.

BIRNIE, P. W., Ph.D. Senior Lecturer, London School of Economics and Political Science, University of London. Barrister (Gray's Inn).

BOYLE, A. E., LL.M., Lecturer in Law, Queen Mary College, University of London

BUTLER, W. E., FSA. M.A., J.D., Ph.D., LL.D. Professor of Comparative Law in the University of London; Director, Centre for the Study of Socialist Legal Systems, University College London; Dean of the Faculty of Laws, University of London (1988-90).

CARTY, J. A., Ph.D. Lecturer in Public International Law, University of Glasgow.

DANILENKO, G. M., doktor iurid. nauk, Senior Research Fellow, Institute of State and Law, USSR Academy of Sciences.

FELDMAN, D. I., doktor iurid. nauk, Professor and Head of the Chair of International Law, Kazan University.

GARDINER, R. K., LL.M. Lecturer, Faculty of Laws, University College London. Barrister (Lincoln's Inn).

KAMENETSKAIA, E. P., kand. iurid. nauk, Senior Research Fellow, Institute of State and Law, USSR Academy of Sciences.

KHAMENEV, I. V., doktor iurid. nauk, Division of Social Sciences, Presidium of the USSR Academy of Sciences.

KHAN, Kabir R., LL.M., Ph.D., Senior Lecturer in Public International Law, University of Edinburgh; Barrister (Gray's Inn)

KORBUT, L. V., kand. iurid. nauk. Secretary, Soviet Association of International Law

KRYLOV, N. B., doktor iurid. nauk. Senior Research Fellow, Institute of State and Law, USSR Academy of Sciences.

LOWE, A. V., Ph.D. University Lecturer and Fellow of Corpus Christi College, Cambridge University.

LUKASHUK, I. I., doktor iurid. nauk, professor. Institute of State and Law, USSR Academy of Sciences.

MENDELSON, M. H., Ph.D. Professor of International Law in the University of London (University College London).

MOVCHAN, A. P., doktor iurid. nauk, professor. Head of Sector, Institute of State and Law, USSR Academy of Sciences.

REDGWELL, C. J. Lecturer in Law, University of Manchester.

SHINKARETSKAIA, G. G., doktor iurid. nauk. Senior Research Fellow, Institute of State and Law, USSR Academy of Sciences.

W. E. Butler, Perestroika and International Law, 329–330.

© 1990 *Kluwer Academic Publishers. Printed in the Netherlands.*

SIMMONDS, K. R., Ph.D. Professor of International Law in the University of London (Queen Mary College); Gresham Professor of Law in the City of London.

TUNKIN, G. I., doktor iurid. nauk, Professor and Head of the Chair of International Law, Moscow State University; Corresponding member of the USSR Academy of Sciences; Chairman of the Soviet Association of International Law.

WARBRICK, C. J., LL.M. Senior Lecturer, University of Durham.